The American
Expeditionary Force
in World War I

ALSO BY GEORGE B. CLARK
AND FROM MCFARLAND

Battle History of the United States Marine Corps, 1775–1945 (2010)

*United States Marine Corps Generals of
World War II: A Biographical Dictionary* (2008)

Decorated Marines of the Fourth Brigade in World War I (2007)

*The Second Infantry Division in World War I: A History of the
American Expeditionary Force Regulars, 1917–1919* (2007)

The Six Marine Divisions in the Pacific: Every Campaign of World War II (2006)

Hiram Iddings Bearss, U.S. Marine Corps: Biography of a World War I Hero (2005)

EDITED BY GEORGE B. CLARK

*United States Marine Corps Medal of Honor Recipients:
A Comprehensive Registry, Including U.S. Navy Medical
Personnel Honored for Serving Marines in Combat*
(2005; paperback 2011)

The American Expeditionary Force in World War I

A Statistical History, 1917–1919

GEORGE B. CLARK

McFarland & Company, Inc., Publishers
Jefferson, North Carolina, and London

LIBRARY OF CONGRESS CATALOGUING-IN-PUBLICATION DATA

Clark, George B., 1926–
　　The American Expeditionary Force in World War I :
a statistical history, 1917–1919 / George B. Clark.
　　　　p.　　cm.
　　Includes bibliographical references and index.

　　ISBN 978-0-7864-7223-9
　　softcover : acid free paper ∞

　　1. United States. Army. American Expeditionary Forces —
Statistics.　2. World War, 1914–1918 — United States.
I. Title.
D570.C58　2013
940.4′1273 — dc23　　　　　　　　　　　　　　2013001542

BRITISH LIBRARY CATALOGUING DATA ARE AVAILABLE

© 2013 George B. Clark. All rights reserved

*No part of this book may be reproduced or transmitted in any form
or by any means, electronic or mechanical, including photocopying
or recording, or by any information storage and retrieval system,
without permission in writing from the publisher.*

On the cover: Barbed Wire Cut — Early 1900's World War I
postcard depicting Americans going through cut barbed wire
with bags of grenades toward Germans (© 2013 Shutterstock)

Manufactured in the United States of America

McFarland & Company, Inc., Publishers
　Box 611, Jefferson, North Carolina 28640
　　www.mcfarlandpub.com

As usual, to my loving wife
of many years,
Jeanne Dansereau Clark,
who has been my inspiration,
I dedicate this volume.

CONTENTS

Acknowledgments	viii
List of Abbreviations	ix
Preface	1
Introduction	5
PART I: THE AMERICAN EXPEDITIONARY FORCE AT WAR	
The Beginnings of the United States' Involvement	11
Battles in Which the American Divisions Participated	20
Statistics of the Meuse-Argonne Battle	46
Conclusion	47
A Summary of American Participation in the War	48
PART II: STATISTICS OF AMERICAN DIVISIONS IN FRANCE	59
Appendix: AEF Units Cited by the French High Command	333
Notes	341
Bibliography	343
Index	351

Acknowledgments

I have had help with this project. The most important person, because she stayed out of my way and didn't call me to wash dishes, was my beloved wife, Jeanne Dansereau Clark. Others who helped were Colonel Douglas Johnson, U.S. Army (ret.) and, though deceased, a comrade who also wrote history, especially of the United States Marine Corps, and of that World War, Colonel Rolfe Hillman II, U.S. Army (ret.).

Many others over many years have supported my writings concerning the 4th Brigade of Marines, Second Infantry Division, in World War I, including Harry Tinney, Curt Bruce, Walter Ford, Bill White, Marty and Pat Wynkoop, Mark Mortensen, Douglas Berry, Rolfe Hillman III, Anthony Klus, Neil Carey, Jacques Naviaux, John McElaney, Patrick Kirby, James Butler, Joe Gorin, Anthony Perash, Pete Owen, Richard Gilbert, Frank Skidmore, Carol and Ray Waldron, Steve Johnson, Richard Schmanke, Gary Cozzens, Rich Hemenez, Rob Singer, Todd Starkey, Troy Thompson, Truman Goodwin, Wayne Pettyjohn, Douglas Bowser, and, frankly, many more.

List of Abbreviations

Adv Det — Advanced detachment
Amb — Ambulance
Am Tn — Ammunition Train
Arty — Artillery
Bn — Battalion
Brig — Brigade
Cav — Cavalry
DHQ — Division Headquarters
Engrs — Engineers
excl — exclusive
F Sig Bn — Field Signal Bn
Hosps — Hospitals
Hq — Headquarters
incl — inclusive
km — kilometer
MG — Machine Gun
MP — Military Police
NA — National Army
NG — National Guard
ORC — Officer Reserve Corps
RA — Regular Army
Regts — Regiment
San Tn — Sanitary Train
Sig Tn — Signal Train
SOS — Services of Supply
Sup Tn — Supply Train
TM Btry — Trench Mortar Battery
Tn — Train

A Few Common French Words

bois — woods
côte — hill
ferme — farm
forêt — forest
pas fini — not passable

Preface

This story, including statistics of the American Expeditionary Force, has never been completely told before, to the best of my knowledge. I am pleased that so many young people are becoming interested in the war and the part played by Americans. A few studies of quality have appeared in the past thirty or so years, mainly about one battle, the Meuse-Argonne.

The data has been derived, mostly, from earlier printed text, primarily because little has been printed on the subject during the past eighty years. The so-called "Great War" will soon have its 100th anniversary and, as with the 100th anniversary of the American Civil War in 1961, the current generations will again take interest. New material will be of interest.

This book was prepared to provide as much detail as possible about the entire American Expeditionary Force. The intent is to supply information about what the American forces rendered to their comrades in arms, French and British, to bring World War I to a successful climax. There is no question, in my mind, that without those members of the AEF, the Allies would not have successfully defeated Germany.

Most of the extant general histories are short on descriptions of events and purposely avoid unpleasantness. One of the few that truly gives sufficient details is *The History of the A.E.F.* by a former first lieutenant named Shipley Thomas. In other words, the complete, unvarnished facts are not broadly published. A few journal articles have been adequate, but every one of them left out some important material, and they have not appeared in academic journals, for the most part.

Some military people prefer that command difficulties should lie dormant, never to be exposed to scrutiny. It is my opinion that only through lessons already learned by others can individuals perform their tasks best. I have tried to tell the complete story, even though several unfortunate incidents have become quite glaring under closer examination. First and foremost, the early senior leadership of the AEF was, in my candid opinion, ineffective. Some few learned while doing. Others were dropped shortly after making blunders that cost many lives. I have decided to let the reader judge who was good and who wasn't. In general, company grade officers were reasonably good at what they did. Most had the hearts of lions. All honor to them.

A statement attributed to Colonel George C. Marshall, U.S. Army, best describes what the American soldier did in France. I believe that it particularly pertains to the Marines and soldiers at Belleau Wood and on the Marne River: "Battles are decided in favor of the troops whose bravery, fortitude, and especially, whose endurance, surpasses that of the enemy; the army with the higher breaking point wins the decision."[1]

Notes have been kept to a minimum. Mostly what has been included are annotations, material that adds to the overall story but does not need to be part of the regular text and can stand by itself. Most of this work is based upon original material; that is, material not published before or, if so, not widely distributed.

The basic ideas for the development of this manuscript have mainly been derived from several publications, including: *The Lions of July*; *The AEF and Coalition Warmaking, 1917–1918*; *The History of the A.E.F.*; *The United States in the First World War: An Encyclopedia*; *The American Army in the European Conflict*; *Pershing's Report*; *Annual Report, Secretary of War, 1919*; *The War with Germany: A Statistical Summary*; and *The American Army in the World War: A Divisional Record*. See the bibliography for further details.

The United States, under its political leadership, primarily the president, Thomas Woodrow Wilson, intended at least for a few years to remain on the sidelines while the World War was being fought. That attitude changed for several reasons. Wilson wanted a place upon the world stage and felt he should play an important part in the final settlement of that war. The only way that could happen soon became clear: he had to lead the nation into the war so he could sit in on the eventual settlement and make decisions.

He had his hour upon the "stage" and it cost the United States nearly 300,000 wartime casualties, not counting the many soldiers, sailors, and Marines who were afflicted and perished with some wartime disease. Not counting the large sums it cost the U.S. to participate. Or the cost of the later Great Depression; many blame the origins upon our part in that war. Or the most important part, the coming of a second, more dreadful war based upon the deplorable settlement imposed upon one nation that unknowingly signed away its rights based upon terms (the "Fourteen Points") that were not adhered too.

Obviously, I am biased against the participation of the United States. I truly believe that the Europeans should have been allowed to settle their own mistakes. We strengthened the one side, while the other side was declining, and in battle provided the necessary power to overwhelm the other. It is quite obvious, to me, that the Allies would have been forced to make arrangements with the Central Powers if the United States had remained on the sidelines. I am sure that if arrangements between exhausted warring powers were of a modest sort, one nation wouldn't have gone irrational and later selected a leader who was obviously insane. That insanity led to a most grievous period.

When I was very young, the veterans of that war thrilled me, every Decoration Day, when those who survived and were mobile paraded in downtown Providence, Rhode Island. My three bravest heroes were my three uncles that served in France, one a member of the 103d Machine Gun Battalion, 26th "YD"; a second that served (I believe) in the 11th Infantry, 5th Infantry Division, and finally the youngest, and the most full of fun to a young nephew, a Marine of the 4th Brigade.

The section devoted to divisional details was taken directly from the semi-official reports. All must have been prepared by different people and many were slightly different in format or spelling of words. I have tried to correct some spelling and eliminate abbreviations, except those which should be obvious.

I have tried to make this a comprehensive study and have therefore included a preponderance of detail that would not normally be found in a book aimed at the general reading public. But I must warn the reader, reliable records about the AEF aren't readily available. Please use this text with discretion. I have done my best, but who knows with certainty that this is any different? I hope it is.

INTRODUCTION

The massive conflict, the Great War, or the World War, as it later became known, was triggered by Bosnian nationalists when they assassinated the Austro-Hungarian archduke Franz Ferdinand, heir to the Austrian throne, and his wife, at Sarajevo, Bosnia, on June 28, 1914. The background is complicated but the real trouble originated with Serbian members of the Black Hand Society who armed the assassins. There seemed to be no question in anyone's mind that the Serbian government, or its employees, sponsored it.[1]

Control of Bosnia had been "awarded" to Austria-Hungary at the 1878 Treaty of San Stefano, which angered the Bosnian nationalists who fought for independence but lost. Serbia, a newly independent nation, was anxious to attach Bosnia and Herzegovina to itself and consequently brooded over the treaty settlement.

Within a few weeks of the assassination, Austria-Hungary demanded that the Serbian government obey a set of rules established by the former, or else. Serbia agreed to obey all but one; that one was tantamount toward eliminating their national independence and they, at the urging of Russia, refused to accept it. Russia had long threatened to intervene should Austria-Hungary attack Serbia.

The background alliances and involvement of the several important nations were quite confused. Russia and Germany had treaties that terminated in 1887 after Chancellor Otto Bismarck refused to allow Berlin banks to loan Russia money, whereas French banks would and did loan them money. That resulted in treaties between France and Russia to come to the other nations' aid if attacked by a third party (Germany). Not long after, Bismarck was unseated and the very young Kaiser Wilhelm II, who desired to control the destiny of a recently united Germany himself, assumed almost complete control. In fact he was not a bad fellow as he has been portrayed, but leaving a powerful growing nation's affairs in his hands was a calamity of huge proportions.

France was anxious for revenge upon a Germany that had defeated it in the 1870–71 war, even though France initiated it by declaring war upon Prussia. Through extraordinary manipulations and treaties France managed in 1904 to entice Great Britain into agreeing to come to France's aid should Germany attack it. France was looking for any possible angle to provoke trouble with Germany, mainly to regain two lost parcels, once originally German states, that France lost in 1871. Now that Russia, with its massive armies, and Britain and its massive navy, were its allies, France had the opportunity.

Great Britain had been the most productive manufacturing nation in the world but had been overtaken, first by the nation across the Atlantic Ocean, the United States, and then Germany. In addition, Germany began building a merchant fleet to project its manufacture around the world, and more slowly a fighting navy to protect it. The former was bad enough, but the latter was not to be allowed. After all, Britain had the world's greatest navy and demanded that no other nation ever contest its right to rule the seas. Besides, the British were becoming convinced that Germany, if it ever defeated France and occupied the coast, would be a solid threat to Britain. There were other reasons, including Germany's late entry into the colony-grabbing hullabaloo, whatever was left and available around the world.

Russia had been in turmoil for most of the nineteenth century. Most of its wars had been opposite Turkey, to obtain passage to the Mediterranean and to "protect her little Slavic brothers" of the Balkan nations. Russia had been badly defeated by the Japanese in their war, 1904–05, and then suffered a disastrous civil war, or rebellious uprising, in 1905. Since then, nearly ten years later, Russia had been looking to create trouble with Austria-Hungary, another nation on the downgrade. To them, they could defeat Austria-Hungary, force separation of its various Slavic nations, and then basically, rule over the Balkans and their Slav "brothers."

Austria, a nation of many nations, had seen rebellious upset for many years, and had joined its crown with its largest and most disaffected subject, Hungary, on December 21, 1868, to try to prevent further trouble. In the mid-nineteen century, Austria had been disastrously beaten in war by Prussia and in another by France, which was aiding the Italians. Meanwhile, its incursions in the Balkans had been continually protested by the Turks, Greeks, Russians, and of course the various Balkan nations themselves. Somehow, Austria-Hungary and a united Germany plus a newly created Italy agreed to fight together should one of those three be attacked by a third nation. The latter united nation had recently been created after centuries of being subjected to the Vatican, or other nations, including Spain, Austria, and France. This treaty gave Austria-Hungary the strength it needed to ward off a threatening Russia. Or, so she thought.

Smaller nations were involved, but none with the impact of the major players. None of the above really thought much about the probable catastrophe a huge war with modern weapons would bring forth.

Austria-Hungary, urged on by Germany, demanded acceptance of its conditions. Serbia, urged by Russia, refused, and on July 29, 1914, Austria began bombarding Belgrade. In the meantime, Wilhelm II learned that Russia had begun to mobilize its army, and he contacted his cousin Nicholas II, the czar of Russia, begging him to cease so he wouldn't have to mobilize the German army. They were "Willy" and "Nicky" to each other, both grandsons of the deceased Queen Victoria of Britain, but even their relatively close relationship didn't stop the movement. Nicky said, "We can't, it's too late." So, Germany mobilized and in the meantime France was also mobilizing. France began advancing its army to the frontiers and briefly invaded Germany.

On August 3, 1914, Germany and France each declared war upon the other, and the following day Germany declared war against Belgium, and then on the 4th Great Britain joined in. For some reason, Russia waited until November 3, 1914, before declaring war against the Central Powers, as Germany and Austria-Hungary became known. The Central Powers, according to their treaty, asked Italy to join them, but Italy found a reason to refuse, and temporarily remained on the sidelines.

Meanwhile, Germany, according to plans made many years before in anticipation of this war, crossed the borders of Belgium, contrary to a treaty they had signed in 1836. That supposedly was what brought Britain in, but as stated before, in 1904 it had secretly agreed to join France in this long anticipated war.

It wasn't long before other nations joined one side or the other. Turkey came in on the Central Powers side on October 29, 1914; Bulgaria on September 6, 1915. Many joined the Allied powers, like Japan on August 23, 1914; Portugal, November 23; Italy on May 23, 1915; Romania, August 27, 1916; Greece, November 23; followed in 1917 by the U.S., Panama, Cuba, Siam, Liberia, China, Brazil; and in 1918 by Guatemala, Nicaragua, Haiti, and lastly, Honduras.

Japan would grab many German colonies in the Pacific Ocean and Shantung, a large section of China which once had been held by Germany. Italy was promised half the world if it would join the Allies, and following the end of the war made a huge fuss when only a modest treasure fell to it.

The war was a horror for all the fighting men. The leaders were generally incompetent and had no idea of what they were leading their men against. Even the Germans, a bit more competent, were at times leading their manpower to a slaughter. The French were the worst; their losses were horrific, and much of that was caused by their beautiful, colorful red and blue uniforms. Machine guns, a specialty of the German army, did the most damage, but they were neck-and-neck with the newest form of artillery. There, at least, the French had some equation with their 75mm field gun, which the men handled with ease and great skill. The British barely fielded an army in Belgium in the early days. Their leader, Field Marshal John French, was worse than most everyone else, although he had quite a few competitors in the three Allied armies.

In time French was replaced by a general named Douglas Haig, who also became a field marshal, and he managed to offer up to the German army most of the British army as casualties. However, he, a member of the Scottish whiskey family, had valuable contacts in London and retained command throughout the balance of the war, though he had many enemies. The French at least kept changing those generals killing Frenchmen, but the replacements always seemed worse than what went before. After the great disasters led by General Robert Nivelle in 1917, and the great mutinies that followed it, they brought in Marshal Henri-Phillipe Petain, who managed to calm the men down and from then on the French army fought an entirely different style war; advancement was almost a mode of the past. "Yielding defense" meant falling back to make a stand where the machine guns and artillery could have an open field to catch the advancing Germans in, or it was a war of "Let the other fellow do it."

During the war's thirty-five months before the United States sent troops to France, Woodrow Wilson and his cabinet tried many times to put forth a reasonable plan to bring the war to a close, but always managed to run into stalemates from one side or the other. The reasons were varied but essentially, both sides wanted the other to surrender something or several things of value. Following is a brief listing of the efforts made to the warring powers.[2]

- On August 3, 1914, President Wilson offered the good offices of the U.S. in mediating between the warring nations. His replies were notes of appreciation, but little substance.
- August 4. Wilson proclaimed neutrality. In fact, he and his government were anything but neutral in selling goods or loaning money. Always to the Allies.
- December 18. Wilson offered a peace proposal. It was, like earlier notes, basically ignored.
- December 26. The U.S. protested British naval policy, which was to interfere with all ships sailing toward any nations that were trading with Germany, mostly the Netherlands and Scandinavia, and bringing the ships into British ports and removing goods. The goods were hardly ever paid for.
- January 24, 1915. U.S. Administration denied discrimination against Germany and Austria. It was making no loans to either nation but

continued loaning heavily to Britain and France. Wilson was really very partial in his negotiations between the Allies and Central Powers.
- February 10. Wilson sent his "strict accountability" note to Germany. This had to do with German submarines sinking ships other than those of the Allies, particularly U.S. ships.
- April 5. The U.S. sent a note to Britain and France protesting the blockade of European waters and impounding U.S. merchant ships with their cargoes. The response was much the same as before. "We'll continue to do so."
- May 10. Wilson made his famous "too proud to fight" speech on why the U.S. wouldn't join the fighting.
- May 14. Wilson made his first *Lusitania* complaint to Germany. American newspapers carried warnings from the German embassy not to travel to Britain on that ship because it would be sunk. That British ship was sunk, and among the nearly 1,200 lives lost, 124 were Americans. The ship, it was later learned, was carrying tons of war material, in a clear violation of Cruiser Laws established at least four hundred years previously. An interesting sidelight: King George V was having a meeting with the U.S. ambassador a few days before the sinking in which the king said: "If that ship is sunk, will the United States declare war on Germany?"
- August 10. The U.S. established a camp at Plattsburgh, New York, for military training of citizen volunteers. The system continued until 1917. It was helpful when the nation went to war.
- September 8. The U.S. requested that Austria recall its ambassador. Ambassador Dumba had been involved in plots to impede American armaments flowing to the Allies. He left the U.S. in November.
- October 21. Wilson again protested the British blockade. There was no positive response.
- November 4. Wilson advocated a stronger national defense policy, though he continued to affirm the neutral stance of the United States.
- December 10. Two attachés of the German embassy were recalled at the request of the U.S.
- April 17, 1916. Several other German attachés were indicted by a federal grand jury for conspiracy to destroy the Welland Canal.
- May 24. Secretary of State Lansing protested to Britain and France against interference with neutral mail. There was no satisfactory response.
- December 20. Wilson issued another peace note. Nothing satisfactory happened.

- January 1917. British intelligence conveyed to Washington the text of the infamous Zimmerman telegram to Mexico. In effect Germany was offering Mexico a return of its lost territories — California, Arizona, and New Mexico — if it would attack the U.S.
- February 3. The U.S. severs diplomatic relations with Germany. The latter, in addition to the Zimmerman telegram, had begun indiscriminate sinking of any ship headed for the British Isles or the French coast. Several U.S. ships went down.
- February 26. Wilson asked Congress for authority to arm merchant ships.
- April 6. At the request of Wilson, the Congress declared war upon Germany.

Part I: The American Expeditionary Force at War

THE BEGINNINGS OF THE UNITED STATES' INVOLVEMENT

Almost minutes after the Congress met and approved Wilson's request for war, two delegations, one from Britain and another from France, arrived in Washington demanding the U.S. send American infantrymen to be blended into their armies commanded by "experienced leaders." Eventually, some Americans served in either the British or French armies. One division, the 93rd, composed of black enlisted men with mainly white officers, was broken up and its units were assigned duty with the French army, at a great loss to the AEF. Two other divisions served the British throughout the war and they too were fine examples of wasted manpower for the AEF.[3]

This only provides a brief telling of what really was happening. Though Wilson protested what the British, especially, were doing to U.S. shipping, which went contrary to the well-established rules of the sea, nothing of genuine consequences was ever done about it. The German navy was utilizing their undersea weapon to try to overcome the preponderance in British ships. Great Britain was slowly squeezing the German nation's food supply.

Hence, the United States went to war. Initially, the plan was not to send any troops to Europe, but simply to have the U.S. Navy help with the blockade. But that changed. The nation did not have a real army and had to build one. First came the volunteers, then a draft, but without suitable camps in which to house and train this large mass. Very few uniforms were available, and many recruits spent many months in their civilian clothes before being issued suitable wear. The first winter was cold and the lack of suitable quarters, which were being built, clothing, and lack of heat caused much discomfort. The nation lacked essential weapons, and spent much money trying to alleviate that problem, never really succeeding. Most weapons the AEF would use came through purchases in France. The army lacked machine guns, artillery, automatic rifles, tanks, gas masks, airplanes, hand grenades, and even enough of that basic rifle, the splendid Springfield 1903.

The enthusiasm of the men, draftees as well as volunteers, was amazing. They maintained most of it through the trying days in the U.S. and even in the few early original battles fought with little training and poor equipment. The French artillery, the so-called "French 75" was splendid, but the exceptionally heavy 8mm Hotchkiss machine gun and the "Chau-chat" automatic rifle were next to useless.[4]

In other words, the United States was in no condition to fight a major war. Its army was always very modest in size, since it had few enemies of consequence, and the few made were minor nations with small populations. Though the U.S. Navy was in considerably better shape, the sea war was easily handled by Great Britain. The U.S. spent at least $25 billion in 1918 dollars, and that does not include the $8 billion to $10 billion it loaned to the Allies, most of which they refused to repay at war's end.

The benefit Wilson sought was a disaster. Though he wanted to have a major role at war's end, he was roundly tossed about in Paris by Clemenceau and Lloyd George, and even the Italian premier, Orlando, got in a few shots. His Fourteen Points, which Germany accepted for the armistice, were mostly ignored. France got its revenge, Britain eliminated an expanding German economy, and Italy was refused most of what it had anticipated.

At the request of President Woodrow Wilson, the Congress of the United States of America declared war against Germany April 6, 1917, and Major General John J. Pershing was made commander-in-chief of the proposed American Expeditionary Forces. To make preparations to receive these troops upon their arrival overseas, he sailed for Europe May 25 on the SS *Baltic*, accompanied by a staff of 53 officers and 146 enlisted men. The *Baltic* arrived at Liverpool, England, on June 8, where General Pershing was received with a guard of honor composed of one of the finest British regiments in the army. As he stepped down the gangplank the regimental band played "The Star Spangled Banner." As soon as the formal ceremonies were concluded, the entire party started by train for London.

In this city the little vanguard of the AEF was paid high honors amid scenes of general rejoicing. Among those who gave the glad hand to General Pershing was King George V, and his words of welcome rang with good cheer.[5]

The few days passed by General Pershing in London, outside of the formalities of reception bestowed upon him with a hearty zest, were devoted to observation of the British army methods. He, however, had pretty much made up his mind to train the AEF in a different method. His handpicked staff had been selected because they agreed with him.

On the morning of June 13, 1917, the American commander landed on French soil, the first American soldier to step upon European shores to conduct a war. On the dock at Boulogne a French regiment in horizon blue battle uniforms awaited the arrival of the foremost of the long-looked for troops, according them a rousing welcome. Upon reaching Paris, General Pershing and his men were wildly cheered, and escorted from the station to their temporary headquarters by a guard of honor, while the band played "The Star Spangled Banner" and then "La Marseillaise." Marshal Joffre, M. Viviani, minister of justice, M. Painleve, minister of war, Generals Foch and Dutail and the U.S. ambassador, William G. Sharp, with many other high dignitaries, were on hand to meet the first Americans to arrive in France. Among the numerous receptions he managed, General Pershing found time to visit the tomb of the great French patriot Lafayette, placing a wreath of American Beauty roses above his resting place, while he is credited with the announcement: "Lafayette, we are here!"[6]

Henceforth General Pershing devoted his entire time to organizing the headquarters of the AEF and planning for the care and disposition of an anticipated American Army of two million men. To facilitate the handling of such a vast body of men, the staff of the General Headquarters was divided into three sections or parts, and, this arrangement found to be unsatisfactory, the number was increased to five, viz.: G-1, Section of Administration, which looked after supplies, transportation, storage and replenishment of men and animals; G-2, Intelligence, devoted to acquiring knowledge of the situation, particularly of the enemy, preparation of maps, charts, and dissemination of propaganda; G-3, Operations, pertaining to the employment of all troops; G-4, Coordination, that is, the distribution of supplies, replacements and ammunition; G-5, Training, which meant having charge of military schools and inspection as well as training of the men.

The staff of the American Expeditionary Forces was given three principal heads: the General, Technical and the Administrative staffs. The command of the entire organization came through the General Staff. The chiefs of the various sections were the assistant chiefs of the staff for their section, and dealt directly with the chief of staff, who commanded them. These chiefs of sections were Pershings' assistants and handled the five subdivisions already mentioned. The most important duty of the staff was to assist troops in preparation for and in combat.[7]

On September 1, the headquarters of the AEF was moved from Paris to Chaumont Haute Marne, placing the American lines of communications midway between the great base depots of Bourges and Tours and the front. Paris was still the center of the French supply lines. General Pershing established his headquarters on September 3 in Room 51 in Building "B" of the French barracks. Chaumont is a pretty little French garrison city of the headwaters of the River Marne, and the huge stone barracks offered good facilities for the installation of the big staff required to manage the two million troops expected for the campaigns to follow.

From the landing on European soil in June 1917 of the first unit of American troops until September 1918, a period of almost fourteen months, the American General Headquarters did not come into actual command of a sector at the front. Yet this was a busy period for soldiers and officers. The paramount issue of the day was in training the American yeomanry so it might become the efficient fighter it was destined to be. An educational system was immediately organized, and as rapidly as the troops arrived the new divisions were instructed in the very latest tactics of war, many of these acquired in the bitter experiences of the previous three years. However, in later times, veterans, usually officers, were highly critical of the end results. This system was founded upon the experiences of the British and French, which of course was a different style than General Pershing and his staff had planned for the Americans. One of the first big challenges was to train officers so they could train men. Most of the junior officers were basically untrained and their seniors had little experience except in small wars against untrained natives.

Somewhat in the nature of an experiment, the first American Division to arrive in France was split up with a French division and trained under its control, but this proved not entirely satisfactory and had to be abandoned. This and succeeding divisions were given supervision by the training section of the General Staff. Originally it was planned to give each division three months of training, but the spring drive of the Germans made it necessary to reduce this time to four weeks — and four strenuous weeks they were.[8]

All through this stage of preparation there never appeared any doubt of the result, and the training of the American forces was largely preparatory with continual emphasis laid on the importance of rifle practice. When the troops were in position and firing against advancing enemy, such was vindicated in the performance of the American riflemen in the various early battles of the following June and July.[9]

When the war was declared there were only 200,000 men in the army. Two-thirds of these were Regulars and one-third National Guardsmen, many of whom had recently been called to federal service for duty along the Mexican frontier. For the Army, their only experience was fighting Filipino natives, and for the few Marines, only the natives of Haiti and Santo Domingo had been of consequence. But certainly neither was like what they would face on the Western Front.

The summer and autumn months of 1917 formed a precarious period on the battle front. Victory for the Allies was still as far removed as before. In April the British, using Canadian troops, began their successful offensives at Vimy Ridge in Flanders. The French under General Neville had a disastrous campaign, though they captured Craonne. Because of this slaughter of French troops, General Petain was made commander-in-chief of the French forces.

In May the Italians opened their great advance towards Trieste which ended in near disaster. June 2 the British took Messines Ridge. Within a month the Russian Army, which for some time had been wavering in a state of uncertainty, began an offensive under Kerensky. Altogether the Allies were apparently on the way to ultimate victory.[10]

This seemed more evident from the fact that the Germans, with a certain amount of disaffection among the Austrians, were anxious for a settlement. On July 19 the Reichstag offered terms of peace, though such terms as could not be honorably accepted by the Allies.[11] The British and French were intent upon conquest and the Germans offered none of that. Still, there was talk of peace in the air, and while this was going on the Hindenburg line on the Western front was strengthening. The Germans had been negotiating with Russia, which was obviously in bad shape, and the latter began to weaken. So much so, they signed a treaty which rankled by giving up sections they had conquered in years past.

Then the British won a victory in Flanders, and in November the French dealt the Germans a furious blow at Chemin des Dames, while the British stormed Passchendaele Ridge on the 6th. In the midst of this promising outlook a sweeping change came over the situation. The British and French victories and modest Italian drives were offset by the widespread Russian mutiny and retreat, and eventual surrender which freed more than 62 divisions of the German Army on the Eastern front. These swung to the West, once more giving Germany a preponderance in numbers and armament on the Western front. The movements of the Allies were changed from an offensive to a defensive. The German attack at Cambrai, which proved so disastrous to the British, showed that the Army of the Kaiser was still far from being defeated.[12]

To add to the seriousness of the situation of the Allies, Italy had been forced to recall its few troops, largely from the Western front, to try and stem the tide of an Austrian invasion. Everywhere was gloom and depression and forebodings for the outcome of the winter. When the contending armies, on account of the miserable weather, went into winter headquarters, Shipley Thomas says candidly in his *History of the A.E.F.*:

> That winter of 1917–18 in Lorraine will ever be remembered by those four divisions for the intense suffering it entailed. The training of the American Army was immediately put on a slightly different basis, and while trench warfare was studied, all the practice marches, all the maneuvers in the snow and rainstorms of that excessively cold winter were in preparation for open warfare.
>
> To practically everyone in the American Army this appeared to be folly. Officers returning from the British schools were full of the new British plan of defense — the policy of "let them come on," which was to prove so costly to the British in the spring drive — the British machine-gun defense in

trench warfare. The French also were practicing the niceties of trench warfare, and the plan of the "yielding defense" was put forth in mid winter, and at once, throughout the French sectors, work was begun on second and third lines of defense with barbed wire ten miles behind the front.

Meanwhile, in the sleet and bitter cold, through snow and over the frozen hills of Lorraine, during that awful winter, the Americans were practicing open warfare. Each evening the junior officers would gather in one room, each bringing with him his precious armful of wood, and while they vainly tried to get warm, they would pour out their troubles which almost amounted to mutiny. They talked — as junior officers always do, in a cocksure way of youthful enthusiasm — of the uselessness of "chasing the Indians," of generals who "had learned nothing since Custer," and apparently couldn't learn, and who did not know that every German artillery shot was plotted days in advance. Night after night in the miserable frozen billets, the junior officers of the 1st Division (for it was the 1st on whom experiments were always tried) poured forth their woes over the incompetence of generals who taught open warfare and attack "when any fool could see that it was the Germans and not us, who were going to attack." And still American G.H.Q. insisted upon open warfare; and now those officers of the 1st Division who are still alive, who suffered those horrors of open warfare that winter of 1917–18 in Lorraine, realize that General Pershing, who insisted upon it, was the wisest of them all, for every moment of this training proved later that it was justified. The actual tactics may have been antiquated; but the confidence and ability it gave to those officers, non commissioned officers, and men of the 1st, and all succeeding divisions, in the use of unfamiliar ground, in fighting in the open, in establishing and maintaining contact, and in ever pushing onward, was what enabled the American divisions, green and unused as they were to the tactics of war, to fill the breach in defense, and then, on July 18, to take tip that most glorious unrelenting offensive which never stopped until the Germans asked for peace.

Too much credit cannot be given to General Pershing and to the General Staff for clinging to their American creed of open warfare, not of defense, but of offense, in the face of utter discouragement.

Those four divisions, who underwent this trial, will never forget that winter of maneuvers, which developed the toughest army, physically and mentally, in the world.

Of food there was plenty, but of all other supplies there was the greatest scarcity. Shoes, for example, were almost impossible to obtain, for many reasons. The chief among these was that in order to keep warm, each soldier was wearing two pairs of heavy knitted socks, and this added to the cold and wet and exception ally heavy packs, which increased the average foot two and three sizes, made the call for shoes much bigger than those sent over according to the old standards. There were plenty of small shoes, but the order for the larger sizes had to go back over such a long line of communication that it was late in the spring before the divisions were fully supplied.[13]

This was but one item, while the training went on, and every man in the American Army had to be counted. Early in the new year, January 15, 1918, the 16th and 18th Infantry Regiments, the 1st Brigade of the 1st Division (Regular) was sent under Maj. Gen. George B. Duncan to relieve the French in the northwest sector of Toul, where the final training was to be made. This became known as the "American Sector." The command of the French here was finally given over to the Americans, who decided to enliven what had been a quiet sector. Accordingly, General Summerall, in command of the 1st Field Artillery Brigade, increased the firing schedules. The Germans were quick to awaken to this fact.

A low, marshy valley lay in front of the forward line, so the trenches were certain to be filled with slimy mud at nightfall, which would require hours of hard work to clear of debris. Behind this line was a rise or ridge of land which constituted the watershed of this section, while almost parallel to this ran the national highway which connected Rambucourt and towns adjoining with Pont-a-Mousson and district beyond. This road, distinguished by its elevated position and twin rows of ancient trees, was the only route of transport for the forces stationed in this vicinity.

Separated from this position of the American forces by a wide marsh on the hillside beyond were the front lines of the German Army, while above this ground rose Mont Sec almost five hundred feet. From the top of the isolated, conical peak the Germans were able to watch every movement of the Americans, and as well as being an observation post commanding a view of the surrounding country for many miles, it was a fortress that could not be assailed with any hope of success.

It was here in the maze of old abandoned trenches, with the marshes of No Man's Land between, that the American Army in France had its beginning in patrol duty. As some Frenchman said, "The Americans were very brave, while the Germans were very skillful." The experience obtained here was costly, but it proved a warning for future action.

The next division to go to the line for its final training was the 26th Division, or New England National Guard, which was assigned to the Eleventh French Army Corps, and sent to the famous sector of Chemin des Dames, which connected Soissons with Rheims, and extended for about 25 miles. March 20, 1918, this division was ordered to proceed to the Barsur-Aube Area, near Chaumont. For gallantry of action many of the officers of this division had been decorated with the Croix de Guerre, while others had been recommended for the American Distinguished Service Cross.

The 42nd Division, known as the "Rainbow" Division of National Guards, was assigned to the Seventh French Army Corps and ordered to the "Baccarat Sector" in the Vosges Mountain near Lunenville. This division went into line February 16, 1918. This sector extended from the forests of Elieux to the village of Badonciller, along the border of Bois Banal to the southern edge of Bois des Pretes, a distance of 15 kilometers. This was a beautiful section of valleys and hills covered with woods. Protected by the mountains on the German side, this retreat was comparatively free from an offensive, an ideal place for rest. This sector, as well as that of Toul, became a noted training school for the American Army. In one respect the method employed here was different from those elsewhere. The various units of the Rainbow Division were assigned to different French divisions for training, these branches of the French Army being the redoubtable 41st, 164th, 14th and 128th Divisions. Eventually the American forces came into command of the position and the French retired.

If resting in a quiet sector, the Americans were not slow in arousing the enemy by patrolling and raiding the German trenches, the result being a number of prisoners. The Americans had not come to France to sit. They were anxious for the enemy to realize who was opposite them.

The fourth combat division to go into training was the 2nd Division, made up from the Regular Army and the U.S. Marines. This division was assigned by the French to the western side of the St. Mihiel salient, near Verdun. The holding of these grounds was not easy, and the 2nd Division suffered its share of casualties, while displaying signal courage. This was especially true of Companies "I" and "L" of the Ninth Infantry during a bitter German raid, when the "Sturm Truppen, five hundred strong thought to surprise and overpower the Americans."[14] So adroitly planned was the raid that a considerable number of the enemy disguised by French uniforms managed to get inside the lines. Then, according to prearranged plans, these daring spirits gave the gas alarms, and simultaneously the main body of the raiders plunged through the intense barrage and leaped into the American trenches. Amid the confusion and hand-to-hand grapple with the unexpected assailants the men of the Ninth gallantly stood their ground. Recovering quickly from the shock of the surprise, with enemies in their midst and on every quarter, the Americans fought like heroes and the Germans were repulsed, leaving 65 dead and eighteen prisoners in the American trenches. While the Boche captured nine soldiers, one of them a battalion surgeon, the victory was a decisive one for the Americans.

The 1st Division in the Toul Sector was relieved on April 4 by the 26th Division, New England National Guard, and the former was assembled to defend Toul. Three sectors were now held by veteran American divisions.

Another division was added to those already mentioned, and consisted of the 32nd Division, made up of the National Guard of Michigan and Wisconsin under command of Major General William G. Haan. This division was stationed at Prauthory, Haute Marne, which was designated as the 10th Training Area. The division was designated as a Replacement Division of the First Corps. Inside of four weeks the activity made it necessary to employ all troops for combat duty, so this was made an active division.[15]

Battles in Which the American Divisions Participated

It would seem as if Providence had showered special favors upon the basin-like valley on the River Seine where Paris was built, in order to protect it from the invasions of the eastern hordes that have periodically overrun the land of the Gaul on an average of every fifty years since more than five centuries before Christ. This natural barrier consists of a series of hills and low mountain ranges, extending, with their sharp shoulders towards Germany, from the marshes of Belgium to the very foot of the Swiss Alps. The ascent from France is generally gradual and not difficult.

Occasional breaks in this bulwark of France against invasion from over the Rhine occur where the French have raised a chain of fortifications and garrisoned cities. The first of these is near the Swiss border reaching from Belfort to Epinal. The Meuse Valley affords a more extended gap and stretches from Verdun to Toul. Between these two passes rise the Vosges Mountains, forbidding and impassable. A little to the west of north from Verdun lie Argonne and the Ardennes forests, where the passage of great bodies of troops is impracticable, if not impossible; although, as you may already be aware, the Nazi armies breached the latter in 1944. Beyond the Ardennes lies the Belgian border. The first of these gaps the French commanded by the presence of an army of a million of trained men, with the ability to increase this defense by the mobilization of four times that number within as many weeks. France had been smarting over the loss of two provinces, Alsace and Lorraine, since their great defeat by the combined German states led by Prussia in 1870–1871, in a war which France declared. In fact, since then they had been planning revenge, and this seemed to their leadership to be the most propitious time to retaliate.

The Belgian frontier was protected by a fortified line running from

Maubeuge and Valenciennes to Lille, with inner circles of protection. Altogether this seemed like an impregnable line of defense, and yet it did not dismay the German leadership and with the examples of previous invasions before them, they were confident of success. The Prussians and most other European states had signed an agreement in 1830 guaranteeing Belgian freedom from any attacking nation; However, notwithstanding, the German plan for invading France included crossing the Belgian border. An interesting sidelight, though Germany was clearly the aggressor insofar as Belgium was concerned, Great Britain had in 1912 failed to renew its signature to that treaty, yet that was its government's stated reason for going to war with Germany.[16] In reality, it was the various points issued earlier: naval threat, potential conquest of the French coast, and the usual balance of power.

There were few sections indeed of the long line of battle known as the Western Front — stretching almost, though not always in a direct course, from the sea to the Alps — which were not at some time in the four years and more of bitter fighting the scene of a furious attack by the Germans in their efforts to break through the barriers besetting their pathway. In the later years of the war and contemporary with the appearance of the American forces, the fighting front was very much reduced in length, and the terms "quiet sectors" and "active sectors" became established. These were determined to a considerable extent by the geography of the country, but became governed somewhat by the earnest drive of the Germans towards Paris, which they naturally had made their objective point. The Germans were well aware that the morale of the French was extremely low and that the loss of Paris would probably induce France to ask for an armistice.

As the physical aspects of a country have much to do with the success or failure of an army, it seems to be in keeping with the subject to describe briefly the situation here as improved by the Germans, and illustrates the extreme difficulty that must be experienced by the troops undertaking to rout them. The River Marne flows between high banks which drop almost perpendicularly to the water's edge, on both the north sides from Essomes-sur-Marne, a little less than two miles west of the town of Château-Thierry, and east as far as Vincelles. A small tributary joins the Marne at Essomes, and in the wedge thus formed is situated Hill 204, frequently mentioned in the accounts of the battle. Less than a mile from the headwaters of this small tributary another small stream has its source and, flowing west almost parallel with the Marne, empties into the Ourcq, which bends abruptly to the south and enters the Marne twenty miles west of Château-Thierry. This tributary to the Ourcq flows through the towns of Bouresches, Belleau, Torcy and Bussiares, which are connected with Essomes and Château-Thierry by a narrow gauge railroad.

Château-Thierry is a town of importance, standing on both banks of the Marne where the river turns sharply to the south, and lying about fifty miles from Paris. Built along the Marne near each other and having bridges across the river are numerous small towns, which became important in the struggle owing to these bridges. The flats or bottomland made famous at the time by the fierce fighting are at the south of the river between Essomes and Château-Thierry. The surrounding country is broken, with patches of woods or belts of forests covering sections of the landscape. Taken altogether the position of the French forces seemed easily breached, whereas the reverse seemed unassailable for the Germans.

As has been said, with the arrival of the American Army, the fighting line of 1914, 1915, 1916 and 1917 was materially shortened. The field of all the actions now became the area about Ypres in Belgium, the Somme Valley, west of Amiens; the Chemin des Dames, north of Soissons; and the Champagne, eastward towards the Argonne Forest and Verdun. The activities died down on the quiet fronts, and No-man's Land soon became a sea of barbed wire.

Aisne Defensive and Belleau Wood

The Aisne Defensive, so-called because Allied forces were called upon to defend themselves against the Germans in their drive for Paris, took place between May 27 and July 5, 1918, and was fought just northeast of Rheims on the Chemin des Dames, "Ladies' Road." It was not in itself a complete combat, but belonged to the series of offensives made by the enemy that in a broader sense was known as the Marne Salient. The Germans reached the River Marne, near Château-Thierry, on June 1. The Second Division, Regulars and Marines, were fighting at Belleau Wood and at Vaux, and Third Division of Regulars participated in this fight south of the river at the city of Château-Thierry. For a better understanding of the situation see Montdidier-Noyon Defensive, Champagne-Marne Defensive, and Aisne Marne Offensive.[17]

The Aisne-Marne defensive left the Allies in a most undesirable position on June 5. The line ran on the south bank of the Marne, with little protection behind, while the Germans occupied a higher situation on the north bank of the river, their front lines a little over the crest of a hill with woods to their rear, being on the western border of Bois-de-Belleau. To improve their position the Allies planned to open a drive with the wooded hill for their objective point.

This task was assigned to the 2nd Division, composed of Regulars and Marines, and was one of the most hotly contested combats during the war, though considered an incident in the Second Battle of the Marne.

Walter A. Dyer, in his introduction to a history of the Marines, says:

> When the history of the Great War is written, it will be no easy task to assign to each of the titanic battles its proper place in the scale of importance, but if justice is done, the Battle of Belleau Wood will take its place beside that of Thermopylae and the other crucial battles of the world history. Here a mere handful of determined, devoted men, as numbers are reckoned today, turned the awful tide, and they were soldiers and Marines of the United States of America....
>
> The Marines were called upon to do the impossible, and because there is no such word in their code, they did it. They left in that wood some of the best blood of America, but, outnumbered and inexperienced as they were, they fought that last fight to a finish and they stopped the Hun.[18]

The secret of the success at Belleau Wood was due largely to the superior marksmanship of the American Marines and soldiers. No doubt the German soldier was the best trained in the world, and a soldier's training marks the upward stride towards victory over defeat. He is no coward, as he demonstrated over and again, especially when amply supported by his comrades and officers. He did lack quick perception, resource, and beyond all he was a poor marksman. General Albertus Catlin, in his report of the Battle of Belleau Wood, declared: "The enemy remained in force to the north of the town [Bouresches], his machine guns were still thick in the greater part of the wood, and his big guns thundered from back of Torcy. He was daunted by our first rush, but he came back. It took the Marines many days to finish the job, but finish it they did."[19]

The fight lasted through the entire month of June, though a battalion of the 5th Marine Regiment was able to take the entire wooded area on June 25. A few days later the 3rd Infantry Brigade then assaulted and took the valuable town of Vaux on the extreme right flank.

Montdidier-Noyon Defensive

This was the second of the series of battles fought between May 26 and August 6, 1918, in order to stop the drive of the Germans toward Paris. The immediate object of this offensive on the part of the enemy was to widen the Marne Salient. The Germans had advanced over thirty miles from the Chemin des Dames and reached the River Marne, but exhausted themselves in the effort. Of equal concern, they had placed themselves on a long, narrow front, twenty-eight miles by twenty-two in width, and were in a position inviting an attack from the Allies against their flank.

Unable to extend their forces on the one hand by the fortified city of

Rheims, held by the French, and on the other by the dense forest of Compiegne, their most promising plan was to push forward to the west of this wooded district and establish a salient running parallel to the Château-Thierry salient, and to connect with it as soon as sufficient advance had been made. This hazardous drive was begun about midnight June 8–9 between Montdidier-Noyon. This threw the Allied forces again on the defensive. The American troops brought into this attack were the Regulars of the First Division.

This drive was checked by the Allies, the enemy coming forward in mighty tides of battle to be mowed down by the artillery and machine guns like grass before the farmer's mowing machine. It was a fearful sacrifice of the German infantry, but the French and American forces stood shoulder to shoulder, while each succeeding wave grew less and less furious, until at the end of five days the Germans gave up hope and fell back upon their arms prostrate. Not only had they failed in this particular line of assault, but the Allies had won back a few points from their previous success.

The Germans now prepared for one more — the final, as it proved — great drive against Paris in their Champagne-Marne offensive. This sector soon became quiet. The 1st American Division, after 78 days of intermittent fighting in the Cantigny Sector, was now ordered to seek a much-needed rest a few miles north of Paris. That arduous campaign had cost this division in lives 238 officers and 5,593 men.[20]

Baccarat Sector

The German attack between Noyon and Montdidier failed, and this failure marked the end of their second attempt to hew their way to Paris. Still the enemy was on the offensive and might be expected to strike again in whatever direction it thought best. But both sides needed time in which to recuperate and prepare for further activity. This period, from June 15 to July 15, an even month, produced some of the most important movements of the troops during the war. The American divisions in this area had proved their dependency, the 1st Division at Cantigny, the 2nd Division at Belleau Wood, Bouresches, and Vaux, the 3rd at Château-Thierry, so they were given important positions without misgivings on the part of the French and British.

The 1st Division was relieved in the Cantigny sector by two French divisions and was assembled in the Beauvais Area; this was on July 5 and four days later the 2nd Division was relieved by the 26th American Division in Belleau Wood, after 40 days of activity, and placed as reserve at Montreuil-St. Aulde. The 3rd Division maintained its line on the banks of the River Marne. All of these divisions were recruited by replacements of men, animals and munitions, and at the end of the month were prepared for another fight with the enemy.

In the midst of these adjustments and preparations, the 77th Division, the first of the National Army Divisions to arrive in France and be placed under command of General George B. Duncan, was sent to relieve the 42nd or Rainbow Division in the quiet sector at Baccarat. The 42nd Division, which had held the Baccarat Sector since March 23 and experienced almost every phase of trench warfare in the Vosges region, was transferred by rail to the Marne Valley, to be stationed near Chalons-sur-Marne on the road from Paris to Nancy. On July 4, 1918, after escaping an armed meeting with the enemy which had threatened it, the Rainbow Division was made a part of the 21st French Army Corps and assigned to defend the Champagne.[21]

Champagne-Marne Defensive

A month of intense suspense followed the Montdidier-Noyon. The Germans made unrelenting preparations for the next drive while the Allies stood waiting for the expected attack, prepared and impatient for action, let it come from any quarter it might. Finally, on the July 15, the suspense was broken by an attack from the Germans and the Champagne-Marne defensive was on. There was no "American Army," as we understand the term and as there was later. The American divisions which did their part so nobly in stopping this last great drive of the enemy did so as units of the different branches of the French Army. The 3rd, 28th, and 42nd divisions participated as follows: the 3rd Division, consisting of Regulars, at Château-Thierry on the River Marne; the 28th Pennsylvania National Guard, near Jaulgonne on the Marne; and the 42nd Rainbow National Guard, to the west of Rheims, on the plateau of Champagne. The struggle comprised three attacks made nearly simultaneously and consisted of distinct battles, and three substantial victories.

The 3rd Division, under command of General Joseph T. Dickman, occupied a compact sector on the south bank of the Marne, and extending from the Jaulgonne Bend on the east to Château-Thierry on the west, just over six miles, or ten kilometers. This sector had been established under heavy fire from hills across the river, and belts of barbed wire were in process of construction, when work was suddenly stopped by the attack of the enemy on July 15. The situation here was hazardous and had characteristic features of its own. The front line was a series of rifle pits dug in the banks of the river, held each succeeding night by a platoon from each company, to be deserted at the breaking of day. Less than four hundred yards in the rear was the Paris-Metz railroad which wound along the top of a high embankment lifted from the lowlands on the south of the river. This embankment became the shelter for the main body of the troops, and naturally the line of resistance when the battle was fairly on. The enemy was effectually screened from the Allies by the steep hills to the north of the Marne, which at places came down to the river bank.

The grand objective of the Germans was to force a crossing of the Marne at Jaulgonne Bend, capture the railroad bridge to the south of the river and thus extend the Château-Thierry Salient and command the road to Paris.[22]

The whole scheme of battle was in keeping with the usual tactics of the Germans. The Germans, in the gloom of the evening of July 14 moved into position, and about midnight their artillery began a terrific cannonade. Besides that they drenched the surrounding country with gas, smoke shell and high explosives, under the cover of which they were able to reach their boats, which had been smuggled down to the river, and in the breaking light of the morning of the 15th start to cross the river. One of the most terrific combats of the war ensued. Lieutenant Lovejoy of the 38th Infantry, 3rd Division, gives a vivid account of this fight:

> Day was just breaking, and through the mist, fog and smoke one could see the boats and rafts loaded to the gunwales with enemy infantry men and machine gunners set out for the southern bank. That was about 3.30 o'clock. Yet not one crossed that day in the middle of the sector, in front of Company H or on the right in front of Company E. Men of the 38th, who had escaped the hours of shelling, met every attempt with rifle and automatic weapon fire. Scores of those boats were shattered and sunk or else disabled and sent drifting harmlessly down the river. Hundreds of Huns jumped into the water and were drowned. Those who reached our side by swimming were either killed or captured.
>
> Soldiers wounded in the early morning, remained at their automatic rifles or in their rifle pits unflinchingly until killed. One man of Company G was later found lifeless with his rifle and pistol empty, and in front of him a heap of twelve dead Germans. Another private's body was found surrounded by five of the enemy, all killed by a bayonet; but his own rifle was clutched in his hands, ready for more work, when he was stopped by a bullet from a machine gun.
>
> At this time Company G was really the pivotal point of the attack, because in front of this company the Germans had erected a pontoon bridge, over which swarmed a host of machine gunners. By means of a second pontoon bridge, the enemy was enabled to direct a flanking fire on the left. But Company G, under Captain Woolnidge, made heroic counter attacks, in the course of which it took more than 400 prisoners, in spite of overwhelming odds.[23]

This part of the attack was east of Château-Thierry, and the brunt of the battle fell on the 3rd Division, but by 8 o'clock on the morning of July 15 the fighting on the center and left of this division had virtually ceased. On the far right, however, the 38th Infantry was holding its outpost line in the rifle pits along the river bank against desperate odds. Its support on the right, the 125th French Division, according to orders had fallen back to make a stand on the heights in the background. The position occupied by this regiment was too important for it to abandon yet, if at all. Its front faced the Surmelin River, a tributary of the Marne flowing down a narrow valley flanked on either side by a broad road the Germans had planned to use to transport their supplies and artillery in anticipation of the splendid victory to be won. So the two roads of the Surmelin River valley were the great factor in this mighty struggle. All other successes would be in vain should the Germans fail here. The task of holding this front had been assigned to the 38th Infantry, with the foremost objective being preventing the Germans from throwing pontoon bridges across the river to connect with roads leading to Montmirail.

Colonel Ulysses G. McAlexander, in command of the 38th, had covered his right flank by rifle pits in "echelon," parallel lines, and so arranged that all could fire at once. These pits were occupied by the reserve battalion which had been brought up under fire. This right of the 38th faced toward Varennes, which had been captured by the enemy. The left flank had been seriously weakened in its support by the withdrawal of the 7th and 30th Infantry in reforming the line since Mezy had fallen into the hands of the enemy. The front held the river bank for a distance of two kilometers. The left flank defended two kilometers, while the right held stubbornly to nine and a half kilometers, the entire distance being about eight and one-half miles.

The 38th Infantry stubbornly defended this position for over fourteen hours against the continuous attacks of some of the best divisions of the German Army, among them the 13th and 36th, made up of such regiments as the 5th and 6th Prussian Grenadier Guards. During all that fateful period, time and again the Germans in their desperate efforts to cross the river in boats or pontoons were beaten back by rifle fire or hand grenades until the river ran red.[24]

General Pershing said in his report to the secretary of war:

> The 3rd Division was holding the bank of the Maine from the bend east of the mouth of the Surmelin to the west of Mezy, opposite Château-Thierry, where a large force of German Infantry sought to force a passage under support of powerful artillery concentrations and under cover of smoke screens. A single regiment of the 3rd wrote one of the most brilliant pages in our military annals on this occasion. It prevented the crossing at certain points on its front, while on either flank the Germans, who had gained a footing, pressed forward. Our men, firing in three directions, met the German attacks with counter-attacks at critical points, which succeeded in throwing two German divisions into complete confusion, capturing six hundred prisoners.[25]

Simultaneously with the preceding attacks by the Germans, they made a drive southward in the Champagne district east of Rheims, midway between that city and the Argonne Forest. Evidence had been accumulating for some time that the Germans were intending to extend their offensive in this direction so as to effect the capture of Rheims and cover the territory as far as Chalons-sur-Marne.

The Fourth French Army under General Gouraud was in command of this section of the salient, and the 28th National Guard Division, commanded by Maj. Gen. Charles M. Clement, was brought up from the vicinity of Montmirail, ten miles in the rear of the 3rd Division. This division had not seen active duty as yet and was now, for obvious reasons, placed by companies and regiments with French units to be tried out. It thus happened that four companies, L and M of the 109th Infantry and B and C of the 110th Infantry, were ordered to help strengthen weak places in the French lines. Company M, 109th Infantry, was stationed below Passy-sur Maine; Company L back of Courtemont-Varennes, in the Jaulgonne Bend, and the two companies from the 110th facing Fossoy and Mezy.

This portion of the Champagne had seen days of furious activity in the earlier stages of the war, but was now a quiet sector. Within two weeks it became active enough to satisfy the most eager warrior. General Gouraud's plan for the coming struggle was simple but daring. It was to hold the first position until it should be considered well to fall back to a second strongly fortified position, from which they should concentrate their fire upon the position just abandoned to the exulting Germans. Signal men were stationed so as to keep the artillery and infantry posted on the situation. There were intervening positions to be evacuated at the proper time. Companies of the 42nd Division were assigned to these places, but the majority of these American troops was sent to the second or main position to which the front line was to retire. It was generally understood the Germans were to open their attack at midnight; they usually moved with the precision of the clock, and fifteen minutes before twelve an unusual silence hung over the scene.

The Germans opened their offensive, as usual, on the night of July 14–15, with over three hours of galling barrage, and at 3:30, under cover of this they threw their pontoon bridges over the river, and then through the fog and smoke came across the gray-green figures until there seemed no end to the marching column. The critical moment had come when it was to be seen if the nervousness of three hours of tense waiting under such fire would transform them into heroes.

The French said afterwards that they were amazed and deeply proud of their American comrades. Nothing seemed to stop the Germans. Though machine gun and rifle fire mowed them down, they continued to come on, and when they had enough men on the south side, they swarmed to assault the Allied line. Up the wooded slopes they swept in waves, regardless of the furious fire of the defenders. One man fell only to have another take his place. They broke into the first line. Gone then was the science and skill of war; there was but one thought: kill or be killed. Hand to hand and breast to breast they fought. Companies were no more. Men fought in little groups, and no group knew what the other group was doing.

And then came the tragedy for those gallant four companies of the 28th Division. Something had gone wrong. Somewhere, due most probably to the difference in language, the order had not been understood, or perhaps the officer to whom the order to retire was given had been killed. At all events, the French had slowly withdrawn to the main line of resistance, and it dawned upon the Pennsylvanians that they were alone!

The French had used their "yielding defense" tactics of which these brave men were ignorant. Alone now, little determined groups a thousand yards apart, they were facing the entire German assault army. Most who remained alive were quickly surrounded — the groups were so small — and were taken prisoners; but some groups, led by officers for whom this was the first battle of their lives, fought their way out, and by a skillful rearguard action brought the survivors back to the lines where the French were making their stand. Such is the heroic story of the four companies of Pennsylvanians in the Second Battle of the Marne.[26]

All along the front, the last, and in some respects the greatest, offensive on the part of the Germans, three days after it had been started, on July 18, was utterly crushed. Frederick Palmer, in summing up the result of the campaign, declared: "We did not dash the cup of victory from his lips; we smashed it to splinters in his face."

So ended gloriously for Allied armies the Champagne-Marne Defensive, the fifth of the German drives towards Paris and London. The first of these drives was made in August and September 1914, through Belgium and northern France, until checked at the Marne, this through the sacrifices of the Belgians and heroism of the French.

The second great offensive was against Verdun in 1916, when again the invader was stopped by the sacrifices of the French troops and the spirit "Thou shalt not pass!"

The third was directed against the British Army at Amiens during the darkest days of the war, in March 1918, when, as Field Marshal Haig said in his report, "The British are fighting with their backs to the wall." Four million men were engaged in this battle on a front of 150 miles.

The fourth drive was made by the Germans in May 1918 and was directed against the Allies between Rheims and Soissons, including Château-Thierry, and was known as the Marne Salient. Gloom hung over armies of the French and British at this stage of the struggle. Already the light of a new day was beginning to break over the night of war, but the sunlight was coming out of the west on the arms of a new ally. Frankly, though neither would ever admit it, the AEF saved the French, who were close to collapse, and if that had happened the British would have rapidly fallen back across the channel, much like they did at Dunkirk. Of course, the huge German forces would have overwhelmed the small numbers of the AEF if they had tried to resist.

The fifth drive of the Germans was directed against the French and Americans in what was known as the Marne Salient. This offensive was undertaken on July 15, 1918, and was another desperate attempt to reach Paris, as well as to deepen and extend their front here. The famous defense of the 3rd Division was made here, and the invasion of the enemy was decisively checked, so the tide of battle no longer ran seaward.

Summing up the expectations of the war from a German viewpoint, Chancellor Hertling said: "On July 1st, 1918, we were convinced the Allies would propose peace before September. We expected grave events in Paris before the 15th of July. But on the 18th, even the most optimistic among us knew that all was lost. The history of the world was played out in those three days."[27]

Aisne-Marne Offensive

The shock of the battle dazed both the Allied and German armies. The Germans were worse; they were seemingly paralyzed. The mighty offensive which they had planned with so much confidence, and which they had undertaken with so much courage, had failed. This was the famed battle fought just south of the ancient city of Soissons. If inferior to their forces, which did not seem apparent now, the Allies had shown themselves strong enough, courageous enough, and skillful enough to stem their tide of aggression; had effectually checked their onward sweep towards Paris. In taking their supreme chance they had not widened this salient but lengthened it. So now they were exposed on a long, narrow front, and no nearer their long-cherished goal.

The American commander, General Pershing, was astute enough to see that a quick, swift action now, while the enemy was getting his breath, would count far more than if taken after a day's delay, when he should have time to rally. This suggestion he conveyed to Marshal Foch, and urged him to have the American troops make a drive at the enemy before he could awaken from his stupor.

Marshal Foch saw the wisdom of this plan and in accepting the proposal decided that the 1st American Division, Regulars, and the 2nd Division, Regular Army and Marines, though worn out with six months of almost continuous fighting, should act in conjunction with that redoubtable French Division known as the Moroccan Division, including the Foreign Legion. No greater compliment could have been paid these battle scarred veterans than to have been chosen from the million or more troops hovering over the Marne Salient. Perhaps many preferred that someone else be chosen for that honor; all of these men had seen recent arduous campaigning and fighting.

This selection of the Americans for this most important move proved that General Pershing's method of training his men had found favor in the eye of the great French commander. The American leader, in the face of opposition, or at least against the advice of those who believed in the French "yielding defense," had trained his men for offensive as well as defensive tactics. The wisdom of this system of warfare had been shown by the heroic action of the 3rd Division Infantry on the outpost line along the River Marne on the night of July 15. It was now to be given a severe test in the grand, yet hazardous, offensive to be undertaken, where a failure spelled disaster, a victory meant greater triumphs ahead.

On the afternoon of July 17 the order was passed down the line to be in readiness for an attack at 4:35 the following morning. The feeling dominating the minds of those brave men awaiting the moment when the first move should be made can neither be described nor imagined. Only those who were there can understand. Fortunately, the elements of nature were in harmony with their work. The night before had been clear and calm, save for the almost constant warfare of the German airplanes making the sky hideous. On this evening an ominous thunderstorm, an unusual occurrence in France, threatened to deluge the earth, while the inky-black clouds rolling low overhead made the scene intensely dark, so dark the German airplanes were obliged to forsake their attentive overlook of the Allied lines. As the success or failure of this movement depended largely upon the secrecy in which it should be carried out, this uncommon darkness seemed providential. In the midst of this murky gloom, as the very floodgates of the heavens were to open with their fire of electrical artillery, the order came for the advance.

And such an advance! Under the canopy of darkness along the three roads leading to the front marched the three divisions, two of the American forces and one of the French, 67,000 men strong, 5,000 animals, 3,000 vehicles, all ordered to a particular point to be reached simultaneously, and each with a separate purpose. Those who lived to recall that memorable march would recall it with wonder and dismay. The road was unfamiliar to the rushing troops, and while the thunderstorm made the passage safer, it also made it more difficult. Artillery pieces and caissons of necessity held the center of the way, while the infantry trudged through the muddy ditches. To make matters worse several battalions of big French tanks came wallowing down the highway, compelling everything to give way to them. Then came the five-ton motor trucks, staff cars, motorcycles, side cars; all these, going at different rates of speed, mixed in an awful congestion with the plodding infantry platoons. By this time the infantry had quite abandoned the road and was picking its way through wheatfields, the soft sod soaked with the pelting rain, the frantic orders of the platoon leaders drowned by the crash and tumult of the grinding trucks, tanks and medley of other vehicles. Amid all confusion and discomfort and uncertainty, the warring forces surging in the pitchy darkness along the overtaxed road entered a small town, where situation grew more hopeless, as the advancing columns no longer had the fields and open country to allow greater space for the advance.

The miracle of that awful night was that every unit of the 1st Division reached its position before 4:30 a.m. Another miracle was that during it all, scarcely a German shell was fired. This showed definitely how certain was the cover of the darkness. So much for the initiative of the 1st Division, which had that night been placed under the command of General Charles P. Summerall, and which was now advancing step by step into the enemy salient. Fortunately for them, that division had been on the scene for several days. How was that enemy prepared to meet them?

The advance of the 2nd Division was fraught with far greater obstacles and uncertainty than the movement already described. They had been rushed to the scene, with little rest for any of the troops. Where the 1st advanced through an open country, this division was forced to march through the dense, almost pathless forest of Retz, black even by daylight. The few narrow roads were quickly blocked by the traffic of the division. Here the plight of the infantry was far more serious than with the preceding division. There were no wheat fields for the infantry to advance through, rather the jungle of Bois de Retz. The confusion, under the blackness of the woods and along the rain-drenched roads, was beyond description.

At 4:30 the order had gone out to open the barrage fire, when the three divisions were expected to go over. Could they hope to make it? Fortunately they had a shorter distance to move than the 1st Division, and again fortunately the French Division, the 1st Moroccan, which was to hold the center of the line, was in position. The 1st American Division was now in position on the French left. Every available means at the command of the last named division was utilized to assist the belated 2nd Division, for rumor had been circulated that the American support had been lost in the woods. They actually had not gotten lost, their pathway was just more difficult than that of the other two divisions.

Small wonder if that was an anxious half hour; small wonder leaders became frantic. In the midst of the awful suspense and out of lower forest emerged at least a portion of the 2nd Division, the 9th and 23rd Infantry Regiments and lastly the 5th Regiment of Marines. Without regard to order these were hurried into position, the infantry making it one minute before the time set for the beginning of the attack, and the 5th Marines after the attack began. At 4:35 the first guns of the great rolling barrage were opened and the battle was at hand. By the light of these guns the last of the Infantry and Marines joined their comrades. The good name of the 2nd Division had been saved, and as it came out of the Bois de Retz, now illuminated far and wide by the flash of the guns, the line was completed. No more need the famous fighters of the Moroccan Division, made up of men whose business it was to fight and die, chafe at the thought of failure on the part of their associates, whose mettle was to be proven to them that morning. In fact, the men of the 2nd Division moved more rapidly and then had to wait for the Moroccan Division to catch up.

To have been selected to fight on either flank of the famous Foreign Legion — then considered some of the best fighters in the world — was incentive sufficient for the 1st and 2nd American Divisions, officers and men, to fill the records of that battle with extraordinary qualities of heroism. The gallant Moroccan Division also tested its mettle that day when brought shoulder to shoulder with these new champions chosen from the entire Allied strength to be its comrades to strike the decisive blow, which was to show to the world the safety or peril of Paris. Upon their action today hung the balance of power.

It proved the Germans were not prepared for this attack. Confident of marching on to Paris in the near future, they had not considered it necessary to "dig in" here. Neither had they expected the Allied forces could recover from their recent efforts to begin anew. They had not come to realize the force of this new element infused into the combat.

Before nightfall, the 2nd Division of the attacking forces had gained the objective set for the drive and prepared to rest upon their arms. This included the 3rd Brigade of Infantry and 5th Regiment of Marines. Moroccans and the 1st American Division had not been able to keep up with their comrades.

Tales of personal valor and heroism abound in the accounts of that and the succeeding days' fighting, until the grand offensive was won. An eyewitness of the thrilling action describes a heroic but useless scene, one among many, which rivals the famous ride of the six hundred horsemen comprising the light brigade of the Earl of Cardigan at Balaklava in the Crimean War. It showed that moronic action, even in this war of multiple machine guns, still persisted. A unit of French cavalry "moving majestically out of the forest of Retz ... at a slow trot, their blue helmets flashing in the sun," at their colonel's command drew their sabers and charged machine guns and artillery. Consequently, they were mowed down.

Before ten o'clock on the night of July 18 the Allied line was fairly fixed for the night, including Breuil, Missy-sur-Bois, near the road to Paris, up the hill to Vierzy, where the 23rd Infantry and 5th Marines of the 2nd Division had performed such prodigious feats, and on the slope of the hill overhanging the little town of Tigny, and thence along to where the Moroccans were holding the slopes.

It was a busy night for both the Allies and the enemy, the artillery of both sides continually belching forth its deadly hail. Ambulances looking after the wounded plied resolutely to and fro despite the rain of fire falling all about. Supply wagons and water carts, with warm food and water for the weary men, performed a gallant part. Munition carts also went forward to replenish the stocks in this essential part of the stern drive. At headquarters no one was idle for a moment. In the seven hours of darkness and prelude of battle, until four in the morning of another day, sleep and rest were unknown. To add to the frightfulness of it all, the red-nosed planes of Baron Richthofen's "Air Circus" whizzed through the air, back and forth, every few minutes dropping their great balls of fire suspended in mid-air by parachutes and lighting the earth far and wide to more than midday brilliancy, a brightness made hideous by the enemy bombs doing fearful havoc among the drivers of munition, food and water carts, brave fellows who followed their line of duty with a courage as great as the veterans who went over the top in battle.

The attack on the second day, July 19, opened under cover of a rolling barrage at four a.m. This drive was made along the entire German front, and with an enemy better prepared than on the previous day, the fighting was more stubborn. To add to the disadvantage of the Allies, all of the American airplanes had been driven from the overhead field of war. The German situation was now desperate. To yield was to court disaster in the end. Each point must be held here at any cost. The price paid in human lives was awful.

This was especially true of the section of the plateau running towards Soissons. Here the Germans had planted three acres of machine guns backed by artillery. Against these the 2nd Brigade of the 1st Division was pitted in one of the fiercest battles waged during the war. Unaware at first of these machine gun nests, the Allied Infantry soon found it had a stiff fight on hand. But, foot by foot, under cover of stiff firing, the line was carried forward until the brow of the hill was reached.

As the troops went over the summit, they were met by a galling fire from 77mm field guns left here by the Germans. The tanks were immediately put out of commission, and the infantry had a tough task to accomplish. But before nightfall the line had been carried forward to Ploisy ravine, where the exhausted infantry rested after one of the hardest days of warfare it had experienced. It had cost this brigade 3000 officers and men.

The 1st Brigade and Moroccans also did some gallant fighting that day, maintaining at great cost their reputations as veterans of war. The glory goes beyond even these divisions. On the previous day, the 2nd Division utilized three regiments and suffered heavy casualties. This day the division had just the 6th Marines coming into the battle fresh, having been held in reserve the first day. They, through no fault of their own, arrived on the battlefront several hours late but swept over the wheat-covered plateau with their usual dash and reckless driving, through, into and past machine gun nests, suffering great casualties until they nearly reached the Château-Thierry road. There they met the full force of the German resistance.

Time after time, by repeated assaults, a few Marines reached the road only to be thrown off again; finally they dug in, facing the village of Tigny, which lay just west of the road. They had not accomplished their mission and had suffered enormous casualties, about half the regiment. However, the road now lay in No Man's Land, and the German communications between Soissons and Château-Thierry were cut. The 2nd Division suffered huge casualties both days and was now finished. It would be sent to a "quiet sector" where it would spend a month or more mending and accepting replacements.

The remaining Allies, with additional French support replacing the 2nd Division, now had pushed their line into the field of the enemy, so they rested on the night of July 19, well satisfied with their work, having advanced seven miles against the very troops selected by the Germans to hew their way to Paris. That night the capital of France must have looked far away to the war-worn men of the disappointed German Army.

The third day's drive is a record of gallant attacks against an equally gallant foe making its last determined stand, but a stand continually yielding before the assaults of the Allies fired with the spirit of victory. To the 1st Division was assigned the herculean task of taking Berzy-le-See. Two regiments of infantry, the 26th and 28th, literally wiped out every vestige of German possession, and the line ran along the western bank of the river Crise. The 16th and 18th infantry, the 1st Brigade of the 1st Division, with the Moroccans cleaned up the Château-Thierry-Soissons highway and rested on the elevated plateau of Bizancy, a fortress which cost severe fighting to capture, but was accomplished, the Allies taking more prisoners on this occasion than their depleted ranks numbered. The Allies now commanded the city of Soissons, three miles down the valley, which was the heaviest blow the Germans had received in all this great offensive of the American divisions and the Moroccans. The cost had been severe to the Allies, and it was the deathblow to the Germans in the Marne region. The best of their soldiery, picked to march on

Paris, had been overwhelmingly defeated and put to rout by the two American divisions and two French divisions.[28]

All indicators pointed toward victory from the first night until the morning of August 6, when the Americans of several other divisions, including the 4th and 26th, and French had reached the Vesle. The rugged lines are now softened by memory, the awfulness of it all forgotten in a measure. For the first time since the Germans had marched into this war, they saw the Fatherland in danger. For them the Marne Salient was no longer an offensive, but a defensive — a retreat, to put it plainly. Their great aim now was to escape disaster and re-establish the army on safer footing nearer home.

The south bank of the Marne was abandoned by the Germans on the morning of July 20, and their machine guns were planted so as to stop any pursuit the Allies might attempt. The 3rd American Division of Regulars was stationed on the Marne east of Château-Thierry as far as Jaulgonne Bend, where it did some sharp lighting, and stopped the first German drive in June. On the morning of July 21 the 26th American Division, New England National Guard, was ordered forward from Belleau Wood, an order they carried out with eagerness, but ending in disappointment inasmuch as the enemy had fled in the night. The order then came to pursue the Germans, which was undertaken with precaution, knowing as they did the still combative nature of the foe.

In the seven days of fighting from July 18 to 24, the 26th Division bore heavy casualties and severe hardship. Losses totaled more than 5,000 officers and men.

In a 1976 interview, Shipley Thomas remembered the afternoon of July 22. He was attempting to contact the division adjutant by phone. Maj. Gen. Summerall grabbed the phone and yelled:

> "Hello, this is General Summerall. Who is this?"
> "Lieutenant Thomas, sir, 26th Infantry."
> "Well, how are things?"
> "I have to report that we have broken through as far as we can. Our colonel is dead, our lieutenant colonel is dead, and all the majors are dead or wounded. And God knows how many captains or lieutenants are down. And the situation with the men is just as bad."
> "Great God, Mr. Thomas! Who is commanding the regiment?"
> "Captain Barney Legge."
> "How is he doing?"
> "Fine, sir, with what he has left."
> "Well, who is his executive officer?"
> "I guess I am...."[29]

The 1st Division remained in the line past its usefulness, for the usual reason — inability because of losses — and was finally relieved on July 25 by the 42nd Division. The Allied forces now held the line from Soissons to Le

Charmel on the south, three miles north of Jaulgonne Bend on the Marne. The key to the southern section was Croix Rouge Fme, with its fortifications, and this was directly in front of the Rainbow Division, recently sent here. On the morning of July 27 the 42nd Division prepared to take this place by crossing the open space which separated it from the forest. This dash was made with the spirit and determination which won the first offensive, and assured the success of the next drive.

In the meantime, the 3rd Division made an attack upon Ronchers and Hill 190, overlooking Ronchers and the Ourcq. That night the north wing of the 42nd cleaned out the forest of Fere of the last of the enemies, while others cleared the slopes of the Ourcq, and at last the Allies commanded the backbone of the German position between the Ourcq and the Marne.

All this had been accomplished against a terrific resistance — the resistance of an army retreating foot by foot, knowing its very existence depended upon the energy with which it coped with a foe that knew only the order "to advance." On July 28 the 3rd Division took the town of Roncheres, while the 42nd Division strengthened its position before Cierges. Those who survived that day's sullen fighting in an atmosphere laden with German gas wonder how they lived through it all. That day the 165th Infantry Regiment of the Rainbow Division captured Hill 184, which made possible the possession of the adjoining towns.

The 3rd Division had been in constant activity since late in May and performed an important part in breaking the German offensive and insuring the success of the Allied offensive, so it had richly earned the rest that came to it on July 30, when it was relieved by the 32nd Division, consisting of the Wisconsin and Michigan National Guard.

On the afternoon of July 30, the 42nd Division took up the task laid down by the 3rd Division, beginning a drive through the woods skirting the little town of Cierges, only to find the village surcharged with gas, so the line was formed at the edge of the woods. The 32nd and 42nd Divisions now held the front on the Ourcq. The following morning, the 32nd Division crossed the opening and took Cierges and Hill 212.[30]

August 1 found the Americans preparing for another advance in the face of bitter opposition, an opposition that seemed to augur further intense work, but on the morning of the 2nd came the great surprise. Where an armed and determined resistance was expected, they were met with the silence of an empty camp! The enemy had quietly and swiftly withdrawn during the night. That was a great day for the Allies. Not only had a hundred small towns fallen with their chain of fortifications, but Soissons had surrendered, Rheims was no longer threatened, while the broken German Army had retreated to the River Vesle. This was the beginning of the German Army falling back on their well-prepared "Hindenburg Line."

The American divisions were ordered to give pursuit, and then followed more skirmishing and driving in of the foe, until the forest of Nesles had been cleared by the 117th. Engineers of the 42nd Division and the last ridge south of the Vesle had been gained. The 42nd Division, under the command of Major General Charles T. Menoher, during its eight days of fighting on this front, had advanced 15 kilometers in the face of bitter resistance and at the cost of 184 officers and 5,469 men. Relieved now by the 4th Division Regulars, on the night of August 2 the Rainbow Division marched triumphantly back to the valley of the Marne.

The final honors in that memorable campaign fell to the fortune of the 32nd Division by driving the Germans out of the town of Fismes and holding the town. This division there completed its mission after three weeks of intense fighting. On August 5 it was relieved by the 28th Division and was assembled on the heights between the Rivers Ourcq and Vesle. In the last seven days of fighting it had lost 77 officers and 645 enlisted killed, with a total casualty list of 3,547, and had advanced twelve miles. Under the command of General William G. Haan, this division of Michigan and Wisconsin troops had entered the fighting area without experience, but covered itself with sufficient glory to place it among the best of the American Army.

On August 4 the 77th Division, New York City National Army, was sent from the Baccarat sector and under the command of General George B. Duncan was given a test in this "Hell Hole of the Vesle," alongside the veterans of the 28th Division. The 4th Division, under Cameron, which had been sent to relieve the 42nd, advanced from the Ourcq to the Vesle. Acting in part with other divisions or together, it had advanced about ten miles, and thrown its line definitely across the Vesle, having suffered during the campaign the loss of over 5,000 men killed and wounded. It was relieved on the night of August 12–13. General John L. Hines was now placed in command, while General Cameron was given the command of the Fifth Army Corps.

August 1, 1918, found five American Divisions in sectors in Alsace and the Vosges Mountains, which was the southeastern end of the Western Front. Another five American divisions were fighting in the direction of Vesles, west of Rheims. One American Division, the 82nd of the American National Army, had been in the Toul sector since June 16. This sector was to the south of St. Mihiel and became designated as the American Area on the Western Front. Next to the Toul Sector on the east was the Saizarais Sector, which ranged from Limey on the east to the Moselle River at Pont-a-Mousson. The French were relieved by the Americans on August 7, 1918. There had been practically no fighting here since 1914, but over the scene rested the horrors of those terrible days and nights of fighting in the Bois-le-Prete, and the old trenches and quarries remained in ruins to keep alive the memory of the sacrifices made to keep the place.[31]

The Aisne-Marne offensive ended when the French and Americans reached the Vesle on August 6. Two days later Marshal Foch ordered the British, with a few American divisions, to begin an offensive towards Cambrai, with the purpose of extinguishing the Amiens Montdidier Salient. The road to Cambrai from Arras to Baupaume and on to Amiens runs through the desolate valley of the Somme. The Germans had depleted this section in order to reinforce the reserves of Vesle front. The American troops with the British along this line of offensive were the 33rd Division of Illinois National Guard, the 27th New York National Guard, and the 30th Old Hickory National Guard and some elements of the 80th Division. On this sector, pitted against the iron front of the Hindenburg line, was waged successfully one of the fiercest battles of the war. Beyond Amiens the road leads to Montdidier, described elsewhere, and to Cantigny, where some of the Americans received their initial action in the Great War.

St. Mihiel Offensive

So far there had been no American Army as such. Instead, the American Divisions, as has been stated, were scattered all along the front as parts of the French and British armies. On September 2, 1918, General Pershing made the request to Foch that the American divisions act as a distinct unit. In his opinion they had won this right through the Aisne-Marne Salient. This demand of the American commander was granted with the condition that the American offensive at St. Mihiel should be limited, and then activities, including most divisions, be transferred to Meuse-Argonne. The American commander in his report says that even then no one present at the conference — Marshals Foch and Petain and other leaders — dared to say the war would end before another year. But Foch had in mind a mighty offensive from Ypres to Verdun, though he had yet to learn of the power of his new Ally.

St. Mihiel is a town of fewer than ten thousand people; its garrison and barracks were an important place during the war, as witness the German battle to capture it in 1914, four years before the time of the coming offensive to wrest it from them. Its seizure by the Germans was not by any means its first taste of war. It became the scene of bitter contention in the days of the French Renaissance, while still earlier in its history it suffered at the hands of the Roman invaders in the days of Caesar.

Strictly speaking the battle did not take place in the town, but as the town capitulated as a result of the victory won nearby it has been given its name. Here as elsewhere, the topography of the country had much to do with the setting of the battle. In times of peace the scene is not without the charm attached to the valley along the River Meuse. On the east southward from Dun-sur-Meuse upstream to Commercy, the landscape lifts sharply for between two and three miles, to the ridge which forms the backbone for the Plain of Woevre. This crest is known as the Heights of the Meuse (Cotes-de-Meuse) in the Verdun section, wherein stood the important strongholds, Forts Vaux and Douaumonth, which the Germans fought hard to capture.

The Plain of the Woevre extends eastward for nearly forty miles until abruptly cut off by the highlands commanding the River Moselle. The Woevre Plain is more strictly speaking a marsh, dotted here and there by bodies of water of varying size, and usually bordered with marshy shore. Through this boggy plain winds leisurely — at places very leisurely — a small stream with the rather startling name of Rupt-de-Mad and which finds its way into the Moselle not many miles south of the German fortifications at Metz.

At this time the German line ran westward from the Moselle Ridge across the Woevre Plain until it came to the Heights of the Meuse at Apremont. Here it turned southward until coming to the Meuse a little south of the old French fort, Camp des Romains. Then the line turned north, crossing the river in front of St. Mihiel and including the ruins of Chauvoncourt, and then re-crossing the Meuse extending northeasterly so as to cross the ridge at an angle to the Woevre Plain east of the battlefield of Les Eparges, the scene of French operations in 1915. From here it ran along the base of Meuse Heights in the Verdun sector.

In the main the enemy was strongly situated. Fort Camp des Romains commanded an extensive and exhaustive view of the Meuse Valley. On the east looking down the side of Meuse Heights were two vantage spots, either nearly or equal to that already mentioned. The first was the church tower at the village of Hattonchatel, which overlooked the swampy plain of Woevre as far as the hills of Metz. The other was from Mont Sec, an isolated peak rising from Woevre Plain, about two miles east of Meuse Heights; it was as important from a military viewpoint as either of the others named. So far we have not found a vulnerable spot. The most promising section for an attack lay between the wooded hills west of Pont-a-Moussan, where the country is open and mostly level to Apremont. An offensive undertaken here and abetted by a determined advance from the Les Eparges corner promised to at least cut off a portion of the enemy's forces, unless a retreat was made.

In Pershing's plan of operations the 1st Division, advancing east of the Meuse Hills and their outlying spur, Mont Sec, would join hands with the 26th Division, coming southeast from the Lea Eparges Corner, and the meeting place would be the village of Vigneulles, just south of Hattonchatel Hill, which is the highest summit of the whole Meuse Heights. Meantime, the rest of Pershing's operative force between Pont-a-Moussan and the 1st Division front would keep step. Thus not only would the St. Mihiel salient be pinched out and the Germans encompassed and captured when the 1st and 26th Divisions joined hands at Vignuelles, but the front would be pushed out eastward towards Metz, beyond the considerable town of Thiaucourt, where the Rupt-de-Mad brook assumes the dignity of a river. This new front would carry a threat both for Metz and for the Briey ironworks and mines far to the north.

Incidentally, the important railroad town of Metz was Pershing's original target, until Foch demanded that he cut the advance short in order to provide most of his First Army to the planned assault in the Meuse-Argonne. The American command considered this a waste since the city was a center of rail traffic and an important supply point for the German army. Taking it would probably compel the Germans to retire from their prepared positions, making the upcoming assault that much easier.

By night marches and concealed action, Pershing's army was in position to advance on the night of September 11, 1918, while the enemy little suspected the struggle was coming so soon. Briefly stated, Pershing had placed his forces on the south side of the salient from the Moselle westward to the First Corps, consisting of the 2nd, 5th, 82nd, and 90th in line, Liggett commanding. On the left, commanded by Dickman, the Fourth Corps, consisting of the 89th, 42nd and 1st Divisions, were placed nearly opposite Mont Sec. From this section round to the northeast corner already mentioned the French troops held the ground, waiting for the outcome of the offensive. At the Corner, under command of Cameron, the Fifth corps awaited action. This comprised the 26th American, the 15th French Colonial, and the 4th American, but only the 26th was expected to participate in the battle. The object of this division was to cross the border of the salient and meet the First Division at Vigneulles.

An interesting sidelight — an American Marine officer, Colonel Hiram I. Bearss, leading the 102nd Infantry, drove his regiment many miles through German lines to actually take the town long before the 1st Division arrived.[32] It will be seen that nine American divisions were on the front, with seven expected to do active duty, and only four of these, the 1st, 2nd, 26th, and 42nd, veteran troops. Three more divisions were held in reserve. The American force numbered in the vicinity of 300,000, and with the reserved American divisions and the French, 70,000, it aggregated 400,000 to 500,000. It was the greatest American army to enter battle and the first to fight in Europe.

The battle and reduction of the St. Mihiel salient was an American offensive — the first — accomplished from September 12 to September 16 with strong French support. Performed wholly under direction of the American command and largely by American troops, it was a distinctive honor to officers and men. The attack began at 5 a.m. on the 12th, and was a continued series of successes, though not accomplished without severe fighting and a casualty list of 7,000.

What mattered most was the fact that the German army was in the process of withdrawing back to join the Hindenburg Line. Its troops were less capable of holding any positions and admittedly, this made the First Army's task simpler. Sixteen thousand prisoners were taken and 443 guns. It not only reduced a dangerous German salient, but it demonstrated the American ability to undertake and execute an extensive and victorious operation. St. Mihiel set a record for concentration of artillery fire by a four-hour artillery preparation, consuming more than 1,000,000 rounds of ammunition.

In overpowering the St. Mihiel salient, the American First Army was aided and protected by the largest concentration of air forces ever made. Of this auxiliary wing of assault, about one-third was American, and the balance was French, British and Italian squadrons operating under American command. Throughout this action the German rear was kept under bombardment day and night; their reserves and ammunition dumps were located for the American long-range artillery, propaganda intended to confuse and distract the enemy; photographs were taken of every movement of the Germans, this information being frequently delivered to headquarters in finished photographs within half an hour.

On account of the fog, which hampered the action during the day, the air forces were compelled to fly low, and the infantry experienced some trouble with the German "strafing" planes. The American air force consisted of eleven observation squadrons, twelve pursuit squadrons, three bombing squadrons and fourteen balloon companies.

Pershing had asked the privilege of demonstrating the ability of the American Army by attempting the capture of one of the oldest occupied sectors on the whole front. Surely the success of the Battle of St. Mihiel had warranted him in his assumption. Cantigny, Belleau Wood and the Aisne-Marne had been the preliminary preparation and St. Mihiel the final test to prove the American soldier and his machinery of war. Pershing had not underestimated his men. On the eve of the second day of battle Foch sent this message: "The American First Army under your command has achieved in this first day a magnificent victory by a maneuver which was as skillfully prepared as it was valiantly executed."[33]

Nothing had gone amiss. The 1st and 26th divisions had met at Vigneulles, as planned, the honor of the actual capture of the town going to the "Yankee Division." The line now ran from Les Eparges 10 miles from Verdun to the Plain of Woevre, passed east of Thiacourt and came to the Moselle beyond Pont-a-Mousson. The tidal battlefields of Gravelotte and Mars-la-Tour, where the French had lost so disastrously in 1870 through the mistakes of Bazaine, and just beyond to Metz, apparently these were within his grasp, but Pershing was not thinking of this, nor yet the iron fields of Briey. His gaze was aimed toward more rugged scenes on the other side of the River Meuse, and the march was taken without any misgivings now as to flank or rear.[34]

Meuse-Argonne Offensive and Blanc Mont Ridge

On September 26, 1918, the First American Army took the place of the Second French Army and began a series of attacks upon the Germans stationed in the broad valley of the River Meuse, destined to be beyond comparison the greatest battle ever fought by American troops until that date, and perhaps the greatest battle in the history of the world up to then. General Pershing said in his report of November 20 that the object of this, the Meuse-Argonne offensive, was "to draw the best German divisions to our front and to consume them."

The main object of the American attack was the Sedan-Mezieres railroad, the principal line of transportation of supplies for the German forces along an important section of the Western Front. Should this way of communication be broken, the entire situation of the enemy would be changed. A retreat of the Germans from this position would not only spell disaster to the morale of the German army but it would mean the evacuation of the Briey iron fields, which had been one source of their supply of this metal. The Germans realized this fully as much as did the Allied powers, and they were resolved to make a desperate stand here. At this critical moment, with the mighty struggle impending, the German commander of the Fifth Army made his memorable appeal in which he called upon his men to stand their ground in defiance of all hazard, acknowledging that defeat here portended disaster to the Fatherland.

This battlefield had a length of over seventy miles, from La Harazee in the Argonne section to Clemrey just north of Nancy, and was fifteen miles in depth. The contour of the country in this territory was calculated to draw out some of the sharpest lines of strategy and afford a battleground of intense offensives and desperate defenses. Fifteen miles west of Verdun rises the abrupt side of the Argonne Forest, which has become inseparably connected with those days of fighting. Leaving this forest and plateau on the left the descent drops into Aire Valley. The German front line was at Boureilles before the beginning of the offensive by the Allies, and was the first to fall on September 26, which marked the opening of the battle. This was accomplished by the 28th Division, and the attack here was followed up by that division and the 35th by bitter fighting at Varennes and Cheppy, the last named town across the Valley of Aire. From Varennes the road leads through Charpentry to

Romange, dotted by half a dozen quaint villages, three of which — Gesnes, Exermont and Sommerance — were the scene of some of the fiercest fighting in those forty-six days of intense combat. The small group of wooded hills comprising this section were in a measure the key to the whole situation, and defended by eight entrenched German divisions, it required the keenest fighting all through the early days of October.

For its gallantry in this action General Pershing issued a general order citing especially the 1st American Division U.S. Regulars. However, the other American divisions, though mostly untrained and suffering huge casualties because they were led by equally untrained officers, fought with magnificent courage.

At Romagne-sous-Montfaucon rest today the bodies of a majority of the brave men who fell in that sanguinary contest, it being the largest American military cemetery in France, having 23,061 graves, one-third of the entire number who fell victims of the war, and one-half of the soldiers killed in action during the battle.

Below Romange lies Bantheville, and then the valley of the River Andon, which winds leisurely through the towns of Aincreville and Dulcon to Dun-sur-Meuse, where on November 5, 1918, the 5th Division began its advance over the Meuse, which was accomplished in three days and a firm footing established at Dun.

Continuing down the valley through Mouzay the river winds into Stenay, where the 90th Division made its hazardous crossing of the Meuse, while just beyond the stream towards Beaumont the 89th Division performed its famous advance to the Meuse. At Beaumont the 2nd Division stole its famous march on the enemy by slipping secretly through the German lines during the night and broke the backbone of the Hun defense. These actions were in the early days of November, and on November 7 the 1st and 2nd Divisions cleared the south bank of the River Meuse, each stroke of the American troops driving the wedge deeper and deeper into the flank of the German Army.

Then the 1st Division was ordered to take Sedan, the city noted as an important position in the Franco German War of 1870.[35] That night this arm of the American troops marched hurriedly along the road through Beaumont, Yoncq, Autrecourt, Villers, Remilly and Wadelincourt, when the order came to halt while it was to be left to the French to have the honor of taking the doomed city. So the French were in possession of Sedan at the time of the Armistice. All this is but an outline of the series of engagements forming the battleground of the Meuse-Argonne, the most stupendous undertaking of the World War.

So at the end of 47 days of continuous battle the goal had been reached; Pershing's words had been fulfilled, for the German divisions had been literally "consumed." And into this bloodthirsty and decisive struggle the Germans had hurled every atom of man power and every grain of ammunition to stem the inevitable tide of war. It is perhaps needless to say that the Allied powers had not been unconscious of the part it was acting. Every available division of the American Army had been called into the battle to crush the enemy.

As was unusual, the battle was in two parts. The first part, late September through mid–October, saw much of the American new-comers, badly trained for the most part, taking the utmost punishment and heavy losses. The second part began on 1 November and lasted until the 11th of that month. It was mostly successful without the heavy losses sustained earlier.[36]

One major battle undertaken by the 2nd Division, and later by the 36th National Guard Division, under the command of the French, has been largely ignored by the historians of the AEF. That was fought to the west of the Argonne Forest and became known as the Battle of Blanc Mont Ridge. It was a height overlooking the city of Rheims the Germans had taken in 1914 and the French had been unable to retake, though they tried many times and lost many thousands of soldiers. The 2nd Division was shattered but they retook the height and the major town on that height, St. Étienne, and the untried, untrained 36th, Texas and Oklahoma "cowboys and Indians" carried on after October 10 and drove the Germans back fifteen miles.[37] Also, two U.S. National Guard divisions, the 27th and 30th, fought valiantly for the British up north and likewise have been ignored.

Statistics of the Meuse-Argonne Battle[38]

Because, until then, it was the greatest battle in which the nation had ever participated, the U.S. government prepared the following data regarding the Meuse-Argonne battle.

Days of battle	47
American troops engaged	1,200,900
Guns employed in the attack	2,417
Rounds of artillery ammunition fired	4,214,000
Airplanes used	840
Tons of explosives dropped by planes on enemy	100
Tanks used	324
Miles of penetration of enemy line, maximum	34
Square kilometers. of territory taken	1,550
Villages and towns liberated	150
Prisoners captured	16,059
Artillery pieces captured	468
Machine guns captured	2,864
Trench mortars captured	177
American casualties	120,000

Conclusion

In June 1917, four regiments of Army Regulars and one of Marines were sent overseas. Colonel Charles A. Doyen was in command of the Fifth Regiment of Marines, landing at St. Nazarre, near Brest, at the northern extremity of the Bay of Biscay. In September, Doyen was made brigadier general and placed in command of the Fifth and Sixth regiments as a Marine brigade. He was also placed in command of the newly created 2nd Division on October 26, 1917, and continued in that role until relieved on November 8 by Major General Omar Bundy, U.S. Army.

The U.S. divisions slowly arrived in Europe, some landing in England and continuing on to France; the delays were caused by lack of American shipping and training in the United States. Some of the worst untrained soldiers were sent overseas to hush the complaints of the British and French, who were suffering heavily from terrible morale problems among their own forces. The British, who had the largest merchant fleet, agreed to transship American troops in their ships but only if the United States would agree to let them have most of the arrivals for "training" purposes. Of course they expected that once the Americans were under their command they would keep them. Military leaders of both nations, France and Britain, had helped through their own lack of skills to slaughter their own men and of course the Americans could expect no better treatment if the Allies were allowed their desires to command the newcomers. Pershing, though not the best field commander, was constantly fighting both groups in efforts to protect his men.

Though Pershing and his staff insisted that the AEF was not going to be handled, as the Allies had their own commands, lack of qualified training for both officers and men was the primary cause for the heavy personnel losses suffered in nearly every engagement.

A Summary of American Participation in the War

While the experiences of a large number of men must be diversified and no strict calculation can be made in regard to any particular phase of service, the average period of training given the American soldiers before being sent overseas was six months. Upon arriving in France a service man was trained two months before entering the battle line, and then given another month in some quiet sector before participating in earnest fighting. This computation applies to the training of the 1,400,000 American men who experienced actual fighting in France. The training in the United States was considered of lesser quality and not much better in France.

The typical division of the American Army which constituted the combat unit was composed of 1,000 officers and 27,000 men. Before the signing of the armistice November 11, 1918, forty-two American divisions had been trained and sent overseas, while the training of twelve more was well advanced, and four others were being organized. The plans under which the War Department was working called for eighty divisions to be sent overseas before July 1, 1919, and 100 divisions by the end of that year. Of course, the war didn't last that long and much fewer divisions actually made it to France.

The following recapitulation of the three branches shows where the divisions of the army were trained, and the states from which they came: The Regulars — 1st, trained in France; 2nd, trained in France; 3rd, trained at Camp Greene, N.C.; 4th, Camp Greene, N.C.; 5th, Camp Logan, Texas; 6th, Camp McClellan, Ala.; 7th, McArthur, Texas; 8th, Fremont, Calif.; 9th, Sheridan, Ala.; 10th, Funston, Kansas; 11th, Meade, Md.; 12th, Devens, Mass.; 13th, Lewis, Wash.; 14th, Custer, Mich.; 15th, Logan, Texas; 16th, Kearny, Calif.; 17th, Beauregard, La.; 18th, Travis, Texas; 19th, Dodge, Iowa; 20th, Sevier, S.C.

National Guard — 26th, New England, trained at Camp Devens; 27th, New York, trained at Camp Wadsworth, S.C.; 28th, Pennsylvania, Camp Hancock, Ga.; 29th, New Jersey, Virginia, Maryland, District of Columbia,

Camp McClellan, Ala.; 30th, Tennessee, North Carolina, South Carolina, Camp Sevier, S.C.; 31st, Georgia, Alabama, Florida, Camp Wheeler, Ga.; 32nd, Michigan, Wisconsin, Camp McArthur, Texas; 33rd, Illinois, Logan, Texas; 34th, Nebraska, Iowa, South Dakota, Minnesota, North Dakota, Camp Cody, N.M.; 35th, Missouri, Kansas, Camp Doniphan, Okla.; 36th, Texas, Oklahoma, Camp Bowie, Texas; 37th, Ohio, Camp Sheridan, Ohio; 38th, Indiana, Kentucky, West Virginia, Camp Shelby, Miss.; 39th, Arkansas, Mississippi, Louisiana, Camp Beauregard, La.; 40th California, Colorado, Utah, Arizona, New Mexico, Camp Kearny, Calif.; 41st, various states, Camp Fremont, Calif.; 42nd, various states, Camp Mills, N.Y.

National Army — 76th, New England, New York, Camp Devens, Mass.; 77th, New York City, Camp Upton, N.Y.; 78th, Western New York, New Jersey, Delaware, Camp Fix, N.J.; 79th, Northeastern Pennsylvania, Maryland, District of Columbia, Camp Meade, Md.; 80th, Virginia, West Virginia, Western Pennsylvania, Camp Lee, Va.; 81st, North Carolina, South Carolina, Florida, Puerto Rico, Camp Jackson, S.C.; 82nd, Georgia, Alabama, Tennessee, Camp Gordon, Ga.; 83rd, Ohio, Western Pennsylvania, Camp Sherman, Ohio; 84th, Kentucky, Indiana, Southern Illinois, Camp Zachary Taylor, Ky.; 85th, Michigan, Eastern Wisconsin, Camp Custer, Mich.; 86th, Chicago, Northern Illinois, Camp Grant, Ill.; 87th, Arkansas, Louisiana, Mississippi, Southern Alabama, Camp Pike, Ark.; 88th, North Dakota, Minnesota, Iowa, Western Illinois, Camp George, Iowa; 89th, Kansas, Missouri, South Dakota, Nebraska, Camp Funston, Kan.; 90th, Texas, Oklahoma, Camp Travis, Texas; 91st, Alaska, Washington, Oregon, California, Idaho, Nebraska, Montana, Wyoming, Utah, Camp Lewis, Wash.; 92nd, various states, Camp Funston, Kan.; 93rd, various states, Camp Stuart, Va. The last two were composed primarily of Negroes and identified as "colored."[39]

A study of this recapitulation shows that the Regular Army Divisions were numbered from 1 to 20, and of these the first eight reached France. The National Guard divisions, made up mainly from the militia of the several states, were numbered from 26 to 42, all of whom went to France. The National Army, made up almost entirely by men called under the selective service law, was composed of Divisions 76 to 92. The 93rd Division did not serve with the rest of the AEF, but was "awarded" to the French Army, in which they served with great distinction. Divisions 95, 96, 97 and 100 were being organized when the war came to an end.

Transportation of the Troops

In a little more than two weeks following the United States' entrance into the war, efforts were being made to transport the troops as fast as they were mustered in and ready for service in Europe. The demand for ships to carry out this task came when there was an uncommon shortage of vessels fit for this purpose. A few U.S. merchant steamers were chartered, and the work began in earnest. Before July seven troop ships and six cargo ships were employed.

The first marked increase in vessels came from German ships interned during the previous months and made to do duty in this cause. For some reason, Dutch ships were taken over in the spring of 1918, and Scandinavian and Japanese ships were chartered, while vessels of other countries were utilized. For every hundred men who were carried over, 49 went in British ships, 45 in American ships, three in Italian ships, two in French and one in Russian shipping under British management. Part of the agreement with the British was that a large number of the men they transported would "learn" their trade under British tutelage. In fact, several of those divisions served under British command in the Belgium campaign.

The round trip or "turn around," as it is known, which is not complete until a transport has taken its load over, discharged it, returned and reloaded ready for another voyage, required on average 52 days for a troop ship and 66 days for a cargo vessel. This record was improved during the summer of 1917, but the following winter, owing to the severe weather, a longer time was required. During 1918, however, this time was reduced so the standard length of a trip was 70 days for cargo ships and 35 days for troop ships.

The fastest ships did better than this and averaged 30 days for a turn around. In the summer of 1918 the *Leviathan*, formerly the German ship *Vaterland*, averaged less than 27 days. This giant craft transported landed in France the equal of a German division, 12,000 men, every month during the summer of 1918. The American ships *Great Northern* and *Northern Pacific* averaged nearly as well, making the turnaround in 25 and 26 days respectively, while under favorable conditions they made turnaround trips in 19 days.

The first year half a million of men were taken over, while in the succeeding half year one million and a half were landed on European soil. During the 19 months of U.S. participation in the war 2,000,000 soldiers were carried to the scene of conflict. A more remarkable feature of this astounding undertaking was the fact that, despite the desperate attempts of the German subs to stop them, no lives were lost from these attacks.

The highest troop-carrying records were in July 1918, when 306,000 soldiers were taken to Europe, and in June 1919, when 346,000 were brought back to America.

The following table shows the number of troops sailing from American and Canadian ports[40]:

Quebec, 11,000
Montreal, 34,000
Portland, ME, 6,000
Boston, MA, 46,000
New York, NY, 1,656,000
  Total, 2,086,000

St. Johns, 1,000
Halifax, 5,000
Philadelphia, PA, 35,000
Baltimore, MD, 4,000
Newport News, VA, 288,000

These troops were landed in Europe as follows: Glasgow, Scotland, 45,000; Manchester, England, 4,000; Liverpool, England, 844,000; Bristol, England, 11,000; Falmouth, England, 1,000; Plymouth, England, 1,000; Southampton, England, 57,000; London, England, 62,000; total, 1,025,000.

The following landed in France: Le Havre, 13,000; Brest, 791,000; St. Nazaire, 198, 000; La Pallice, 4,000; Bordeaux, 50,000; Marseilles, 1,000; total, 1,057,000.

Two thousand landed in Italy. This was a regiment sent to serve directly under British command.

During the entire period of transportation no American transport was lost, and only 200,000 tons of transports, 142,000 of this, were sunk by torpedoes.

The Crisis of the War

The most serious crisis of the war was early in the spring of 1918, when the German Army began its great drive against the British and French Armies between St. Quentin and Cambrai, a battle in which 4,000,000 men were engaged on a front of 150 miles. The Germans had been able to concentrate on the Western Front their strongest forces following the downfall of the Russian Army, leaving them the opportunity to withdraw 63 divisions from the Eastern front. They now had total of 206 divisions to hurl against the Allies. It was before American troops in any number were anywhere near the front lines.

This critical time called for decisive action by the Allies. While the American forces were eager to begin work, until then a complete unity of the three Allies—British, French, and now the Americans—had not been perfected. Field Marshal Haig had said the British were fighting with "their backs to the wall." He was correct; the British were in bad shape and genuinely expected to withdraw across the English Channel. Someone was needed to take supreme command, and that man was unanimously chosen. March 28, 1918, the French Marshal Ferdinand Foch, a soldier of considerable skill, was made commander-in-chief of the Allied Armies in France.

General Pershing immediately placed the American forces under the command of Marshal Foch, and from this time until the St. Mihiel offensive in September, General Pershing acted under the advice of the French commander. Although with some reservations, he continued that association until the war's end. The American divisions entered the ranks as units of the British or French armies as fast as they were trained.

General Pershing said in his final report: "We had four divisions with experience in the trenches, all of which were equal to any demands of battle action. The crisis which this offensive developed was such that our occupation of an American sector must be postponed. At the request of Marshal Foch the 1st Division was transferred from the Toul Sector to a position in reserve at Chaumont-en-Vixen. This was about thirty miles northwest of Paris.

On April 4 the 26th Division was sent to relieve the 1st Division in the Toul Sector, and this transfer of troops was the first test of the administrative ability of the American staff. Captain Thomas says in his narrative: "Moving 28,000 men, 1,700 animals and 1,000 vehicles three hundred miles, at the same time turning over a sector to another division, giving the men a chance to rest and bathe, all in twelve days, proved the efficiency of the staff."[41]

The 1st Division was given a week of open warfare maneuvers at Chaumont-en-Vixen, in preparation for the coming ordeal under the careful attention of French and American generals, at the close of which General Pershing, after witnessing the final maneuvers, delivered to the officers of the division his famous speech referred to as his "Farewell to the First." After declaring that they had been selected to uphold the good name of the American Army fighting with the best units in the British and French Armies in Picardy, closing by telling them the command had passed to the French. It was a memorable day to the officers present. That the 1st Division did not betray the confidence of their old or new leader has become history. Since it was his favorite division, his confidence never failed.

American troops saw service on practically every section of the western front from the British base in Belgium to the quiet sectors in the Vosges Mountains near Epinal. Their first entrance into the line was in the quiet sector of Toul on October 21, 1917. From that date to the day of the Armistice, American units were in line somewhere continuously. This activity brought them into thirteen battles which have been recognized in order to distinguish them from minor operations that from time to time fell to their lot. One of these battles occurred in Italy, the others on the Western Front. The following table shows their names in order of engagement and number of Americans involved in the fight.[42]

Thirteen Major Battles	*Americans Engaged*
Cambrai, November 20 to December 4, 1917	2,500
German offensives, March 21 to July 18, 1918:	

Somme, March 21 to April 6, 1918	2,200
Lys, April 9 to 27, 1918	500
Aisne, May 27 to July 5	27,500
Noyon-Montdidier, June 9 to 15	27,000
Champagne-Marne, July 15 to 18	85,000
Allied offensives, July 18 to November 11, 1918:	
Aisne-Marne, July 18 to August 6	270,000
Somme, August 8 to November 11	54,000
Oise-Aisne, August 18 to November 11	85,000
Ypres-Lys, August 19 to November 11	108,000
St. Mihiel, September 12 to 16	550,000
Meuse-Argonne, September 20 to November	1,200,000
Italian front, Campaign of 1918:	
Vittorio-Veneto, October 24 to November 4	1,200

Out of every three American men who went overseas, two participated in battle. Thus of the 2,084,000 men who reached France 1,390,000 saw active service on the front line. Of the forty-two divisions sent overseas twenty-nine took an active part in the war, while others were used for replacements, unless they had arrived too late to participate. The history of these twenty-nine combat divisions practically covers the history of American participation in the war. Seven of these combat divisions were of the Regular Army; eleven were organized from the National Guard, and eleven were composed of National Army troops. One, the 93rd, served entirely with the French to their benefit.

The activity of these American combat divisions covered a period of two hundred days, from April 25 to November 11, 1918. During this strenuous period they were engaged in thirteen battles, two of which were entirely American. The greatest activity was in the second week of October, when all of the American combat divisions were in action, holding 101 miles of the front, or 23 percent of the entire line of battle.

From the middle of August to the Armistice, the American forces defended a front longer than that held by the British, and their numbers added to those already in the field and gave a preponderance of numbers to the Allied powers.

The battle advance of the American divisions amounted to 782 kilometers, or 485 miles, an average advance for each division of 17 miles, nearly all of it against the resistance of a desperate enemy. They captured 63,000 prisoners, 1,378 pieces of artillery, 708 trench mortars and 9,650 machine guns.

In June and July they assisted in a successful defensive against the Germans' march upon Paris and participated in a triumphant offensive which shattered the hopes of the enemy of ever reaching the capital of France. At St. Mihiel they captured a German salient which had been a constant source of danger to the French for four years. In the Argonne and on the Meuse they broke down the enemy lines and stopped their communication and means of supply for half of the Western battle front.

Another advantage made by the rapid arrivals of the American troops was the great increase of rifle men on the front line of service. On April 1, 1918, the Germans had a superiority of 324,000 riflemen on the Western front. This strength increased until about the middle of June, when the Allied Powers were their equal. Despite the fact that the French and British forces were losing strength, the Allied forces continually gained upon the enemy, due to the ever-increasing stream coming from the American shores. The significance of this is proved by the superiority of the allied rifle strength on November 1, which had out distanced the Germans by over 600,000 rifles.

The comparative numbers of the contending forces on the Western front during the two hundred days of active combat is in the following table.[43]

Month	Germans	Allied Forces
April	1,569,000	1,245,000
May	1,600,000	1,343,000
June	1,639,000	1,496,000
July	1,612,000	1,556,000
August	1,412,000	1,672,000
September	1,395,000	1,682,000
October	1,223,000	1,694,000
November	666,000	1,485,000

Mortality of the War

It has been officially stated that the war with Germany was "undoubtedly the bloodiest war that was ever fought." One possible competitor would be the Second World War, in which the casualty rate per hundred men was equally heavy but the civilian deaths far exceeded any casualties in any other conflict in modern times. In the First World War two were killed or died of disease out of every one hundred, including sailors as well as soldiers. Among the other leading nations engaged in the great conflict, approximately twenty-three in each 100 were killed or died of disease. The number of battle deaths of the different armies engaged in the struggle are shown by the following figures.[44]

Number Killed in the World War, 1914–1918

Russia	1,700,000
Germany	1,600,000
France	1,385,300
Great Britain	900,000
Austria	800,000

Italy	330,000
Turkey	250,000
Serbia and Montenegro	125,000
Belgium	102,000
Romania	100,000
Bulgaria	100,000
United States	48,900
Greece	7,000
Portugal	2,000
Total	7,450,200

In the above table only deaths resulting directly from action are included, and because these figures were derived from early publications, it is probable these figures are larger in the cases of some of the belligerents. The entire list of casualties in some cases will be doubled when the account of those who were wounded and died an early death or from disease, privations and other causes is taken into consideration.

According to one estimate, the total battle deaths in the war were greater than all the deaths in all wars for more than one hundred years previous. From 1793 to 1914 total deaths in the wars may safely be estimated at something under 6,000,000. Battle deaths alone from 1914 to 1918 totaled about 7,500,000. This does not take into consideration civilian deaths.

According to the table, though Russia retired from the war in the fall of 1917, it suffered the heaviest losses. Germany is a close second, with France only a little behind them in losses. Germany, Austria-Hungary and Turkey combined suffered over one-third of the battle casualties. Yet they were fighting against a total of thirteen nations, including Japan.

The rate of death in the infantry, obviously, was much higher than in any other branch of the service. Of every one thousand men enlisted in the infantry fifty-two were killed in action or died of wounds. Among the officers the rate was higher. In connection with the death rate of the American Army in comparison with the other losses, it should be borne in mind that the Americans were in heavy fighting for but two hundred days, as opposed to the average of 1,500 of all the other powers, except Russia.

The United States' Casualties

Six men were wounded, taken prisoners or reported missing for every man killed in battle. The horror of this was mitigated by the number of the wounded who were returned to duty from the hospital, the percentage being 85. About half of those reported as injured were only slightly wounded and would not have been included in the casualties of other wars. The high water mark of the list of missing ran up to 78,000, but this has been steadily reduced to fewer than fifty.[45]

Battle Casualties

Killed in action	34,180
Died of wounds	14,729
Total dead	48,909
Wounded severely	80,130
Wounded slightly	110,544
Wounded, degree undetermined	39,400
Total wounded	230, 074
Missing in action	2,913
Taken prisoner	4,434
Summary	260,496

The number of lives lost in both Army and Navy from the declaration of war to July 1, 1919, was 125,500. Deaths in the army, including the Marines, were 115,660. About two-thirds of these deaths occurred overseas. There were 768 lost at sea, 381 of whom are included in the list of battle deaths, from the fact that their loss was due to submarine activity. About one-half of the losses were from diseases. A government report states that this is the first war in which the United States was engaged that showed a lower death rate from disease than from battle. In previous wars unsanitary conditions at camps and ravages of epidemic diseases resulted in disease deaths far in excess of the number killed on the battlefield. The highest death rate from disease occurred in the Mexican War, when 110 died in every thousand during a year, while those killed in battle numbered only fifteen. In the American Civil War sixty-five died of disease out of every 1000, while thirty-three were killed in battle.

In conclusion it can be said that of every 100 soldiers and sailors who served in the First World War, two were killed or died of disease. The number of American lives lost was 125,500; 10,000 of these belonging to the Navy. The casualty rate for the infantry was higher than for any other branch of the service, while the rate for the officers was higher than for the men. In this war the death rate from disease was lower and that from battle was higher than in any previous American war. For every man killed in battle six were wounded, while the wave of influenza, which swept the world in 1918, took more victims than fell in battle (exact figures were elusive). The British battle fatalities were 18 times greater than for the United States; while those of France were 28 times in excess; for Germany 32; for Russia, with its two years of bitter experience, 34 times as great. The record for Russian wounded and prostrated from the service showed a still greater difference.

The Financial Cost of the War

If the cost of the war in the number of lives was great, the financial loss fairly staggers today's mind unaccustomed to reckon above nine figures. For from the period of April 6, 1917, to May 6, 1919, exactly two years and one month, it cost the United States government $1,000,000 each hour. The treasury disbursements during the time reached the enormous sum of $23,500,000,000, of which $1,650,000,000 may be charged to the normal expenses that would have been required had there been peace, leaving $21,850,000,000 which may be considered the direct cost of the war in dollars. That sum was nearly sufficient to pay the entire expense of the government from the ratification of the Constitution in 1791 to the declaration of war against Germany in April 1917. This expenditure was sufficient to have met the cost of maintaining the War for American Independence continuously for over a thousand years. Those figures, revised to today's dollars, would certainly be at least twice that amount and probably three times.

Besides meeting this enormous burden, the United States loaned to the European Allies money at the rate of almost half a million dollars an hour, or in round numbers $8,850,000,000. Much of that was long before the U.S. entered the war. Eight billion dollars and for three years, the Untied States loudly proclaimed its neutrality. The government made an estimate of the cost belonging to each department, and its report shows that for each dollar spent in conducting the war, 44 cents was paid to the Quartermaster's Department, 29 cents to Ordnance, 13 cents to the paymaster for wages and salaries, six cents for air service, four cents for engineers, two cents for the medical department, and two cents for signal service and miscellaneous expenses.

The following table of estimated war expenditures of the principal countries engaged in the war afford interesting comparisons; the figures are given in billions of dollars without including normal expenses and loans to allies.[46]

Country	Amount
America and Allies	
Great Britain and Dominions	$38,000,000,000
France	26,000,000,000
United States	22,000,000,000
Russia	18,000,000,000
Italy	13,000,000,000
Belgium, Romania, Portugal, Yugoslavia,	5,000,000,000
Japan and Greece	1,000,000,000
Total	$123,000,000,000
Teuton Allies:	
Germany	39,000,000,000
Austria-Hungary	21,000,000,000

Turkey and Bulgaria	3,000,000,000
Total	$63,000,000,000
Grand total	$186,000,000,000

The United States spent about one-eighth of the entire cost of the war, and less than one-fifth of the expenditures on the side of the Allies.

Assets

To offset some degree the mighty expenditures of the war, the American government acquired certain valuable property and improvements which may have been considered as permanent assets at that time. As a result it owned some of the finest docks in the world; sixteen National Army cantonments and three National Guard camps which would be temporarily retained as training grounds. It had a number of aviation fields, depots and balloon schools, some of which would be sources of value in the years to come. In other lines of war preparation and utilities it was sufficient to equip an army of a million men and maintain them in active combat for six months. These munitions and weapons, some of which were of the best quality and recent designs, served the AEF well while in combat. The government had also Liberty motors, service planes and equipments of various kinds which were of value for several years following the war.

The United States also had many permanent casualties to care for. It was also considered by many, most of whom didn't go, to be a commitment for future United States involvement in the affairs of foreign nations.

Part II: Statistics of American Divisions in France

THE FIRST DIVISION, REGULAR ARMY

The First Division was organized from troops of the regular army. The command of the division changed from Major General William L. Sibert on December 12 to Major General Robert B. Bullard on the night of the 14th. Brigadier General Charles P. Summerall took command of the division and was later succeeded by Brigadier General Frank E. Bamford, and he in turn by Brigadier General Frank Parker. This division was the first in line and the first to enter an active sector. It reached France in June 1917, went into line in October and into an active sector in April 1918. The First Division was quiet 127 days and active 93 days. Its advance was 51 kilometers. It captured 6,469 German prisoners. Its total casualties were 21,612, including 4,411 battle deaths and 17,201 wounded. It received 30,206 replacements.

First Infantry Brigade

16th Infantry
18th Infantry
2nd Machine Gun Battalion

Second Infantry Brigade

26th Infantry
28th Infantry
3rd Machine Gun Battalion

First Field Artillery Brigade

5th Field Artillery
6th Field Artillery
7th Field Artillery
1st Trench Mortar Battery

Divisional Troops

1st Machine Gun Battalion
1st Engineers
2nd Field Signal Battalion
Headquarters Troop

Trains

1st Train Headquarters
1st Military Police
1st Ammunition Train
1st Supply Train
1st Engineer Train
1st Sanitary Train
Ambulance Cos. and
Field Hospitals 2, 3, 12, 13

For a period from June 1917, the 5th Regiment of Marines was attached to the First Division until transferred in late September 1917 to join the newly forming Second Division.

Record of Events

SECTORS WHERE THE 1ST DIVISION WAS ENGAGED IN WARFARE

Sommerviller sector, France, October 21 to November 20, 1917.
Ansauvllle sector, France, January 15 to April 3, 1918.
Cantigny sector, France, April 25 to June 8, 1918.
Montdidier-Noyon defensive, France, June 9 to 13, 1918.
Cantigny sector, France, June 14 to July 7, 1918.
Aisne-Marne offensive, France, July 18 to 23, 1918.
Saizerais sector, France, August 7 to 24, 1918.
St. Mihiel offensive, France, September 12 to 13, 1918.
Meuse-Argonne offensive, France, October 1 to 12, 1918.
Meuse-Argonne offensive, France, November 5 to 8, 1918.

Organization and Movement Overseas

MAY 24–DECEMBER 22, 1917

May 24, War Department directs organization of the First Expeditionary Division, later designated 1st Division, Regular Army. The majority of the troops selected are in service near the Mexican border at Brownsville, Douglas, El Paso, San Benito, and Forts Bliss, Ringgold, and Sam Houston; others are at Washington Barracks and Fort Oglethorpe; new organizations join at the ports of embarkation.

June 3, the first contingent, consisting of the 16th, 18th, 26th, and 28th Regt's of Infantry, Field Hospital 6 later designated FH 13, Ambulance Co 6 later designated A 13, and Co C, 2nd Field Signal Bn, after being increased to authorized strength by transfers and voluntary enlistments, moves to Hoboken, NJ.

June 7, 2nd Infantry Brigade, which includes the 26th and 28th Regt's of Infantry, is formed in New York City.

June 8, Brig. Gen. William L. Sibert assumes command of the Division. He becomes Maj. Gen. Sibert on 27 June.

June 9, 1st Infantry Brigade, which includes the 16th and 18th Regt's of Infantry, is formed in New York City.

June 14, Division Hdqs, Hdqs 1st Infantry Brig, Hdqs 2nd Infantry Brig, and the first contingent sail from New York and Hoboken, and arrive 26 June at St. Nazaire.

July 22, the second contingent, consisting of the 5th, 6th, and 7th Regt's of Field Artillery, and Cos A and B 2nd Field Signal Bn, begins the journey from Texas and Arizona to Hoboken, sails on July 31 from Hoboken, and arrives August 13 at St. Nazaire.

August 6, the 1st Engineers and Train move from Washington Barracks to Hoboken, sail on August 7, and arrive August 20 at St. Nazaire.

August 7, the Motor Bn of the Ammunition Train and 1st Trench Mortar Battery sail from Hoboken and arrive August 21 at St. Nazaire.

August 13, the Horse Bn of the Ammunition Train, Field Hospitals 2 and 12. Ambulance Cos 2 and 12 of the 1st Sanitary Train, and the 1st and 2nd Military Police Cos sail from Hoboken, land September 1 and 3 at Liverpool, England, and after a short stay in rest camps move to Le Havre, France.

December 1, Field Hospital 3 leaves Fort Bliss, Texas, and Ambulance Co 3 leaves Fort Oglethorpe, for Hoboken, sail December 5, and arrive December 22 at St. Nazaire, completing the overseas movement of the division. On 14 December Maj. Gen. Robert L. Bullard assumes command of the division.

Completion of Organization in France
JULY 5, 1917–FEBRUARY 17, 1918

July 5, the first contingent moves to 1st Gondrecourt Training Area, where the division less artillery is ordered to assemble. At this time the First Expeditionary Division is re-designated the 1st Division, AEF.

July 14, division trains with the French 47th Division Chasseurs.

August 6, Headquarters Field Artillery Brigade moves to Le Valdahon preparatory to the organization and assembly of the brigade at that camp.

August 16, 1st Field Artillery Brigade is organized at Le Valdahon and includes the 5th, 6th and 7th Regiments of Field Artillery. which arrive 21–24 August from St. Nazaire.

August 21, Companies A and B, 2nd Field Signal Bn arrive in Gondrecourt Area, where they are joined by the Motor Bn, Ammunition Train and 1st Engineers and Train on 30 August and 4 September, respectively.

August 30, The concentration is completed and systematic training is begun.

September 6, Horse Bn, Ammunition Train, Field Hospitals 2 and 12, Ambulance Cos 2 and 12, and the 1st and 2nd MP Cos arrive.

September 10, division trains with French 18th Division which replaces the French 47th Division Chasseurs. During the winter the infantry units furnish the personnel for the 1st, 2nd, and 3rd Machine Gun Bns, which are formed in the Gondrecourt Area.

February 17, The 1st Supply Train is organized in this area.

Training and Operations
OCTOBER 19, 1917–NOVEMBER 11, 1918

October 19, the artillery moves from Le Valdahon to the area of the French IX Corps, French Eighth Army north of Lunéville, and 20 October infantry battalions from Gondrecourt follow.

October 21, elements of the division enter the sector of French 18th Division, French IX Corps, with whom they are affiliated for training, along the front 1¼ km southwest of Parroy, south shore of Etang de Parroy, Bures inclusive, Arracourt, including Fme de Ranzey 2 km south of Bezange-la-Grande. The infantry enters the line by battalion; the artillery also trains by battalion, one from each regiment, with the French sector artillery; units, after completing duty in the sector, train in the Gondrecourt Area.

October 21 to November 20, division participates in the occupation of the Sommerviller Sector, Lorraine.

November 20, troops withdraw from the line and continue training at Gondrecourt.

January 15, division, less 2nd Infantry Brig and two battalions of artillery, which remain in the Gondrecourt Area, moves to the area of the French 32nd Corps, French First Army northwest of Toul. (near Verdun).

January 18 to February 5, 1st Infantry Brigade, with 5 battalions of field artillery attached, participates in occupation of Ansauville Sector Lorraine.

Night of January 18–19, elements of 1st Infantry Brigade begin the relief of French 1st Moroccan Division on the front of the Ansauville sector western part of the Royaumeix Corps sector, which extends along east edge of Bois de Remiêres, north edge of Bois Carré, 1 km north of Seicheprey, ½ km south of Richecourt, Marvoisin (incl.), east shore of Etang de la Grande-Croix, south shore of Etang de Vargévaux 1¼ km northeast of Bouconville, and includes the Beaumont and Rambucourt zones.

January 20 to July 14, division is under the administrative control of the I Corps.

January 21, command passes to French 69th Division, which retains control, although no French units are in line; local actions.

February 5–April 3, division occupies Ansauville Sector Lorraine.

February 5, division assumes command of sector; French 69th Division French 32nd Corps on right, French 10th Colonial Division French II Colonial Corps on left.

February 28, 2nd Infantry Brig moves from Gondrecourt and begins the relief of 1st Infantry Brig, which returns to the Gondrecourt Area.

March 9, command passes.

March 26, Ansauville sector is designated de la Reine sector.

March 29–30, division takes over sub-sector Broussey.

April 3, 26th Division relieves division, and the 2nd Infantry Brig and divisional units return to the Gondrecourt Area.

April 5, division moves to area of French Fifth Army near Gisors, northwest of Paris, where it resumes training. Brig. Gen. Beaumont B. Buck assumes command of the division until Gen. Bullard returns on April 13.

April 17, division moves north by stages to the area of the French 6th Corps French First Army, and takes station near Froissy.

Night of April 24–25, division inserts the 1st Infantry Brig between the French 162nd and French 45th Divisions in the Cantigny Sector, 5 km west of Montdidier, the French divisions moving to the northwest and east, respectively.

April 27–June 8, division occupies Cantigny Sector Picardy. The zones of Broyes, Tournelle, and Coullemelle comprise the sector which extends from Bois Céléstin (excl.), 1 km west of Fontaine-sons-Montdidier, along the northern edge of Bois de Cantigny, Cantigny (excl.), to 1 km south of St. Aignan; French 162nd Division on right, French 45th Division, French IX Corps, on the left.

April 27, division assumes command of the sector.

April 30, French 152nd Division, French IX Corps on left.

May 5, division passes to French X Corps when this corps relieves French VI Corps.

May 7, French 60th Division, French X Corps, on right.

May 16, 2nd Infantry Brig relieves 1st Infantry Brig.

May 22–24, 28th Infantry withdraws, receives special training, and May 26–28 relieves elements of its own and the French 152nd Division on a 2¼ km front west of Cantigny.

May 28, 28th Infantry captures Cantigny and the heights; the gains are consolidated.

May 31–June 8, division reorganizes sector and places the brigades abreast, 1st Infantry Brig on left.

June 1–3, 1st Infantry Brig relieves elements of French 152nd Division on the left and occupies the Esclainvillers Zone, the front of which extends northward through St. Aignan and Grivesnes both included to a point ½ km east of Bois Poignard; French 3rd Division French IX Corps on left; local actions.

June 9, Cantigny Sector occupation merges into the Montdidier-Noyon Defensive. Enemy attacks on the front of French First and French Third Armies between Montdidier and Noyon.

June 9–13, division participates in Montdidier-Noyon Defensive. Division, holding the Cantigny Sector, is alerted during the artillery bombardment.

June 14, Montdidier-Noyon Defensive stabilizes and the Division resumes routine duties.

June 14–July 8, division occupies Cantigny Sector, Picardy.

Night of July 5–6, French 152nd and French 166th Divisions begin the relief of 1st Division.

July 8, command passes; division less 2nd Infantry Brig and 7th Field Artillery moves to the area between Beauvais and Breteuil subject to the orders of the French GAR; 2nd Infantry Brig and 7th Field Artillery move to the northern part of the area between Froissy and Breteuil in the reserve of French X Corps.

July 11, division is at the disposal of French Tenth Army, and the following day moves to the Dammartin-en-Goele Area.

July 14–22, division is under the administrative control of the III Corps.

Night of July 15–16, division is under control of French 20th Corps, moves into the Compiègne Forest preparatory to relieving the 1st Moroccan Division southwest of Soissons.

Night of July 17–18, division relieves French 1st Moroccan Division on a 2 km front from 1¼ km northeast of St. Pierre-Aigle to ½ km east and 1¼ km northeast of Cutry, command passing July 18.

July 18, division attacks east, captures Missy-aux-Bois and establishes a line ½ km northeast of Chaudun, ½ km east of Missy-aux-Bois, ¼ km northeast of Montplaisir Fme; French 1st Moroccan Division on right, French 153rd Division, French I Corps on left.

July 18–23, division participates in Aisne-Marne Operation.

July 19, division attacks and occupies Ploissy.

July 20–21, division extends zone to the north to include Berzy-le-Sec, which is captured by the 2nd Infantry Brig, and establishes a front from the northwestern outskirts of Buzancy to the northern outskirts of Berzy-le-Sec; French 87th Division on right, elements of French 69th Division on left.

July 23, Scottish 15th and French 69th Divisions relieve 1st Division less Artillery and Signal Train, which remain in the sector until July 24; the latter assembles in Forêt de Villers-Cotterêts and then returns to the Dammartin-en-Goële Area.

July 28, division moves to the area of the French Eighth Army near Toul preparatory to the relief of the 2nd Moroccan Division.

July 30–August 22, division is under the administrative control of the IV Corps.

Night of August 4–5, division, under French 32nd Corps, begins relief of French 2nd Moroccan Division in the Saizerais sector northwest of Pont-à-Mousson.

August 7–24, division occupies Saizerais Sector, Lorraine. Division occupies the line from Haut de Rieupt 2 km northwest of Pont-à-Mousson, through Forêt du Bois-le-Prêtre, Fey-en-Haye (incl.), Régniéville-en-Haye (incl.), to ¼ km south of Remenauville, with brigades abreast, 2nd Infantry Brig on right; French 64th Division on right, 82nd Division on left; local actions, consolidation of position, and reconstitution during the occupation.

August 9, 2nd Division on right.

August 11, 89th Division on left.

August 18, division is ordered to join the First Army.

August 19, 82nd Division on right.

August 24, 90th Division relieves division less Artillery, which remains in the sector, now called Villers-en-Haye, until August 28, and the latter assembles in the 5th Vaucouleurs Training Area for special instruction.

August 24–26, division is under administrative control of IV Corps.

August 28, 1st Field Artillery Brig and 1st Ammunition Train, relieved from duty with 90th Division, move to Forêt de la Reine near the south face of the St. Mihiel salient.

September 1, division less Artillery moves via Pagny-sur-Meuse to the area of IV Corps on south side of St. Mihiel salient and assembles in and near the Forêt de La Reine, in the rear of the Ansauville Sector.

September 6, division begins the relief of elements of 89th Division in the main line of resistance in the west part of the Lucey Sector; command passes September 8.

September 8–11, division occupies that part of Lucey Sector between Seicheprey and Marvoisin, known as the Ansauville Sector Lorraine. Elements of 89th Division, under command of 1st Division, hold the outpost line north of and parallel to the Beaumont-Rambucourt road. The main line of resistance is in northern part of the Forêt de La Rome.

September 12, sector occupation merges into the St. Mihiel Operation.

September 12–16, division participates in St. Mihiel Operation.

September 12, division, brigades abreast, 2nd Infantry Brig on right, on the left of the IV Corps, attacks north on a 2½ km front from 1 km north of Seicheprey to ¼ km northwest of Marvoisin, crosses the Rupt-de-Mad, advances through Richecourt, Lahayvile, Quart-de-Réserve woods, Bois Rate, Bois de l'Etang, east part of Bois de Pannes, Nonsard, enters Bois de Nonsard and Bois de Lamarche, occupies Lamarche-en-Woëvre, and establishes a line 1 km northwest of Lamarche-en-Woëvre, through Bois de Lamarche, narrow-gauge railroad through the north part of Bois de Nonsard, eastern edge of Bois de Pannes, through Bois de La Belle Ozière, Etang de Champrez (excl.), ¾ km southeast of Gerard Bois Fme, through Bois de Gargantua; 42nd Division on right, French 39th Division on left.

September 13, 2nd Infantry Brig continues the advance through the Bois de Vigneulles to outskirts of Vigneulles-les-Hattonchâtel and Hattonville, closes all exits leading east from the towns, and establishes contact with the 26th Division (V Corps) which is attacking southeast; the junction of the 1st Division with the 26th Division completes the reduction of the St. Mihiel salient.

September 14, the French 39th Division relieves the 1st Division which retires, assembles in and near the Bois de La Belle Ozière, and passes to the reserve of the IV Corps; rehabilitation.

September 19, division moves to the rear of the III Corps area in vicinity of Benoitevaux, where it passes into army reserve.

September 27, division moves via Nixéville to the area of the I Corps near Neuvilly, pending entry into line east of the Argonne Forest.

Night of September 30–October 1, division begins the relief of the 35th Division along a front extending from Sérieux Fme, to the ridge north of Baulny, and October 1, occupies, in general, the front extending from Sérieux Fme to Chaudron Fme, to L'Espérance, command passing October 1; 91st Division (V Corps) on right, 28th Division on left.

October 1–13, division participates in Meuse-Argonne Operation.

October 2, division front is extended on right to include Côte 231 north of les Bouleaux Bois when 91st Division elements are withdrawn from the sector.

October 4, division, brigades abreast, 2nd Infantry Brig on right of the I Corps, attacks, advances through the Bois de Montrebeau, and establishes a line ¼ km northwest of Tronsol Fme, south slope of Côte 200 west of Rau du Gouffre, is Neuville-le-Comte Fme, Fme de Beauregard, Exermont (incl.) south and southwest edges of Bois de Boyon, slope ¼ km southeast of Fléville; 32nd Division V Corps on right, 28th Division on left.

October 5, division captures Côte 240 in Bois do Boyon and reaches Fme d'Ariétal.

October 7, division passes to V Corps and extends the front on the right to include Côte 269; 164th Infantry Brig, 82nd Division on left.

October 8, elements of 181st Infantry Brig, 91st Division, holding left flank of 32nd Division front along north edge of Bois du Chêne-Sec, west of Gesnes, are attached to 1st Division.

October 9, division, as left of V Corps, attacks, advances through le Petit-Bois into Bois de Romagne, and establishes a line Côte 269 in Bois de Moncy, Côte 263 in north part of le Petit-Bois, south of Côte de Maldah, 1½ km south of Sommerance, northern outskirts of Fléville; the attached elements of 181st Infantry Brig, 91st Division, are in line east of Hill 269.

October 10, I Corps moves its right boundary to a line from the west edge of the Bois de Boyon to Sommerance (excl.), thereby reducing the Division zone of action by 1¼ km; Division advances through Bois de Romagne, crosses Côte de Maldah and establishes line 1¼ km southeast and ¾ km south of La Musarde Fme, along northern edge of Bois de Romagne, across northwest slope of Côte de Maldah to a point ¾ km southeast of Sommerance; 181st Infantry Brig, 91st Division on the right of the division is attached to the 32nd Division after reaching a line from ¼ km southwest of Hill 286 to 1¼ km southeast of La Musarde Fme in the Bois de Gesnes.

October 11, 181st Infantry Brig relieves elements of the Division which are in line east of a point in Bois de Romagne ¼ km south of la Musarde Fme.

October 12, 42nd Division relieves division, less Artillery, which remains in line until October 31, and the latter assembles in the woods near Choppy in the rear zone of the I Corps.

October 13, division less Artillery moves via Los Islettes to the Vavincourt Area, where it passes to the reserve of the First Army; rehabilitation and training.

October 25, division less Artillery moves to area of V Corps north of Récicourt.

October 29, division passes to the reserve of V Corps.

October 29–November 11, division participates in Meuse-Argonne Operation.

October 31, division less Artillery moves north of the road between

Eclise-Fontaine and Ivoiry to the vicinity of Gesnes and Cierges, then into the Bois de Romagne.

November 3, division less Artillery bivouacs in Bois de la Folie, east of Buzancy.

November 4, division less Artillery follows advance of V Corps in close support of 2nd Division.

November 5, division moves from vicinity of Nouart toward the Stonne-Beaumont road preparatory to relieving 80th Division, I Corps in front line; 1st Field Artillery Brig and 1st Ammunition Train rejoin.

November 6, division, on a 6 km front extending from the northwestern outskirts of Beaumont, along Beaumont-Yoncq road to the crossroad 1 km northeast of la Harnoterie Fme, Hill 255, Hill 275, 1 km west of Yoncq, passes through 80th Division in the direction of Mouzon, pursues the enemy to the heights of the Meuse, and sends patrols into Villemontry Le Faubourg and Autrecourt; 2nd Division on right, 77th Division, I Corps on left.

Night of November 6–7, division marches upon Sedan.

November 7, division reaches heights south and southwest of Sedan; later in the day, division is recalled and withdraws south of a line from La Besace to Autrecourt in compliance with orders of First Army; thereafter the division moves to Vaux-en-Dieulet Area

Post Armistice Activities

NOVEMBER 12, 1918–AUGUST 14, 1919

November 12, division moves into Bois de Romagne.

November 13, division moves via Malancourt and Verdun-sur-Meuse into billets near Domrémy-la-Canne and Gondrecourt, and prepares for the advance into Germany as a part of the Army of Occupation.

November 17, division moves via Audun-le-Tiche, Hesperange (Luxemburg), Canach, Konz (Germany), Schweich, Hetzerath, Wittlich, Alf, and Treis, and arrives December 12 in Coblenz.

November 17–December 12, advance into Germany.

December 13, 1918–August 21, 1919, division occupies Coblenz Bridgehead as part of the Army of Occupation.

December 13, division moves into the Bridgehead and occupies stations at and near Montabaur. Training predominates.

April 18, units relieve part of 32nd Division east of the line from Dierdorf to Immendorf.

June 18, division concentrates, prepared for further advance, pending signature of the Treaty of Versailles.

June 28, troops return to billets.

July 19, division relieves 2nd Division and occupies the entire Bridgehead.

Return to United States and Demobilization
AUGUST 15–SEPTEMBER 27, 1919

August 15, division moves to Brest.
August 21, Advance Detachment sails.
August 22, Division Headquarters sails.
August 24, Headquarters 2nd Infantry Brig sails, followed August 25 by Headquarters, 1st Infantry Brig, and Headquarters, 1st Field Artillery Brig.
September 6, the last elements of the division arrive at Hoboken. During September the emergency personnel are demobilized at Camp Meade and the division thereafter proceeds to Camp Taylor for station.

THE SECOND DIVISION, REGULAR ARMY

The Second Division was composed in France of units from the regular army and the United States Marine Corps during the fall of 1917. Brigadier General Charles A. Doyen, U.S. Marine Corps, organized the division and was in command until November 7, 1917, when he was relieved and returned to command the 4th Brigade. One of several senior officers rejected for ill health, Doyen was returned to the United States in May 1918 and died there the following spring. He was succeeded in command of the Fourth Brigade by Brigadier General James A. Harbord, U.S. Army. The Second Division was commanded by Major General Omar Bundy, who was succeeded by Major General James G. Harbord on July 14, 1918, until July 28, 1918, when Major General John A. Lejeune of the United States Marine Corps assumed command.

The division captured 12,026 men. Its total advance was 60 kilometers. It was quiet 71 days and active 66 days. Its total casualties were 22,230, the largest of any division of the army. It had 4,478 battle deaths and 17,752 wounded. The division received 35,343 replacements.

Third Infantry Brigade

9th Infantry
23rd Infantry
5th Machine Gun Battalion

Fourth Marine Brigade

5th Regiment Marines
6th Regiment of Marines
6th Machine Gun Battalion

Second Field Artillery Brigade

12th Field Artillery
15th Field Artillery
17th Field Artillery
2nd Trench Mortar Battery

Divisional Troops

4th Machine Gun Battalion
2nd Engineers
1st Field Signal Battalion
Headquarters Troop

Trains

2nd Train Headquarters
2nd Military Police
2nd Supply Train
2nd Sanitary Train
Ambulance Cos
Field Hospitals 1, 15, 16, 23.

Record of Events

SECTORS WHERE THE 2ND DIVISION WAS ENGAGED IN WARFARE

Toulon-Troyon sectors, Verdun, France, March 15 to May 9, 1918.
Aisne defensive, France, May 31 to June 5, 1918.
Château-Thierry sector, France, June 6 to July 9, 1918.
Aisne-Marne offensive, France, July 18 to 19, 1918.
Marbache sector, France, August 9 to 16, 1918.
St. Mihiel offensive, France, September 12 to 16, 1918.
Meuse-Argonne offensive, Champagne, France, October 1 to October 10, 1918.
Meuse-Argonne offensive, France, November 1 to 11, 1918.

Organization and Movement Overseas

22 SEPTEMBER 1917–30 MARCH 1918

September 22, the War Department directs the organization of the 2nd Division, Regular Army. The division includes troops of the United States Marine Corps which are at Quantico or already in France, and units of the Regular Army stationed at Chickamauga Park, El Paso, Gettysburg, Governors Island, Philadelphia, Syracuse, Forts Benjamin Harrison, Ethan Allen, Myer, Oglethorpe, Riley, Sam Houston, and Camps Robinson and Vail as well as others en route to, or already in, Europe. The Marine contingent, designated to form the 4th Brig (infantry), includes the 5th Marines (formed in June at Philadelphia) which sailed June 14–17 from Philadelphia and landed June 26–July 2 at St. Nazaire, and the 6th Marines and 6th Machine Gun Bn, Marines (both formed in August at Quantico), which are preparing to embark. The 3rd Infantry Brig, then known as the 1st Provisional Brig, is en route to France, and includes the 9th Infantry, which sailed September 7 and 18 from Hoboken and New York and landed September 20 at St. Nazaire and October 3 at Liverpool; the 23rd Infantry, which sailed September 7 from Hoboken and arrived September 20 at St. Nazaire, and the 5th Machine Gun Bn (formed in August 1917 as a provisional machine gun battalion), which sailed September 18 from New York and arrived October 5 at Le Havre. The 2nd Engineers, which sailed September 10 from Hoboken via Glasgow, arrives October 6 at Le Havre. Field artillery units are at their old stations and include the 12th Field Artillery at Fort Myer (formed from personnel of the 3rd Field Artillery in June), the 15th Field Artillery at Syracuse (formed from personnel of the 4th Field Artillery in June), and the 17th Field Artillery at Camp Robinson (formed from personnel of the 8th Field Artillery in June). The components continue to move overseas. The 1st Bn 6th Marines sails from New York on September 23 and arrives at St. Nazaire on October 5.

October 18–31, two detachments, 6th Marines, leave New York and arrive November 4 at St. Nazaire and November 12 at Brest.

November 24, Field Hospital 1 and Ambulance Co 1 leave El Paso, sail December 5 from Hoboken, and land December 22 at St. Nazaire.

December 1, Field Hospital 15 and Ambulance Co 15 leave Fort Benjamin Harrison, sail December 4 from Hoboken, and arrive December 21 at Brest; Field Hospital 23 and Ambulance Co 23 move from Fort Oglethorpe, sail December 5 from Hoboken, and arrive December 22 at St. Nazaire.

December 12, The enlisted personnel for Division Headquarters and Headquarters 2nd Field Artillery Brig sail from Hoboken and arrive December 27 at Brest; 15th Field Artillery sails from New York and arrives December 25 at Liverpool.

December 13, 17th Field Artillery sails from Hoboken and arrives December 28 at Brest.

December 14, 6th Machine Gun Bn, Marines (then known as the 1st MG Bn, Marines), sails from New York and arrives December 28 at St. Nazaire.

December 15, 4th Machine Gun Bn and 2nd Trench Mortar Battery (recently organized) move from Gettysburg to Camp Merritt, sail December 24 from Portland and arrive January 8 at Liverpool.

December 22, 2nd Ammunition Train, 2nd Supply Train, 2nd Train Headquarters and Military Police leave Chickamauga Park for Camp Merritt, sail January 8 from New York and arrive January 24 at Liverpool.

December 25, 1st Field Signal Bn, en route from Camp Vail, sails from New York and arrives January 8 at Liverpool.

January 11, 12th Field Artillery sails from New York and arrives January 19 at Liverpool, England.

January 16, The remaining hospital units, Field Hospital 16 and Ambulance Co 16, move from Fort Riley to Camp Merritt, sail January 23 from Hoboken and arrive February 5 at Brest. **January 24,** 2nd Bn, 6th Marines, sails from New York and arrives February 6 at St. Nazaire. Units arriving in England proceed to Le Havre after a brief stay in rest camps.

March 30, The last element arrives at Bordeaux.

Completion of Organization and Training

SEPTEMBER 24, 1917–MAY 13, 1918

September 24, the concentration of the Division (less Artillery) begins with the arrival of a detachment of 5th Marines in the 3rd Bourmont Training Area. Soon the 23rd Infantry and elements of the 9th Infantry arrive from St. Nazaire.

October 6, the 1st Provisional Brig is designated the 3rd Infantry Brig.

October 23, the 4th Marine Brig (Infantry) is formed at Bourmont.

October 26, Brig. Gen. Charles A. Doyen, U.S. Marine Corps, assumes command of the division. During October the 9th Infantry completes its concentration and the 5th Machine Gun Bn arrives.

November 8, Maj. Gen. Omar Bundy arrives and assumes command of the division; Doyen reverts to command the 4th Brigade.

January 1, 1918, 2nd Field Artillery Brig is organized at Le Valdahon, where the 15th Field Artillery arrived on December 30 from Le Havre, and where the concentration is completed on January 30 and systematic training is begun. During January the 2nd Engineers and elements of the 6th Marines, which have been with the Services of Supply since arrival join; they are the 1st Field Signal Bn, 4th Machine Gun Bn, 6th Machine Gun Bn Marines, Field Hospital 15, and Ambulance Co 15.

January 20–July 4, division is under the administrative control of the I Corps. In February the concentration of the Division (less Artillery) is completed. March 13, Division (less Artillery) moves to the area of the French Second Army near Sommedieue, southeast of Verdun-sur-Meuse.

March 17–30, division participates with the French in the occupation of the Toulon, Rupt, and Troyon Sectors (Lorraine). The division is affiliated with troops of the French X Corps (French Second Army) along the entire corps' front on the line 3 km northwest of St. Mihiel on Route Nationale No. 64, 1½ km northwest of Lamorville, ¾ km south of Seuzey, ½ km east of Vaux-lès-Palameix, south and east edges of Bois Loclont, le Saillant, east slope of Côte de Senoux, Bois des Eparges, Lea Eparges, Côte 346, Monville Ancne Fme, Trésauvaux, Bonzée-en-Woëvre, and ½ km south of Haudiomont.

Night, March 17–18, units, except artillery, enter the line and train successively by battalion, regiment, and brigade. The troops serve with the French 33rd Division in the Toulon Sector, which includes the Eparges and Bonchamp sub-sectors, with the French 34th Division in the Rupt Sector, which includes the Ranzières, Mouilly, and Sonvaux sub-sectors, and with the French 52nd Division in the Troyon Sector, which includes the Rouvrois, Lacroix, and Chevaliers sub-sectors; French 15th Colonial Division (French II Colonial Corps) on right, and French 131st Division (French XVII Corps) on left.

March 21, 2nd Field Artillery Brig and 2nd Ammunition Train join from Le Valdahon.

March 30, French X Corps extends its sector north to include the Ronvaux and Moulainville sub-sectors, relieving the French 131st Division on the front, ¼ km south of Haudiomont, Haudiomont (incl.), Ronvaux (incl.), ½ km north of Watronville, ½ km northeast of Châtillon-sous-les-Côtes, 1 km northeast of Moulainville, ½ km north of Eix; the French 34th Division is withdrawn from the Rupt sector, which is divided between the Toulon and Troyon sectors; the Toulon sector is extended south 2 km to include the Sonvaux and the north half of the Mouilly sub-sectors; the Troyon sector is extended north 2 km to include the Ranzières and the south half of the Mouilly sub-sectors; French 32nd Corps on right, and the French 17th Corps on left.

March 30–May 13, division participates with the French in the occupation of the Toulon and Troyon Sectors (Lorraine). The division is brigaded with troops of the French X Corps, and, later, French II Colonial Corps (French Second Army).

April 17, French II Colonial Corps relieves the French X Corps in the Toulon and Troyon sectors.

April 25, 3rd Infantry Brig assembles in the Rouvrois and Lacroix subsectors and the 4th Marine Brig in the Ronvaux and Moulainville sub-sectors, where the brigade commanders assume charge of the fronts.

May 9, division begins a withdrawal from the front and moves to the south and west of Bar-le-Duc; training.

May 18, division moves to the vicinity of Chaumont-en-Vexin in the rear area of the French Fifth Army; training.

May 27, the enemy attacks the Chemin des Dames and threatens Paris.

May 31, division, at the disposal of the French Sixth Army, moves toward the front of the French 21st Corps northwest of Château-Thierry.

Operations in France

MAY 31, 1918–NOVEMBER 11, 1918

May 31–June 5, division participates in the Aisne Defensive Operation. During this period, French units fell back through the lines held by the members of the 2nd Division.

June 1, division begins the occupation of a second line position on a 20 km front astride the road from Château-Thierry to Paris in support of the French 43rd, French 73rd and French 164th Divisions, which are holding the French 21st Corps' front. This support position passes through Bonneil, La Nouette Fme, east edge of Bois de La Marchette, Le Thiolet, Bois des Clérembauts, Triangle, Lucy-le-Bocage, Hill 142, east and north edges of Bois de Veuilly, woods southwest of Veuilly-la-Poterie, and Bremoiselle.

June 2–3, the enemy captures Bussiares, Torcy, Belleau, Bouresches, and Veuilly-la-Poterie, and advances to the line from Triangle to Le Thiolet and into the Bois de Belleau; almost the entire position of the 2nd Division becomes the corps' front; a few French units which are in line withdraw during the following night.

June 4–5, division commands the front with brigades abreast, 3rd Infantry Brig on right, on a line from the eastern and northern edges of the Bois de La Marchette, the eastern edge of the Bois des Clérembauts, the 4th Marine Brig on left from Triangle, Lucy-le-Bocage and woods to the northwest, Hill 142, to ¼ km north of Champillon on the Champillon-Bussiares road, north edge of the Bois de Veuilly; it withdraws units of the 3rd Infantry Brig in a support position east of the Bois de La Marchette (in the zone of the French 38th Corps); French 4th Cavalry Division (French 38th Corps) on the right, and French 167th Division (French 21st Corps) on the left. On June 6, units formerly with the French 43rd Division west of Champillon are withdrawn; the Aisne Operation merges into sector occupation.

June 6–July 10, division occupies the Château-Thierry Sector (Ile de France); June 6, division attacks; it advances toward Vaux, captures Bouresches, and clears the south portion of the Bois de Belleau; French 10th Cl Division (French 38th Corps) on right.

June 8–13, division engages in a series of attacks and counterattacks, during which, on June 12, it temporarily occupies the Bois de Belleau.

June 14, the sector of the 3rd Infantry Brig is extended to the left to include Bouresches, relieving elements of the 4th Marine Brig.

June 15–18, 7th Infantry (3rd Division), attached, relieves the front line battalions of the 4th Marine Brig, which withdraw to support positions; the Division sector is reduced by moving the left boundary 1 km to the east, elements of the French 167th Division executing the relief.

June 21, French III Corps assumes command of the corps sector.

Night of June 21–22, 4th Marine Brig reenters the front line, and the night of June 23–24, completes the relief of the 7th Infantry.

June 25, 4th Marine Brig completes the capture of Bois de Belleau.

June 26–30, local actions.

June 28, French 39th Division on right.

July 1, 3rd Infantry Brig captures Vaux and clears the Bois de La Roche.

July 4, I Corps relieves the French III Corps; 52nd Infantry Brig, 26th Division, relieves the 4th Marine Brig, which retires to the second position (army line) 10 km to the rear.

July 7, 26th Division continues the relief, completes that of the 3rd Infantry Brig on the night of July 8–9, and on July 10 assumes command of the Château-Thierry sector, designated on July 2 the Pas Fini sector.

July 10–16, Division occupies the Second Position in the Pas Fini Sector (Ile de France). Division occupies the position with brigades abreast, 4th Marine Brig on the right, from 1 km south of Villiers-sur-Marchne, through Bézu-le-Guéry, Montreuil-aux-Lions, La Sablonnière, Chambardy, to les Brulis (all incl.), and consolidates the position.

July 14, division is assigned to the French Tenth Army and moves to the southwest of Soissons, where it joins the French 20th Corps near Taillefontaine.

July 14–22, division is under the administrative control of the III Corps.

July 18, division attacks east, captures Beaurepaire Fme, Vauxcastile, Vierzy, and establishes a front 1½ km east of Vierzy; French 38th Division (French 30th Corps) on right, French 1st Moroccan Division on left; command passes.

Night of July 17–18, division relieves the French 38th Division on a 2 km front northwest of Longpont from ¼ km northeast of Chavigny to 1¾ km west of Verte-Feuille Fme.

July 18–20, division participates in the Aisne-Marne Operation.

July 19, the 6th Marine Regt continues the attack and reaches a line ½ km east of Parcy-Tigny, Côte 160, la Ràperie.

July 20, French 58th Division relieves the division (less Artillery) which concentrates in the woods east of Verte-Feuille Fme in army reserve. Second Field Artillery Brig remains in line, supports French 58th Division until July 24, the French 12th Division until July 26, and then reverts to the division.

Night of July 20–21, division (less Artillery) moves to the vicinity of Pierrefonds and Taillefontaine, on July 24 to Nanteuil-le-Haudouin, on July 30 to the Nancy Area, where it joins the French Eighth Army, and again on August 4 to the area of the French 32nd Corps, north of Nancy.

July 31–August 27, division is under the administrative control of the IV Corps.

Night of August 5–6, division begins the relief of the French 64th Division in the Marbache Sector.

August 9–19, division occupies the Marbache Sector (Lorraine). The front line of the sector is 1 km southeast of Port-sur-Seille, Morville-sur-Seile, along the south bank of the Seille River to the northeast edge of Bois de Cheminot, Lesménils, La Vitrée, Pont-à-Mousson, Montrichard, Haut de Rieupt (all incl.); French 32nd Division (French XV Corps) on right, 1st Division on left; local actions.

August 15, the U.S. 82nd Division begins the relief of the Division (less Artillery), which moves to the 6th (Colombey-les-Belles) training area; the artillery supports the 82nd Division until August 22.

August 18, division is ordered to join the First Army.

August 19, the command passes to the 82nd Division.

August 27, division receives orders to join the I Corps and on September 1 moves to the vicinity of Francheville where, on September 3, 9th Infantry enters corps reserve.

Night of September 9–10, division moves to the woods north of Noviant-aux-Prés and Manonville and relieves units of 89th and 90th Divisions in the Limey Sector; September 10, command passes.

September 10–12, division occupies the Limey Sector (Lorraine). The front line of this sector on the south Face of the St. Mihiel salient extends from ½ km southeast of Remenauville to 1 km north of Limey; 5th Division on right and 89th Division (IV Corps) on left.

September 12, the Limey Sector occupation merges into the St. Mihiel Operation.

September 12–16, division participates in the St. Mihiel Operation.

September 12, division attacks on a 2 km front as the left division of the I Corps, brigades in column, 3rd Infantry Brig leading, advances through the Bois du Four, Bois La Haie-l'Evéque, east part of Bois du Beau Vallon, Bois d'Heiche, Bois du Fey, Thiaucourt, and over the heights to the north; 5th Division on right, 89th Division (IV Corps) on left.

September 13, division captures Jaulny and advances a short distance beyond; 4th Marine Brig relieves the 3rd Infantry Brig.

September 14–15, division renews the attack and establishes the line, Bois de Blainchamp, Moulin de Rembercourt, east and northwest edges of Bois de La Montague, 1½ km north of Xammes.

September 16, 78th Division relieves the Division (less Artillery, which supports the 78th Division until September 18) and the latter moves to the north of Toul near Ansauville and Royaumeix.

September 20, division moves to Toul; rehabilitation.

September 25, division moves to the south of Châlons-sur-Marne, where it passes to the reserve of the French Group of Armies of the Center.

September 28, division moves to the vicinity of Souain and Suippes in the rear area of the French 21st Corps and enters the reserve of the French Fourth Army, which is attacking between the Argonne Forest and Rheims.

September 30–October 10, division participates in the Meuse-Argonne (Champagne) Operation.

Night of September 30–October 1, division begins the relief of the French 61st Division (French 21st Corps) and elements of the French 21st Division (French XI Corps) north of Sommepy on a 3 km front which extends from 1¾ km northeast of the Sommepy railroad station to 1½ km west thereof.

October 2, command passes; the 4th Marine Brig is in the front line; the 3rd Infantry Brig is in reserve south of the ridge between Butte-de-Souain and Navarin Fme; French 170th Division is on the right, French 21st Division (French XI Corps) on the left. During that day and the night of October 2–3 the 4th Marine Brig clears and occupies Essen Trench, which is ¼ km north of and parallel to the original front, and the 3rd Infantry Brig moves toward the Bois des Pins and occupies attack positions.

October 3, division attacks, the 3rd Infantry Brig advances northwest from a line which extends from ¼ km west of Pavon-et-Puits to 2¾ km northeast of the Sommepy railroad station; the 4th Marine Brig advances northward in the left half of its zone on a 1½ km front; the 2 km gap between it and the 3rd Infantry Brig closes as the attacks converge at the intersection of the Médéah Fme, Blanc-Mont, and Somme-Py, St. Étienne-à-Arnes roads. The division front now extends from Médéah Fme to ½ km south of Hill 160, thence southward along the road from St. Étienne-à-Arnes to Somme-Py as far as the Médéah Fme, Blanc-Mont road, thence westward to the heights of Blanc-Mont; French 167th Division on right, French 21st Division (French XI Corps) on left.

October 4–5, 4th Marine Brig clears the Blanc-Mont ridge and extends its front from ½ km south of Hill 160 to 1½ km south of St. Étienne-à-Arnes; the French divisions on each flank fail to advance alongside the 2nd Division, causing heavy casualties. The French 22nd Division relieves the French 21st Division and re-establishes contact with the 2nd Division.

October 5, French 73rd Division on the right alongside the 3rd Brig.

October 6, division uses the 71st Infantry Brig (36th Division), attached, to relieve its front line units from ¾ km northwest of Médéah Fme to 1 km southeast of St. Étienne-à-Arnes, and the latter then withdraw to Pylone Hill and the Blanc-Mont ridge.

October 7, command passes to the 71st Infantry Brig. Division reorganizes the front line preparatory to an attack; French units enter the west outskirts of St. Étienne-à-Arnes.

October 8, 71st Infantry Brig, with 2 battalions, 6th Regt of the 2nd Division attached for flank protection, attacks, captures St. Étienne-à-Arnes, and pushes its right to the north of, and parallel to, the road from St. Étienne-à-Arnes to Orfeuil; French 7th Division (French XI Corps) on left.

October 9, the trenches ¾ km north of St. Étienne-à-Ames are occupied.

October 10, 36th Division relieves the division (less Artillery and Engineers, which support the 36th Division until October 28 when they revert to the 2nd Division) and the latter assembles near Souain and Suippes; the 3rd Infantry Brig passes into corps reserve, the 4th Marine Brig into army reserve.

October 14, division (less detached units) moves north of Châlons-sur-Marne to positions near Bouy and Vadenay; training.

October 19, 4th Marine Brig is placed at the disposal of the French IX Corps in order to relieve the French 73rd Division near Attigny.

October 20, the 4th Brigade moves by stages to the vicinity of Leffincourt expecting to make the relief on the night of October 22–23, but the plan is changed and during night of October 23–24 this brigade reverts to the division.

October 21, division is ordered to join the First Army.

October 22, division (less detached units) moves via Herpont and Valmy to the vicinity of Les Islettes in the Argonne Forest where it enters the reserve of the V Corps (1st Army).

Night of October 25–26, 3rd Infantry Brig concentrates near Charpentry, where the 4th Marine Brig joins it the following night.

October 27–November 11, division participates in the Meuse-Argonne Operation.

Night of October 30–31, division relieves the 42nd Division, except the outposts which are relieved on November 1, from ½ km northwest of Tuilerie Fme, through the north edge of the Côte de Chatillon, 1¼ km south of Landres-et-St. Georges, to 1 km south of St. Georges.

October 31, command passes.

November 1, division, on a 4 km front, as the left of the V Corps, attacks toward Bayonville-et-Chennery, advances through Landres-et-St. Georges, the east portion of St. Georges, Bois des Hazois, Landreville, Bayou-ville-et-Chennery, and establishes a line, which is held by the 4th Marine Brig, from ¾ km southwest of Barricourt, through a point ¼ km south of Magenta Fme, Côte 313, to Fontaine des Parades; 89th Division on right, 80th Division (I Corps) on left.

Night of November 2-3, 3rd Infantry Brig advances through the 4th Marine Brig toward an exploitation line from Nouart to Fossé and causes the enemy to withdraw from the Bois de la Folie.

November 3, 3rd Infantry Brig advances to the line from Champy-Haut to Bellevue Fme, and that night pursues the enemy via the Belval-Bois-des-Dames, Beaumont road, through the north part of the Bois du Port-Gérache to la Tuilerie Fme.

November 4, 3rd Infantry Brig establishes outposts from near Belle Tour Fme to the high ground 1½ km south of Beaumont, the enemy withdrawing to the east bank of the Meuse; the 4th Marine Brig moves to the ridge southeast of Vaux-en-Dieulet.

Night of November 4-5, division, 3rd Infantry Brig leading, advances toward the Meuse.

November 5, division enters Beaumont and Létanne and occupies the heights of the Meuse from the south edge of the Bois de la Vache to 1½ km east of Beaumont and ¾ km north of Létanne.

November 6, 1st Division on left.

November 6-7, elements of the 3rd Infantry Brig occupy positions north and south of la Sartelle Fme and along the east edge of the Bois de l'Hospice and Bois Luquet; the 4th Marine Brig assembles in the Bois du Four north of la Forge Fme.

November 7, the boundaries are moved to the left; the 89th Division relieves elements south of Létanne and the 2nd Division sends patrols into Villemontry and Le Fabourg relieving the 1st Division; the new front extends from Létanne to Le Fabourg (both incl.); 77th Division on left.

November 8, 3rd Infantry Brig, with one regiment in support, holds the front; part of the 4th Marine Brig moves toward the Bois du Fond-de-Limon, which it reaches the next day.

November 10-11, two battalions of the 4th Marine Brig cross the Meuse east of the Bois de l'Hospice and reach the heights south of Moulins, the north and south ridge through Sénégal Fme, and Warmonterne Fme.

Post Armistice Activities

NOVEMBER 12, 1918–JULY 14, 1919

November 12, division consolidates the position east of the Meuse.

November 14, 77th Division relieves the 2nd Division.

November 16, division (less one regiment sent to Stenay) assembles near Pouilly.

November 17–December 13, advance into Germany.

November 17, division advances via Virton (Belgium), Anon, Brouch (Luxemburg), Mersch, Larochette, Mettendorf (Germany), Rittersdorf, Prüm, Gerolstein, Nohn, Adenau, Ahrweiler, and Heddesdorf, and arrives on December 13 near Coblenz and northwest of Heddesdorf.

December 13, division moves into the Bridgehead and occupies stations in and northwest of Heddesdorf. Training predominates.

December 13, 1918–July 14, 1919, division occupies the Coblenz Bridgehead as part of the Army of Occupation.

April 18, units relieve part of the 32nd Division west of the line from Dierdort to Bendorf.

June 18, division concentrates near Dierdorf, prepared for a further advance, pending the signature of the Treaty of Versailles.

June 28, the troops return to billets.

Return to the United States and Demobilization

JULY 15–AUGUST 10, 1919

July 15, division moves to Brest.

July 23, 5th Machine Gun Bn sails.

July 25, Division Headquarters, Headquarters 3rd Infantry Brig and Headquarters 4th Marine Brig sail.

July 30, Headquarters 2nd Field Artillery Brig follows.

August 8, 4th Marine Brig, detached, moves to Quantico.

August 10, the last element, Ambulance Co 1, arrives in the United States. During August the emergency personnel are demobilized and the division proceeds to Camp Travis for station.

THE THIRD DIVISION, REGULAR ARMY

The Third Division was organized at Camp Greene, Charlotte, North Carolina, from units of the regular army. Major General Joseph F. Dickman was the first commander. He was followed by Major General Beaumont B. Buck, who assumed command August 31, 1918, and continued until October 17, when he was succeeded by Brigadier General Preston Brown. This division arrived in France May 30, 1918. The division captured 2,240 German prisoners. It was quiet zero days and active 86 days. It advanced 41 kilometers. Its casualties totaled 16,117. It had 3,177 battle deaths and 12,940 wounded. This division received 24,033 replacements.

Fifth Infantry Brigade

4th Infantry
7th Infantry
8th Machine Gun Battalion

Sixth Infantry Brigade

30th Infantry
38th Infantry
9th Machine Gun Battalion

Third Field Artillery Brigade

10th Field Artillery
18th Field Artillery
76th Field Artillery
3rd Trench Mortar Battery

Divisional Troops

6th Engineers
7th Machine Gun Battalion
5th Field Signal Battalion
Headquarters Troop

Trains

3rd Train Hdqs
3rd Military Police
3rd Ammunition Train
3rd Supply Train
6th Engineer Train

3rd Sanitary Train
Ambulance Cos and Field Hospitals 5, 7, 26, 27

Record of Events

SECTORS WHERE THE 3RD DIVISION WAS ENGAGED IN WARFARE

Peronne sector, France, February 10 to March 29, 1918 (6th Eng.).
Somme defensive, France, March 21 to April 6, 1918 (6th Eng.).
Amiens sector, France, April 7 to June 7, 1918 (6th Eng.).
Aisne defensive, France, June 1 to 5, 1918.
Château-Thierry sector, France, June 6 to July 14, 1918.
Champagne-Marne defensive, France, July 15 to 18, 1913.
Aisne-Marne offensive, France, July 18 to 27, 1918.
St. Mihiel offensive, France, September 12 to 14, 1918.
Meuse-Argonne offensive, France, September 30 to October 27, 1918.

Organization and Training in the United States

NOVEMBER 12, 1917–MARCH 6, 1918

November 12, the War Department directs the organization of the 3rd Division, Regular Army, at Camp Greene.

November 21, the organization begins in accordance with the Tables of Organization of August 8, 1917, and includes Regular Army troops stationed at Camps Greene, Forrest, Shelby, Stanley, Stuart, and Travis, and Forts Bliss, Clark, Douglas, Leavenworth, and Washington Barracks. The infantry brigades and the 7th Machine Gun Bn are formed at Camp Greene; the 5th Infantry Brig includes the 4th Infantry, 7th Infantry, and 8th MG Bn; the 6th Infantry Brig includes the 30th Infantry, 38th Infantry (formed from personnel of the 30th Infantry in 1917) and 9th MG Bn.

November 26, Organization of Hq 3rd Field Artillery Brig is begun at Camp Stanley; the brigade includes the 10th Field Artillery at Fort Douglas (formed from personnel of the 6th Field Artillery in 1917), the 18th Field Artillery at Fort Bliss (formed from personnel of the 5th Field Artillery in 1917), and the 76th Field Artillery at Camp Shelby (formerly the 18th Cav).

November 28, Maj. Gen. Joseph T. Dickman assumes command; systematic training begins. During December and January drafts — largely from Camps Devens, Dix, Lee, Meade, and Upton, totaling 10,000 — complete the division.

December 4–5, 6th Engrs and Tn sail from Hoboken and land December 21–22 at Brest and St. Nazaire.

December 28, Hq 3rd Field Artillery Brig moves from Camp Stanley to Camp Travis.

February 27, Adv Det and 5th F Sig Bn sail from Hoboken and arrive March 11 at Brest.

Movement Overseas

MARCH 7–MAY 13, 1918

March 7, units move from their respective stations to the ports of embarkation (Halifax, Hoboken, Newport News, and New York) via Camps Merritt and Stuart.

March 14–April 19, Division (less Arty and Engrs) sails, and debarks at St. Nazaire, March 27, F Hosp 5, April 29, 1st Bn 4th Inf; at Liverpool, March 29, 3rd Am Tn, and 3rd Tn Hq and MP, April 12, Hq 6th Inf. Brig, 30th Inf., 7th, 8th, and 9th MG Bns; at Bordeaux, March 30–April 6, DHQ, Amb Cos 7 and 27, and F Hosp 27; at Glasgow, April 4, part of the 38th Inf; at Brest, the remainder, including, April 7, 38th Infantry (less 1st and 3rd Bns and MG Co), April 13, 3rd Bn 38th Inf., April 15, Hq 5th Inf. Brig, 7th Infantry 4th Inf. (less 1st Bn), April 28, 3rd Sup Tn, 3rd San Tn. March 25, units of the 3rd Field Artillery Brig move to Camp Merritt, where the brigade is concentrated for the first time.

April 23 and 30, 3rd Field Artillery Brig sails from Hoboken and debarks at Brest, May 6, 76th Field Artillery (less 2nd Bn); at Bordeaux, May 7, 10th Field Artillery and 3rd Bn 18th FA; at St. Nazaire, May 12–13, the remainder of the artillery.

Final Training and Operations

MARCH 16–NOVEMBER 11, 1918

March 16, Division (less Arty and Engrs) concentrates in the 9th (Château-villain) Training Area.

March 21–April 6, certain elements of the 6th Engrs, attached to the British Fifth Army, participate as infantry in the Somme Defensive Operation when they occupy the front line from 34 km west of Warfusée-Abancourt to the Bois des Tailloux (incl.).

April 7, 3rd Am Tn, the leading element of the 3rd Field Artillery Brig, moves from Le Havre to Camp Coëtquidan, where the concentration of the brigade is completed on May 27; training follows.

May 30, division (less Arty and Engrs) moves to Château-Thierry and the vicinity.

May 31–June 5, division (less Arty and Engrs) participates in the Aiane Operation.

May 31, 7th MG Bn, attached to the French 10th Colonial Division, enters the line along the south bank of the Marne at Château-Thierry.

June 1, the enemy occupies Château-Thierry and the north bank of the Marne.

June 2, division moves to the south bank; units of 5th Infantry Brig, attached to the French 20th Division, occupy a position from 1 km southeast of Tréloup to Sauvigny; units of 6th Infantry Brig attached to the French 10th Colonial Division take position from 134 km west of Mézy to 34 km west of Fossoy.

June 3, 2nd Bn, 30th Infantry, attached to the French 4th Cavalry Division, occupies a support position at Mont-de Bonneil, west of Château-Thierry; units of 6th Infantry Brig extend west, along the south bank of the Maine, to 34 km southeast of Brasles.

June 4, the commanding general, 3rd Division, now commands the French 38th Corps Reserve consisting of French and 3rd Division units.

June 5, Co E, 30th Infantry, relieves units of the French 10th Colonial Division and occupies part of the front north of Crogis.

June 6, division assumes command of a sector along the south bank of the Maine from Mézy (incl.) to Chierry (excl.); elements of the French 33rd Colonial Infantry remain in line under the 3rd Division.

June 6–7, 2nd Bn, 30th Infantry, moving north from Mont-de-Bonneil, attacks through Monneaux toward Hill 204 and reaches a line midway between Monneaux and Vaux; French 10th Colonial Division on right, 2nd Division on left.

June 6–July 14, division occupies the Château-Thierry Sector (Champagne).

June 7–11, units of the 5th Infantry Brig relieve elements of the French 20th Division and occupy the south bank of the Marne from Sauvigny to 34 km north of Reuilly, east of 3rd Division sector; units of 5th Infantry Brig in line east of Sauvigny are relieved.

June 11, 6th Engrs and Tn rejoin.

June 14, two subsectors are organized and held by regiments, 30th Infantry on the right, 38th on the left; French 20th Division on right, French 10th Division on left.

June 15, 7th Infantry is detached and operates.

June 16–23, with the 2nd Division in the Château-Thierry (Pas Fini) sector.

June 16, the sector is extended west as far as the eastern limits of Château-Thierry.

June 16–17, the remaining French units are relieved and the sector is held with three regiments in line, 4th Infantry on the left.

June 21–July 18, division is under the administrative control of the I Corps.

June 25–28, three subsectors are created, Chierry, Gland, and Mont–St. Père; French 125th Division relieves the French 20th Division on the right; French 39th Division relieves the French 10th Colonial Division on the left.

July 3, the sector is extended east to a point 1 km west of Varennes and four subsectors are created — Brasles, Gland Mont–St. Père, and Chartèves — which are held with brigades abreast, four regiments in line.

July 4–14, local actions occur.

July 5–13, 3rd Field Artillery Brig and 3rd Am Tn join from Camp Coëtquidan.

July 8, French 125th Division (French III Corps) is on the right.

Night of July 14–15, the enemy launches an offensive, crosses the Marne near Mezy, penetrates into Surmelin Valley, and reaches the line Les Etangs Fme, 34 km east of Launay, 34 km east of Moulins, Fossoy.

July 15, the Château-Thierry sector occupation merges into the Champagne-Marne Operation.

July 15–17, division participates in the Champagne-Marne Operation. Division is in line along the south bank of the Maine from 1 km west of Varennes to Château-Thierry (excl.); French 125th Division (French III Corps) on right, French 39th Division on left.

July 16, the enemy advances his line to 1 km east of Launay, the northern outskirts of Connigis, le Chanet, Crézancy (excl.); 3rd Division with 111th Infantry (28th Division) attached, advances to the line from 1 km north of Crózancy to 34 km north of Fossoy.

July 17, division retakes Mózy and reoccupies its position along the south bank of the Marne west of that village; French 73rd Division on right, French 39th Division on left. The Champagne-Marne Operation merges into the Aisne-Marne Operation.

July 18, the counter-offensive of the Allies begins with a penetration of the west face of the Marne salient by the French Sixth and French Tenth Armies.

July 18–30, division participates in the Aisne-Marne Operation.

Night of July 19–20, the enemy retires to the north bank of the Marne; division advances its right front to the line from Varennes to Mézy.

July 21, division pursues northeast; 5th Infantry Brig crosses the Marne at Mézy, Fossoy, Chierry and Château-Thierry, and occupies Mont–St. Pêre; French 73rd Division (French III Corps) on right, French 39th Division on left.

July 22, 6th Infantry Brig crosses the Marne at Mézy and captures Jaulgonne; 5th Infantry Brig advances its left through the Bois du Chanois to la Théoderie; division front extends from Jaulgonne to the northeast edge of the Bois du Chanois.

July 23, division advances its left to La Tieulerie Fme.

July 24, division pursues the retiring enemy to the line from Argentol, through the southern outskirts of Le Charnel, to the east edge of the Forêt de Fère; French 4th Division (French III Corps) on right.

July 25, the pursuit continues; Le Charnel is captured and held.

Night of July 26–27, the enemy withdraws to the Ourcq River,

July 27, division advances the 5th Infantry Brig to a north and south line from Villardelle Fme to Côte 190 (incl.) and withdraws the 6th Infantry Brig to the south bank of the Marne.

July 28, the pursuit continues and Ronchêres is captured; French 4th Division on right, 28th Division on left.

July 29, 4th Infantry, in conjunction with an attack of the 42nd Division on the left, attacks the Bois des Grimpettes.

July 30, 32nd Division relieves the division, which moves south of the Marne to the vicinity of Château-Thierry; rehabilitation and training.

July 31–August 3, division is under the administrative control of the III Corps.

Night of August 2–3, 6th Infantry Brig, detached, moves to join the French III Corps near St. Gilles.

Night of August 3–4, the leading elements arrive at Mont-sur-Courville.

August 3–6, 6th Infantry Brig participates in the Aisne-Marne Operation.

August 5, III Corps relieves the French III Corps; elements of the 6th Infantry Brig relieve the French 18th Bn Chasseurs in the support position 2 km southwest of St. Gilles.

August 6, elements of the 6th Infantry Brig relieve the French 147th Infantry south of the Vesle River; French 4th Division on right, 32nd Division on left. This operation merges into sector occupation.

August 7, after an attempt to establish a bridgehead, the brigade holds the south bank of Vesle River until relieved on August 11 by the French 164th Division, when it rejoins the 3rd Division.

August 7–11, 6th Infantry Brig occupies the Vesle Sector, holding the front from Villette to Fismes (excl.).

August 14, division moves from the vicinity of Château-Thierry to the 1st (Gondrecourt) Training Area.

August 18, division is ordered to join the First Army.

August 19–September 4, rehabilitation and training.

August 27, division is assigned to V Corps.

Night of September 4–5, division moves to the 5th (Vaucouleurs) Training Area.

September 9, division (less Arty and 7th MG Bn) moves to a position in readiness in the Forêt de la Reine, where, on September 11, it passes into corps reserve; 3rd Field Artillery Brig and 3rd Am Tn are detached to support the 1st and 42nd Divisions, and the 7th MG Bn is attached to the 1st Division.

September 12, division, in corps reserve, moves to Beaumont and the vicinity.

September 12–15, division participates in the St. Mihiel Operation.

September 13, elements of the division occupy a position in readiness between Nonsard and Pannes.

September 15, all detached units revert to the division, which moves to the vicinity of Nixéville.

Night of September 25–26, division moves to the Forêt de Hesse, where it passes to corps reserve.

September 26–October 27, division participates in the Meuse-Argonne Operation.

September 30, division relieves the 79th Division along the Ridge 300 in northwest of Nantilois and along the north edge of the Bois de Beuge; 4th Division (III Corps) on right, 32nd Division on left.

October 1, 4th Division units in line within 3rd Division sector are relieved.

October 3, the sector is extended west to include Cierges by the relief of units of the 32nd Division.

October 4, division attacks north-northwest and advances 1 km along the entire front; 80th Division on right, 32nd Division on left.

October 5, division attacks and retains a line from the north edge of Woods 250, 300 m south of Hill 253, to 1¾ km east of Gesnes.

October 9, the sector is reduced 1 km on the left (west) by relinquishing the line to the 32nd Division. Division captures Hill 253, Bois de Cunel, and La Mamelle Trench ¾ km south of the road from Cunel to Romagne-sous-Montfaucon, and establishes a front from the north edge of the Bois de Cunel to 1 km southeast of Romagne-sous-Montfaucon.

October 11, division advances its right to the ridge Hill 272 and Hill 255.

October 12, 5th Division is on the right.

October 13, 4th Division is on the right.

October 12–13, the sector is extended northeast to a point on the south edge of the Bois de Forêt, 2¾ km west of Brieulles, by the relief of elements of the 5th and 4th Divisions southeast of Cunel and in the Bois de Forêt.

October 14–15, 5th Division passes through the 3rd Division along La Mamelle Trench; 3rd Division attacks across the Fond-Diné, reaches a line from the southwest edge of les Aiséments Bois to the Bois de la Pultière, and, later, makes a further advance and occupies the Bois de Peut-de-Faux; 5th Division on left.

October 15–19, local actions occur.

Night of October 18–19, 6th Infantry Brig relieves units of the 4th Division which are along the northeast edge of the Bois de Fays, north edge of the Bois de Brieulles and northwest edge of the Bois de la Côte Lémont to Fond de la Côte Laimont on the Meuse; 33rd Division (French 17th Corps) on fight.

October 20–23, division attacks northeast, occupies la Grève, Clairs-Chênes woods, la Mi-Noel, the entire Bois de Forêt, and the small woods southwest of Clery-le-Grand; 33rd Division on right until relieved, October 21, by the French 15th Colonial Division.

October 22, 90th Division is on the left.

October 24, the gains are consolidated.

October 27, 5th Division relieves the 3rd Division (less Arty, which remains in position and supports the 5th Division until November 11) and the latter moves to Montfaucon.

October 30, division (less Arty) moves to the vicinity of Tronvilie-en-Barrois and Tannois; rehabilitation and training.

Post Armistice Activities

NOVEMBER 12, 1918–AUGUST 4, 1919

November 14, division (less Arty) moves to the region south of Champion; the artillery rejoins.

November 17, division moves via Remich (Luxemburg), Saarburg (Germany), Morbach, Sin-morn, and Boppard, and arrives for station in the Kreis of Mayen on December 12.

November 17–December 16, advance into Germany.

December 18, 1918–August 4, 1919, division forms part of the Army of Occupation in Germany. Training predominates.

March 9, 3rd TM Btry sails from St. Nazaire.

June 19–27, division (less elements forming part of the Reinforced Brigade, III Corps) concentrates along the Rhine, prepared for a further advance, pending the signature of the Treaty of Versailles. The Reinforced Brigade, III Corps, concentrates near Mayen.

June 28, the troops return to billets.

Return to the United States and Demobilization

AUGUST 5–31, 1919

August 5, division moves to Brest.

August 10, elements of the 38th Infantry 9th MG Bn and 18th Field Artillery sail.

August 14, DHQ sails, and arrives August 23 at Camp Merritt, via Hoboken.

August 28, the last elements arrive in the United States. During August the emergency personnel are demobilized and the division proceeds to Camp Pike for station.

THE FOURTH DIVISION, REGULAR ARMY

The Fourth Division was organized at Camp Greene, Charlotte, North Carolina, on December 10, 1917. It was composed of units of the regular army brought to full strength by drafted men. It left Camp Greene on April 18, 1918, and had all organizations in France by June 3. General George H. Cameron was the first commander and was succeeded by Major General John L. Hines. On October 11, General Cameron resumed command of the Fourth. The division captured 2,756 German prisoners. It was quiet 7 days and active 38 days. It advanced 24½ kilometers. It had 12,504 total casualties, including 2,611 battle deaths and 9,893 wounded.

Seventh Infantry Brigade

39th Infantry
47th Infantry
11th Machine Gun Battalion

Eighth Infantry Brigade

58th Infantry
59th Infantry
12th Machine Gun Battalion

Fourth Field Artillery Brigade

13th Field Artillery
16th Field Artillery

77th Field Artillery
4th Trench Mortar Battery

Divisional Troops

4th Engineers
Tenth Machine Gun Battalion
Eighth Field Signal Battalion
Headquarters Troop

Trains

4th Train Hdqs
4th Military Police
4th Supply Train
4th Engineer Train
4th Sanitary Train
Ambulance Cos and Field Hospitals 19, 21, 28, 33

Record of Events

Sectors Where the 4th Division Was Engaged in Warfare

Aisne-Marne offensive, France, July 18 to August 8, 1918.
Vesle sector, France, August 7 to 12, 1918.
Toulon sector, France, September 6 to 13, 1918.
St. Mihiel offensive, France, September 14, 1913.
Meuse-Argonne offensive, France, September 26 to November 11, 1918.

Organization and Training in the United States

November 19, 1917–April 21, 1918

November 19, the War Department directs the organization of the 4th Division, Regular Army, at Camp Greene.

December 3–January 5, the division is organized in accordance with the Tables of Organization of August 8, 1917, and includes Regular Army troops stationed at Camp Greene, Monterey, Vancouver Barracks, and other places.

December 10, Major General George H. Cameron assumes command. The infantry and artillery brigades are organized at Camp Greene; the 7th Infantry Brig includes the 39th and 47th Regts of Infantry (formed from personnel of the 30th and 9th Regts of Infantry respectively, in 1917; the 8th Infantry Brig includes the 58th and 59th Regts of Infantry (formed from personnel of the 4th Infantry in 1917); the 4th Field Artillery Brig includes the 13th Field Artillery (formed from personnel of the 5th Field Artillery in 1917), the 16th Field Artillery (formed from personnel of the 8th Field Artillery in 1917) and the 77th Field Artillery (formerly the 19th Cav).

December 31, the division consists of 13,000 regulars.

January 5, the organization is completed and systematic training begins. During and after late February, men who had been voluntarily inducted from all sections of the United States are sent to the division.

March 1–21, drafts, aggregating 10,000 from Camps Custer, Grant, Lewis, Pike, and Travis, complete the division.

Movement Overseas

APRIL 21–JUNE 9, 1918

April 21, division (less Arty and certain Tns) moves to Camp Mills.

April 30, 4th Engrs and Tn sail from New York and arrive May 13 at Bordeaux.

May 2, Adv Det sails, arriving May 10 at Brest.

May 3–10, DHQ, 16th FA, all the infantry, and some of the Divisional units sail, and the major units land at Brest on May 23, 7th Infantry Brig (less elements of the 39th Inf) and 16th FA; in England, May 13–25, DHQ and the 8th Infantry Brig. May 23, the SS *Moldavia* with part of the 58th Infantry is torpedoed by a submarine off the English coast with the loss of 56 men.

May 14, 4th Field Artillery Brig (less 16th FA) leaves Camp Greene for Camp Merritt.

May 19–22, 4th Field Artillery Brig (less 16th FA) sails, and lands May 30–31 at Brest and Liverpool.

May 19–27, the remaining trains sail, and land May 31 to June 9 at Brest or Liverpool.

Final Training and Operations

MAY 18–NOVEMBER 11, 1918

May 18, division (less Arty, 8th F Sig Bn, 4th Sup Tn, 4th San Tn, and elements 58th Inf) moves from Brest, Le Havre, and Calais to the Saner Training Area.

May 18–June 10, division is under the administrative control of the II Corps. Training with the British in Picardy.

May 27, 4th Field Artillery Brig and 4th Am Tn move from Le Havre and Brest to Camp de Souge, where they train.

May 31–June 5, division (less detached units) trains with the British 16th (Irish) Division

June 9, division moves to entraining stations on the Hesdin-Montreuil railroad.

June 11, division (less detached units) moves to the vicinity of Meaux.

June 11–July 17, training with the French Sixth Army.

June 13, 7th Infantry Brig is attached to the French 4th Division and proceeds to the Rosoy-en-Multien Area for training.

June 14, division (less 7th Infantry Brig and other units), attached to the French 164th Division for training, moves to the south and west of La Ferté-sous-Jouarre.

June 17, 8th F Sig Bn and 4th Sup Tn rejoin; 4th Engrs moves to Crouttes to construct, with the assistance of infantry, a second position extending from Crouttes to Crouy-sur-Ourcq.

June 21, 4th Am Tn rejoins.

June 21–July 27, the division is under the administrative control of the I Corps.

July 1, 7th Infantry Brig is placed at the disposal of the French II Corps with a view to occupying a second position, located between Autheuil and Varinfroy, in case of a German attack; it occupies this position from July 5 to 7 and again on July 15.

July 5, division (less Arty and 7th Infantry Brig) moves to the vicinity of Lizy-sur-Ourcq and May-en-Multien along the Ourcq Canal; it occupies a second position in anticipation of a German attack.

July 16, 39th Infantry (7th Infantry Brig) is attached to the French 33rd Division.

Night of July 16–17, division (less Arty and 7th Infantry Brig) moves to the front line; infantry battalions reinforced by machine gun companies are affiliated with units of the French 164th Division (French VII Corps).

Night of July 17–18, 39th Infantry (7th Infantry Brig), reinforced by Cos A and C 11th MG Bn, relieve the French 11th Infantry in the left sector of the French II Corps from Troësnes (incl.) to Faverolles (excl.).

July 18, 39th Infantry attacks east through Buisson de Cresnes and captures Noroy-sur-Ourcq; French 33rd Division on right, French 41st Division (French Tenth Army) on left. Elements of the 8th Infantry Brig, affiliated with the French 164th Division, attack east from a line of departure extending from 1 km east of Vinly to a point on Ru d'Alland 1 km northeast of Chézy-en-Orxois; 2nd Bn, 58th Infantry, captures Chevillon.

July 18–22, division (less Arty) participates in the Aisne-Marne Operation. The 7th Infantry Brig is with the French II Corps, the remainder of the division with the French VII Corps on the right; the entire line extends from Ancienville to Hautevesnes.

July 19, the attack is pushed to Rau de Pudeval and to a line extending south for 1 km from a point 1 km southeast of Lo Bout du Mont. The 59th Infantry attacks, captures Bois de Cassel, Bois de l'Orme, Bois de Leipzig, and reaches the line, Courchamps, Bois de Leipzig, 1 km west of Sommelans.

Night of July 19–20, 39th Infantry is relieved and moves to rejoin the 7th Infantry Brig.

July 20, 1st Bn 58th Infantry and 3rd Bn 59th Inf resume the attack; the former reaches Hill 145, the latter the unimproved road between Bonnes and Sommelans.

July 21, French units relieve the front line battalions of the division.

July 22, 7th Infantry Brig reverts to the control of the division; the latter is placed to the east and south of La Ferté–Mion in the reserve of the French Sixth Army; rehabilitation.

July 24, 7th Infantry Brig (less 47th Inf) is placed at the disposal of the French II Corps; the 47th Infantry at the disposal of the French VII Corps, mops up the Bois du Châtelet.

July 28, division (less Arty and 7th Infantry Brig) moves to the Bois du Châtelet, where it passes into corps reserve. The 4th Field Artillery Brig and 4th Am Tn move from Camp de Souge to rejoin the Division near Château-Thierry.

July 28–August 6, division participates in the Aisne-Marne Operation.

July 29, the concentration of the Division (less detached units) in the Bois du Châtelet is completed.

July 29–31, 1st and 3rd Bns 47th Infantry are attached to the 42nd Division and participate in an attack on Sergy. July 30, 7th Infantry Brig is placed at the disposal of the 42nd Division in case of emergency.

Night of August 1–2, the enemy begins a retreat from the Ourcq River to the Vesle River.

August 1–6, 4th Field Artillery Brig and 4th Am Tn participate in the Aisne-Marne Operation; 16th Field Artillery supports the 42nd Division.

August 3, division passes through the lines of the 42nd Division along the east, northeast, and northwest edges of the Fort de Nesles, pursues the enemy northeast, and establishes a line from ¼ km northeast of Chery Chartreuve to 1½ km southeast of Mont-Notre-Dame, along the road connecting these villages; 7th Infantry Brig reverts to the division on the passage of the lines; 32nd Division (French 38th Corps) on right, French 62nd Division (French II Corps) on left.

August 4–6, division continues its advance to the Vesle River; on the right, elements cross the Vesle River and reach and hold ½ km of the Route Nationale east of le Trou-Baret; on the left, elements enter St. Thibaut and reach the river; 32nd Division (III Corps) is on the right, French 62nd Division (I Corps) on the left.

August 7, the Aisne-Marne Operation merges into sector occupation. Elements of the division cross the Vesle River northeast of St. Thibaut and entrench along the railroad track; 28th Division on right.

August 7–12, division occupies the Vesle Sector (Champagne).

August 8, troops along the Route Nationale are withdrawn to the railroad north of the Vesle River.

August 9, Bazoches is attacked; patrolling follows.

Night of August 11–12, division (less Arty, which remains in line supporting 77th Division until August 17) is relieved by the 77th Division; August 12, command passes.

August 12–13, division concentrates in the Forêt de Fère.

August 14, division (less Arty) moves to entraining stations near Montmirail and La Ferté–Gaucher, and thence on August 18 to the 4th (Rimaucourt) Training Area and to stations in and near Reynel.

August 21, division is ordered to join the First Army.

August 21–30, rehabilitation and training.

August 22, 4th Field Artillery Brig and 4th Am Tn rejoin.

August 29, division moves to Vavincourt Area; training.

Night of September 5–6, 8th Infantry Brig (less 58th Infantry) begins the relief of elements of the French 10th Colonial Division and French 2nd Dismounted Cavalry Division from Trésauvaux (incl.) to Watronville (incl.), and completes the relief on September 7, the commanding general, 8th Infantry Brig, assuming command of the sector; 58th Infantry in support.

September 7–11, elements of the 4th Field Artillery Brig support the 26th Division in the Rupt Sector and the French 15th Colonial Division in the Sommedieue Sector along the west face of the St. Mihiel salient.

September 7–12, division (less Arty) occupies the Toulon Sector (Lorraine).

Nights September 9–10 and 10–11, division (less Arty and 8th Infantry Brig) moves to an area between Sommiedieue and Haudainville, where it becomes corps reserve.

September 12–13, patrolling.

September 12–15, division participates in the St. Mihiel Operation. The 8th Infantry Brig is in front line, the remainder of the division (less Arty) in corps reserve; French 15th Cl Division is on the right, French 10th Cl Division (French 17th Corps, French Second Army) on the left. Units of the 4th Field Artillery Brig and 4th Am Tn support the 26th Division and French 15th

Colonial Division during the St. Mihiel Operation until September 14, when this brigade is withdrawn and concentrated in the Forêt de Souilly.

September 13–14, 7th Infantry Brig is located east of Mouilly.

September 14, elements of the 59th Infantry advance into Fresnes-en-Woecrre and Manheulles, where they establish outposts; the original line of resistance from Trésauvaux to Watronville is retained.

Night of September 14–15, French 15th Colonial Division relieves the 8th Infantry Brig, and on September 15 assumes command.

September 15–18, training.

September 16, division is ordered to join the III Corps.

Night of September 19–20, division moves to the vicinity of Lemmes.

Night of September 21–22, elements of the 7th Infantry Brig relieve elements of the 33rd Division in the front line of the Verdun-Fromeréville Sector, but are under the command of the 33rd Division until the beginning of the Meuse-Argonne Operation.

September 22–25, division moves into assembly positions for the Meuse-Argonne Operation.

September 25, division occupies a sector north of Esnes, which extends from 1 km southwest of Béthincourt to Haucourt (excl.).

September 26–October 19, division participates in the Meuse-Argonne Operation.

September 26, division attacks north-northwest, 7th Infantry Brig leading, captures Cuisy and Septsarges, and occupies the Bois de Septsarges; 80th Division on right, 79th Division (V Corps) on left.

September 27–28, division pushes through the Bois de Brieulles to the Brieulles-Nantillois road against increasing resistance; the right gains the north edge of the Bois de Brieulles; the left assists the 79th Division in the capture of Nantillois, approaches the Bois des Ogons and Bois de Pays, but retires; the division now holds the line from Hill 280 to a point 1 km north of Nantillpis.

September 28–29, 33rd Division replaces the 80th Division on right.

September 29–October 3, 8th Infantry Brig, reinforced by the 318th Infantry (80th Division) until October 5, relieves the 7th Infantry Brig.

September 30, 3rd Division replaces the 79th Div on left.

October 3, elements of the 58th Inf. are relieved by the 4th Inf. (3rd Division) on the left.

October 4–12, division, in a series of attacks, captures the Bois de Fays, Bois de Malaumont, Bois de Peut-de-Faux, the western part of the Bois de Forét; 80th Division (III Corps) on left.

October 11–12, the sector is extended east; the 316th Meridian becomes the right boundary of the div; 5th Division on left.

October 13, elements of the division in the Bois de Forêt are relieved by the 3rd Div; elements in the Bois de Peut-de-Faux are withdrawn; the new left boundary extends from the north edge of the Bois de Fays to the Meuse 1 km north of Brieulles; patrolling.

October 14–18, 58th Infantry is in the reserve of the 5th Division in the Bois de Beugc.

October 16, division occupies Moulin-d'en-Haut; the front line extends along the west edge of the Bois de la Côte Lémont, the north edge of the Bois de Brieulles, and the northeast edge of the Bois de Pays.

Night of October 18–19, division is relieved by the 6th Infantry Brig (3rd Division).

October 19–20, division (less Arty, which supports the 3rd, 5th, and 90th Divisions until November 11) assembles in the Forôt de Hesse.

October 21, division is ordered to join the Second Army and moves by stages to the Commercy Area; training.

November 4, division is ordered to join First Army.

November 6, division (less Arty) starts for Blercourt, but returns on November 9 and resumes training.

Post Armistice Activities

NOVEMBER 12, 1918–JULY 8, 1919

November 14, 4th PA Brig and 4th Am Tn revert to the control of the division.

November 20, division moves via Briey, Hayange, Remich (Luxemburg), Saarburg (Germany), Cues, and Alf, and on December 17 takes station in the Kreise of Cochem and Adenau.

November 20–December 17, advance into Germany.

December 17–July 8, division forms part of the Army of Occupation in Germany. Training predominates.

April 8, 4th TM Btry sails from St. Nazaire.

April 13, Division establishes itself in the Kreise of Ahrweiler.

May 20–June 5, the infantry regiments are detached from the division and function under Third Army, guarding property at railheads and supply depots in the Third Army area.

June 19–27, division is concentrated along the Rhine, prepared for a further advance, pending the signature of the Treaty of Versailles.

June 28, the troops return to billets.

Return to the United States and Demobilization

JULY 9–AUGUST 31, 1919

July 9, division moves to Brest.
July 16, Hq 7th mt Brig, 47th Tnt, and 10th MG Bn sail.
July 24, DHQ sails, and arrives August 1 at Hoboken. Other units follow rapidly.
August 5, division (less detachments) moves from Camp Merritt to Camp Dodge.
August 10, the last elements arrive in the United States. The emergency personnel are demobilized during the latter part of July and August.

THE FIFTH DIVISION, REGULAR ARMY

The Fifth Division was organized at Camp Logan, Texas, made up of regular army units. Major General James E. McManor commanded the division until October 24, 1918, when he was succeeded on this date by Major General Hanson E. Ely. The overseas movement took place in March, April and May 1918. The division captured 2,356 German prisoners. It was quiet 71 days and active 32 days. It advanced 29 kilometers. Its total casualties were 8,840, with 1,976 battle deaths, 6,864 wounded and 12,611 replacements.

Ninth Infantry Brigade

60th Infantry
61st Infantry
14th Machine Gun Battalion

Tenth Infantry Brigade

6th Infantry
11th Infantry
15th Machine Gun Battalion

Fifth Field Artillery Brigade

19th Field Artillery
20th Field Artillery
21st Field Artillery
5th Trench Mortar Battery

Divisional Troops

7th Engineers
13th Machine Gun Battalion
9th Field Signal Battalion
Headquarters Troop

Trains

5th Train Hdqs
5th Military Police
5th Ammunition Train
5th Supply Train
7th Engineer Train
5th Sanitary Train
Ambulance Cos and Field Hospitals 17, 25, 29, 30

Record of Events

Sectors Where the 5th Division Was Engaged in Warfare

Anould sector, Vosges, France, June 14 to July 16, 1918.
St. Die sector, Vosges, France, July 17 to August 23, 1918.
St. Mihiel offensive, France, September 12 to 16, 1918.
Meuse-Argonne offensive, France, October 12 to 22, 1918.
Meuse-Argonne offensive, Prance, October 27 to November 11, 1918.

Organization and Training in the United States

November 17, 1917–April 1, 1918

November 17, the War Department directs the organization of the 5th Division, Regular Army, with DHQ at Camp Logan. December 1, the organization begins in accordance with the Tables of Organization of August 8, 1917, and includes Regular Army units stationed at Camps Forrest, Greene, Johnston, Logan, and Stanley, and Fort Leavenworth; the 9th Infantry Brig is formed at Camp Greene and includes the 60th and 61st Regts of Infantry (formed from personnel of the 7th Infantry in 1917) and 14th MG Bn.

December 11, Maj. Gen. Charles H. Muir assumes command.

December 12, organization of 5th Field Artillery Brig begins, and includes the 19th and 20th Regts of Field Artillery (formed from personnel of the 7th Field Artillery in 1917) and 21st Field Artillery (formed from personnel of the 3rd Field Artillery in 1917).

January 1, 10th Infantry Brig is formed at Camp Forrest and includes the 6th and 11th Regts of Infantry and 15th MG Bn. Recruits and drafts arrive during the winter and complete the Division. Systematic training is conducted.

February 14, Hq 5th Field Artillery Brig moves to Camp MacArthur.

February 25, 7th Engrs (formed from personnel of the 1st Engrs in 1917) moves from Fort Leavenworth, via Camp Merritt, to Hoboken. March 6, 7th Engrs sails for England, moves on March 23 to Le Havre, and on March 29 to Gièvres for duty with the SOS.

Movement Overseas

April 2–June 19, 1918

April 2, units of the division (less Engrs) move from their respective stations via Camps Merritt and Upton to the ports of embarkation (Hoboken, Montreal, and New York).

April 7, Adv Det sails from Hoboken, and lands April 15 at Brest.

April 9–30, division (less Arty, Engrs, and Tns) sails. April 22, 28, and May 2, 6th Infantry, 61st Infantry, Hq 10th Infantry Brig, 11th Infantry and 15th MG Bn debark at Brest in the order stated.

April 22 and 28, 14th MG Bn, 13th MG Bn, DHQ, Hq Troop, and the 2nd Bn and one-half of the 3rd Bn 60th Infantry land at Liverpool.

April 28, 29, and May 12, 60th Infantry (less 1½ bns), Hq 9th Infantry Brig, and 9th F Sig Bn debark at St. Nazaire.

May 11, 5th Tn Hq and MP lands at Bordeaux.

May 27–June 10, 5th Field Artillery Brig and Tns sail from New York, Montreal, and Hoboken.

June 8, 11, and 12, Hq 5th Field Artillery Brig, 5th Am Tn, 5th TM Btry, 7th Sn Tn, and 19th, 20th, and 21st Regts of Field Artillery debark at Liverpool in the order stated.

June 19, 5th Sup Tn lands at Brest. Units in England, after a brief stay in rest camps, proceed to Le Havre.

Final Training and Operations

April 25–November 11, 1918

April 25, division (less Arty, Engrs, Sup Tn, and Sn Tn) moves to the 13th (Bar-sur-Aube) Training Area; training follows.

May 31–June 10, division is under the administrative control of the I Corps.

June 1, division (less Arty, Engrs, and Sup Tn) moves to the Vosges front, east of Epinal, where it trains with French divisions in the rear areas; DHQ and 9th Infantry Brig (less 60th Infantry) are affiliated with the French 70th Div, 60th Infantry with the French 62nd Division; 10th Infantry Brig (less 6th Infantry) trains with the French 77th Div.

June 1–July 14, training with the French in Lorraine.

June 2–14, 6th Infantry and 13th MG Bn are stationed near Pagny-sur-Meuse as a reserve of the 26th Division, which occupies the Toul-Boucq Sector.

June 12, 5th Field Artillery Brig and 5th Am Tn move to Le Valdalion; training.

June 13–July 13, division is under the administrative control of the mini Corps.

June 14–15, division (less detached units), affiliated with the French 21st Div, enters the line, Rospel-Wald, ½ km west of Stosswihr, le Linge, ½ km west of Faing, 1 km west of Bonhomme, east edge of Bois de Brehaingoutte, ½ km east of Wisembach, ¾ km south of Lusse.

June 14–July 16, division (less Arty and Sup Tn) participates with the French in the occupation of the Anould Sector (Lorraine).

June 15, 6th Infantry and 13th MG Bn rejoin.

June 16, the command of the sector passes from the French 70th Division to the French 21st Division. Local actions occur during the occupation.

June 30, 7th Engrs and Tn join.

July 1, 10th Infantry Brig assumes command of Groupement Sud, near Stosswihr, which extends from Muhlbach (excl.) to Weiss Creek, ¾ km southwest of Orbey.

July 3, 9th Infantry Brig is relieved and moves to the Arches Training Area.

July 12, 9th Infantry Brig and 13th MG Bn move to the St. Die Sector.

July 14–August 19, division is under the administrative control of the V Corps.

Night of July 14–15, division, brigades abreast, 9th Infantry Brig on left, begins the relief of the French 62nd Division in the St. Die Sector.

July 15, 10th Infantry Brig moves from the Anould Sector to the St. Die Sector.

July 19–August 23, division occupies the St. Die Sector (Lorraine).

July 19, division assumes command of the sector on the front, ¾ km south of Lusse, Fme des Fées, 1 km west of Beulay, 1½ km east of St. Jean d'Ormont, 1 km west of Ménil, ½ km west of Senones, 2 km east of Celles-sur-Plaine, ½ km south of Allencombe; French 21st Division on right, 77th Division on left; local actions.

July 20, 5th Sup Tn rejoins. **July 28,** 5th Field Artillery Brig and 5th Am Tn join.

August 4, 37th Division on left.

August 8, the command of the sector artillery passes to the 5th Field Artillery Brig.

August 15, division relieves the French 25th Territorial Infantry in the Fave Valley.

August 17, 6th Infantry attacks and captures Frapelle and Hill 451.

August 19–29, division is under the administrative control of the VII Corps.

August 23, division is relieved by the French 87th Division and moves to the Arches Training Area; training.

August 26, division is ordered to join the First Army, and on August 27 to join the I Corps.

August 29, division moves to the southwest of Lunéville, and proceeds September 4 to the vicinity of Martincourt.

September 8–9, the leading elements of the 5th Field Artillery Brig enter the Villers-en-Haye Sector.

September 10, division relieves units of the 90th Division (less elements in the outpost area) in the central part of this sector from 1 km east of Regniéville to ½ km southeast of Remenauville, preparatory to the St. Mihiel Operation.

September 10–11, division occupies part of the Villers-en-Haye Sector (Lorraine).

September 12, division attacks north, 10th Infantry Brig leading, from the front line of the Viéville-en-Haye Sector, advances through the Bois de la Rappe and woods north and northwest thereof, captures Viéville-en-Haye, occupies the Bois Gerard, and reaches the line 1 km southeast and 1 km northeast of Viéville-en-Haye, north edge of the Bois Gerard, 2½ km southeast of Jaulny; 90th Division on right, 2nd Division on left.

September 12–16, division participates in the St. Mihiel Operation.

September 14, division resumes the attack on the left and penetrates the Bois de Grand-Fontaine north of the Bois de Bonvaux; the right occupies the north slope of Hill 361.4. **September 15,** division advances its right toward Tautecourt Fme and reaches the southwest edge of the Bois du Troude-la-Haie; division withdraws its left to the northeast edge of the Bois de Bonvaux.

September 16, division advances its right towards la Souleuvre Fme and its left ¾ km into the Bois de Grand-Fontaine where it reaches the south slope of ridge 310.2–287.1, southeast of Rembercourt; 78th Division is on the left.

September 17, division (less Arty and Engrs, which remain in position) is relieved by the 78th Division and moves to the vicinity of Domêvre-en-Haye; rehabilitation and training.

September 17–29, 7th Engrs and Tn serve with the 78th Division in Limey Sector and with the IV Corps.

September 17–October 3, 5th Field Artillery Brig and 5th Am Tn participate with the 78th Division in the occupation of the Limey Sector.

September 26, elements of the 1st Bn 60th Infantry and 14th MG Bn participate with the French 69th Division in a raid in the Pont-à-Mousson Sector; 11th Infantry and elements of the 15th MG Bn are placed at the disposal of the French 69th Division; 13th MG Bn is attached to the 90th Div.

Night of September 27–28, division (less detached units) moves to the Pagny-sur-Meuse Area, where it is rejoined by the detached units, except the artillery.

October 3, division (less Arty) moves to the Nixéville Area via Souilly.

October 4–10, 5th Field Artillery Brig and 5th Am Tn participate with the 90th Division in the occupation of the Puvenelle Sector.

Night of October 5–6, division (less Arty) moves into the Forêt de Hesse where it is in corps reserve.

October 5–November 11, division (less Arty) participates in the Meuse-Argonne Operation.

Nights of October 9–10, 10–11, division advances through the Bois de Montfaucon to the vicinity of Nantillois.

October 10–November 11, 5th Field Artillery Brig and 5th Am Tn participate with the 7th Division in the occupation of the Puvenelle Sector.

October 11–12, 9th Infantry Brig relieves the 80th Division from 1 km east of Cunel to 400 meters south of that village.

October 12, command of the sector passes to the 5th Division, which attacks towards the Bois de la Pultière.

Night of October 12–13, 3rd Division relieves the 9th Infantry Brig; division reorganizes in positions south of the Bois de Cunel.

Night of October 13–14, division forms for attack along Mamelle Trench ½ km south of the road from Cunel to Romagne-sous-Montfaucon; 58th Infantry (4th Division), attached, forms the division reserve.

October 14, division attacks, brigades abreast; 9th Infantry Brig advances elements through Cunel into the Bois de la Pultière; 10th Infantry Brig moves to the line from ¾ km northwest of Cunel to ¾ km northeast of Romagne-sous-Montfaucon; 3rd Division on right, 32nd Division on left.

October 15, 9th Infantry Brig attacks and clears the Bois de la Pultière.

October 16–17, 10th Infantry Brig extends the sector to the east, relieves units of the 9th Infantry Brig along the north edge of the Bois de la Pultière and of the 3rd Division along the northeast edge of that woods; 9th Infantry

Brig, after withdrawal, assembles near Nantillois; 58th Infantry reverts to the 4th Division.

October 19–20, division resumes the attack.

October 20, 89th Division on left.

October 21, division captures the Bois des Rappes.

October 22, 90th Division relieves the 5th Division, which moves to the vicinity of Montfaucon; rehabilitation.

Night of October 26–27, division (less Arty) relieves the 3rd Division on the line, north edge of the Bois de la Côte Lémont, Têton Trench, northeast edge of Bois de Fays, east edge of Bois de Peutde-Faux, south and east edges of Bois de Forêt, 1 km south of Cléry-le-Grand, 1½ km south of Aincrevile; French 15th Colonial Division on right, 90th Division on left.

October 27, command passes.

October 30, division units are in Aincreville.

November 1, division captures Cléry-le-Grand and Brieulles-sur-Meuse and reaches the Meuse near the latter town.

November 2, division enters Cléry-le-Petit, reaches the Meuse east thereof, and occupies the Bois de Babiémont.

November 3, division enters Doulcon and holds the Meuse along almost the entire front; patrols cross the Meuse northeast of Brieulles-sur-Meuse.

November 4–5, division forces crossings of the Meuse and the canal, establishes bridgeheads near Brieulles-sur-Meuse and Cléry-le-Petit, advances through the Bois de Châtillon, Liny-devant-Dun, Bois de Bussy, Bois de Chénois, Dun-sur-Meuse and Milly, and reaches a line from the Bois de Châtillon to Milly.

November 6, division attacks northeast, occupies the Bois de Sartelle, Bois de l'Epinois, Bois de Fontaines, Fontaines, Bois des Tailles-Forgettes, les Fonzy Bois, Bois du Fayel, Murvaux, Côte-Saint-Germain, and part of the Bois du Corrol, and sends patrols into Viosnes-sur-Meuse to assist the French in crossing the river; 128th Infantry (32nd Division), attached, is on the right flank of the division.

November 7, division enters Lion-devant-Dun, mops up the Bois du Corrol, and captures the southern portion of the Bois de Brandeville. The following day it clears the Bois de Brandeville, reaches a position on le Haut Gron, and enters Brandeville.

November 9, division captures Mouzay and advances through the Bois de Rémoiville and Bois de Murvaux, patrols reaching the north edge of the Bois de Jametz, Rémoiville, and a position 1 km northeast of Chamois; 32nd Division is on the right.

November 10, division occupies Jametz, advances into the Forêt de Woëvre, clears the Bois de Juvigny, occupies Louppy-sur-Loison; it establishes a front from Jametz through Rémoiville, Louppy-sur-Loison, along northeast edge of Bois de Juvigny, and into the Forêt de Woëvre 1 km southwest of Bois Robert; patrols establish connection with the 90th Division in the Bois du Chênois.

Post Armistice Activities

NOVEMBER 12, 1918–JULY 3, 1919

November 12, division establishes outposts on the line held at the armistice.

November 14, elements of the 32nd and 90th Divisions relieve the 5th Division, which moves to positions near Dun-sur-Meuse, east of the river.

November 17, 11th Infantry returns to the front and occupies the line from Louppy (incl.) to Vilers-les-Mangiennes (excl.); enforcement of armistice terms, salvage, and training.

November 22, division is assigned to duty with the SOS, Army of Occupation, and moves to the vicinity of Longwy and Longuyon.

November 27–July 3, occupation of the Grand Duchy of Luxemburg.

November 27, division (less detachments) moves into the southern part of the Grand Duchy of Luxemburg, where it performs service of supply duties and controls circulation along the frontier between Luxemburg and Germany; 6th Infantry moves to Trier; detachments proceed to Belgian Area No. 2 near Anon and Virton, where they guard enemy war materiel; other units remain in France.

December 5, 5th Field Artillery Brig and 5th Am Tn rejoin.

February 7, 6th Infantry rejoins.

February 28, 5th TM Btry sails from St. Nazaire.

April 12, division relieves the 33rd Division in the northern part of Luxemburg, assumes all service of supply duties for the Army of Occupation in the Grand Duchy, and controls the entire border separating it from Germany.

Return to the United States and Demobilization

JULY 4–JULY 31, 1919

July 4, division begins to concentrate at Brest from Belgium, France, and Luxemburg.

July 9, elements of the 11th Infantry sail, followed on July 13 by the division and brigade headquarters.

July 31, the last unit arrives in New York. During July the emergency personnel are demobilized at Camps Merritt and Mills, and on July 24 the division (less Arty) moves to Camp Gordon, the artillery to Camp Bragg.

The Sixth Division, Regular Army

The Sixth Division was organized from regular army units at Camp Forest, Georgia, and Camp McClellan, Alabama. Many of the units were trained in England, and the final arrival of the complete division in France was August 28, 1918. Brigadier General James B. Erwin, who commanded the division until August 31, 1918, was succeeded on that date by Major General Walter P. Gordon. The division captured 12 prisoners and was quiet 40 days. It had 546 casualties, including 93 battle deaths and 453 wounded. The division received 2784 replacements.

Eleventh Infantry Brigade

51st Infantry
52nd Infantry
17th Machine Gun Battalion

Twelfth Infantry Brigade

53rd Infantry
54th Infantry
18th Machine Gun Battalion

Sixth Field Artillery Brigade

3rd Field Artillery
11th Field Artillery
78th Field Artillery
6th Trench Mortar Battery

Divisional Troops

318th Engineers
16th Machine Gun Battalion
6th Field Signal Battalion
Headquarters Troop

Trains

6th Train Hdqs
6th Military Police

6th Supply Train
318th Engineer Train
6th Sanitary Train
Ambulance Cos and Field Hospitals 20, 37, 38, 40

Record of Events

SECTORS WHERE THE 6TH DIVISION WAS ENGAGED IN WARFARE

Geradmer sector, Vosgee, France, September 3 to October 18, 1918.
Meuse-Argonne offensive, France, November 1 to 11, 1918.
Meuse-Argonne offensive, France, October 19 to November 11, 1918 (11th FA).

Organization and Training in the United States

NOVEMBER 17, 1917–JUNE 27, 1918

November 17, the War Department directs the organization of the 6th Division, Regular Army.

November 26, the organization begins in accordance with the Tables of Organization of August 8, 1917, from Regular Army units stationed at Camps Forrest and Logan, Forts Leavenworth, Riley, and Sam Houston, Vancouver Barracks, and other places; DHQ is established initially at Camp McClellan, Col. Charles E. Tayman commanding; training begins. In November and December the 12th and 11th Infantry Brigs, respectively, are organized at Camp Forrest; the 11th Infantry Brig includes the 51st and 52nd Regts of Infantry (both formed from personnel of the 11th Infantry in June 1917), the 12th Infantry Brig includes the 53rd and 54th Regts of Infantry (both formed from personnel of the 6th July in June 1917).

December 29, Brig. Gen. James B. Erwin assumes command.

March 13, DHQ moves to Camp Forrest. The 6th Am Tn, 6th Sup Tn, and 6th Tn Hq and MP are also at Camp Forrest.

April 4, the 6th Field Artillery Brig, Hq formed in April, which includes the 3rd FA, 11th Field Artillery (formed from personnel of the 6th Field Artillery June 1, 1917), and 78th Field Artillery (organized from the 20th Cav in June 1917), is ordered to concentrate at the Artillery Training Center at Camp Doniphan for ten weeks' instruction.

May 4–June 2, DHQ, 12th Infantry Brig, 16th and 17th MG Bns, 6th F Sig Bn, and 6th Tn Hq and MP move to Camp Wadsworth. On May 8, 318th Engrs and Tn sail; they land May 18 at Brest. During May and June drafts totaling 15,000 arrive from Georgia, Indiana, Kentucky, Maryland, Minnesota, Ohio, Pennsylvania, South Carolina, and Wisconsin; as finally constituted the division includes personnel of the Regular Army and selective service men.

June 13, units stationed at Camps Doniphan, Forrest, and Wadsworth are ordered to ports of embarkation via Camps Mills and Upton.

Movement Overseas

JUNE 28–JULY 26, 1918

June 28, Adv Det sails from New York and arrives July 10 at Glasgow.

June 29, DHQ leaves Camp Wadsworth.

July 6–7, DHQ, all infantry and some divisional troops and trains sail, and debark at Le Havre on July 19, 6th F Sig Bn, 6th Sn Tn, July 22, DHQ, Hq 12th Infantry Brig, 17th and 18th MG Bns, 6th Tn Hq and MP; at Liverpool and Glasgow, July 17, other units.

July 12–14, 6th Field Artillery Brig, 6th Am Tn, and 6th Sup Tn sail, and debark July 19 and 26 at Southampton and Liverpool. Units in England, after a brief stay in rest camps, move to Le Havre and Cherbourg.

Final Training and Operations

JULY 23–NOVEMBER 11, 1918

July 23, division (less Arty and Sup Tn) moves to the 9th (Château-villain) Training Area; 6th Field Artillery Brig and 6th Am Tn move to the Le Valdahon Area; training.

August 23–26, division is under administrative control of VI Corps.

August 27, division (less Arty) moves to the Remiremont Area.

August 27–October 26, division is under administrative control of VII Corps.

August 31–September 6, division (less Arty) participates with the French in the occupation of the Gêrardmer Sector (Alsace).

August 31, division is affiliated with French 131st Division and that night, August 31–September 1, the leading elements enter the line to relieve the 35th Division in the Gëratdmer Sector.

September 2, the command of the sector, which extends from Lauch Creek, 1 km west of Sengeren, to Weiss Creek, ½ km west of Faing, passes to the French 131st Division.

September 6, division assumes command of the sector except the centers of resistance of le Linge and Noirmont; the northern limit is near Grossmatt.

September 6–October 12, division (less Arty) occupies the Gérardmer Sector (Alsace).

September 9–11, the sector is extended north to Weiss Creek, including le Linge and Noirmont; elements of the French 131st Division are relieved; local actions.

October 12, division, relieved by the French 162nd Division in the north half of the sector and by the French 1st Division in the south half, moves to the staging areas near Corcieux and Saulxures-sur-Moselotte.

October 13, 3rd and 78th Regts of Field Artillery move to Liffol-le-Grand; training.

October 20, 11th Field Artillery moves to the west of Romagne, where it is attached to the 58th Field Artillery Brig.

October 26, Division (less Arty) moves to the south of Les Islettes and Clermont-en-Argonne; training follows.

October 26–November 1, supports the 89th Division in the Meuse-Argonne Operation.

November 1, division, in corps reserve, moves north through the Forêt d'Argonne.

November 1–8, division (less Arty) participates in the Meuse-Argonne Operation.

November 2, division arrives near Pont-à-l'Aune, Camp de Bouzon and Champ-Mahaut; elements relieve the 82nd Division in a reserve battle position which extends along the ridges south of the Aire River, from a point on the river west of Hill 174, along the north edge of Bois de Marcq and thence along the east and north edges of the Bois de Negremont.

November 3–6, division moves north via Briquenay and the region of Authe and St. Pierremont, to the vicinity of Stonne and Artaise-le-Vivier.

November 6, units move into line to fill a temporary gap which exists between the French and the I Corps near Artaise-le-Vivier, and caused by the movement of the latter toward the northeast.

November 9, division moves via Authe, the Thénorgues Briquenay Area, the Montblainville-Cornay Area, and Montfaucon to the Verdun-sur-Meuse Area.

Post Armistice Activities

NOVEMBER 12, 1918–MAY 19, 1919

November 14, division relieves the 26th Division and French 10th Colonial Division northeast of Verdun-sur-Meuse in the former Neptune Sector, which extended from Abaucourt, through Bezonvaux, to Vile-devant Chaumont; 81st Division on right, 79th Division on left.

November 18, the front is reduced on the left and extended on the right, when the 79th Division relieves the 11th Infantry Brig as far as Bezonvaux, and the 11th Infantry Brig relieves the 81st Division from the crossroads 2km west of Pintheville to Abaucourt (incl.); the enforcement of armistice terms follows.

November 20, 79th Division relieves the 6th Division except the artillery; the division (less Arty) moves to the 14th (Aignay-le-Duc) Training Area.

December 6, 6th Field Artillery Brig reverts to the division.

December 9, training is resumed.

April 9, 6th TM Btry sails from St. Nazaire for the United States.

April 28, division moves toward the Coblenz Bridgehead, but, May 7, the transfer is suspended, at which time the 6th Field Artillery Brig, 6th Am Tn, 16th and 18th MG Bns, part of 6th F Sig Bn, eleven companies of infantry, and attached units are still in the 14th Training Area.

April 28–May 19, division (less detachments) forms part of the Army of Occupation in Germany.

Return to the United States and Demobilization

MAY 20–JUNE 30, 1919

May 20, division moves to Brest.

May 25, DHQ leaves Coblenz.

June 2, 17th MG Bn, 318th Engrs and Tn, 6th Am Tn, and 6th Tn Hq and MP sail.

June 3, DHQ sails, arrives June 10 at Hoboken and moves to Camp Mills the same day.

June 30, the last element of division, a detachment of 18th MG Bn, arrives at New York. During June the emergency personnel are discharged and the division proceeds to Camp Grant for station.

THE SEVENTH DIVISION, REGULAR ARMY

The Seventh Division was organized January 1, 1918, at Chickamauga Park, Georgia, and was trained at Camp McArthur, Waco, Texas. Its overseas movement began July 31 and continued until the arrival of the last unit in France on September 3. The division captured 69 prisoners; it was quiet 31 days and active 2 days. It advanced 1 kilometer. Its total casualties, 1,693. It had 296 battle deaths and 1,397 wounded. The division received 4,112 replacements.

Thirteenth Infantry Brigade

55th Infantry
56th Infantry
20th Machine Gun Battalion

Fourteenth Infantry Brigade.

34th Infantry
64th Infantry
21st Machine Gun Battalion

7th Field Artillery Brigade

8th Field Artillery
79th Field Artillery
80th Field Artillery

Divisional Troops

Fifth Engineers
19th Machine Gun Battalion
Tenth Field Signal Battalion

Trains

7th Train Hdqs
7th Military Police
7th Supply Train
5th Engineer Train
7th Sanitary Train
Ambulance Cos and Field Hospitals 22, 34, 35, 36

Record of Events

SECTOR WHERE THE 7TH DIVISION WAS ENGAGED IN WARFARE

Meuse-Argonne offensive, France, September 28 to November 11, 1918.

Organization and Training in the United States

DECEMBER 6, 1917–JULY 17, 1918

December 6, the War Department directs the organization of the 7th Division, Regular Army, in accordance with the Tables of Organization of August 8, 1917, and designates Camp Wheeler, Macon, Georgia, as the location for DHQ. The Regular Army units selected to form the nucleus of the Division are stationed as follows: at Chickamauga Park, the 55th and 56th Regts of Infantry (formed from personnel of the 17th Infantry in 1917), and 80th Field Artillery (organized as the 22nd Cav in 1917); at Fort Bliss, the 34th Infantry (formed from personnel of the 7th, 20th, and 23rd Regts of Infantry in 1916) and the 64th Infantry (formed from personnel of the 34th Infantry in 1917); at Camp Logan, the 79th Field Artillery (organized as the 21st Cav in 1917); at Camp Wheeler and Fort Sill, the 8th Field Artillery (formed from personnel of the 5th and 6th Regts of Field Artillery in 1916); at Camp Vail, the 10th F Sig Bn (formed from Regular Army Signal Corps personnel in 1917); at Camp Greenleaf, the 22nd, 34th, 35th, and 36th F Hosps and Amb Cos; and in Texas, the 5th Engrs (formed from personnel of the 2nd Engrs in 1917). Regular Army officers and graduates of the First and Second Training Camps form the commissioned personnel of the division.

December 18, the Hq 13th Infantry Brig is formed at Chickamauga Park, and on December 20 the Hq 14th Infantry Brig is formed at Camp Bliss.

January 1, Brig. Gen. Charles H. Barth, commanding 13th Infantry Brig, assumes command of the division; Gen Barth remains at Chickamauga Park, but an adjutant opens an administrative headquarters for the division at Camp Wheeler. During January the machine gun battalions are formed from personnel of the infantry regiments.

January 8, the Hq 7th Field Artillery Brig is formed at Camp Wheeler.

February 2, the 13th Infantry Brig and 80th Field Artillery move to Camp MacArthur, and on May 5, DHQ follows. During the spring and early summer systematic training is conducted in spite of numerous losses.

May and June, 20,000 new men join, the greater part from Camps Travis and Wheeler and Columbus Barracks, many originally drafted from Illinois, Iowa, Michigan, Missouri, and Pennsylvania.

June 11, the War Department directs the concentration of the 7th Field Artillery Brig at Camp McClellan, which is accomplished and training begins during the month.

June 16, the 14th Infantry Brig moves to Camp MacArthur. The division receives additional drafts prior to departure for the ports of embarkation.

Movement Overseas

July 18–September 3, 1918

July 18, division moves to the ports of embarkation (Hoboken and New York) via Camp Merritt, where it is completed by additional drafts and casuals. The division sails for Brest, except 21st MG Bn en route to Liverpool and 7th Sup Tn and 7th Tn Hq and MP to Bordeaux, as follows, July 26, Adv Det, arriving August 6; July 31, 5th Engrs, arriving August 12; August 3, DHQ and 13th Infantry Brig, arriving August 11; August 8–17, 34th Infantry 21st MG Bn and the trains, except the ammunition train, arriving August 20–28; August 18–22, the artillery and other divisional troops; August 25–26, the remainder of the 14th July Brig. The last units land on September 3.

Final Training and Operations

August 17–November 11, 1918

August 17, division (less Arty) moves to the 15th (Ancy-le-Franc) Training Area; training.

August 23, 13th Infantry Brig sends 2000 replacements to the 4th and 26th Divisions.

August 31, 7th Field Artillery Brig and 7th Am Tn proceed to the Ploërmel Area; training.

September 2–14, division is under the administrative control of the VI Corps.

September 21, the artillery is concentrated at Camp de Meucon for training.

September 27, division (less Arty) moves to the Toul Area; training.

October 10, division relieves the 90th Division on the front, Sablière, Vandières (incl.), Côte 327, north edge of Bois des Rappes, la Souleuvre Fme, 1½ kms south of Rembercourt-sur-Mad; 92nd Division is on the right, 37th Division on the left.

October 10–November 11, division (less Arty) occupies the Puvenelle Sector (Lorraine).

October 16, 28th Division is on the left.

October 23, 92nd Division (VI Corps) is on the right.

October 26, the sector is reduced by moving the east boundary to a line between Villers-sous-Prény and Prény (both incl.), elements of the 92nd Division relieving the 56th Infantry.

October 29, the sector is extended west to a line from Xammes to Charey, 64th Infantry relieving elements of the 28th Division, on a front along the eastern edge of Bois de Blainchamp, northern edge of Bois de Hailbat, eastern edge of Bois du Rupt, northern edge of Bois de La Montague; local actions occur.

November 1, division attacks and establishes outposts in the Bois du Trou-de-la-Haie and Bois de Grand-Fontaine.

November 9–11, division executes local attacks and it gains; on November 9, the temporary occupation of a hill west of Prény, on November 10, the Hill 323 (1 km southeast of Rembercourt), and on November 11, the line from 310.2 to 287.1 in the Bois de Grand-Fontaine, the quarry near 278.7, west of Rembercourt, and the small woods ¼ km south of Mon Plaisir Fme.

Post Armistice Activities

NOVEMBER 12, 1918–JUNE 2, 1919

November 12–January 9, division remains in the vicinity of the former Puvenelle Sector and engages in the enforcement of the armistice terms, salvage, and training.

December 10, Hq and 2nd Bn 34th Infantry move to the vicinity of Longuyon, where they guard the railroad lines and abandoned enemy materiel.

January 8, the entire 34th Infantry is detached and concentrated in the Briey Basin for guard duty.

January 9, Division (less Arty and 34th Infantry) moves to the northeast of Toul; training.

January 10, 7th TM Btry sails from St. Nazaire for the United States.

February 2, 5th Engrs and Tn 1 sail February 15 from Brest.

February 14, 7th Field Artillery Brig and 7th Am Tn leave Camp de Meucon, and on February 16 are at Pont-à-Mousson, where they revert to the division.

April 6, division (less Arty) moves to the 6th (Colombey-les-Belles) Training Area.

April 8, 7th FA Brig moves to Commercy.

May 14, division moves to the Conlie Area, American Embarkation Center, Le Mans.

Return to the United States and Demobilization

JUNE 3–JUNE 30, 1919

June 3, the leading contingents of the division leave the American Embarkation Center en route to Brest.

June 9, Hq 14th Infantry Brig and other infantry units sail.

June 12, DHQ, Hq 13th July Brig, and Hq 7th Field Artillery Brig embark.

June 26, the division leaves Camp Mills for Camp Funston.

June 30, the last element of the division arrives at Newport News.

June and July, the emergency personnel and certain units are demobilized.

THE TWENTY-SIXTH DIVISION, NATIONAL GUARD

The 26th Division was organized near Boston, Mass., from a combination of the New England National Guard and National Army troops from Camp Devens. It was commanded by Major General Clarence B. Edwards from August 22, 1917, until October 24, 1918, when he was relieved and succeeded by Brigadier General Frank E. Bamford. The overseas movement began September 7, 1917, and headquarters were established in Newfchateau, France, October 31, 1917. It was known as the Yankee Division. The 26th Division captured 3148 prisoners. It was quiet 148 days, active 45 days. It advanced 37 kilometers. Its total casualties were 13,460. It had 2135 battle deaths and 11,325 wounded. It had 14,411 replacements.

51st Infantry Brigade

101st Infantry
102nd Infantry
102nd Machine Gun Bn

52nd Infantry Brigade

103rd Infantry
104th Infantry
103rd Machine Gun Bn

51st Field Artillery Brigade

101st Field Artillery
102nd Field Artillery
103rd Field Artillery
101st Trench Mortar Battery

Divisional Troops

101st Machine Gun Bn
101st Engineers
101st Field Signal Bn
Headquarters Troop

Trains

101st Train Hdqs
101st Military Police
101st Ammunition Train
101st Supply Train
101st Engineer Train
101st Sanitary Train
Ambulance Cos And Field Hospitals 101–104

Record of Events

SECTORS WHERE THE 26TH DIVISION WAS ENGAGED IN WARFARE

Chemin des Dames sector, France, February 6 to March 21, 1918.
Toul (Boucq) sector, France, April 3 to June 28, 1913.
Champagne-Marne defensive, France, July 15 to 18, 1918.
Aisne-Marne offensive, France, July 18 to 25, 1918.
St. Mihiel offensive, France, September 12 to 16, 1918.
Troyon sector, France, September 17 to October 8, 1918.
Meuse-Argonne offensive, France, October 18 to November 11, 1918.

Organization and Training in the United States

JULY 18–SEPTEMBER 5, 1917

On July 18, 1917, the War Department designated National Guard troops of Connecticut, Maine, Massachusetts, New Hampshire, Rhode Island, and Vermont to form the 26th Division at Camp Greene, Charlotte, North Carolina, which was selected for the training.

July 25, the National Guard units of Connecticut, Maine, Massachusetts, New Hampshire, Rhode Island, and Vermont are called into federal service.

August 3, the War Department directs the concentration of the Division at Camp Greene, but this is subsequently rescinded.

August 5, the National Guard units of Connecticut, Maine, Massachusetts, New Hampshire, Rhode Island and Vermont are drafted into federal service, and during the month units are concentrated at Allston, Boxford, Westfield, and Framingham, Massachusetts, at New Haven and Niantic, Connecticut, and at Quonset Point, Rhode Island.

August 18, the 51st Field Artillery Brig is organized and ultimately includes the 1st and 2nd Regts of Massachusetts Field Artillery and detachments of Connecticut, Maine, New Hampshire, and Rhode Island Field Artillery of New England, and of Rhode Island Cavalry.

August 19, the 51st Infantry Brig is organized and ultimately includes the 5th and 9th Regts of Massachusetts Infantry the 1st and 2nd Regts of Connecticut Infantry and detachments of the 1st Vermont Infantry of the 6th Massachusetts Infantry and of Massachusetts Cav.

August 20, the 52nd Infantry Brig is organized and ultimately includes the 1st New Hampshire, 2nd Massachusetts, and 2nd Maine Regts of Infantry and detachments of the 6th Massachusetts, 8th Massachusetts, and 1st Vermont Regts of Infantry and of Rhode Island and New Hampshire Cav.

August 22, Maj. Gen. Clarence R. Edwards assumes command; the division is reorganized in accordance with the Tables of Organization of August 8, 1917.

September 13, the reorganization is completed. During September a draft of 900 men from the 76th Division completes the division.

Movement Overseas

SEPTEMBER 6, 1917–JANUARY 2, 1918

September 6, the division moves to the ports of embarkation of Hoboken, Montreal, Newport News, and New York.

September 7, Hq 51st Infantry Brig, 101st Infantry, 101st F Hosp, and 101st Amb Co sail from Hoboken and arrive September 20 at St. Nazaire.

September 9, 22–23, Hq 51st Field Artillery Brig, 101st FA, 102nd FA, elements of the 102nd Inf, the 102nd MG Bn, 101st F Sig Bn, and elements of the 101st San Tn sail from Hoboken; the 101st Field Artillery and elements of 102nd Infantry arrive September 24 at Liverpool, the remainder arrive October 6 at St. Nazaire.

September 16–October 6, Hq 52nd Infantry Brig, 102nd Infantry, part of 104th Infantry, and part of 101st San Tn sail from Montreal and arrive October 3–23 at Liverpool.

September 18–October 9, DHQ, 103rd Infantry, elements of the 104th Infantry, the 101st MG Bn, 103rd MG Bn, 103rd FA, 101st Am Tn, 101st TM Btry, 101st Engrs and Tn, part of the 101st San Tn, the 101st Sup Tn, and

101st Tn Hq and MP sail from New York and arrive October 3-23 at Liverpool.

December 10, the last element of the division, a detachment of the 102nd FA, sails from Newport News and arrives January 2 at St. Nazaire. The troops which land in England stay a short time in rest camps and then proceed to Le Havre.

Final Training and Operations

SEPTEMBER 25, 1917–NOVEMBER 11, 1918

September 25, 51st Field Artillery Brig and 101st Am Tn move to Camp Coëtquidan, where they arrive September 26–November 2 for training.

September 29, division (less Arty, and Engrs and Tn) moves to the 2nd (Neufchâteau) Training Area, where the last element arrives on November 15 for training.

October 20, 101st Engrs and Tn, upon arrival in France, move to Rolampont, and later to Doulaincourt and Bazoilles, where they are on duty with the SOS until January 4, when they rejoin the division.

January 20–June 21, division is under the administrative control of the I Corps.

February 1, 51st Field Artillery Brig and 101st Am Tn move to the area of the French Sixth Army north of Soissons.

February 6–March 22, division, affiliated with the French, participates in the occupation of the Chemin des Dames Sector (Ile de France). This sector, north of Soissons, is held by the French XI Corps.

February 4, the leading element, 101st Field Artillery, enters the sector of the French 22nd Division, where it goes into action the next day.

February 5, division (less Arty) moves to the area of the French XI Corps (French Sixth Army), where it is affiliated at various times with the French 21st, French 22nd, French 51st, French 61st, and French 151st Divisions for training.

February 6 and thereafter, the units enter front lines successively by company, battalion, and regiment along the line from 1 km south of Chevregny, along the southern bank of the Oise-Aisne Canal, Fort de Mortier, Quincy, to Aulers, and local actions follow.

March 18, division moves to the vicinity of Brienne-le-Château.

March 27, division arrives at the 4th (Rimaucourt) Training Area and on March 30 moves to the area of the French Eighth Army north of Toni.

Night of March 31–April 1, division begins the relief of the 1st Division in de la Reine Sector (known as the Ansauville Sector prior to March 26) and in the center of resistance Broussey to the west thereof, and also the relief of elements of the French 10th Colonial Division in the centers of resistance of Brichauchard and St. Agnant on the left of the 1st Division sector.

April 3–June 28, division occupies the Toul-Boucq Sector (Lorraine).

April 3, division, brigades abreast, 51st Infantry Brig on the right, assumes command of the Toul-Boucq Sector, which includes de la Reine Sector and the centers of resistance of Brichauchard and St. Agnant, and which extends from the Bois de Remières to the Bois Brûlé along the line of the northern edge of the Bois de Remières, ½ km south of Richecourt, Marvoisin in Etang de la Grande Croix, southern shore of Etang de Vargevaux, 2 km east of Apremont, 1 km southeast of Apremont, to the Bois Brûlé; French 69th Division on right, French 10th Colonial Division on left.

April 10–13, local actions in the Bois Brûlé.

April 20–21, local actions at Seicheprey.

May 24, the sector is extended 3½ km on the east, to a point 1½ km northwest of Flirey, by the relief of the French 162nd Infantry; the sector is reduced 6½ km on the west by moving the boundary to the Etang de Vargévaux; the French 34th Division occupies the centers of resistance Broussey, Brichauchard, and St. Agnant.

May 27, the sector is extended 1½ km on the east to Haut de Fouché, by the relief of the French 151st Infantry (French 69th Division).

June 4, French 65th Division is on the right.

June 16, at Xivray-et-Marvoisin.

June 21–29, division is under the administrative control of the IV Corps.

June 24–28, the French 154th Division and the 82nd Division relieve the division, which concentrates near Toul.

June 28, command passes to the French 154th Division.

June 29, division moves to the region about Meaux and St. Cyr-sur-Morin and prepares to relieve the 2nd Division northwest of Château-Thierry.

June 30–July 4, division is under the administrative control of the I Corps.

Night of July 3–4, 52nd Infantry Brig moves to support positions near Montreuil-aux-Lions.

Night of July 4–5, division begins the relief of the 2nd Division in the Pas Fini Sector.

July 10, division, brigades abreast, 51st Infantry Brig on the right, assumes command of the sector from Vaux (incl.), through the northern edge of the Bois de la Roche, northern edge of the Bois de la Côte 192, northern edge of the Bois des Haies, Bouresches (incl.), eastern and northern edges of the Bois de Belleau, to ¾ km southwest of Torcy; French 39th Division (French 38th Corps) on right, French 167th Division (I Corps) on left.

July 10–14, division occupies the Pas Fini Sector (Lorraine).

July 10–15, division organizes the position and local actions occur.

July 15–18, division participates in the Champagne-Maine Operation. July 15, the Pas Fini Sector occupation merges into the Champagne-Marne Operation when the enemy attacks on the front Château-Thierry, Reims, and Argonne Forest; local actions take place.

July 17, French 39th Division (French 38th Corps, French Ninth Army) is on the right.

July 18–25, division participates in the Aisne-Marne Operation.

July 18, 52nd Infantry Brig, in conjunction with the French 167th Division on the left, attacks and captures Belleau, Givry, and Torcy; 51st Infantry Brig remains in position.

July 20, division, brigades abreast, attacks toward Trugny, and reaches the line from Vaux (incl.), along the eastern and northeastern edges of the Bois de la Ealmardière, eastern edge of the Bois de Bouresches, la Gonétrie Fme, Hill 190 which is 1¼ km southwest of Etrépilly, ¾ km east of Belleau, Givry (md), to Torcy (md); French 39th Division (French 38th Corps, French Sixth Army) on right, French 167th Division on left.

Night of July 20–21, the enemy withdraws to the prepared position from l'Hermitage, through Epieds, to Mont–St. Père.

July 21, division pursues, passes through Etrépilly, and reaches a line from ¾ km north of Verdilly, along the eastern and northeastern edges of the Bois de Breteuil, to 1¼ km south of Bézu–St. Germain.

July 22, the troops temporarily occupy parts of Trugny and Epieds, and the right of the division extends along line from 1 km southeast of Trugny to 1 km southwest of that town.

Night of July 23–24, 56th Infantry Brig (28th Division), attached, relieves the 52nd Infantry Brig, which moves to a support position; the enemy withdraws to a north and south line through la Croix Rouge Fme.

July 24, division pursues and advances through the Bois de Trugny, the Bois de Fary, and the northern part of the Forêt de Fère, to a line lying west of the road between Le Charnel and Fère-en-Tardenois, from a point in the Forêt de Fère 2 km northwest of Le Charmel to 1¼ km west of la Croix Rouge Fme.

Night of July 25–26, 42nd Division relieves division, except the artillery and engineers, by passage of lines; division assembles in the Bois la Sacerie and Bois de Chante-Merle west of Château-Thierry.

July 25–August 5, 51st Field Artillery Brig and 102nd Am Tn participate in the Aisne-Marne Operation supporting the 42nd Division until August 3, and the 4th Division until August 5.

July 25–August 3, 101st Engrs and Tn participate in the Aisne-Marne Operation under the I Corps.

July 26–29, division (less Arty and Engrs) is in the reserve of French Sixth Army north and northwest of Château-Thierry.

July 30, division moves to La Ferté-sous-Jouarre Area where the detached units rejoin; training follows.

August 13, division moves to the 12th (Châtillon-sur-Seine) Training Area; rehabilitation and training follow.

August 18, division is assigned to the First Army.

August 28, division moves north of Bar-le-Duc, and thence via the Sommedieue Area to the western face of the St. Mihiel salient.

Night of September 3–4, 52nd Infantry Brig moves to the Sommedieue Area in support of the French 2nd Dismounted Cavalry Division.

September 5, division moves into the Rupt Sector, and during the night of September 6–7 the leading units enter the front line.

September 8, division relieves the French 2nd Dismounted Cavalry Division in the centers of resistance Terrasse, Liège, and Venise, and occupies the front from le Saillant, along the eastern slope of Côte de Senoux, Bois des Eparges, to ½ km southwest of Les Eparges; French 2nd Dismounted Cavalry Division (French II Colonial Corps) on right, French 15th Colonial Division on left.

September 8–12, division occupies the Rupt Sector (Lorraine).

September 12, sector occupation merges into the St. Mihiel Operation. Division, brigades abreast, 51st Infantry Brig on the right, attacks southeast from the front line of the Rupt Sector, advances through the Bois des Eparges, Bois de St. Remy, and le Chanot Bois, and reaches a line from ½ km southwest of Côte 381 in the Bois de Dommartin, along the eastern edge of le Chanot Bois, to ¾ km northwest of Dommartin-la-Montagne; French 2nd Dismounted Cavalry Division (French II Colonial Corps) on right, French 15th Colonial Division on left.

September 12–16, division participates in the St. Mihiel Operation.

September 13, the enemy retires and the division pursues through Dommartin-la-Montagne, along the Grande Tranchée de Calonne, and through the northern part of the Forêt de la Montagne, to a line from Côte 412, through a point 1 km south of Vigneulles-les-Hattonchâtel, Hattonville, Billysous-les-Côtes, St. Maurice-sous-les-Côtes (all incl.), to Thillot-sousles-Côtes (excl.), establishes contact with the 1st Division (IV Corps), which is advancing from the south along the road from Vigneulles-lès-Hattonchâtel to Hattonville, and thus completes the reduction of the St. Mihiel salient.

September 14–15, French 2nd Dismounted Cavalry Division relieves the division from Hattonchâtel to Thillot-sous-les-Côtes (both incl.), and the French 39th Division executes the relief from Vigneulles-lês-Hattonchâtel to Côte 412, after which the division occupies and organizes the New England

Sector, including the Massachusetts and Connecticut subsectors, relieves elements of French 15th Colonial Division from Thillot-sous-les-Côtes to Combres (both excl.), and at outposts in St. Hilaire and Wadonville-en-Woëvre.

September 15, units of the division repel a raid on St. Hilaire but withdraw from the village.

September 16, the New England Sector becomes a subsector of the Troyon Sector; division extends its front to include Trésauvaux with outposts near Champion and Saulx-en-Woevre.

Night of September 16–17, division begins the relief of the French 15th Colonial Division (French II Colonial Corps) on the new front; French 2nd Dismounted Cavalry Division on right, French 15th Colonial Division on left.

September 16–October 8, division occupies the Troyon Sector (Lorraine).

September 19, division extends the sector to the north to include Fresnes-en-Woëvre, and on September 20, relieves elements of the French 15th Colonial Division (French 17th Corps), and organizes the position.

September 26, division participates in a demonstration by the French II Colonial Corps and engages in local actions from Riaville to Marchéville.

October 6, 79th Division, elements of the French 2nd Dismounted Cavalry Division, and the French 39th Division, relieve the division, except the artillery which supports the 79th division, until October 11, and the engineers which remain until October 10.

Night of October 7–8, division (less Arty and Engrs) moves to the vicinity of Verdun to the zone of the French 17th Corps, where it enters army reserve and the detached units rejoin. **October 8,** the command passes to the 79th Division.

October 11, elements of the 29th Division are near Côte de L'Oie, east of the Meuse, in the reserve of the French 17th Corps.

October 13–14, Haumont-près-Samogneux, and Samogneux.

October 14–17, division, brigades abreast, 52nd Infantry Brig on the right, relieves the French 18th Division and the 57th Infantry Brig (29th Division), along the southeastern edge of the Bois de Haumont 1¾ km southwest of Flabas, the eastern edge of Bois d'Haumont, center of Bois d'Ormont, northern edges of the Bois des Chênes and Bois de la Reine, to 1 km southeast of Molleville Fme; French 26th Division on right, 29th Division on left.

October 18, the command passes from the French 18th Division.

October 23, 51st Infantry Brig, in conjunction with 29th Division, attacks and advances through le Houppy Bois to the southern edge of Belleu Bois.

October 24–25, 51st Infantry Brig attacks the enemy line from Belleu Bois to Bois de Moirey but without material gain; the 29th Division reduces the sector ½ km on the left when it relieves the 26th Division troops west of Belleu Bois.

October 27, 51st Infantry Brig renews the attack, advances into Belleu Bois, and consolidates the position.

Night of October 31–November 1, 79th Division begins the relief of the 51st Infantry Brig in Belleu Bois and Bois d'Ormont along the line, 1¾ km west of Flabas, Côte 360 in Bois d'Ormont, eastern edge of Bois des Chênes, and Belleu Bois.

November 1–2, 51st Infantry Brig relieves units of the French 26th Division and occupies the sector on the right of the 52nd Infantry Brig along the line, 1 km north of Beaumont, 1¼ km northeast of Côte 345, northern edge of Bois des Caures, as far as the southeastern edge of the Bois d'Haumont.

November 3, division completes the relief of the French 26th Division and assumes command of the Neptune Sector on a front extending from 1 km north of Beaumont to 1¾ km west of Flabas; French 10th Colonial Division on right, 79th Division on left.

November 8, the enemy retreats and the division, pivoting on its right, advances through Flabas to the line Sousla-fosse-à-terre, heights north of Flabas.

November 9, division advances east to a line from 1½ km northeast of Beaumont, along the eastern edge of la Wavrille, the ravine le Fond-des-Vaux, to ¼ km west of Ville-devant-Chaumont.

November 10, division advances to Fme St. André, the eastern edge of the Bois de Ville, and Ville-devant-Chaumont (incl.).

Post Armistice Activities

NOVEMBER 12, 1918 – MARCH 17, 1919

November 14, the 6th Division relieves the division in the former Neptune Sector and the latter, except the artillery which goes to the Bar-le-Duc Area, moves to Benoitevaux and Nicey Area, and from thence, on.

November 17, to the 8th (Montigny-le-Roi) Training Area; training follows.

December 20, the artillery rejoins.

January 18, division moves to the American Embarkation Center, Le Mans.

February 28, 101st TM Btry sails from Brest.

Return to the United States and Demobilization

MARCH 19 – MAY 3, 1919

March 19, the division moves to Brest.

March 27, DHQ, and Hq 52nd Infantry Brig, 104th Infantry, and elements of the 101st Engrs and Tn, Hq 51st Infantry Brig, and March 31, Hq 51st Field Artillery Brig, sail from Brest.

April 11, the last unit, a detachment of the 103rd FA, sails, and arrives April 22, at Boston. The demobilization at Camp Devens includes, April 29, Hq 51st Infantry Brig, Hq 52nd Inf. Brig, Hq 51st Field Artillery Brig, and May 3, DHQ.

THE TWENTY-SEVENTH DIVISION, NATIONAL GUARD

The 27th Division was organized at Camp Wadsworth, South Carolina, from the New York National Guard. Major General John O'Ryan of the New York National Guard commanded the Division during its entire service. The overseas movement began on May 8, 1918, and was completed July 7, 1918, when the last unit arrived in France. This division was loaned to the British government and served with that army in Belgium. It captured 2358 prisoners. It was quiet zero days and active 57 days. It advanced 11 kilometers. Its total casualties were 8986. It had 1785 battle deaths and 7201 wounded. The replacements were 5355.

53rd Infantry Brigade

105th Infantry
106th Infantry
105th Machine Gun Battalion

54th Infantry Brigade

107th Infantry
108th Infantry
106th Machine Gun Battalion

52nd Field Artillery Brigade

104th Field Artillery
105th Field Artillery
106th Field Artillery

Divisional Troops

102nd Engineers
104th Machine Gun Battalion
102nd Field Signal Battalion
Headquarters Troop

Trains

102nd Train Hdqs
102nd Military Police
102nd Ammunition Train
102nd Supply Train
102nd Engineer Train
102nd Sanitary Train
Ambulance Cos and Field Hospitals 105–108

Record of Events

SECTORS WHERE THE TWENTY-SEVENTH DIVISION WAS ENGAGED IN WARFARE

Dickebush Lake and Scherpenberg sectors, Belgium, July 9 to August 30, 1918.
Ypres-Lys offensive, Belgium, August 31, to September 2. 1918.
Somme offensive, France, September 24 to October 30, 1918.

Organization and Training in the United States

JULY 15, 1917–APRIL 27, 1918

July 15, the National Guard of New York, including the 6th Division commanded by Maj. Gen. John F. O'Ryan, is called into federal service.

July 18, the War Department re-designates the 6th Division, New York National Guard, as the 27th Division and selects Camp Wadsworth, Spartanburg, South Carolina, for the training.

August 3, the War Department directs the concentration and reorganization of the division at Camp Wadsworth.

August 5, the National Guard of New York is drafted into federal service.

September 1, the concentration of the division at Camp Wadsworth begins.

October 1, division is reorganized in accordance with the Tables of Organization of August 8, 1917; the brigades are organized and ultimately include 53rd Infantry Brig, the 2nd, 23rd, 71st, and detachments of the 12th and 14th, Regts of New York Infantry, and a detachment of New York Cav; 54th Infantry Brig, the 1st, 3rd, 7th, 74th, and a detachment of the 12th Regts of New York Infantry, and a detachment of New York Cav, 52nd Field Artillery Brig, the 1st, 2nd, and 3rd Regts of New York FA, detachments of the 1st, 12th, 14th, 71st, and 74th Regts of New York Infantry , and a detachment of 1st New York Cav.

October 8–April 27, systematic training is conducted. In the spring 2,500 recruits and selective service men join and complete the division.

Movement Overseas

April 28–July 12, 1918

April 28, the leading units leave Camp Wadsworth for Newport News.

May 2, Adv Det sails from Hoboken and arrives May 10 at Brest.

May 9–18, DHQ and the infantry sail from Newport News, except the 106th Infantry, which embarks at Hoboken and arrives May 23 and 30 at Brest and St. Nazaire.

May 16, the field artillery and remaining trains leave Camp Wadsworth, sail June 6–30, from Newport News, and arrive June 19, 27, and July 12 at Brest, except the 106th Field Artillery, which lands at St. Nazaire.

Final Training and Operations

May 26–November 11, 1918

May 26, division (less Arty, 102nd Sup Tn, and 102nd Sn Tn) moves to the Rue-Buigny Training Area.

May 28–June 8, division (less Arty, 102nd Sup Tn, and 102nd San Tn) arrives in the Rue-Buigny Training Area, where it is affiliated with the British 66th Div.

May 28–July 24, training with the British in Picardy and Flanders.

May 31–September 24, the division is under the administrative control of the II Corps.

June 10, the training begins.

June 16, division (less detached units) moves to the vicinity of Abbeville, southwest of the Somme Canal, in the St. Valery-Gamaches Area.

June 21, division (less troops previously detached, and the machine gun units which remain in the St. Valery Area) moves to the Beauval-Doullens Area; the infantry trains in the forward areas, but all troops are available for the defense of the rear lines.

July 2, division (less Arty, 102nd Sup Tn, and 102nd San Tn) moves to the Arques Area; the machine gun units rejoin.

July 3, the leading artillery troops arrive at Camp de Souge from the base ports.

July 5, division (less Arty, 102nd Sup Tn, and 102nd San Tn) moves to the vicinity of Cassel and St. Omer.

July 9, 27th and 30th Divisions are assigned to the organization and defense of the East Poperinghe Line, which is the third position in the British system in the Dickebusch Lake and Scherpenberg Sectors; elements of division begin front line training.

July 25–August 18, division (less Arty and 102nd Sup Tn), affiliated with British, participates in the occupation of the Dickebuach Lake and Scherpenberg Sectors (Flanders). The machine gun and infantry units serve by battalion, and other divisional troops serve by detachments, with the British 6th and British 41st Divisions in the front line of the sector, which extends from 1 ½ km north-northwest of Kemmel to the woods ½ km west of Elzenwalle.

August 19, sector occupation merges into the Ypres-Lys Operation.

August 19–September 3, division (less Arty and 102nd Sup Tn), participates in the Ypres-Lys Operation.

Nights of August 22–23 and 23–24, division relieves the British 6th Division in the front line of the Dickebusch Sector from a point near Kaaleput to the vicinity of Elzenwalle.

August 23, the command passes to the 27th Division; British 34th Division on the right, 30th Division (British H Corps) on the left.

August 30, the enemy withdraws to western slopes of the Wytschaete Ridge.

August 31, division, 53rd Infantry Brig leading, advances southeast to the road from Neuve-Eglise to Ypres, where the front extends from Rossignol Bois (incl.), through Vierstraat, to ½ km south of Voormezeele. September 1, division advances its right to a line extending from Haringhe Creek 1 km east of Goethals Fme to the road 1 km northeast of Vierstraat.

September 1, 52nd Field Artillery Brig and 102nd Am Tn begin the move from Camp de Souge to the vicinity of Longeville.

September 2–3, division crosses the line of Haringhe Creek and Wytschaete Creek and in addition establishes a front west of the Bois Confluent, holding 1 km of the road between Wytschaete and Voormezeele.

Night of September 2–3, British 41st Division relieves the division.

September 3, the command passes and the division moves to the Winnezeele Area.

September 4, division moves to the zone of British Third Army and takes station in the Beauquesne Area near Doullens; training follows.

September 10–25, they participate in the occupation of the Verdun-Fromeréville Sector (Lorraine) where they support the 33rd Division.

September 22, division moves to the Tincourt-Boucly Area, near Péronne, which is in the advance zone of the British Fourth Army, where it becomes corps reserve.

September 24–October 1, division (less Arty and 102nd Sup Tn) participates in the Somme Offensive Operation.

Night of September 24–25, division relieves the British 18th and British 74th Divisions (British III Corps), between Malakoff Fme and le Tombois Fme, command passing September 25. The II Corps, to which division is assigned, is affiliated with the Australian Corps.

September 26–October 21, 52nd Field Artillery Brig and 102nd Am Tn, attached to the 33rd Division, participate in the Meuse-Argonne Operation.

September 27, division, 53rd Infantry Brig leading, attacks to capture the outlying defenses of the Hindenburg Line west of the St. Quentin Canal Tunnel; 30th Division on right, British 12th Division on left. Severe fighting takes place around Quennemont Fme, Guillemont Fme, and The Knoll; the gains are slight.

September 28, 54th Infantry Brig relieves the 53rd Infantry Brig.

September 29, division, cooperating with general attack of British Fourth Army, attacks; at 11 A.M. the front line of the 27th Division extends from ¾ km northeast of Bois de Malakoff, east of and along the road from Bellicourt to Bony, through points 400 in south of Bony, 200 in west of Bony, 500 in northwest of Quennemont Fme, west of Guillemont Fme, to 400 in east of The Knoll; in the afternoon the Australian 3rd Division reinforces the lines and assists in the capture of Guillemont Fme; British 18th Division on the left.

September 30, the command of the forward area passes to the Australian 3rd Division, but many units of the 27th Division are still in line and participate in the operations of the Australians.

October 1, division moves to the Péronne Area; rehabilitation follows.

October 5, II Corps prepares to relieve the Australian Corps in the front line; the 30th Division moves into line, the 27th Division to reserve.

October 6–21, division (less Arty and 102nd Sup Tn) participates in the Somme Offensive Operation.

October 7–11, division moves by stages toward Busigny, following the 30th Division which is pursuing the enemy.

October 12, division relieves the 30th Division; the 54th Infantry Brig, one battalion 105th Infantry attached, takes over front line west of La Selle River extending from Vaux-Andigny through St. Souplet to St. Benin (excl.);

British 6th Division (British IX Corps) on the right, British 50th Division (British XIII Corps) on the left.

Night of October 14–15, the sector is reduced so that the front then extends from ½ km north of Vaux-Andigny to ½ km north of St. Souplet.

Night of October 15–16, 30th Division relieves 27th Division units in the southern half of the sector; the boundary between the American divisions lies north of St. Martin-Rivière.

October 17, division, brigades abreast, attacks northeast, captures Bandival Fme, l'Avantage Fme, Arbre-Guernon, and reaches the highway between Ribeauville and Le Cateau; the front extends from Arbre-Guernon (incl.) to l'Avantage Fme, thence along the ridge to the farm which lies northeast of Bandival Fme; 30th Division on right, British 50th Division on left.

October 18, the attack is resumed; Jonc de Mer Fme and la Roue Fme are captured; the east crest of Jonc de Mer ridge is occupied; the front line, extending north and south, lies slightly east of Jonc de Mer Fme; British 25th Division on the left.

October 19, division crosses the valley of Jonc de Mer Creek, captures la Jonquière Fme and the ridge, and advances to a front which extends from ½ km southeast of la Jonquière Fme along the eastern crust of the ridge, to the southern edge of Basuel; British 1st Division on the right.

October 20, the main line of resistance is established along the western bank of St. Maurice Creek; patrolling follows.

October 21, British 6th Division relieves the division, which becomes corps reserve, later army reserve; it moves to the vicinity of Roisel and Tincourt-Boucly.

October 23, division moves toward Amiens to the Corbie Training Area and training follows.

October 28–November 11, 52nd Field Artillery Brig and 102nd Am. Tn, attached to 79th Division, participate in the Meuse-Argonne Operation.

Post Armistice Activities

NOVEMBER 12, 1918–FEBRUARY 16, 1919

November 18, 52nd Field Artillery Brig and 102nd Am Tn move to the vicinity of Verdun-sur-Meuse.

November 23, division (less Arty) moves to the American Embarkation Center, Le Mans.

December 12–14, 52nd Field Artillery Brig and 102nd Am Tn arrive in the Laval Area and revert to the division; training follows.

January 8, 102nd TM Btry sails from Brest for the United States.

Return to the United States and Demobilization

FEBRUARY 17–APRIL 1, 1919

February 17–26, the division (less 102nd Engrs and Tn) moves to Brest, the 102nd Engrs and Tn to Le Havre.

February 18, 102nd Engrs and Tn sail from Le Havre.

February 26, DHQ and about one half of the division sail from Brest aboard SS *Leviathan*, arriving March 6 at New York.

March 19, the last units arrive at New York.

April 1, the Division demobilizes at Camp Upton.

THE TWENTY-EIGHTH DIVISION, NATIONAL GUARD

The 28th Division was organized at Camp Hancock, Georgia, from the Pennsylvania National Guard. The generals in command of the division were Major General Charles M. Clement to December 11, 1917, succeeded by Major General Charles H. Muir, who served until October 24, 1918, when Major General William H. Hay took command and served until the end of the war. The 28th Division captured 921 prisoners, was quiet 31 days and active 49 days. It advanced 10 kilometers. It had a total casualty list of 13,980. It had 2551 battle deaths; 11,429 were wounded.

55th Infantry Brigade

109th Infantry
110th Infantry
108th Machine Gun Battalion

56th Infantry Brigade

111th Infantry
112th Infantry
109th Machine Gun Battalion

53rd Field Artillery Brigade

107th Field Artillery
108th Field Artillery
109th Field Artillery

Divisional Troops

103rd Engineers
107th Machine Gun Battalion
103rd Field Signal Battalion
Headquarters Troop

Trains

103rd Train Hdqs
103rd Military Police
103rd Ammunition Train
103rd Supply Train
103rd Engineer Train
103rd Sanitary Train
Ambulance Cos and Field Hospitals 109–112

Record of Events

SECTORS WHERE THE TWENTY-EIGHTH DIVISION WAS ENGAGED IN WARFARE

Château-Thierry sector, France, July 9 to 14, 1918.
Champagne-Maine defensive, France, July 15 to 18, 1918.
Aisne-Marne offensive, France, July 18 to August 6, 1918.
Flames sector, France, August 7 to 17, 1918.
Oise-Aisne offensive, France, August 18 to September 7, 1918.
Meuse-Argonne offensive, France, September 26 to October 9, 1918.
Meuse-Argonne offensive, France, October 16 to November 11, 1918.

Organization and Training in the United States

JULY 15, 1917–APRIL 20, 1918

July 15, the National Guard of Pennsylvania, including the 7th Division commanded by Maj. Gen. Charles M. Clement, was called into the federal service.

July 18, the War Department re-designates the 7th Division, Pennsylvania National Guard, as the 28th Division, and selects Camp Hancock, Augusta, Georgia, for the training.

August 5, the National Guard of Pennsylvania is drafted into federal service.

August 19, the concentration of the Division at Camp Hancock begins.

September 1, Maj. Gen. Charles M. Clement assumes command.

September 14, the concentration, totaling 27,000, is completed and systematic training is begun.

September 22, division is reorganized in accordance with the Tables of Organization of August 8, 1917; the brigades are organized and ultimately include 55th Infantry Brig, the 1st, 3rd, 10th, 13th, and a detachment of the 4th Regts of Pennsylvania Infantry, a detachment of the 1st Pennsylvania Cav; 56th Infantry Brig, the 6th, 8th, 16th, 18th, and a detachment of the 4th Regts of Pennsylvania Infantry; 53rd Field Artillery Brig, the 1st, 2nd, and 3rd Regts of Pennsylvania Field Artillery and a detachment of 1st Pennsylvania Cav. In March several thousand National Army men from Camps Lee, Meade, and Travis are assigned to replace losses and complete the division.

Movement Overseas

April 21–June 11, 1918

April 21, the leading units leave Camp Hancock en route to Camp Upton.

April 29, Adv Det sails, and arrives May 7 at Liverpool.

May 3, 5, and 7, DHQ and the infantry sail, and arrive May 13, 14, and 16 at Liverpool, except the Hq 56th Infantry Brig and the 111th Infantry which land May 13 at Southampton.

May 18–19 and 27, 53rd Field Artillery Brig and the remaining divisional troops and trains sail, arriving May 31 at Liverpool, except the 103rd Sup Tn, which lands June 8. The troops, after a brief stay in rest camps, proceed via Dover and Southampton to Calais and Le Havre.

June 11, the last unit arrives in France.

Final Training and Operations

May 17–November 11, 1918

May 17, division (less Arty, and divisional troops and trains) moves from Calais to the Lumbres Training Area, east of Boulogne, where, May 21–June 8, it trains with the British 34th Division.

May 17–June 11, training with the British in Picardy.

May 18–June 13, division is under the administrative control of the II Corps.

June 7, 53rd Field Artillery Brig and 103rd Am Tn move from Le Havre to Camp de Meucon for training.

June 9, division (less Arty, 103rd Sup Tn, 103rd F Sig Bn, 103rd Tn Hq and MP) moves to entraining stations between St. Pol and Montreuil-sur-Mer in the area of the British First Army. **June 12–14,** division (less detached units) arrives near Gonesse, northeast of Paris, where it trains; 55th Infantry Brig is attached to the French 125th Division, 56th Infantry Brig to the French 39th Division; 103rd Sup Tn, 103rd F Sig Bn, and 103rd Tn Hq and MP rejoin.

June 12–28, training with the French northeast of Paris and south of Château-Thierry.

June 21–July 28, division is under the administrative control of the I Corps.

June 23–24, division (less Arty) moves with the French 39th Division and French 125th Division to the south of Château-Thierry, where it occupies stations along the Montmirail-Rebais railroad.

June 29, division (less Arty) moves to the Hondevihiers Area; 55th Infantry Brig, attached to French 125th Division, takes station near Artonges, and the 56th Infantry Brig, attached to French 39th Division, near Bassevelle.

July 1, units of the division are affiliated for training with the French 39th and French 125th Divisions, which are in line along the Marne near Château-Thierry.

July 1–14, division (less Arty and 103rd Sn Tn), affiliated with the French, participates in the occupation of the Château-Thierry Sector (Champagne).

July 7, the 56th Infantry Brig occupies a second position in the so-called West Sector, extending from Los Trinité Fme, 6 km southwest of Château-Thierry, to the Bois de Gravelles, 2 km west of Nogent-l'Artaud; the French 39th Division holds the front; the 3rd Division is on the right, 2nd Division is on the left until it is replaced on July 10 by the 26th Division.

July 9, the 55th Infantry Brig occupies a second position extending west for 6 km from the center of the Bois de Rougis to a point north of Coufremaux; the French 125th Division holds the front; the French 51st is on the right, the 3rd Division on the left. Units of the division are attached to French regiments and serve in the front line.

July 15–18, division (less Arty and 103rd Sn Tn) participates in the Champagne-Marne Operation.

July 15, the enemy attacks, crosses the Marne at Reuily and points east thereof, advances through the Bois de Condé, and reaches the second position near St. Agnan; the French 73rd Division is now assisting the French 125th Division.

July 16, units of the 109th Infantry join the French 20th Division, which has replaced the French 51st Division in line, in a counterattack east of St. Agnan.

July 16–19, 111th Infantry (56th Infantry Brig) is attached to the 3rd Division, which holds the line between the French 39th Division and French 73rd Division.

July 17, 56th Infantry Brig moves to the right and occupies the second position on the left of the 55th Infantry Brig near Coufremanx; French 73rd Division relieves French 125th Division of command of the sector.

July 18–August 6, Division (less Arty) participates in the Aisne-Marne Operation.

July 19, 56th Infantry Brig is placed under the tactical control of the French 73rd Division.

Night of July 19–20, the enemy withdraws to the north bank of the Marne.

July 20, French 73rd Division attacks and advances to the south bank of the river; 111th Infantry reverts to the 56th Infantry Brig. July 21, 56th Infantry Brig is placed at the disposal of the French 39th Division and moved north of the Marne to the vicinity of Saulchery and Charly.

July 24, 55th Infantry Brig is moving to the vicinity of Saulchery and Charly; 56th Infantry Brig, attached to 26th Division, relieves the 52nd Infantry Brig (26th Division) in the line near Trugny and pursues the enemy.

July 25, 56th Infantry Brig is relieved by the 84th Infantry Brig (42nd Division) and passes from the 26th Division to the reserve of the I Corps.

July 26, 55th Infantry Brig guards the Marne bridges between Mézy and Château-Thierry (both incl.).

Night of July 26–27, the enemy withdraws to the Ourcq River; French 39th Division pursues and the 28th Division units follow.

July 28, 55th Infantry Brig relieves the French 39th Division from Courmont (incl.) to 1¼ km north of Fresnes, advances northeast, crosses the Ourcq and holds the river line south of Bois des Lutes; 3rd Division on right, 42nd Division (I Corps) on left. The 56th Infantry Brig is in the reserve of the French 38th Corps.

July 29, 55th Infantry Brig makes a series of attacks, in conjunction with the attack of the 3rd Division, and gains some ground.

Night of July 29–30, 32nd Division relieves the 3rd Division.

July 30, 55th Infantry Brig again attacks, cooperating with one brigade of the 32nd Division on the right, captures the Bois des Grimpettes and Hill 188 on the right, and holds the line from that hill to ½ km southeast of Moulin Caranda.

July 31, 63rd Infantry Brig (32nd Division) relieves the 55th Infantry Brig; 28th Division passes to the reserve of the French 38th Corps in a second line position north of the Marne near Le Charnel.

July 31–August 3, division is under the administrative control of the III Corps.

August 3, division, in corps reserve, follows the advance of the 32nd Division toward the Vesle River.

August 4, division continues to support the 32nd Division and reaches the vicinity of Dravegny.

August 6, 53rd Field Artillery Brig and 103rd Am Tn revert to the division and leave Camp de Meucon.

Night of August 6–7, division relieves 32nd Division along the Vesle River from Fismes (incl.), through Tannerie, to los Grands-Marais; 56th Infantry Brig is in the front line, 55th Infantry Brig is in support; 6th Infantry Brig (3rd Division) on right, 4th Division (I Corps) on left.

August 7–17, division occupies the Fismes Sector (Champagne).

August 7–8, division (less Arty) attacks Fismettes and occupies the southern and eastern parts of the town.

August 8–13, 53rd Field Artillery Brig and 103rd Am Tn rejoin.

August 10, Fismettes is occupied.

August 11, French 164th Division is on the right.

August 13, division relieves the French 164th Division on the right; 77th Division on the left relieves elements of 28th Division west of Fismes; the new sector extends from west of Ormont Fme to Fismes (incl.); French 20th Division (French V Corps, French Fifth Army) is on the right; local actions follow.

August 18–September 8, division participates in the Oise-Aisne Operation.

August 22, Fismettes is cleared of the enemy.

August 26, French 9th Division is on the right.

August 27, the enemy recaptures Fismettes.

Night of September 3–4, the enemy withdraws toward the Aisne.

September 4, division pursues across the Vesle River and advances to an east and west line 3 km north of Basiieux.

September 6, division attacks several strong points and reaches a line extending from the northern edge of the Bois Vigneux toward the northwest, along the high ground, to the vicinity of la Croisette.

September 8, French 62nd Division relieves the division which, September 10, moves by stages through the Epernay, Revigny and Triaucourt areas to the vicinity of Clermont-en-Argonne.

Nights of September 18–19 and 19–20, division relieves units of the French 73rd and French 120th Divisions, except in the outpost area, from southeast of Boureuilles, through los Merliers, to Pierre-Croisée; preparations for the Meuse-Argonne Operation follow; 35th Division on right; 77th Division on left.

September 20, division is assigned to I Corps.

September 20–25, division occupies the Clermont Sector (Lorraine).

September 26, division attacks northwest; the 55th Infantry Brig captures part of Varennes west of Aire River and occupies the high ground ½ km south of La Forge and the Tranchée des fils Do for 1½ km northwest of Boureulles; the 56th Infantry Brig advances to the south slope of Cote des Peinnieres, and Bas-Jardinet.

September 26–October 9, division participates in the Meuse-Argonne Operation.

September 27, division captures Montblainville but on the left progress is slow due to the German resistance at Champ-Mahaut.

September 28, division attacks, the right progresses along the Montblainville-Apremont road and captures Apremont; the high ground of Jo Chêne Tondu is occupied; the left reaches the northern edge of the Bois de Bouzon.

September 29–October 6, division advances its right along the Aire River to ½ km south of Flévile and its left organizes the high ground of le Chêne Tondu.

October 1, 1st Division replaces 35th Division on the right.

October 6, 82nd Division relieves elements of the 28th Division north of La Forge.

October 7, 55th Infantry Brig attacks west and captures Châtel-Chéhéry and eastern slopes of Cote 244; 56th Infantry Brig attacks Cote 244 from the direction of Apremont, and prolongs the front to the southwest, ¾ km south of Drachen.

October 8, division advances its right, west of Châtel-Chéhéry, to the Pylone-Drachen road in the Bois de Cornay, and its left, west of Cote 244, to ¼ km south of Drachen and thence southwesterly to a point 2 km west of le Ménil Fme.

October 9, 326th Infantry (82nd Division) relieves the division, except the artillery and engineers, which are attached to the 82nd Division, which then assembles near Varennes and Montblainvile as corps reserve.

October 10, division moves to army reserve in the vicinity of Thiaucourt.

October 16, division relieves the 37th Division in this sector from 1½ km south of Rembercourt, in Bois de Blainchamp, along northern edges of Bois de Hailbat, along the Bois de la Monagne, Bois de Charey, and Bois de la Grande-Souche to the southern edge of Etang de Lachaussee; 7th Division on right, French 39th Division (French II Cl Corps) on left.

October 16–November 11, division (less Arty) occupies the Thiaucourt (Pannes) Sector (Lorraine).

October 18, the 53rd Field Artillery Brig is detached and moves from the Argonne Forest to Belgium.

October 24–29, division occupies Haumont-lès-Lachaussée.

Night of October 28–29, the sector is reduced on the east when the boundary is moved to a point midway between Xammes and Charey, the 7th Division executing the relief, but is enlarged on the west to include the western edge of the Bois des Haravillers when the 28th Division relieves units of the French 39th Division; local actions follow; 33rd Division (French II Cl Corps) on left.

November 4, the front is advanced to the northern edge of Bois des Haudronvilles Bas.

November 6, the French 17th Corps is on the left.

November 10–11, division advances to the Bois Dommartin, Marimbois Fme, the northern edge of the Bois des Haravillers, and the Fme des Hauts-Journaux.

October 30–November 11, 53rd Field Artillery Brig participates in the Ypres-Lys Operation, supporting the 91st Division.

Post Armistice Activities

NOVEMBER 12, 1918–MARCH 15, 1919

November 12, the training is resumed.

January 6, division (less Arty) moves to the 6th (Colombey-les-Bôlles) Training Area.

February 1, 53rd Field Artillery Brig is relieved from 91st Division and placed under the administrative control of the II Corps pending the arrival of the 28th Division in Le Mans Area.

March 12, 103rd TM Btry sails from Brest for the United States.

Return to the United States and Demobilization

MARCH 16–MAY 22, 1919

March 16, the division moves to the American Embarkation Center, La Mans.

April 12–20, division entrains for St. Nazaire. April 16, the loading elements sail.

April 19, DHQ sails from St. Nazaire and arrives April 30 at Philadelphia.

April 27, 53rd Field Artillery Brig sails from St. Nazaire.

May 22, the last elements arrive at New York. The demobilization at Camp Dix includes, May 3, Hq 56th Infantry Brig, May 17, DHQ, May 18, Hq 55th Infantry Brig, May 22, Hq 53rd Field Artillery Brig.

The Twenty-Ninth Division, National Guard

The 29th Division was organized at Camp McClellan in Alabama and was composed of National Guard organizations from Maryland, Virginia, District of Columbia and New Jersey. They went overseas and arrived at Brest and St. Nazaire in the month of June 1918. The division was commanded by Major General Charles G. Morton. The division captured 2148 prisoners. It was quiet 59 days and active 25 days. It advanced 4 kilometers. It suffered a casualty list of 5219. It had battle deaths of 950 and 4268 were wounded. The division received 4977 replacements.

57th Infantry Brigade

113th Infantry
114th Infantry
111th Machine Gun Battalion

58th Infantry Brigade

115th Infantry
116th Infantry
112th Machine Gun Battalion

54th Field Artillery Brigade

110th Field Artillery
111th Field Artillery
112th Field Artillery
104th Trench Mortar Battery

Divisional Troops

104th Engineers
110th Machine Gun Battalion
104th Field Signal Battalion

Trains

104th Train Hdqs
104th Military Police

104th Supply Train
104th Engineer Train
104th Sanitary Train
Ambulance Cos. and Field Hospitals 113–116

Record of Events

SECTORS WHERE THE TWENTY-NINTH DIVISION WAS ENGAGED IN WARFARE

Center sector, Haute-Alsace, France, July 25 to September 22, 1918.
Meuse-Argonne offensive, France, September 28 to October 5, 1918 (104th Eng).
Meuse-Argonne offensive, France, October 8 to 30, 1918.

Organization and Training in the United States

JULY 18, 1917–JUNE 3, 1918

July 18, the War Department designates National Guard troops of Delaware, Maryland, New Jersey, Virginia, and the District of Columbia to form the 29th Division. Camp McClellan, Anniston, Alabama, is selected for the training.

July 25, the National Guards of Delaware, Maryland, New Jersey, Virginia and the District of Columbia are called into federal service.

July 28, Brig. Gen. Charles W. Barber assumes command of Division.

August 3, the War Department directs the concentration and reorganization of the division at Camp McClellan.

August 5, the National Guards of Delaware, Maryland, New Jersey, Virginia and the District of Columbia are drafted into federal service.

August 25, the concentration of the division at Camp McClellan begins; the 58th Infantry Brig is organized and ultimately includes the 1st and 5th Regts of Maryland Infantry, the 1st and 2nd Regts of Virginia Infantry and detachments of the 4th Maryland and 4th Virginia Regts of Infantry.

September 4–June 3, systematic training is conducted.

September 6, 57th Infantry Brig is organized and ultimately includes the 1st, 5th, and detachments of the 2nd, 3rd, and 4th Regts of New Jersey Infantry.

September 8, 54th Field Artillery Brig is organized and ultimately includes the 1st Virginia and 1st New Jersey Regts of FA, the 1st District of Columbia Cav, and detachments of the 4th Virginia and 5th Maryland Regts of Infantry, of New Jersey Field Artillery and Cav, and of Virginia Sig Corps.

September 15, division is reorganized in accordance with the Tables of Organization of August 8, 1917.

November 5, drafts totaling 1,000 join from Delaware, Maryland, New Jersey, and the District of Columbia.

January 8, the 1st Delaware Infantry and Delaware National Army men are relieved from the division. During May 5,000 National Army men from New York, the New England states, and the Middle West join and complete the division.

May 26, Adv Det sails from Newport News and arrives June 8 at Brest.

Movement Overseas

MAY 26–JULY 22, 1918

June 4, the division moves via Camps Stuart, Hill, and Mills to the ports of embarkation of Baltimore, Hoboken, Newport News, New York, Norfolk, and Philadelphia.

June 14–15 and 19, DHQ, the infantry, 104th F Sig Bn, and 104th Engrs and Tn sail, and arrive June 26–27 at Brest, Bordeaux, and St. Nazaire.

June 28–July 6, the field artillery units and remaining divisional troops sail, and arrive July 10–17, at Liverpool, except the 104th Am Tn which lands July 22 at London. The 54th Field Artillery Brig and divisional troops, after a brief stay in rest camps, proceed to France via Cherbourg and La Havre.

Final Operations and Training

JUNE 30–NOVEMBER 11, 1918

June 30, division (less Arty) moves to the 10th (Prauthoy) Training Area for training.

July 13, 54th Field Artillery Brig and 104th Am Tn move to the Poitiers Area.

July 17, division (less Arty) moves to the vicinity of Belfort.

July 18–August 19, division is under the administrative control of the V Corps.

July 24, division moves into the defensive sector of Haute-Alsace (French XL Corps) along the line from the Swiss border southwest of Moos, through Seppois-le-Haut, Largitzen, 1 km west of Carspach, Eglingen, Ammertzwiller, Pont-d'Aspach, Aspach-le-Haut, to 1 km north of Aspach-le-Haut on the Aspach-le-Haut-Thann road; the 57th Infantry Brig is affiliated with the French 151st Division in the Boron Sector, the 58th Infantry Brig with the French 53rd Division in the Rougemont Sector; all the infantry is north of Largitzen.

July 25–August 8, division (less Arty) participates with the French in the occupation of the Center Sector (Alsace).

August 9, division takes command of the recently created Center Sector, which lies astride the Rhine-Rhône Canal, from the railroad 1 km west of Carspach, through Eglingen to Spech-Bach Creek 3 km northwest of Ammertzwiller; French 151st Division on right, French 53rd Division on left; local actions follow.

August 9–September 22, division (less Arty) occupies the Center Sector (Alsace).

August 19–September 23, division is under the administrative control of the VII Corps.

August 25, 54th Field Artillery Brig and 104th Am Tn move to Camp de Meucon for training.

September 20, division is ordered to join First Army and V Corps.

September 22, French 38th Division relieves the division, which, September 23, moves to First Army Area near Condé-en-Barrois.

September 30, division continues to the vicinity of Nixéville, and again, October 3, moves to the Vérdun-sur-Meuse Area.

October 8, 58th Infantry Brig, on the front from Samogneux to Brabant-sur-Meuse, attached to the French 18th Division (French XVII Corps), attacks north, captures Malbrouck Hill, and reaches a line from the Ravin de Coassinvaux 1½ km north of Haumont-près-Samogneux (excl.), through the Bois de Brabant-sur-Meuse, Cote 338, ½ km south of Cote 382 to ¾ km east of the Fme de Régivaux; French 18th Division on right, 33rd Division on left.

October 8–18, units of the division are affiliated with and operate under French 18th Division.

October 8–30, division (less Arty) participates in the Meuse-Argonne Operation.

October 9–10, 58th Infantry Brig advances into the Molleviule Bois and Bossois Bois and establishes a line from the junction of the Ravin de Molleville and Fond de Walonsevaux, through a point ¾ km south of Molleville Fme, to ½ km northeast and ¼ km northwest of Hill 382 near Richêne.

October 10, elements of the 57th Infantry Brig, attached to the French 18th Division, attack on the right of the 58th Infantry Brig, and establish a front along the eastern and northern edges of the Bois des Chênes and Bois de la Reine.

October 11, 58th Infantry Brig reverts to the division.

October 11–16, division (less 57th Infantry Brig), in a series of attacks, advances to a line from the Ravin de Molleville, through the road junction north of Bultruy Bois, south of Hill 370 in the Bois de la Grande-Montagne, to ¾ km southeast of Magenta Fme; elements of the 57th Infantry Brig, attached to the French 18th Division, advance on the right of the 29th Division and penetrate the Bois d'Ormont.

October 18, 57th Infantry Brig reverts to the division, which then organizes the Grande-Montagne Sector; 26th Division on right.

October 21, French 15th Colonial Division is on the left.

October 23, division advances its right and occupies Hill 361 in the Bois d'Etrayes, from which point the line extends West to a saddle south of Hill 370 in the Bois de la Grande-Montagne.

October 30, division is relieved by the 79th Division and moves to the Vavincourt Area.

Post Armistice Activities
NOVEMBER 12, 1918 – APRIL 10, 1919

November 17, the division (less Arty) moves to the 11th (Bourbonne-les-Bains) Training Area via the Tronville Area; training follows.

December 8, 54th Field Artillery Brig rejoins.

February 23, 104th TM Btry sails from St. Nazaire for the United States.

Return to the United States and Demobilization
APRIL 11 – MAY 30, 1919

April 11, the division moves to the Ballon Area, American Embarkation Center.

April 21, division moves to St. Nazaire.

April 24, the leading elements, part of the 114th Infantry, sail.

May 6, DHQ sails.

May 26, the last elements arrive at New York. The demobilization includes, at Camp Dix, May 16, Hq 57th Infantry Brig, May 30, DHQ; at Camp Lee, May 26, Hq 54th Field Artillery Brig; at Camp Meade, May 29, Hq 58th Infantry Brig.

THE THIRTIETH DIVISION, NATIONAL GUARD

The 30th Division was organized at Camp Sevier, Greenville, South Carolina, from the National Guard organizations of Tennessee, North Carolina and South Carolina, and contained men from Indiana, Illinois, Iowa, Minnesota and North Dakota. Major General George W. Read was in command of the division from April 27, 1918, to August 10, 1918, when he was succeeded by General Edward M. Lewis. The overseas movement took place between May 7, 1918, and June 24, 1918, when the complete division was landed in Calais, France. This division captured 3848 prisoners, was active 56 days and advanced 29½ kilometers. It suffered 8954 casualties. It had 1629 battle deaths and 7325 were wounded. This division received 2384 replacements.

59th Infantry Brigade

117th Infantry
118th Infantry
114th Machine Gun Battalion

60th Infantry Brigade

119th Infantry
120th Infantry
115th Machine Gun Battalion

55th Field Artillery Brigade

113th Field Artillery
114th Field Artillery
115th Field Artillery

Divisional Troops

105th Engineers
113th Machine Gun Battalion
105th Field Signal Battalion
Headquarters Troop

Trains

105th Train Hdqs
105th Military Police
105th Ammunition Train
105th Supply Train
105th Engineer Train
105th Sanitary Train
Ambulance Cos, and Field Hospitals 117–120

Record of Events

SECTORS WHERE THE THIRTIETH DIVISION WAS ENGAGED IN WARFARE

Canal sector, Belgium, July 16 to August 30, 1918.
Toul sector, France, August 23 to September 11, 1918 (55th FA).
Ypres-Lys offensive, Belgium, August 31 to September 2, 1918.
St. Mihiel offensive, France, September 12 to 16, 1918 (55th FA).
Somme offensive, France, September 24 to October 20, 1918.
Meuse-Argonne offensive, France, September 26 to October 8, 1918 (55th FA).
Woevre sector, France, October 11 to November 8, 1918 (55th FA).

Organization and Training in the United States

JULY 18, 1917–APRIL 30, 1918

July 18, the War Department designates National Guard troops of North Carolina, South Carolina, and Tennessee to form the 30th Division. Camp Sevier, Greenville, South Carolina, is selected for the training.

July 25, the National Guard units of North Carolina, South Carolina and Tennessee are called into federal service.

August 3, the War Department directs the concentration and organization of the division at Camp Sevier.

August 5, the National Guard units of North Carolina, South Carolina and Tennessee are drafted into federal service. During August the concentration is in progress.

August 25, the 55th Field Artillery Brig is organized and ultimately includes the 1st North Carolina and 1st Tennessee Regts of FA, the 1st Tennessee Infantry, Troop D Tennessee Cav, and detachments of the 1st North Carolina and 2nd Tennessee Regts of Infantry.

August 28, Maj. Gen. John F. Morrison assumes command of the division.

September 12, division is reorganized in accordance with the Tables of Organization of August 8, 1917; the infantry brigades are organized and ultimately include 59th Infantry Brig, the 3rd Tennessee and 1st South Carolina Regts of Infantry, and detachments of the 1st North Carolina and 2nd South Carolina Regts of Infantry and of Pennsylvania Cav; 60th Infantry Brig, the 2nd, and 3rd North Carolina Regts of Infantry, and detachments of the 1st North Carolina, and 2nd Tennessee Regts of Infantry and of North Carolina Cav.

September 17–April 30, systematic training is conducted. During October selective service men from Camps Gordon, Jackson, and Pike complete the division.

Movement Overseas

MAY 1–JUNE 25, 1918

May 1, DHQ and the infantry organizations leave Camp Sevier, the 59th Infantry Brig en route to Camp Mills, the 60th Infantry Brig en route to Camp Merritt.

May 7, Adv Det sails, and lands May 14 in England.

May 11–19, DHQ and the infantry sail from New York and Hoboken, and arrive May 23–June 5 in England.

May 18, 55th Field Artillery Brig begins the move from Camp Sevier to Camp Mills.

May 27–June 12, the artillery and divisional troops and Infantry sail from New York and Hoboken and arrive in England, June 8–25. The troops, after a brief stay in rest camps, proceed to Calais and Le Havre, infantry to the former, artillery to the latter.

Final Training and Operations

MAY 27–NOVEMBER 11, 1918.

May 24–September 24, division is under the administrative control of the II Corps.

May 27–June 17, division (less Arty, 105th Sup Tn, and 105th San Tn) arrives in the Recques Training Area between Calais and St. Omer, where it is affiliated with the British 39th Division for training.

May 27–August 18, training with the British in Picardy and Flanders.

June 13–21, 55th Field Artillery Brig and 105th Am Tn arrive at Le Havre and proceed to the artillery school at Camp Coëtquidan, where they train until August 20.

June 22 and 30, 105th San Tn and 105th Sup Tn arrive at Calais and Cherbourg respectively, and on June 28 and July 5 they proceed to the 17th (Fays-Billot) Training Area.

July 2, division (less detachments) moves to the area west of Poperinghe, Belgium.

July 9, the 27th and 30th Divisions are assigned the organization and defense of the East Poperinghe Line, a third defensive position in the Dickebusch Lake and Scherpenberg Sectors.

July 10, the machine gun troops and engineers complete their training and follow the division.

July 11, division assumes responsibility for the East Poperinghe trench system.

July 16–August 9, Division Infantry in the front line; the 59th Infantry Brig is affiliated with the British 49th Division, the 60th Infantry Brig with the British 33rd Division; the machine gun and infantry units serve by battalions, and the other divisional troops serve by detachments.

July 16–August 18, division (less Arty and 105th Sup Tn), affiliated with the British, participates in the occupation of the Canal Sector (Canal d'Ypres, Flanders).

August 10–18, the training is continued in the rear areas.

Nights of August 16–17 and August 17–18, division relieves the British 33rd Division in the front line of the Canal Sector from the vicinity of Elzenwalle to the railroad southeast of Transport Fme.

August 18, division assumes command; British 6th Division on right.

August 19, the Canal Sector occupation merges into the Ypres-Lys Operation.

August 19–September 4, division (less Arty and 105th Sup Tn) participates in the Ypres-Lys Operation.

August 23, the 27th Division is on the right.

August 26–September 11, 55th Field Artillery Brig and 105th Am Tn participate in the occupation of the Lucey Sector with the 89th Division.

August 31, combat patrols investigate the report of a German withdrawal; the British 14th Division is on the left.

September 1, division, 60th Infantry Brig leading, captures Moated Grange, Voormezeele, Lock No. 8, and Lankhof Fme, and occupies a line connecting these localities with the original front at Gunners' Lodge; 27th Division on right, British 14th Division on left.

Night of September 3–4, September 4, and Night of September 4, command passes.

September 4–5, the British 35th Division relieves the division.

September 5–6, division concentrates near Proven and moves to the St. Pol Area in the zone of the British First Army, where it arrives on September 7 for training.

September 12–15, 55th Field Artillery Brig and 105th Am Tn participate in the St. Mihiel Operation, again supporting the 89th Division.

September 15, 55th Field Artillery Brig and 105th Am Tn are detached from the 89th Division and ordered to the V Corps to support the 37th Division in the Avocourt Sector.

September 17–18, division moves to the Puchevillers (British Third Army) Area for training.

Nights September 21–22, 22–23, and 23–24, division moves to the Tincourt-Boucly (British Fourth Army) Area; the II Corps is affiliated with the Australian Corps.

September 22–October 1, division (less Arty and 105th Sup Tn) participates in the Somme Offensive Operation.

September 23, Night of September 23–24, division relieves the Australian 1st Division east of Villeret and Hargicourt from 300 in east of Buisson-Gaulaine Fme, through La Haute Bruyère, la Terrasse Trench, Bois des Tuyas; Boyau du Chevreau, to Malakoff Fme; the 59th Infantry Brig occupies the forward area.

September 23–25, 55th Field Artillery Brig and 105th Am Tn participate in the occupation of the Avocourt Sector with the 37th Division.

September 24, the command passes to the 30th Division.

September 26–October 8, 55th Field Artillery Brig and 105th Am Tn participate in the Meuse-Argonne Operation supporting the 37th and 32nd Divisions.

September 26–27, the division attacks from a line of departure between 300 and 400 in east of line between La haute Bruyère and Malakoff Fme; British 46th Division (British IX Corps) on right, 27th Division on left.

Night of September 27–28, 60th Infantry Brig relieves the 59th Infantry Brig.

September 29, division breaks through the Hindenburg Line, crosses the canal tunnel, captures Bellicourt and enters Nauroy; the Australian 5th Division, moving up to pass through the 30th Division, joins, and both divisions advance and establish a front from the intersection of Wattling Street road and canal, east and northeast to the hill south of Nauroy, Nauroy (incl.), 300 in west of the Fme du Bois du Cabaret, 800 in northeast of the Bois de Malakoff.

September 30, the command of the forward area passes to the Australian 5th Division, but units of the 30th Division that are in line participate in the operation until noon.

October 1–2, division moves to the Herbécourt and Mesnil-Bruntel Areas.

October 5, the II Corps prepares to relieve the Australian troops in the front line; division returns to the front, the 59th Infantry Brig moves to Nauroy, the 60th Infantry Brig and other units move to the Tincourt-Boucly Area.

Night of October 5–6, 59th Infantry Brig relieves the Australian 2nd Division from Montbrehain (incl.) to Beaurevoir (excl.).

October 6, 60th Infantry Brig takes position in support near Hargicourt and Bellicourt.

October 6–20, division (less Arty and 105th Sup Tn) participates in the Somme Offensive Operation.

October 7, 59th Infantry Brig attacks to realign the front.

October 8, division, assisted by tanks, the 59th Infantry Brig and one battalion 60th Infantry Brig leading, attacks northeast, captures Brancourt-le-Grand and Prémont, and reaches a line from the Fme de la Piété (incl.), to the eastern outskirts of Prémont; British 6th Division (British IX Corps) on right, British 25th Division (British XIII Corps) on left.

October 9, the 60th Infantry Brig passes through the 59th Infantry Brig and captures Busigny and Becquigny.

October 10, the division front now extends along the western outskirts of Vaux-Andigny, through La Haie-Menneresse, and St. Souplet, to St. Benin (incl.).

October 11, division occupies Vaux-Andigny, La Haie-Menneresse, and reaches the northwestern outskirts of St. Martin-Rivière; its front extends north thereof, along the west bank of La Selie River to St. Benin.

Night of October 11–12, 27th Division relieves the division, which then rests near Prémont, Brancourt-le-Grand, and Montbrehain.

October 11–November 11, 55th Field Artillery Brig and 105th Am Tn participate in occupation of the Troyon Sector supporting the 79th and 33rd Divisions.

October 12, command passes.

Night of October 15–16, division returns to line, the 59th Infantry Brig relieves the 54th Infantry Brig (27th Division) in the right sector of the II Corps from Vaux-Andigny (excl.) to ½ km west of St. Martin-Rivière; British 6th Division (British IX Corps) on right, 27th Division on left.

October 17, division attacks northeast, crosses La Selle River, captures Molain and establishes a line from ¾ km north of La Demi-lieue to l'Arbre-de-Guise (incl.).

October 18, Ribeauville is occupied.

October 19, the front now extends from Rejet-de-Beaulieu (excl.) to ¾ km southeast of la Jonquiere Fme.

Night of October 19–20, the British 1st Division relieves the division, which moves, October 20–23, to the vicinity of Tincourt-Boucly and Roisel.

October 23, division moves to the Querrieu Area for rehabilitation; training follows.

Post Armistice Activities

NOVEMBER 12, 1918–MARCH 3, 1919

November 19, the division (less Arty) moves to the American Embarkation Center, Le Mans; training follows.

December 6, 55th Field Artillery Brig and 105th Am Tn, attached to the 33rd Division, move to Mersch, Luxemburg, but on January 20 they revert to the control of the division.

February 18, 105th TM Btry sails from Brest for the United States.

Return to the United States and Demobilization

MARCH 4–MAY 7, 1919

March 4, the division moves to St. Nazaire.

March 6, 113th Field Artillery sails and other units follow in rapid succession.

March 17, DHQ leaves.

April 18, the last elements arrive at Charleston, South Carolina. The demobilization includes, at Fort Oglethorpe, April 10, Hq 55th Field Artillery Brig, April 12, Hq 59th Infantry Brig; at Camp Jackson, April 19, Hq 60th Infantry Brig, May 7, DHQ.

THE THIRTY-SECOND DIVISION, NATIONAL GUARD

The 32nd Division was organized at Camp MacArthur, Waco, Texas, and contained the National Guard of Wisconsin and Michigan. The first commander was Major General James Parker until September 19, 1917; he was succeeded by Brigadier General William G. Haan, who continued in command until the war ended. The overseas movement of the division occurred between January 19, 1918, and March 12, 1918, when the last unit reached France. This division was the only National Guard unit detailed to the army of occupation on the Rhine. This division captured 2153 prisoners. The 32nd was quiet 60 days and active 35 days. It advanced 36 kilometers. It had 2915 battle deaths and 10,477 wounded. Its total casualties were 13,392, and it had 20,140 replacements.

63rd Infantry Brigade

125th Infantry
126th Infantry
120th Machine Gun Battalion

64th Infantry Brigade

127th Infantry
128th Infantry
121st Machine Gun Battalion

57th Field Artillery Brigade

119th Field Artillery
120th Field Artillery
121st Field Artillery

Divisional Troops

107th Engineers
119th Machine Gun Battalion
107th Field Signal Battalion
Headquarters Troop

Trains

107th Train Hdqs
107th Military Police
107th Ammunition Train
107th Supply Train
107th Sanitary Train
Ambulance Cos and Field Hospitals 125–128

Record of Events

SECTORS WHERE THE THIRTY-SECOND DIVISION WAS ENGAGED IN WARFARE.

Haute-Alsace sector, Alsace, France, May 18 to July 21, 1918.
Aisne-Marne offensive, France, July 30 to August 6, 1918.
Oise-Aisne offensive, France, August 28 to September 2, 1918.
Meuse-Argonne offensive, France, September 30 to October 20, 1918.
Meuse-Argonne offensive, France, November 8 to 11, 1918.

Organization and Training in the United States

JULY 15, 1917–JANUARY 1, 1918

July 15 the National Guard of Michigan and Wisconsin is called into federal service.

July 18, the War Department designates National Guard troops of Michigan and Wisconsin to form the 32nd Division. Camp MacArthur, Waco, Texas, is selected for the training.

August 3, the War Department directs the concentration and organization of the division at Camp MacArthur.
August 4, the concentration begins.
August 5, the National Guard units of Michigan and Wisconsin are drafted into federal service.
August 25, the 57th Field Artillery Brig is organized and ultimately includes the 1st Wisconsin FA, 1st Wisconsin Cav, and detachments of the 4th Wisconsin, 6th Wisconsin, and 31st Michigan Regts of Infantry, and of Michigan Cav and FA.
August 26, Maj. Gen. James Parker assumes command.
September 8, the 64th Infantry Brig is organized and ultimately includes the 1st, 2nd, and 3rd Regts of Wisconsin Infantry and detachments of the 4th, 5th, and 6th Regts of Wisconsin Infantry.
September 11, the 63rd Infantry Brig is organized and ultimately includes the 31st, 32nd, and 33rd Regts of Michigan Infantry.
September 22–October 20, division reorganizes in accordance with the Tables of Organization of August 8, 1917.
September 29, systematic training begins.
October 26–November 3, drafts aggregating 3,000 arrive from Camp Custer, and during December an additional 1,000 come from Camps Custer and Grant. The division is about 3,500 under the authorized strength at the time of embarkation.

Movement Overseas

JANUARY 2–MARCH 12, 1918

January 2, the division moves to the ports of embarkation of Hoboken, Newport News, and New York, via Camps Merritt and Stuart. January 13, Adv Det sails from Hoboken, and lands January 24 at Brest.
January 23–February 18, a large part of the division (less Arty Regts) sails, and lands in England February 6, the 107th F Sig Bn, February 15, the 107th Sup Tn and 107th Engr Tn (which were aboard SS *Tuscania* when torpedoed on February 5 off the British coast, February 16, DHQ, February 17, 107th Am Tn; at St. Nazaire, February 6, Amb Cos 125 and 128.
February 24, 1st Bn 125th ml; at Brest, February 16, 24, March 4, the remainder of the division.
February 26 and March 4, the artillery regiments sail and land at Liverpool, March 6, 119th FA, March 12, the remainder. Troops who land in England stay a short time in rest camps and then proceed to Le Havre.

Final Training and Operations

FEBRUARY 4–NOVEMBER 11, 1918

February 4, division is designated as the Replacement Division, I Corps.

February 10, division (less Arty, Engrs, 125th, 126th, 127th Regts of Infantry, and 119th MG Bn) moves to the 10th (Prauthoy) Training Area.

February 20–June 10, division is under the administrative control of the I Corps.

February 22, 57th Field Artillery Brig and 107th Am Tn move from the base ports to Camp Coëtquidan, where the last element arrives on March 22.

February 28, 125th Infantry moves from the base ports to Is-sur-Tille and vicinity for duty with the SOS.

February 24–April 10, division (less detached units) functions as the Replacement Division, I Corps.

March 6–7 and 9, 126th Infantry 127th Infantry and 119th MG Bn move from the base ports to Bordeaux, Dijon, St. Nazaire, and Vaucouleurs for duty with the SOS.

March 12, 128th Infantry arrives in the 10th (Prauthoy) Training Area. During March the division forwards 7,000 replacements, which include all captains and privates of the 128th Infantry who join the 1st Division. In the latter part of March steps are taken to reconstitute the division as a combat unit.

March 31, the infantry and machine gun troops on duty with the SOS are ordered to rejoin.

April 10, division transfers the duties of a replacement division to the 41st Division. The division equalizes the strength of the infantry units by local transfers. Subsequent replacements received from depots raise it to approximately full strength; training follows.

May 14, division (less Arty and Engrs) moves to the vicinity of La Chapelle-sous-Rougemont in the area of the French Seventh Army.

Night of May 16–17, division (less Arty and Engrs) moves to the front.

May 20–July 19, division, affiliated with the French, participates in the occupation of the Centre Sector (Alsace). The division (less Arty, 64th Infantry Brig and 107th Engrs) is attached to the French 9th Division north of the Rhône-Rhine Canal in the La Chapelle sector, which on June 24 becomes the North Sector; the 64th Infantry Brig is attached to the French 10th Division south of the canal in the Suarce Sector, which on June 24 becomes the South Sector; the entire line runs from 1½ km northeast of Largitzen, through the Bois d'Iuirtzbach, ¼ km west of Carspach, the northern and eastern edges of the Bois de Carspacb, Eglingen, ½ km west of Ammertzwiller, ¼ km southwest of Burnhaupt-le-Bas, eastern edge of Langlittenbag, 1 km west of Aspach-le-Bas, to 1½ km north of Aspach-le-Haut.

Night of May 20–21, the leading unit enters the line; raids and patrolling follow.

June 9, 57th Field Artillery Brig (less 119th Field Artillery attached to 26th Division in Toul-Boucq Sector) and 107th Am Tn rejoin.

June 13–July 14, division is under the administrative control of the III Corps.

June 14, division assumes command of La Chapelle Sector, retaining elements of the French 9th Division.

June 25, French 53rd Division relieves French 9th Division; 107th Engrs and 119th Field Artillery rejoin.

June 30, French 151st Division relieves French 10th Division.

July 14–22, division is under the administrative control of the V Corps.

July 19, French 53rd Division relieves the division; and on July 21 the last elements of the 64th Infantry Brig leave.

July 22, division moves to the vicinity of Pont-Ste.-Maxence and Béthisy-St. Martin.

July 27–30, division is under the administrative control of the I Corps.

July 27, division proceeds to the region of Château-Thierry, and thence into the Forêt de Fère near Jaulgonne.

July 30–August 6, division participates in the Aisne-Marne Operation.

Night of July 29–30, 64th Infantry Brig relieves the 3rd division on a 1 km front north of Ronchères.

July 30, the command passes to the 32nd Division which, together with the 28th Division on left, attacks north, occupies the southwestern corner of the Bois de Cierges, advances through the eastern part of the Bois des Grimpettes and organizes along the northern edge; French 4th Division (French Ill Corps) on right, 28th Division on left.

July 31–August 3, division is under the administrative control of the III Corps.

Night of July 30–31, 63rd Infantry Brig relieves the 55th Infantry Brig (28th Division) in, and to the west of, the Bois des Grimpettes; the enemy retires to the fringe of woods north of Cierges.

July 31, division extends its front to the west by the relief of the 28th Division and holds the entire front of the French 38th Corps, which extends from the southwestern edge of the Bois de Cierges, through the eastern, northern, and western edges of the Bois des Grimpettes, to southeast of Moulin Caranda; it attacks, brigades abreast, and captures Cierges; 42nd Division (I Corps) on left.

August 1, division clears les Jomblets and the woods to the east thereof.

Night of August 1–2, the enemy begins to retire to the Vesle River, and, August 2, the division resumes the advance and reaches le Mouline Ray 1 km north of Cohan, Dravegny, and Bois Chenet.

August 3, division advances to a line from St. Gilles to Mont–St. Martin (both incl.); 4th Division (I Corps) on left.

August 4, III Corps relieves the French 38th Corps and assumes command of the corps sector; division enters Fismes and reaches a front extending from Tir, through Fismes, Tannerie, Bois du Larribonnet (incl.), to northeast of Villesavoye; the enemy holds the line of the Vesle River in force.

August 5–6, division captures Fismes; 6th Infantry Brig (3rd Division) on right; the Aisne-Marne Operation merges into sector occupation.

August 7, division (less Arty and Engrs) participates in the occupation of the Fismes Sector (Champagne). The 28th Division relieves the division (less Arty and Engrs), which then passes to the corps reserve and to stations between Dravegny and Cierges; training follows.

August 7–11, 107th Engrs participate in the occupation of the Fismes and Vesle Sectors with the 3rd and 28th Divisions.

August 7–17, 57th Field Artillery Brig and 107th Am Tn participate in the occupation of the Fismes Sector, supporting the 28th Division until August 12, and then the 77th Division, August 13–17.

August 11, 64th Infantry Brig, is at the disposal of the French 164th Division (III Corps), as division reserve, and moves to the Bois de Reims and Bois de Vézilly.

August 18–24, 57th Field Artillery Brig and 107th Am Tn participate in the Oise-Aisne Operation, where two regiments support the 77th Division, and one regiment forms part of the III Corps artillery.

August 24, 57th Field Artillery Brig and 107th Am Tn revert to the control of the division; division moves to the vicinity of Pierrefonds and Hautefontaine.

Night of August 26–27, division moves to the vicinity of Tartiers and passes to the reserve of the French 30th Corps.

Night of August 27–28, division relieves the French 127th Division west of Juvigny from 2 km northwest of Chavigny to 2 km east of Bagneux, establishes its right along the Chaussée-Brunehaut, and places its left east of the Bois de la Domaine.

August 28, division assumes command and attacks, 63rd Infantry Brig leading, in conjunction with the French 59th Division (French I Corps) on the right; the right approaches the railroad leading north from Chavigny; French 64th Division on left.

August 28–September 2, division participates in the Oise-Aisne Operation.

August 29, French Tenth Army advances; the division attacks east and advances its left to within 1 km of Juvigny; French 66th Division (French 30th Corps) on left.

August 30, division resumes the attack, 64th Infantry Brig leading, cleans the Bois du Couronné and occupies Juvigny.

August 31–September 2, division again attacks and reaches the line, Beaumont Fme, the Râpcrie, Route Nationale No. 37.

September 2, 1st Moroccan Division relieves the division (less Arty which remains in line supporting 1st Moroccan Division until September 6), and the latter passes to corps reserve and moves to the vicinity of Tartiers and Bieuxy.

September 6, division moves to the Attichy-Hautefontaine Area, where it passes to army reserve; 57th Field Artillery Brig and 107th Am Tn revert to the control of the division.

September 9, division moves to the vicinity of Joinvile; training follows.

September 17, 57th Field Artillery Brig and 107th Am Tn move from Joinvile to the vicinity of Dombasle-en-Argonne and Jouy-en-Argonne, where, September 22–25, they are attached to the 79th Division in the Avocourt Sector.

September 22, division (less Arty) moves to the vicinity of Autrécourt and Lavoye, where, September 24, it passes to corps reserve.

Night of September 25–26, division (less Arty) moves, via Brabanten-Argonne, to the Forêt de Hesse.

September 26–29, division (less Arty) remains in the Forêt de Hesse in corps reserve.

September 26–October 6, 57th Field Artillery Brig and 107th Am Tn participate in the Meuse-Argonne Operation supporting the 79th Division until September 30, and thereafter the 3rd Division.

September 26–November 11, division participates in Meuse-Argonne Operation.

September 30–October 1, division (less Arty) relieves the 37th Division from the Bois de Beuge, Hill 254, Fme de Brisegueule as far as la Grange-aux-Bois Fme.

October 1, division (less Arty) advances, 63rd Infantry Brig leading, occupies Cierges, and establishes connection with the 91st Division on the left at la Grange-aux-Bois Fme; 3rd Division on right.

Night of October 3–4, a readjustment of the corps' front extends the division sector to the west, and the new front extends from Cierges (excl.), through la Grange-aux-Bois Fme, the northern edge of the Bois Communal de Cierges, the northern edge of the Bois Communal de Baulny, to Tronsol Fme; the 64th Infantry Brig relieves the 91st Division west of la Grange-aux-Bois Fme; the 3rd Division relieves elements of the 32nd Division in, and east of, Cierges.

October 4, division (less Arty), cooperating with the 1st Division (I Corps), attacks toward Gesnes, and establishes a line from the crossroads 1¼ km east of Gesnes, through Gesnes (excl.), to Tronsl Fme (incl.); 3rd Division on right, 1st Division on left.

October 5, division continues the attack, captures the Bois de la Morine and Bois du Chêne-Sec, and enters Gesnes.

October 6, 57th Field Artillery Brig and 107th Am Tn revert to the division.

October 8–9, in a change of boundaries, the division gains one km from the 3rd Division on the right and relinquishes that part of the front which extends from Gesnes (excl.) along northern edge of the Bois du Chêne-Sec (incl.), to the Rau du Gouffre; 181st Infantry Brig (91st Division), attached to the 1st Division, on the left.

October 9, division attacks, 63rd Infantry Brig leading, reaches Mainelle Trench, and occupies the line from ¾ km southeast and ½ km south of Romagne-sous-Montfaucon, through the Bois de Valoup, to ¾ km northwest of Gesnes.

October 10, division clears the enemy from the vicinity of the Fme du Transvaal, reaching Côte Dame-Marie; 181st Infantry Brig is attached.

October 12, division relieves the 181st Infantry Brig along the northern edge of the Bois de Romagne from ½ km northwest of Fme du Transvaal to ½ km south of la Musarde Fme; 42nd Division on left.

October 13, the sector is reduced by moving the western boundary to ½ km northwest of Fme du Transvaal, the 42nd Division making the relief.

October 14, division attacks north, captures Romagne-sous-Montfaucon, Côte Dame-Marie, the eastern portion of the Bois de Gesnes, and reaches a line from the northern outskirts of Roinagne-sous-Montfaucon, a point ½ km south of Hill 264, 1 km east of Tuilerie Fme, to ½ km northwest of Hill 286 in the Bois de Gesnes; 5th Division (III Corps) on right.

October 15–16, the attack continues and the division occupies the Bois de Chauvignon and the eastern part of Bois de Romagne.

October 17–19, division enters the Bois de Bantheville, and holds a line from ½ km north of Romagne-sous-Montfaucon, east of, and along the northern edge of the Bois de Chauvignon, eastern edge of the Bois de Bantheville, an east and west line through the Bois de Bantheville 1 km north of Hill 262, western edge of the Bois de Bantheville, to 1 km north of la Tuilerie Fme.

October 20, 89th Division relieves the division, except the artillery, which supports the 89th Division until November 1, when it reverts to the 32nd Division.

October 21–November 8, division (less Arty) is in corps reserve (with the V Corps to October 27, and the III Corps thereafter) in the Bois de

Cheppy, Bois de Very, and western part of the Bois de Montfaucon; rehabilitation and training follow.

Night of November 2–3, division (less Arty) moves to the vicinity of Romagne-sous Montfaucon.

Night of November 3–4, division (less Arty) moves to the Bois des Rappes and Bois de la Pultière.

November 6–8, 128th Infantry, attached to the 5th Division, enters the line in the Bois de Fontaines, advances on the right flank of the 5th Division, and, on November 8, occupies Brandeville.

November 8–11, 57th Field Artillery Brig and 107th Am Tn participate in Meuse-Argonne Operation near Brocourt as part of the army artillery of the First Army.

November 9, 128th Infantry reverts to the division, and the leading elements of the regiment relieve units of the French 15th Colonial Division at Peuvillers and 1½ kin east of Bréhéville.

Night of November 9–10, the remainder of the division crosses the Meuse; the 127th Infantry enters line east of Bréhéville and relieves part of the 128th Infantry.

November 10, division (less Arty) pursues, 64th Infantry Brig leading, advances so that part of the 128th Infantry reaches a line from the Bois Dombras to the Côte du Mont but later withdraws; division finally holds a line from ¾ km south of Peuvillers, along the road from Damvillers to Jametz, the southwestern edge of the Bois Demange, the woods west of Thinte Rau, to 2¼ km south of Jametz; French 15th Colonial Division on right, 5th Division on left.

Post Armistice Activities

NOVEMBER 12, 1918–APRIL 17, 1919

November 12–16, the division (less Arty) bivouacs near Ecurey and Haraumont, outposts the armistice line, and prepares to march to the Rhine.

November 14, elements relieve the 5th Division on the line, Jametz, Rémoiville, Louppy (incl.). Current activities include the enforcement of armistice terms, salvage, and training.

November 17, the division (less Arty) moves via Marville, Petange (Luxemburg), Consdorf, Welschbillig (Germany), Daun, Mayen, Ochtendung, Bassenheim and Sayn.

November 17–December 13, advance into Germany.

December 14–April 17, division (less Arty) forms part of the Army of Occupation in Germany. The division (less Arty) moves to the vicinity of

Dierdorf and Rengsdorf in the Coblenz Bridgehead where training continues.

January 25, 107th Am Tn rejoins.

Return to the United States and Demobilization

APRIL 18–MAY 23, 1919

April 18, the division (less Arty) moves to Brest, where the 57th Field Artillery Brig rejoins.

April 20, the leading element, 107th TM Btry, sails.

April 25, Hq 57th Field Artillery Brig and Hq 64th Infantry Brig sail, followed on April 27 by DHQ.

May 22, the last elements, detachments of the 125th and 126th Infantry, arrive at New York. The demobilization includes, at Camp Devens, May 7, Hq 57th Field Artillery Brig; at Camp Grant, May 17, Hq 64th Infantry Brig; at Camp Custer, May 23, DHQ and Hq 63rd Infantry Brig.

THE THIRTY-THIRD DIVISION, NATIONAL GUARD

The 33rd Division was organized at Camp Logan, Houston, Texas, in August 1917 from the Illinois National Guard. It was commanded by Major General George Bell, Jr. The complete Division arrived in France June 11, 1918. It captured 3987 prisoners. It was quiet 32 days and active 27 days. It advanced 36 kilometers. Its total casualties were 7255. It had 989 battle deaths and 6266 wounded. This division received 20,140 replacements.

65th Infantry Brigade

129th Infantry
130th Infantry
123rd Machine Gun Battalion

66th Infantry Brigade

131st Infantry
132nd Infantry
124th Machine Gun Battalion

58th Field Artillery Brigade

122nd Field Artillery
123rd Field Artillery
124th Field Artillery

Divisional Troops

108th Engineers
122nd Machine Gun Battalion
108th Field Signal Battalion
Headquarters Troop

Trains

108th Train Hdqs
108th Military Police
108th Ammunition Train
108th Supply Train
108th Engineer Train
108th Sanitary Train
Ambulance Cos and Field Hospitals 129–132

Record of Events

SECTORS WHERE THE THIRTY-THIRD DIVISION WAS ENGAGED IN WARFARE

Amiens sector, France, July 1 to August 7, 1918.
Somme offensive, France, August 8 to 20, 1918.
Verdun sector, France, September 10 to 25, 1918.
Meuse-Argonne offensive, France, September 24 to October 21, 1918.
Meuse-Argonne offensive, France, October 26 to November 11, 1918.

Organization and Training in the United States

JULY 18, 1917–APRIL 30, 1918

July 18, the War Department designates National Guard troops of Illinois to form the 33rd Division. Camp Logan, Houston, Texas, is selected for training.

July 25, the National Guard of Illinois is called into federal service.

August 3, the War Department directs the concentration and organization of the division at Camp Logan.

August 5, the National Guard of Illinois is drafted into federal service. During August the concentration begins.

August 24, the 65th Infantry Brig is organized and ultimately includes the 3rd and 4th Regts of Illinois Infantry and a detachment of the 5th Illinois Infantry.

August 25, Maj. Gen. George Bell, Jr., assumes command.

September 10, the 58th Field Artillery Brig is organized and ultimately includes the 2nd and 3rd Regts of Illinois Field Artillery and the 6th Ill Infantry.

September 11, the 66th Infantry Brig is organized and ultimately includes the 1st and 2nd Regts of Illinois Infantry and detachments of the 5th and 7th Regts of Illinois Infantry.

September 22, Division is reorganized in accordance with the Tables of Organization of August 8, 1917.

October 1–April 30, systematic training is conducted.

October 25–November 14, transfers of 5,600 National Army men arrive from the 86th Division, Camp Grant, and 1,000 from the 88th Division, Camp Dodge.

April 5–29, 7,000 National Army men from the 84th, 86th, and 88th Divisions at Camp Taylor, Grant, and Dodge, respectively, complete the division.

Movement Overseas

April 23–June 15, 1918

April 23, 108th Engrs and Tn leave for Camp Merritt.

May 1, the leading infantry units leave for Camp Upton.

May 8, Adv Det and 108th Engrs and Tn sail from Hoboken, arriving, May 18 at Brest.

May 10–22, DHQ, the infantry, 108th Sup Tn, and 108th Tn Eq and MP sail, and the majority arrive May 23–24 and 30 at Brest, others at Bordeaux.

May 26–June 5, 58th Field Artillery Brig and remaining units sail, arriving June 8–15 at Liverpool.

Final Training and Operations

May 25–November 11, 1918

May 24–August 25, division is under the administrative control of the II Corps.

May 25, DHQ, the infantry except part of 129th Infantry, the 108th Engrs and Tn, and 108th Tn Eq and MP move from Brest to the Martainneville and Huppy Training Areas, and, on June 9, to the Eu Training Area for training.

May 25–August 23, training with the British in Picardy.

June 13, 58th Field Artillery Brig and 108th Am Tn arrive from England, via Le Havre, and go to the artillery training areas of Le Valdahon and Ornans for training.

June 14, 108th F Sig Bn rejoins.

June 21, division (less 58th Field Artillery Brig, 108th Engrs, and the trains) moves toward Amiens to the Long and Martainneville Areas.

July 4, Cos C and E, 131st Infantry, and Cos A and G, 132nd Infantry, affiliated with the Australian 4th Division, take part in the attack which captures Hamel and the high ground beyond.

July 5, the detached companies rejoin.

July 17, the 65th Infantry Brig joins the Australian Corps and the 66th Infantry Brig joins the British III Corps on a front that extends from Villers-Bretonneux through Hamel and Ville-sur-Ancre to Bouzincourt. Troops enter the line successively by platoon, battalion, and regiment.

Night of July 17–18, the leading elements of the 66th Infantry Brig enter the front line near Albert, and on the night of July 27–28 the leading elements of the 65th Infantry Brig enter near Villers-Bretonheux.

July 17–August 7, division (less Arty and divisional troops) participates in the occupation of the Amiens Sector (Picardy).

August 6, 65th Infantry Brig passes from the Australian Corps to the Br III Corps, and moves to the vicinity of Allonville.

August 8–21, division (less Arty and 108th Sup Tn) participates in the Somme Offensive Operation.

August 9–10, 131st Infantry, attached to and on the right of the British 58th Division, takes part in the attack by the British III Corps between the Somme and the Ancre Rivers, and clears Chipilly Ridge and Gressaire Wood.

August 12, 131st Infantry and Australian 13th Brig form the liaison force north of the Somme; the 132nd Infantry, arriving near Harbonnières, replaces the Australian 13th Brig and operates as the reserve of the Australian 4th Division.

August 13, troops of the 131st Infantry participate in the capture of Etinehem Spur by the Australian 13th Brig.

August 13–20, 131st Infantry occupies the right sector along the eastern slope of Etinehem Spur from ¾ km southwest of the Bois du Canal to 1 km west of La Neuville-lès-Bray.

Night of August 23–24, division — after the four infantry regiments, including the 129th Infantry from the British III Corps in the vicinity of Albert north of Ancre River, having been relieved — begins to entrain to join the First Army; it moves to Tronville-en-Barrois and the vicinity; training follows.

August 26–September 11, 58th Field Artillery Brig and 108th Am Tn participate in the occupation of the Lucey (Ansauville) Sector, in support of the 89th and 1st Divisions.

September 2, 108th Sup Tn rejoins.

September 3, 52nd Field Artillery Brig (27th Division), attached to the 33rd Division, begins to arrive.

September 5–8, division moves to a sector north of Verdun-sur-Meuse.

Night of September 7–8, 129th Infantry relieves the 372nd Infantry (French 157th Division) in Subsector 304 between Haucourt and Béthincourt.

Nights of September 8–9 and 9–10, the 132nd Infantry relieves parts of the French 120th Division in the adjacent sector, extending the front to the Meuse opposite Samogneux.

September 10, command of the sector, which extends from the Meuse opposite Samogneux to Haucourt, passes to the 33rd Division; French 18th Division (French 17th Corps) on right, French 157th Division (French 17th Corps) on left.

September 10–14, division is under the administrative control of the III Corps.

September 10–25, division (less Arty) occupies the Verdun-Fromeréville Sector (Lorraine).

September 12, the attached divisional artillery participates in a demonstration fire to cover the attack on the St. Mihiel salient.

September 12–15, 58th Field Artillery Brig and 108th Am Tn participate in the St. Mihiel Operation in support of the 1st Division.

Night of September 21–22, elements of the 4th Division and one battalion of the 80th Division relieve two battalions in the front line where they function under the 33rd Division.

September 23–Night of September 25–26, division holds the front line of the III Corps; units of division, under 79th Division command, hold V Corps' front from Haucourt to 1½ km west of Avocourt.

September 26, the sector occupation merges into the Meuse-Argonne Operation. The division, on the right of the III Corps, 66th Infantry Brig leading, attacks from the line of departure of Bois Trench (north of Regneville), Mary Trench (south of Forges), and Massin Trench (1½ km north of le Mort-Homme), captures Forges, the Bois de Forges and Gercourt-et-Drillancourt, and reaches the Meuse from 1 km north of Forges to Laiterie de Belhaine; French 18th Division on right, 80th Division on left. It then organizes and holds the line of the Meuse until it vacates the right sector, south of Côte des Grands-Prés, on October 7, and the left sector, north of Côte des Grands-Prés, on October 9.

September 26–October 15, 58th Field Artillery Brig and 108th Am Tn participate in the Meuse-Argonne Operation, where they support the 91st Division until October 4 and then the 32nd Division until October 11.

September 26–October 21, division participates in the Meuse-Argonne Operation.

September 29, the front is extended along the left bank of the Meuse from Laiterie de Belhaine to the Bois de la Côte Lémont (incl.), when the 65th Infantry Brig relieves the 80th Division; 4th Division on left.

Night of October 6–7, 3rd Bn and MG Co 132nd Infantry relieve elements of the 4th Division in the Bois de Fays.

October 7, division (less units attached to the 4th Division) passes to the tactical control of the French 17th Corps, which is operating east of the Meuse, and assembles three battalions in the Bois de Forges preparatory to crossing this river.

October 8, two battalions of the 132nd Infantry cross the Meuse at Brabant-sur-Meuse, move north-northwest in contact with the French 18th Division, of which the 58th Infantry Brig (29th Division) forms the left half, and reach a line from ½ km north of the Fme de Regivaux, along the southern edge of the Bois de Chaume, to the northern outskirts of Consenvoye; one battalion of the 131st Infantry crosses the Meuse south of Consenvoye in support of troops of the 132nd Infantry.

October 9, one battalion of the 129th Infantry crosses the Meuse at Consenvoye.

Night of October 9–10, the remaining infantry units, except two machine gun companies, one machine gun battalion, and four infantry battalions, cross to the east bank, where they all pass to the 66th Infantry Brig.

October 10, division attacks and reaches a line, ½ km northwest of Hill 382 in the Bois Plat-Chêne, ¼ km south of Magenta Fme, along the ridge to Dans-les-Vaux, ½ km north of Hill 316, the Route Nationale No. 64 east of Vanne.

October 12, a new line of resistance south of the front line is organized.

October 13, division evacuates the old front line and occupies the new line that extends east and west through the Bois Plat-Chêne and to the north of Hill 316 in the Bois de Cliaume; units detached with the 4th Division rejoin.

October 16, division makes a slight advance in Bois Plat-Chêne.

Nights October 18–19, 19–20, and 20–21, French 15th Colonial Division relieves the division.

October 23, division rests near Sommedieue, Dieue-sur-Meuse, and Rambluzin-et-Benoitevaux.

October 24, division begins the relief of the 79th Division from Doncourt-aux-Teinpliers (excl.) to Fresnes-en-Woëvre (incl.); the 52nd Field Artillery Brig passes to the 79th Division and the 55th Field Artillery Brig (79th Division) to the 33rd Division.

October 24–November 11, 58th Field Artillery Brig and 108th Am Tn support the 89th Division in the Meuse-Argonne Operation.

October 26–November 11, division (less Arty) occupies the Troyon Sector (Lorraine).

October 26, the division assumes command of the Troyon Sector extending from Doncourt-aux-Teinpliers (excl.) to Fresnes-enWoëvre (incl.); French 39th Division on right, 35th Division (French 33rd Corps) on left.

October 29, the sector is extended east to the northern edge of le Rebois wood, by relief of elements of French 39th Division; 28th Division (IV Corps) on right; local actions follow.

November 7, 81st Division (French II Cl Corps) is on the left.

November 9–10, division occupies la Vachère Bois, Bois les Hautes-Epines, Bois de Wavrile, and St. Hilaire.

November 11, division advances its left to Marchéville, Riaville, and the crossroads 1½ km north-northeast of Fresnes-en-Woëvre.

Post Armistice Activities

NOVEMBER 12, 1918–APRIL 24, 1919

November 12–December 6, the division engages in the enforcement of armistice terms, salvage, and training.

December 7–16, division moves to the vicinity of Saarburg, Germany

December 7–April 24, Occupation of Grand Duchy of Luxemburg.

December 17–20, division proceeds to the Diekirch Area in the northern part of Luxemburg.

January 8, 55th Field Artillery Brig reverts to the 30th Division; 58th Field Artillery Brig and 108th Am Tn rejoin.

March 1, 108th TM Btry sails from St. Nazaire for the United States.

Return to the United States and Demobilization

APRIL 25–JUNE 8, 1919

April 25–May 5, the division moves to Brest.

May 9, DHQ, 132nd Inf, 122nd and 124th MG Bns sail, arriving, May 17, at Hoboken.

May 27, the last units arrive at Hoboken. The demobilization at Camp

Grant includes, May 28, Hq 65th Infantry Brig, June 5, Eq 66th Infantry Brig, June 6, DHQ, June 8, Eq 58th Field Artillery Brig.

THE THIRTY-FIFTH DIVISION, NATIONAL GUARD

The 35th Division was organized at Fort Sill, Oklahoma, from the Missouri and Kansas National Guards. The division was commanded by Major General William M. Wright from its organization until June 15, 1918, when he was succeeded by Major General Peter M. Traub. The movement overseas commenced April 25, 1918, and the division arrived in France via England on May 11, 1918. The 35th Division captured 781 prisoners. It was quiet 92 days and active 5. It advanced 12½ kilometers. It suffered 7283 casualties, had 1067 battle deaths and 6216 wounded. It received 10,605 replacements.

69th Infantry Brigade

137th Infantry
138th Infantry
129th Machine Gun Battalion

70th Infantry Brigade

139th Infantry
140th Infantry
130th Machine Gun Battalion

60th Artillery Brigade

128th Field Artillery
129th Field Artillery
130th Field Artillery
110th Trench Mortar Battery

Divisional Troops

110th Engineers
128th Machine Gun Battalion
110th Field Signal Battalion

Trains

110th Train Hdqs
110th Military Police
110th Ammunition Train
110th Supply Train
110th Engineer Train
110th Sanitary Train
Ambulance Cos and Field Hospitals 137–140

Record of Events

SECTORS WHERE THE THIRTY-FIFTH DIVISION WAS ENGAGED IN WARFARE

Gerardmer sector, France, July 8 to September 2, 1918.
Meuse-Argonne offensive, France, September 26 to October 1, 1918.
Meuse-Argonne offensive, France, October 15 to November 7, 1918.

Organization and Training in the United States

JULY 18, 1917–APRIL 12, 1918

July 18, the War Department designates National Guard troops of Kansas and Missouri to form the 35th Division. Camp Doniphan, Fort Sill, Oklahoma, is selected for training.

August 3, the War Department directs the concentration and organization of the Division at Camp Doniphan.

August 5, the National Guards of Kansas and Missouri are drafted into federal service.

August 23, the concentration of the division at Camp Doniphan begins.

August 25, Maj. Gen. William M. Wright assumes command of the division; the 69th Infantry Brig is organized and ultimately includes the 1st and 2nd Kansas and the 1st and 5th Missouri Regts of Infantry, and a detachment of the 2nd Missouri Infantry.

September 8, systematic training begins.

September 13, division is reorganized in accordance with the Tables of Organization of August 8, 1917.

September 18, the 70th Infantry Brig is organized and ultimately includes the 3rd, 4th, and 6th Missouri and 3rd Kansas Regts of Infantry and a detachment of the 2nd Missouri Infantry.

September 22, the 60th Field Artillery Brig is organized and ultimately includes the 1st and 2nd Missouri and 1st Kansas Regts of Field Artillery and detachments of the 2nd Missouri Infantry and of Missouri Cav.

October 22, a draft of 3,000, the majority from Kansas and Missouri, joins from Camp Funston. During October the concentration and reorganization is completed.

October 31, the strength is 26,000. During the spring additional selective service men arrive from Camps Funston and Travis and Fort Leavenworth.

Movement Overseas

APRIL 3–JUNE 11, 1918

April 3, the division moves via Camps Merritt and Mills to the ports of embarkation of Brooklyn, Hoboken, New York, and Philadelphia.

April 13, 69th Infantry Brig moves to Camp Mills. Early in May the engineers and artillery leave for Camps Merritt and Mills, respectively. While at Camp Mills the division receives 2,000 replacements and reaches its full strength.

April 16, Adv Det sails from New York, arriving April 28 at Liverpool.

April 22–May 7, DHQ and the infantry sails, and arrives May 7–16 at Liverpool, except Co F, 138th Infantry, which lands May 25 at London.

May 2, 110th Engrs and Tn sail and arrive May 10 at Brest. **May 19, 20, and 27,** the 60th Field Artillery Brig, 110th Am Tn, 110th Sn Tn, 110th Sup Tn, and 110th F Sig Bn sail; the 128th and 129th Field Artillery arrive June 5 at London, the remainder, May 31 and June 8, at Liverpool, and complete the movement of the division. Troops which land in England stay a short time in rest camps and then proceed via Southampton to Le Havre.

Final Training and Operations

MAY 12–NOVEMBER 11, 1918

May 11–June 8, division is under the administrative control of the II Corps.

May 12, division (less Arty, 110th F Sig Bn, and certain trains) moves from Le Havre to the Gamaches Training Area near Eu, where, May 20–June 5, it trains with the British 30th Division under control of the British 19th Corps.

May 12–June 8, training with the British in Picardy.

June 6, division (less detachments) moves from the area of the British Fourth Army to entraining stations in the Neufchâtel Area, and, on June 8, to the Arches Training Area, southeast of Epinal, where all the detached units, except the artillery, rejoin.

June 9–September 2, training with the French in Alsace.

June 11, 60th Field Artillery Brig and 110th Am Tn move from Le Havre to Angers and the vicinity for training.

June 13–July 13, division is under the administrative control of the III Corps.

June 18, a part of the division moves to the Wesserling Area, and the leading elements of the 69th Infantry Brig follow the next day.

June 20, the leading elements of the 69th Inf Brig enter the line which extends from 1 km north of Aspach-le-Haut to Röspel-Wald.

June 20–July 26, elements of the division, affiliated with the French 22nd Division, participate in the occupation of the Wesserling Sector (Alsace).

July 4, the 69th Infantry Brig completes the move and occupies the Benoit, Robinson, De Galbert, and Collette Subsectors.

July 8, 60th Field Artillery Brig and 110th Am Tn move to Camp Coëtquidan and continue training until August 10.

July 14, 69th Infantry Brig assumes command of the Wesserling Sector; the remainder of the division moves from the vicinity of Arches to the Wesserling Area.

July 14–August 19, division is under the administrative control of the V Corps.

July 23, 70th Infantry Brig relieves the 69th Infantry Brig, which goes to a training area near Cornimont.

July 27, the command of the Fecht Sector from 1 km east of Lao du Ballon to Röspel-Wald passes from the French 22nd Division to the 35th Div; the 70th Infantry Brig and certain French units are in the line; the 69th Infantry Brig is in corps reserve; the Thur Sector (southern half of the Wesserling Sector) passes to the French 22nd Division.

July 27–August 13, division (less Arty) occupies the Fecht Sector (northern half of the Wesserling Sector, Alsace).

August 11, 69th Infantry Brig moves into a sector immediately north of the Wesserling Sector and the new division front extends from the vicinity of Muhlbach to ½ km west of Faing.

August 14, the command passes to the division, French 80th Territorial Infantry attached, which holds the front with brigades abreast from Lauch Creek to Weiss Creek along a line from 1 km west of Sengeren, through Breitstein, ½ km east of Metzeral, Röspel-Wald, ¾ km north of Stosswihr, le Linge, Noirinont Fme, to 1¼ km southwest of Orbey, and which is now called the Gérardmer Sector; local actions follow.

August 14–September 2, division occupies the Cêrardmer Sector (southern part of the Anould Sector, Alsace).

August 15, 60th Field Artillery Brig and 110th Am Tn rejoin.

August 19–September 4, division is under the administrative control of the VII Corps.

August 27, division is assigned to the I Corps. The 60th Field Artillery Brig assumes control of the artillery in the Gérardmer Sector.

September 2, 6th and French 131st Divisions relieve the division; command passes to latter; division moves to Corcienx and the vicinity.

September 4, division moves near Rosières-aux-Salines in the area of the French Eighth Army.

September 10, division moves to the area of the First Army and takes station in the Forêt de Haye, where it remains in army reserve during the St. Mihiel Operation.

September 15, division moves to the vicinity of Charmontois-le-Roi.

September 19–20, 69th Infantry Brig moves to the vicinity of Clermont-en-Argonne.

Night of September 20–21, the remainder of the division moves into the woods to the west and south of Grange-le-Comte Fme, where it enters the Grange-le-Comte Sector; 69th Infantry Brig relieves the French 73rd Division, except the troops in the outpost area, which remain until the night of September 25–26.

September 21–25, division occupies the Grange-le-Comte Sector (Lorraine). The front extends from southeast of Vauquois (hill), north of la Cigalerie Fme, and over Hill 253 to ½ km southeast of Boureuilles; 91st Division (V Corps) on right, 28th Division on left.

Night of September 25–26, the division relieves the outpost of the French 73rd Division.

September 26–October 1, division participates in the Meuse-Argonne Operation.

September 26, division, on the right of the I Corps, 69th Infantry Brig and one battalion 70th Infantry Brig, attached, leading, attacks north, captures Cheppy, clears that part of Varennes east of the Aire River, and establishes a line from ½ km northwest of Very to the Aire River east of La Forge.

September 27–28, division continues the attack, 70th Infantry Brig in line, 69th Infantry Brig in support, and captures Charpentry, Baulny, and Chaudron Fme on the first day.

September 28, it captures Montrebeau Wood and reaches a line from 1 km northeast of Chaudron Fme, along the northern and western limits of Montrebeau Wood, to l'Espérance.

September 29, division attacks, reaches Exermont and captures the Fme de Beauregard and la Neuville-le-Comte Fme, north of Exermont Creek, but during the afternoon enemy counterattacks north of Exermont Creek, reaches the southern edge of Montrebeau Wood, and causes the division to withdraw to a prepared position on the ridge northeast of Baulny.

September 30, division organizes the line for defense from 1 km northwest of Sérieuz Fme, toward Chaudron Fme, along the ridge north of Baulny, to the Aire River; 91st Division on the right holds a line within the sector of the 35th Division from a point near the road ½ km northwest of Sérieux Fme to the western edge of the Bois Communal de Baulny; 327th Infantry (82nd Div) attached to the 28th Division on the left.

October 1, 1st Division relieves the division, which assembles in the Véry-Cheppy Area.

October 2–3, division assembles in the Bois de Beaulieu, south of Clermont-en-Argonne, and on October 4 moves to the vicinity of Vavinçourt.

October 5–11, rehabilitation.

October 12, division moves to the Sornmedieue Area in the zone of the French 33rd Corps east of the Meuse.

Night of October 14–15, division relieves the French 15th Colonial Division on the front from Bonzée-en-Woëvre, through Haudiomont, Watronville, Moulainvile-la-Basse, 1 km east of Eix, to Daniloup (excl.); 139th Infantry is in corps reserve; 79th Division (French II Colonial Corps, Second Army) on right, French 10th Colonial Division on left. October 24, 139th Infantry relieves units of the French 10th Colonial Division on the front from Damloup to Vaux Creek.

October 15–November 7, division participates in the Meuse-Argonne Operation.

October 26, division extends its front to the north to include the Ravin du Pré; patrolling follows.

November 7, 81st Division relieves the division, except the Arty, which remains in line until November 11, and the division then moves to the St. Mihiel Area via the Chainnont-sur-Aire Area.

Post Armistice Activities

NOVEMBER 12, 1918–MARCH 5, 1919

November 13–December 6, the division engages in the enforcement of armistice terms, salvage, and training.

December 7, division (less Arty) moves to the Commercy Area and training follows.

January 22, the artillery, stationed in the Resson Area, rejoins.

February 8, 110th Engrs and Tn move to Brest for duty with the SOS.

Return to the United States and Demobilization

MARCH 6–MAY 14, 1919

March 6–10, the division entrains for the American Embarkation Center, Le Mans.

March 29, division moves to the ports of embarkation; the 60th Field Artillery Brig, 110th Am Tn, and 137th Infantry proceed to Brest, the remaining units to St. Nazaire.

April 6, the leading unit, 110th Sn Tn, sails.

April 7, DHQ sails.

April 11, 110th Engrs and Tn sail from Brest.

April 30, the last element, 110th TM Btry, arrives at Philadelphia. The demobilization includes, at Camp Pike, April 29, Eq 60th Field Artillery Brig, at Camp Funston, May 8, Eq 69th Infantry Brig, May 13, Eq 70th Infantry Brig, May 14, DHQ.

THE THIRTY-SIXTH DIVISION, NATIONAL GUARD

The 36th Division was organized at Camp Bowie, Texas, from the National Guards of Oklahoma and Texas. Major General John E. St. John Greble organized the division and was succeeded by Major William R. Smith, who continued in command throughout the war. The overseas movement which began on July 18, 1918, was concluded on July 30, when the division landed in France and was ordered to Bar-sur-aube for training. The division captured 549 prisoners and was active 23 days. It advanced 21 kilometers. It had 2528 casualties, including 600 battle deaths and 1928 wounded. The Division had 3397 replacements.

71st Infantry Brigade

141st Infantry
142nd Infantry
132nd Machine Gun Battalion

72nd Infantry Brigade

143rd Infantry
144th Infantry
133rd Machine Gun Battalion

61st Field Artillery Brigade
131st Field Artillery
132nd Field Artillery
133rd Field Artillery
111th Trench Mortar Battery

Divisional Troops
111th Engineers
131st Machine Gun Battalion
111th Field Signal Battalion

Trains
111th Train Hdqs
111th Military Police
111th Ammunition Train
111th Supply Train
111th Engineer Train
111th Sanitary Train
Ambulance Cos and Field Hospitals 141–144

Record of Events

SECTORS WHERE THE THIRTY-SIXTH DIVISION WAS ENGAGED IN WARFARE

Gerardmer sector, France, July 8 to September 2, 1918.
Meuse-Argonne offensive, France, September 26 to October 1, 1918.
Meuse-Argonne offensive, France, October 7 to November 11, 1918 (111th Eng).

Organization and Training in the United States

JULY 18, 1917–JULY 7, 1918

July 18, the War Department designates National Guard troops of Oklahoma and Texas to form the 36th Division. Camp Bowie, Fort Worth, Texas, is selected for the training.

August 3, the War Department directs the concentration and organization of the division at Camp Bowie.

August 5, the National Guard units of Oklahoma and Texas are drafted into federal service.

August 17, the concentration of the division at Camp Bowie begins.

August 23, Maj. Gen. Edwin St. J. Greble assumes command.

August 25, the 61st Field Artillery Brig is organized and ultimately includes the 1st and 2nd Regts of Texas Field Artillery and a detachment of the 1st Texas Cav.

August 29, the 71st Infantry Brig is organized and ultimately includes the 1st, 2nd, and 7th Regts of Texas Infantry and 1st Oklahoma Infantry (less MG Co and Band).

September 1, the 72nd Infantry Brig is organized and ultimately includes the 5th and 6th Regts of Texas Infantry, the 3rd and 4th Regts of Texas Infantry (less MG Cos and Bands) and detachments of the 1st Texas Cav.

October 1–July 7, systematic training is conducted.

October 15, division reorganizes in accordance with the Tables of Organization of August 8, 1917. During November the division reaches a strength of 25,000. In the spring drafts aggregating 4,000 replace losses.

Movement Overseas

JULY 8–AUGUST 12, 1918

July 8, the division moves to the ports of embarkation of Halifax, Hoboken, and Newport News, via Camp Mills, except the 143rd Infantry, which proceeds directly to Newport News.

July 15, Adv Det sails from Hoboken and arrives July 22 at Brest.

July 18, DHQ, the majority of the infantry, and part of the divisional troops sail, and arrive July 30 in France.

July 26–27, the remainder of the infantry and divisional troops sail; the 143rd Infantry lands, August 8, in England, the others, August 6, in France.

July 31, 61st Field Artillery Brig (less 111th TM Btry which sails August 31) leaves; the brigade arrives August 12 at Brest, the TM Btry, August 11 at Liverpool. The majority of the units which sail directly for France land at Brest, the remainder at Bordeaux, Le Havre, and St. Nazaire.

Final Training and Operations

AUGUST 2–NOVEMBER 11, 1918

August 2, division (less Arty) moves to the 13th (Bar-sur-Aube) Training Area for training.

August 17, 61st Field Artillery Brig and 111th Am Tn move to Redon and the vicinity for training.

August 23–September 14, division is under the administrative control of the VI Corps.

September 4, the artillery moves to Camp Coëtquidan for training.

September 10, 111th Engrs and Tn are attached to First Army, and, September 12–16, participate in the St. Mihiel Operation, and September 26–November 11, in the Meuse-Argonne Operation.

September 26, division (less Arty and Engrs) moves to area between Epernay and Chálons and becomes a reserve of the French Group of Armies of the Center.

October 4, division is attached to French Fourth Army; the 71st Infantry Brig and 111th F Sig Bn move by stages via Somme-Suippes to the north of Sommepy, where, October 6, they are attached to the 2nd Division, and on the night of October 6–7 occupy that part of the front extending from 3 km west of Orfeuil to 1 km southeast of St. Etienne-à-Arnes.

October 7, the command passes to the brigade.

October 8, 71st Infantry Brig, with liaison battalions of the 2nd Division on the right and left, attacks toward Machault, advances its right about ½ km, and with elements of the 2nd Division captures St. Etienne-à-Arnes.

October 9, the brigade advances north of St. Etienne-à-Arnes; the division (less Arty, Engrs, and 71st Infantry Brig) marches north from the vicinity of Suippes-Souain.

October 10, division completes the relief of the 2nd Division in the Blanc-Mont Sector; the 71st Infantry Brig, after relieving the elements of 2nd Division in front line, advances its right by a local attack, French 73rd Division on right.

Night of October 10–11, the enemy begins to withdraw toward Dricourt and Attigny.

October 10–28, division (less Arty) participates in the Meuse-Argonne Operation.

October 11, division passes the 72nd Infantry Brig through the 71st Infantry Brig, enters Machault, and reaches a line from 1¼ km east of Machault, to a point ¾ km north of Machault, French 7th Division on left.

October 12, division pursues the retreating enemy through Dricourt and establishes a front from 1½ km north of Vaux-Champagne, through points ¼ km southeast of Beaumont Fme, ½ km west of Vaux-Champagne, to 1¼ km southeast of Saulces-Chainpenoises.

October 13, division advances to the line of the Aisne from Attigny (excl.) to Givry (incl.).

Night of October 13–14, the sector is extended east to include the Briqueterie east of Attigny, the 71st Infantry Brig relieving the French 73rd Division.

October 21, the sector is extended west to include La Charité, the 144th Infantry relieving the French 7th Division.

October 23, the sector extends from Fontenille Fme (excl.) to Givry (incl.); the French 53rd Division is now on the right, the French 61st Division is on the left.

October 27, division in a local attack captures Forest Fme, clears the bend of the Aisne about Rilly-aux-Oies, and occupies a line from 2 km west of Voncq to 1 km west of Forest Fme. October 28, division is ordered to join the First Army; the French 1st and French 22nd Divisions relieve the division, which then moves by stages to the Triaucourt Area.

November 3–17, the division undergoes rehabilitation and training.

Post Armistice Activities

NOVEMBER 12, 1918–MAY 16, 1919

November 16, 111th Engrs and Tn, relieved from the First Army, revert to the control of the division.

November 18, division (less Arty) moves to the 16th (Tonnerre) Training Area, where the last elements arrive on November 29 and training follows.

February 2, 61st Field Artillery Brig and 111th Am Tn move to St. Nazaire.

February 26, the artillery sails.

May 2, division (less Arty, Engrs, and Sup Tn) moves to the Montfort Area, American Embarkation Center, Le Mans.

Return to the United States and Demobilization

MAY 17–JUNE 20, 1919

May 17, the leading elements leave the American Embarkation Center, Le Maps, for Brest.

May 19, the leading infantry units sail.

May 23, DHQ and Eq 71st Infantry Brig sail.

June 11, the last element, part of the 111th Engrs, arrives at New York. The demobilization at Camp Bowie, includes, March 25, Hq 61st Field Artillery Brig, June 18, DHQ, June 19, Hq 71st Infantry Brig, June 20, Hq 72nd Infantry Brig.

The Thirty-Seventh Division, National Guard

The 37th Division was organized from the Ohio National Guard at Camp Sheridan, Montgomery, Alabama. It was transferred to Camp Lee, Virginia, where it was filled to war strength and began its overseas movement June 15, 1918. It captured 1495 prisoners. It was quiet 50 days and active 11 days. It advanced 30 kilometers. It had 5243 casualties. It had 977 battle deaths, and 4266 were wounded. The division received 6282 replacements.

73rd Infantry Brigade

145th Infantry
146th Infantry
135th Machine Gun Battalion

74th Infantry Brigade

147th Infantry
148th Infantry
136th Machine Gun Battalion

62nd Field Artillery Brigade

134th Field Artillery
135th Field Artillery
136th Field Artillery

Divisional Troops

112th Engineers
134th Machine Gun Battalion
112th Field Signal Battalion

Trains

112th Train Hdqs
112th Military Police
112th Ammunition train
112th Supply Train

112th Engineer Train
112th Sanitary Train
Ambulance Cos and Field Hospitals 145–148

Record of Events

SECTORS WHERE THE THIRTY-SEVENTH DIVISION WAS ENGAGED IN WARFARE

Baccarat sector, France, August 4 to September 16, 1918.
Meuse-Argonne offensive, France, September 26 to 30, 1918.
Meuse-Argonne offensive, France, October 7 to 16, 1918.
Ypres-Lys offensive, Belgium, October 31 to November 4, 1918.
Ypres-Lys offensive, Belgium, November 9 to 11, 1918.

Organization and Training in the United States

JULY 15, 1917–MAY 19, 1918

July 15, the National Guard of Ohio is called into federal service.

July 18, the War Department designates National Guard troops of Ohio and West Virginia to form the 37th Division. Camp Sheridan, Montgomery, Ala., is selected for the training.

August 3, the War Department directs the concentration and organization of the Division at Camp Sheridan. August 5, the National Guard of Ohio is drafted into federal service.

August 25, the concentration of the Ohio National Guard at Camp Sheridan begins.

August 26, Brig. Gen. William R. Smith assumes command.

September 3, the brigades are organized and ultimately include, 73rd Infantry Brig, the 5th and 8th and detachments of the 1st, 2nd, 7th, and 10th Regts of Ohio Infantry, 74th Infantry Brig, the 3rd and 6th, and detachments of the 1st, 2nd, 7th, and 10th Regts of Ohio Infantry; 62nd Field Artillery Brig, the 1st, 2nd, and 3rd Regts of Ohio Field Artillery and detachments of the 7th and 10th Regts of Ohio Infantry.

September 15, division is reorganized in accordance with the Tables of Organization of August 8, 1917.

September 30, division aggregates 21,700.

October 16–18, drafts aggregating 1,000 arrive from Camp Sherman.

October 29, systematic training begins. During the winter and spring the losses approximate 3,000. However, replacements, received prior to embarkation, complete the division.

Movement Overseas

MAY 20–JULY 18, 1918

May 20, the division moves to Camps Lee and Upton, where it reaches its full strength upon the receipt of drafts from Camps Jackson, Lee, Meade, Mills, and Upton, and then proceeds to the ports of embarkation of Baltimore, Brooklyn, Hoboken, Montreal, Newport News, New York, and Philadelphia.

June 6–15, Adv Det, DHQ, and 73rd Infantry Brig sail, and arrive June 18–27 at Brest.

June 22, 74th Infantry Brig, 112th Engrs and Tn, and 112th F Sig Bn sail, and arrive July 5 at Brest.

June 27–28, the artillery and the remaining divisional troops and trains sail, and arrive July 10–18, the 62nd Field Artillery Brig and the Military Police land at Liverpool, the 112th Sup Tn at Birkenhead, the 112th TM Btry and 112th San Tn at Glasgow, and the remainder at Brest. The troops in England stay a short time in rest camps and then proceed via Le Havre and Cherbourg, the 62nd Field Artillery Brig and 112th Sup Tn through the former, the 112th, TM Btry and 112th San Tn through the latter.

Final Training and Operations

JUNE 25–NOVEMBER 11, 1918

June 25, division (less Arty) moves to the 3rd (Bourmont) Training Area for training.

July 15, 62nd Field Artillery Brig and 112th Am Tn move to the southwest of Bordeaux and thence to Camp de Souge for training.

July 22, division (less Arty) moves to the vicinity of Baccarat in the Vosges.

July 23–August 27, division is under the administrative control of the IV Corps.

July 28–August 4, division (less Arty) is affiliated with the 77th Division in the Baccarat Sector on the front from 1 km west of Hill 487.8 (4½ km east of Badonviller), through Neuviller and Ancerviller, to a point 2 km west of Domèvre.

August 4, division relieves the 77th Division and patrolling follows.

August 4–September 16, division (less Arty) occupies the Baccarat Sector (Lorraine).

September 15, the sector is reduced by moving northern boundary to the vicinity of le Pètit-Bois-de-Bouleaux, the French 75th Infantry effecting the relief.

September 16, French 131st Division relieves the division, which moves, September 17, to the Robert-Espagne Area and thence to the Argonne front.

September 23, 62nd Field Artillery Brig moves from Camp de Souge to Revigny Area. Division relieves portions of the 79th and 91st Divisions on main line of resistance in rear of a front which extends from 1¾ km northeast of Avocourt in the Bois d'Avocourt, along the northern outskirts of Avocourt, to ½ km north of La Cour, held temporarily by units of the 33rd Division, and prepares for Meuse-Argonne Operation.

September 23–25, division (less Arty) occupies the Avocourt Sector (Lorraine).

September 26, division, in the center of the V Corps, attacks from the front line of the Avocourt Sector toward Cierges and Rémonville, and reaches the northern edge of the Bois de Montfaucon, the Tranchée de Montfaucon southwest of Montfaucon, the road from Montfaucon to Ivoiry 1 km west of Montfaucon, to a point ¾ km south of Ivoiry; 79th Division on right, 91st Division on left.

September 26–30, division (less Arty) participates in the Meuse-Argonne Operation.

September 27, the front line extends from ¾ km northwest of Montfaucon to ¾ km south of Ivoiry.

September 28–29, division attacks and advances to a line along the northwestern edge of the Bois de Beuge, east and south of Cierges, to south of la Grange-aux-Bois Fme, where it organizes a position.

September 30, 32nd Division relieves the division, which concentrates near Récicourt.

October 3, division moves to Pagny-sur-Meuse and the vicinity.

October 7, division relieves the 89th Division on the front from 1¼ km northeast of Jaulny, along the northern edge of the Bois de in Montagne, the northern edge of the Bois de Charey, Fme de Champ-Fontaine, to the southern corner of the Etang de Lachaussée; patrolling follows, 90th Division on right, French 39th Division on left.

October 7–16, division (less Arty) occupies the Pannes Sector (Lorraine).

October 10, the 7th Division is on the right.

October 12–23, 62nd Field Artillery Brig and 112th Am Tn participate in the occupation of the Marbache Sector supporting the 92nd Div.

October 16, 28th Division relieves the division which moves, October 18, to the Hooglede Area, near Roulers (Flanders).

October 22–January 11, division is under administrative control of the II Corps.

October 23, 62nd Field Artillery Brig (less 136th FA, which remains in the Marbache Sector until October 30) proceeds to the vicinity of Avrainville.

October 26, division moves by stages to the vicinity of Thielt and Meulebeke (Belgium).

October 28–November 11, troops of the 62nd Field Artillery Brig participate in sector occupations as follows: Paiines Sector, 134th Field Artillery supporting the 28th Division, October 28–November 11; 136th Field Artillery as corps artillery of French II Colonial Corps and IV Corps, November 3–11; Troyon Sector, 135th FA supporting 33rd Division, October 28–November 11.

Nights of October 29–30 and October 30–31, division relieves the French 132nd Division along the Courtrai-Ghent railroad between Waalesstraat and Vossenhol.

October 30–November 4, division (less Arty) participates in the Ypres-Lys Operation.

October 31, division attacks southeast and reaches the heights west of Cruyshautem between De Biest and Hoogemolen; French 128th Division (French VII Corps) on right, French 12th Division (French 30th Corps) on left.

November 1, division attacks east, occupies Cruyshautem, and reaches the Scheldt River between Eyne and Meerschkant.

November 2–4, division forces the crossings of the Scheldt River at Eyne, Heurne, and Heuvel, and advances ¾ km beyond the river.

November 4, French 12th Division relieves the division which moves to the Thielt Area for rest.

November 8, division moves to the front east of Heuvel, Syngem, and Asper.

November 9–11, division (less Arty) participates in the Ypres-Lys Operation.

November 10, division passes through elements of the French 11th and French 12th Divisions along the line from Meerschkant, through Groot-Meersch, to Klein-Meersch, attacks east, crosses the Scheldt River against enemy opposition at Heuvel and Herinelgem, occupies Nederzwalm, and gains the region north of Hermelgem and ¼ km east of the river near Grootenberg; French 132nd Division on right, French 5th Division on left.

November 11, patrols occupy Munckzwalm, Hundelgem, Zwarten-broek, Dickele, Bouchaute Fme and reach the crossroad 800 m southwest of Keerken.

Post Armistice Activities

NOVEMBER 12, 1918–FEBRUARY 26, 1919

November 18, division (less Arty) moves east toward Brussels to the vicinity of Leeuwergem, midway between Most and Audenarde, Belgium.

November 21–December 17, division (less Arty) marches west via Ootroosebeke and Hondschoote to the Wormhoudt Area; training follows.

January 9, division (less Arty) moves to the Alençon Area and continues training.

February 3, 112th Engrs and Tn go to the American Embarkation Center, Le Mans.

February 9, 62nd Field Artillery Brig, stationed in Château-Gontier Area, reverts to the Division.

February 17, the remainder of the division moves to the American Embarkation Center.

*Return to the United States
and Demobilization*

FEBRUARY 27–JUNE 23, 1919

February 27, the division moves to Brest.
March 10, the leading elements sail.
March 12, DHQ sails, and other units follow in rapid succession.
April 30, the last element, 112th TM Btry arrives at Philadelphia. The demobilization at Camp Shernian includes, April 8, Hq 74th Infantry Brig, April 10, Hq 73rd Infantry Brig, April 11, Hq 62nd Field Artillery Brig, June 23, DHQ.

THE FORTY-SECOND DIVISION, NATIONAL GUARD

The 42nd or Rainbow Division was organized at Camp Mills from the National Guard organizations from every section of the United States. The division was organized by General William A. Mann, who commanded it until December 14, 1917, when he was succeeded by Major General Charles T. Menoher, who remained in command until November 7, 1918, when Major General Charles D. Rhodes succeeded him. The overseas movement began October 18, 1917, and was completed December 4, 1917, when the last unit reached France. This division captured 1317 prisoners. It was quiet 142 days and active 39 days. It advanced 55 kilometers. Its total casualties, 13,919. It had 2,644 battle deaths and 11,275 wounded. It received a replacement of 17,253.

83rd Infantry Brigade

165th Infantry
166th Infantry
150th Machine Gun Battalion

84th Infantry Brigade

167th Infantry
168th Infantry
151st Machine Gun Battalion

67th Field Artillery Brigade

149th Field Artillery
150th Field Artillery
151st Field Artillery
117th Trench Mortar Battalion

Divisional Troops

117th Engineers
149th Machine Gun Battalion
117th Field Signal Battalion

Trains

117th Train Hdqs
117th Military Police
117th Ammunition Train
117th Supply Train
117th Engineers Train
117th Sanitary Train
Ambulance Cos and Field Hospitals 165–168

Record of Events

SECTORS WHERE THE FORTY-SECOND DIVISION WAS ENGAGED IN WARFARE

Luneville sector, Lorraine, France, February 21 to March 23, 1913.
Baccarat sector, Lorraine, France, March 31 to June 21, 1918.
Esperance-Souain sector, Champagne, France, July 4 to 14, 1918.

Champagne-Marne defensive, France, July 15 to 17, 1918.
Aisne-Marne offensive, France, July 25 to August 3, 1918.
St. Mihiel offensive, France, September 12 to 16, 1918.
Essey and Pannes sector, Woevre, France, September 17 to 30, 1918.
Meuse-Argonne offensive, France, October 12 to 31, 1918.
Meuse-Argonne offensive, France, November 5 to 10, 1918.

Organization and Training in the United States

AUGUST 1–OCTOBER 17, 1917

August 1, the War Department directs the formation of a composite National Guard Division, the personnel to be selected from the United States at large.

August 14, the organization of the 42nd Division begins according to the Tables of Organization of August 8, 1917, and includes National Guard units from Alabama, California, Colorado, Georgia, Illinois, Indiana, Iowa, Kansas, Louisiana, Maryland, Michigan, Minnesota, Missouri, Nebraska, New Jersey, New York, North Carolina, Ohio, Oklahoma, Oregon, Pennsylvania, South Carolina, Tennessee, Texas, Virginia, Wisconsin, and the District of Columbia.

August 20, the concentration of the division begins at Camp Mills, where the following brigades are organized: August 21, the 83rd Infantry Brig, which includes the 69th New York, 4th Ohio, and Cos B, C, and F, 2nd Wisconsin Regts of Infantry; September 1, the 84th Infantry Brig which includes the 4th Alabama, 3rd Iowa, and Cos B, C, and F, 2nd Georgia Regts of Infantry; September 5, the 67th Field Artillery Brig, which includes the 1st Illinois, 1st Indiana, and 1st Minnesota Regts of FA, and a TM Btry of Maryland CA.

September 5, Maj. Gen. William A. Mann assumes command of the division.

September 10, systematic training begins.

September 13, the concentration is completed.

September 23, Adv Det sails from Hoboken and lands October 6 at St. Nazaire.

October 8, division numbers about 27,000 officers and men.

Movement Overseas

OCTOBER 18–DECEMBER 8, 1917

October 18, the division moves to the ports of embarkation of Hoboken, Montreal, and New York.

October 18 and 31, DHQ, 83rd Infantry Brig (less one battalion 165th Infantry) 151st MG Bn, 67th Field Artillery Brig, 117th Am Tn, 117th Engrs, 117th Sup Tn, 117th San Tn (less two ambulance companies and one field hospital), and 117th Tn Hq and MP sail from Hoboken, and arrive November 1 and 14, at St. Nazaire; the battalion of the 165th Infantry sails October 27 from Montreal, and lands November 11 at Liverpool.

November 3–23, the remainder sails from New York and arrives November 20 and December 1 at Liverpool. The troops in England stay a short time in rest camps and then proceed to Le Havre.

Final Training and Operations

NOVEMBER 5, 1917–NOVEMBER 11, 1918

November 5, division (less Hq 84th Infantry Brig, 168th Infantry, 149th MG Bn, Arty, and part of the Sn Tn) moves to the 5th (Vaucouleurs) Training Area.

November 9, 67th Field Artillery Brig (less TM Btry) and 117th Am Tn move to Camp Coëtquidan, and the TM Btry to the vicinity of Langres, for training.

December 9, 117th Engrs and Tn moves to the 7th (Rolampont) Training Area for duty with the SOS.

December 12, the troops in the Vaucouleurs Training Area move to the 4th (Rimaucourt) Training Area, where the Hq 84th Infantry, 168th Infantry, 149th MG Bn and the detached parts of the San Tn rejoin.

December 26, division (less 168th Infantry, Arty, and Engrs) moves to the 7th (Rolampont) Training Area.

January 20–June 21, division is under the administrative control of the I Corps.

January 31, the last elements of the 168th Infantry rejoin; training follows.

February 16, division moves to the vicinity of Lunéville and St. Clement.

February 17–June 21, training with the French in Lorraine.

February 18, the artillery rejoins from Camp Coëtquidan.

February 21, the leading elements enter the line of the French VII Corps which extends from a point 4 km north of Celles-sur-Plaine, through Neuviller-lès-Badonviller, Ancerviller, the eastern edge of the Bois Banal, 2 km west of Domèvre, 1 km east of Reillon, Embermenil, the eastern and northern edges of the Forêt de Parroy, to 1½ km southwest of Parroy, where they are affiliated with the French 128th, French 14th, and French 164th Divs in the respective divisional sectors of Baccarat, St. Clement, and Lunéville;

elements of the artillery are with the French 41st Division in the Dombasle Sector; local actions follow.

February 21–March 23, division, affiliated with the French, occupies the Luneville Sector (Lorraine).

March 23, division is relieved and concentrates near Gerbéviller and Baccarat West, preparatory to the return to the 7th (Rolampont) Training Area; rehabilitation.

March 28, the orders for return to the 7th Training Area are cancelled; the division moves to the Baccarat Sector and the leading elements enter the line to relieve the French 128th Division in the subsectors of Neufmaisons and Merviller.

March 31–June 21, division occupies the Baccarat Sector (Lorraine).

March 31, division, on the right of the French Eighth Army, with brigades abreast, 84th Infantry Brig on the right, relieves the French 128th Division, except in the center of resistance Chasseurs, from 4 km north of Celles-sur-April Plaine, through Neuviller-lês-Badonviller and Ancerviller, to the southeastern edge of the Bois Banal; local actions follow; French 170th Division (French 21st Corps, French Seventh Army) on right, French 128th Division on left.

April 23, French 12th Division is on the left.

April 30, French 62nd Division is on the right.

May 31, division relieves French troops in the center of resistance Chasseurs.

June 15, French 247th Field Artillery relieves the 151st Field Artillery, which moves to the vicinity of Châtel-sur-Moselle. **June 21,** 77th Division and the French 61st Division, the command passing to the latter, relieve the division, which assembles near Châtel-sur-Moselle in the reserve of the French Eighth Army.

June 21–23, the division is under the administrative control of the IV Corps.

June 22, division moves to vicinity of St. Gennain-la-Ville, where it is at the disposal of the French Armies of the North as a reserve.

June 28, division moves to Camp de Chalons and to the south of the Espérance and Souain Sectors; special training follows.

July 3, division moves into the Espérance and Souain Sectors near Sommepy.

July 5–15, division occupies the Second Position in the Espérance and Souain Sectors (Champagne).

July 5, division, affiliated with the French 13th and French 170th Divisions, assumes charge of the second position within the Espérance and Souain divisional sectors; these sectors, with the Trou-Bricot Sector, comprise the zone of the French 21st Corps, the front of which extends from Tahure to Vaudesincourt. Elements of division are also affiliated with the French 13th and French 170th Divisions in the Intermediate Position within the same sectors. The French 43rd Division is on the right, French 132nd Division (French IV Corps) on the left.

July 15, the enemy attacks on the front of the Argonne Forest, Reims, and Château-Thierry. In zone of the French 21st Corps the troops are withdrawn from the Main Line of Resistance to the Intermediate Position which is defended and held, and where elements of the 42nd Division participate.

July 15–17, division participates in the Champagne-Maine Operation.

July 18, division withdraws and assembles near Chàbons-sur-Marne.

July 21, division moves, via the Meaux and La Ferté-sous-Jouarre Areas, to the area of the I Corps near Epieds and Verdilly.

July 25–August 6, division participates in the Aisne-Marne Operation.

Night of July 25–26, division, 84th Infantry Brig leading, passes through the 26th Division and attached 56th Infantry Brig (28th Division), which is holding the line in the Forêt de Fére from 2 km east of la Logette Maison to 1¼ km west of Croix Rouge Fme; French 39th Division (French 37th Corps) on right, French 167th Division (I Corps) on left.

July 26, division, cooperating with the French 39th Division, attacks and captures la Croix Rouge Fme, whereupon the French 39th Division relieves the elements of the Division south thereof.

Night of July 26–27, 83rd Infantry Brig relieves the French 167th Division on the left of the 84th Infantry Brig from 1½ km southwest of la Croix Blanche Fme to the northeastern outskirts of Beuvardes; the division now holds the entire corps' front; the enemy retires toward the Ourcq River.

July 27, division extends its sector to Villemoyenne (excl.) on the west by relieving the French 164th Division (French VII Corps) and units of the French 52nd Division (French II Corps), and then advances through the Forêt de Fére and Bois de Villemoyenne to the line, the western slope of Côte 188, a point ½ km northeast of Favière Fme, Villers-sur-Fére (incl.), northern edge of the Bois de Villemoyenne. The French 52nd Division (French II Corps) is on the left.

July 28, division attacks, forces a crossing of the Ourcq River, and reaches a line from a point ¼ km southeast of Moulin Caranda, along the crest of Côte 212, Sergy (excl.), Côte 124, to the southeastern exit of Fère-en-Tardenois; 28th Division on right, French 62nd Division (French II Corps) on left.

July 29–30, division, two battalions of the 47th Infantry (4th Division) attached, resumes the attack and captures Sergy and Seringes-et-Nesles.

July 31–August 1, division occupies the Bois Briûle; 32nd Division (French 38th Corps) on right.

Night of August 1–2, the enemy withdraws to the Vesle River.

August 2, division pursues, occupies Nesles and the Forêt de Nesles, and reaches a line from Cote 142, along the eastern, northeastern, and northwestern edges of the Forêt de Nesles, to the eastern edge of the Bois de ha Porte-d'Arcy; patrols enter Mareuil-en-Dole, les Bons-Homines Fme, and, on August 3, Chartreuve Fme.

August 2–3, 4th Division passes through the division and the latter, except the artillery, assemble as corps reserve and bivouacs in the Forêt de Fêre.

August 3–6, 67th Field Artillery Brig and 117th Am Tn support the 4th Division in the Aisne-Marne Operation, and, August 7–11, support the same division in the Vesle Sector.

August 10, division moves to La Ferté-sous-Jouarre Area, and thence, August 16, to the 3rd (Bourmont) Training Area; rehabilitation and training follow.

August 18, division is ordered to join the First Army.

August 28, division (less Arty, which goes to Toul and thence into the Forêt de la Reine) moves to the 2nd (Neufchâteau) Training Area.

September 4, division (less Arty) moves by stages via the 6th (Colombey-les-Belles) Training Area to the Forêt de ha Reine, where it occupies assembly positions during the night of September 9–10 in the rear of the 89th Division.

Night of September 10–11, elements of the division relieve units of the 89th Division in support positions near Beaumont, Mandres-aux-Quatre-Tours, and Hamonville.

September 11, division occupies that portion of the Lucey Sector between Flirey and Seicheprey. Command passes to the 42nd Division.

Night of September 11–12, division relieves the remaining elements of the 89th Division on a line from a point 1¼ km west of Flirey, along the northwestern edge of the Bois du Jury, the Bois Carré, to 1 km north of Seicheprey, and the sector occupation merges into the St. Mihiel Operation.

September 12, division, brigades abreast, 84th Infantry Brig on the right, attacks toward St. Benoît-en-Woëvre, advances through the Bois de la Sonnard, St. Baussant, Maizerais, Essey, and Pamies, and reaches a line from 1¼ km southwest of Beney, through point 220.1 south of the Bois Millot, along the southeastern edge of the Bois de Thiaucourt, to ¾ km south of Lamarche-en-Woevre; 89th Division on right, 1st Division on left.

September 12–16, division participates in the St. Mihiel Operation.

September 13, division advances through the Bois de Thiaucourt, Bois de Beney, St. Benoît-en-Woëvre, and reaches the line, northern edge of the Bois de Charey, Fme de Champ-Fontaine, Etang d'Afrique (excl.), east of Etang des Anceyiennes, ¼ km north of Hassavant Fme, le Repiquage.

September 14–16, division consolidates its position; local actions occur; French 39th Division on left.

September 17, the French 39th Division takes over that part of the front west of a point ½ km north of Etang des Anceyiennes; the 89th Division is on the right; the 84th Infantry Brig now holds the front line; the 83rd Infantry Brig is in reserve.

September 17–October 1, division occupies the Pannes Sector (Lorraine).

September 19, division advances through the Bois de la Grande-Souche to the southwestern outskirts of Hauinont-lès-Lachaussée; local actions follow.

September 28, 83rd Infantry Brig relieves the 84th Infantry Brig in the front line.

September 30, 89th Division extends toward the west and relieves the 42nd Division.

October 1, the command passes and the 42nd Division moves to the vicinity of Souilly, where it joins the reserve of the First Army.

October 4, division moves to the Récicourt Area and passes to corps reserve.

October 4–November 10, division participates in the Meuse-Argonne Operation.

October 5, division moves to the Bois de Montfaucon.

October 6, 67th Field Artillery Brig and 117th Am Tn move to the vicinity of Romagne-sous-Montfaucon, where they support the 32nd Division in Meuse-Argonne Operation, October 7–12.

October 10, division (less Arty) moves to the vicinity of the Bois Communal de Cierges and Bois Emont, and then to the woods south and southeast of Exermont.

October 11, division (less Arty) begins the relief of the 1st Division in the Bois de Romagne and along the northwestern slope of Côte de Maldah north of Exermont; 181st Infantry Brig (attached to 32nd Division) on right, 82nd Division (I Corps) on left.

October 12, division (less Arty) assumes command and occupies a line from ½ km south of la Musarde Fme in the Bois de Romagne, along the northern edge of the Bois de Romagne and the northwestern slope of Côte de Maldah, to Sommerance; 32nd Division on right, 82nd Division on left.

October 13, division extends its sector toward the east and relieves such elements of the 32nd Division as are west of a point ¼ km northwest of the

Transvaal Fme in the Bois de Gesnes; 67th Field Artillery Brig and 117th Am Tn rejoin.

October 14, division attacks toward Landres-et-St. Georges and establishes a line from ¼ km northwest of Hill 286 in Bois de Gesnes, along the southern slope of Hill 288, ¼ km south of la Musarde Fme, the northern edge of the Bois de Romagne, the western slope of Côte de Châtillon, to 1¼ km north of Sommerance.

October 15, division continues the attack, progresses through the eastern part of the Bois de Romagne, and captures Hill 242.

October 16, division captures Tuilerie Fme and occupies Côte de Châtillon.

October 17–30, division consolidates the position and local actions follow.

October 20, 89th Division is on the right.

October 21, the sector is reduced ¼ km when Tuilerie Fme and the eastern slopes of Côte de Chàtillon pass to the 89th Division; 83rd Infantry Brig is in line; 84th Infantry Brig is in reserve. **October 31,** division (less outposts, which revert to the division on November 1, and less Arty, which reverts on November 2) is relieved by the 2nd Division on the line, ½ km northwest of Tuilerie Fme, northern slope of Côte de Châtillon, 1¼ km south of Landres-et-St. Georges, 1 km south of St. Georges.

November 1, division (less Arty) assembles near Sommerance.

November 2, division moves to the vicinity of Authe-Fontenoy.

November 4, the enemy begins the withdrawal to the Meuse.

Midnight November 4–5, division moves forward.

November 5, division passes through the 78th Division between Sy and Tannay, pursues the retreating enemy through the Bois du Fay and Bois du Mont-Dieu, and reaches a line from 1 km southwest of Stonne, along the heights of la Grange du Mont, la Raillère Fme, the northern edge of the Bois du Mont-Dieu, to 1 km south of La Neuville-à-Maire; 77th Division on the right, French 40th Division (French IX Corps, French Fourth Army) on the left.

November 6, the zone of action is extended to the west to include the road from Chémery to Chéhéry and Sedan; division reaches a line extending from 1 km southwest of Angecourt, 1¼ km south of Thélonne, 1 km north of Bulson, Fme de St. Quentin, to the high ground ¾ km northeast of Connage.

November 6–9, division pursues toward Sedan.

November 7, division reaches the heights of the Meuse on a front extending from west of Reinilly-sur-Meuse to Cheveuges.

November 8, on the left the zone is reduced to the boundary Chemery, Bulson, Thélonne, and Bazeilles, when the French 40th Division relieves the

83rd Infantry Brig which then withdraws to the vicinity of Chemery; 84th Infantry Brig remains in line.

November 9, 77th Division begins the relief of the division.

November 10, the command passes to the 77th Division, and the 42nd Division assembles in area of Artaise-le-Vivier and Les Petites-Armoises.

November 11, division moves to the vicinity of Buzancy.

Post Armistice Activities

NOVEMBER 12, 1918 – APRIL 4, 1919

November 14, division assembles near Landres-et-St. Georges.

November 16–17, division concentrates east of the Meuse in the Brandeville, Stenay and Baalon Areas, and prepares for the advance into Germany.

November 20, division moves as a reserve division via Montmedy, Virton (Belgium), Anon, Mersch, Consdorf (Luxemburg), Welschbillig (Germany), Speicher, Birresborn, Dreis, and Adenau, and, on December 14, takes station in the Kreis of Ahrweiler.

November 20–December 14, advance into Germany.

December 15–April 4, division forms part of the Army of Occupation in Germany. Training predominates.

Return to the United States and Demobilization

APRIL 5 – MAY 12, 1919

April 5, the division moves to Brest.

April 9, 117th TM Btry sails from St. Nazaire.

April 15, Hq 83rd Infantry Brig, April 17, Hq 67th Field Artillery Brig, and, April 18, DHQ and Hq 84th Infantry Brig sail from Brest.

May 1, the last unit, 117th Am Tn, arrives at Newport News. The demobilization includes, at Camp Upton, May 5, Hq 83rd Infantry Brig; at Camp Dix, May 9, DHQ; at Camp Dodge, May 12, Hq 84th Infantry Brig; at Camp Grant, May 12, Hq 67th Field Artillery Brig.

THE SEVENTY-SEVENTH DIVISION, NATIONAL ARMY

The 77th Division was organized at Camp Upton, New York. The overseas movement began on March 28, 1918, and landed in France in April. The first commander was Major General J. Franklin Bell; he was succeeded May 18, 1918, by Major General George B. Duncan. He was relieved of the command on August 27, 1918, by Major General Robert Alexander, who commanded the division until the end of the war. The division captured 750 prisoners. The famous Lost Battalion consisted of six companies of the 308 Infantry commanded by Lieutenant Colonel Charles Whittlesey. The 77th was quiet 47 days and active 66. It advanced 71½ kilometers. The total casualties were 10,497. It had 1992 battle deaths and 8505 wounded. It received 12,728 replacements.

153rd Infantry Brigade

305th Infantry
306th Infantry
305th Machine Gun Battalion

154th Infantry Brigade

307th Infantry
308th Infantry
306th Machine Gun Battalion

152nd Field Artillery Brigade

304th Field Artillery
305th Field Artillery
306th Field Artillery
302nd Trench Mortar Battery

Divisional Troops

302nd Engineers
304th Machine Gun Battalion
302nd Field Signal Battalion

Trains

302nd Train Hdqs
302nd Military Police
302nd Ammunition Train
302nd Supply Train

302nd Engineer Train
302nd Sanitary Train
Ambulance Cos and Field Hospitals 305–308

Record of Events

SECTORS WHERE THE SEVENTY-SEVENTH DIVISION WAS ENGAGED IN WARFARE

Baccarat sector, France, June 21 to August 4, 1918.
Vesle sector, France, August 12 to 17, 1918.
Oise-Aisne offensive, France, August 18 to September 16, 1918.
Meuse-Argonne offensive, France, September 26 to October 16, 1918.
Meuse-Argonne offensive, France, October 21 to November 11, 1918.

Organization and Training in the United States

AUGUST 5, 1917–MARCH 27, 1918

August 5, the War Department establishes the 77th Division, National Army, which is to be organized at Camp Upton, Yaphank, New York; drafts aggregating 42,000, anticipated for 1917 from New York City and the adjoining counties, are designed to furnish personnel.

August 13, the organization of DHQ is directed, and its commissioned personnel are ordered to report on or before August 15.

August 16, the commanding general of Camp Upton is directed to organize the division in accordance with the Tables of Organization of August 8, 1917.

August 18, Maj. Gen. J. Franklin Bell assumes command.

August 25, the program for the movement of selective service men to camps is announced. During the last week in August the organization begins from a cadre of officers and men of the Regular Army and from ORC and NA officers of the First Officers Training Camp at Plattsburg.

September 10, the initial draft of 2,000 selective service men arrives at camp.

September 19–24, an additional 19,000 arrive. In September systematic training begins.

October 31, the division numbers about 23,000. During November the many transfers, in spite of a fresh draft of 750, reduce the division to less than 18,000.

December 5–10, the last drafts of 1917 furnish the camp with 8,500.

December 31, the strength again reaches 23,000. During the winter fresh drafts are received from Camp Devens and other places; 4,500 are transferred from the division during January and February; in March new arrivals complete the division. On March 22, the Adv Det sails from New York and arrives March 31 at Liverpool.

Movement Overseas

MARCH 28–MAY 13, 1918

March 28, division moves to the ports of embarkation of Boston, Brooklyn, Hoboken, New York, and Portland.

March 29–April 16, division (less Arty, 302nd Sup Tn, 302nd Am Tn, 308th Amb Co, and 308th F Hosp) sails, and arrives April 12–28, at Liverpool.

April 23–26, 152nd Field Artillery Brig, 302nd Am Tn, 302nd Sup Tn, and 308th Amb Co sail, and arrive May 2–6 at Brest. May 13, the last element of the Division, 308th F Hosp, arrives at St. Nazaire. The units in England, after a brief stay in rest camps, proceed to Calais.

Final Training and Operations

APRIL 15–NOVEMBER 11, 1918

April 15–May 4, division (less Arty, 302nd Sup Tn, and 308th F Hosp) moves to the Eperlecques and Recques Training Areas, where it is attached to the British 39th Division (British Second Army) for training.

April 15–June 5, training with the British in Picardy and Artois.

April 15–June 12, division is under the administrative control of the II Corps.

May 7, 152nd Field Artillery Brig and 302nd Am Tn move to Camp de Souge for training.

May 13, 154th Infantry Brig moves to the vicinity of Couturelle and trains with the British 2nd and British 42nd Divisions (British Third Army) with a view to its employment along the support line between Marieux and Pas, east of Doullens, in case of hostile attack.

June 6, division (less Arty, Sup Tn, and 308th F Hosp) moves to entraining stations, the 153rd Infantry Brig, from the British Second Army, marching to vicinity of Hesdin, the 154th Infantry Brig, from the British Third Army, marching to vicinity of Longpré-les-Corps-Saints.

June 9, division (less detached units) moves to the vicinity of Rambervillers in the Vosges in the area of the French Eighth Army.

June 12–21, division is under the administrative control of the I Corps.

June 14, 302nd Sup Tn rejoins.

June 19, division (less Arty and 308th F Hosp) moves to the Baccarat Sector.

June 21, troops of the 77th Division, affiliated with the French 61st Division, enter the front line of the sector, which includes the subsectors of Badonviller, Ste. Pôle, Montigny and La Blette, and extends from a point 2½ km northeast of Pierre-Percée, through Neuviller-lès-Badonviller and Ancerviller, to a point on the Vezouse River 1½ km northeast of Herbéviller. On this date the command of the sector passes from the 42nd Division to the French 61st Division; local actions follow.

June 21–July 15, division participates in the occupation of the Baccarat Seètor (Lorraine).

June 21–August 8, division is under the administrative control of the IV Corps.

June 24, 308th F Hosp rejoins.

July 8–18, 152nd Field Artillery Brig and 302nd Am Tn rejoin.

July 16, 77th Division assumes command of the Baccarat Sector and the French 61st Division begins to withdraw.

July 16–August 4, division occupies the Baccarat Sector (Lorraine).

August 4, 37th Division relieves the 77th Division.

August 6, division moves from the vicinity of Charmes to the vicinity of Fère-en-Tardenois in the zone of the French Sixth Army.

August 11, division moves toward the front.

August 12–17, division occupies the Vesle Sector (Champagne).

August 12, division relieves the 4th Division and part of the French 62nd Division in the Vesle Sector from the Château du Diable, along the railroad north of the Vesle River, the slopes east and north of St. Thibaut, to the railroad north of la Gravière; 28th Division on right, French 62nd Division (French XI Corps) on left.

Night of August 13–14, the division extends its front to the western edge of Fismettes, relieving troops of the 28th Div.

August 15, French 164th Division is on the left.

August 18, the sector occupation merges into the Oise-Aisne Operation.

August 18–September 16, division participates in the Oise-Aisne Operation.

August 18–September 3, the French Sixth Army attacks the enemy positions north of the Vesle River. The division establishes bridgeheads north of the river near the Château du Diable and Bazoches.

August 21, division occupies Tannerie, and on August 22, captures the Château du Diable.

August 27, 2nd Bn 306th Infantry raids Bazoches from the southwest and retires to its original position before a hostile counterattack.

Night of September 2–3, division extends its sector toward the right to include Fismes.

Night of September 3–4, the enemy begins his withdrawal to prepared positions north of the Aisne.

September 4, division advances, crosses the Vesle, and reaches an east and west line from Grotte to les Terres-Noires, southwest of Perles.

September 5, division captures Merval and Serval and farther west reaches a line from Barbonval (excl.) to Pierre-Laroche, captures Longueval, and occupies les Champs–Ste. Macre. **September 6,** division reaches a line from a point east of la Butte de Bourmont to Villers-en-Prayères (incl.), thence along the road connecting Villers-en-Prayères and Vieil-Arcy, to the Ruines-du-Tordoir (excl.); patrols cross the Aisne Canal.

Night of September 7–8, French 62nd Division relieves the 28th Division on the right; French 164th Division (French III Corps) is on the left.

September 7–14, several attacks gain some ground in the direction of Glennes and Révillon and toward the Aisne.

Night of September 11–12, the sector is reduced when the French 164th Division relieves the 306th Infantry west of the Bois de Mauchamp.

Nights of September 14–15 and 15–16, the Italian 8th Division relieves the division.

September 16, the command passes to the Italian 8th Division, and the 77th Division moves, via Epernay and Châlons-sur-Marne, to the area of the French Second Army near Givry-en-Argonne.

September 19, division (less Arty and trains) moves to the vicinity of Le Neufour, Florent, and Les Islettes.

Nights September 19–20 and 20–21, division (less Arty and trains) relieves the French 120th Division in the Forêt d'Argonne.

September 21–25, division occupies the Forêt d'Argonne Sector (Lorraine). The division reorganizes this sector which extends from Pierre-Croisée, through Courtechaussee and Le Four de Paris, to 1 km north of La Harazée.

Nights of September 23–24, the artillery and trains enter the sector.

September 26, division, on the left of the I Corps, attacks toward Grand-pré and advances about 2 km; the 28th Division is on the right; the 368th Infantry (92nd Division), as part of a Franco-American liaison detachment of the Groupement Durand between the First and French Fourth Armies, is on the left.

September 26–November 11, division participates in the Meuse-Argonne Operation.

September 27–October 1, a series of attacks through the Bois de la Grurie establishes a line from a point southwest of Le Chêne Tondu, through the Bois de la Naza, to 1 km east of Binarville.

September 30, French 1st Dismounted cavalry Division (French 38th Corps, French Fourth Army) is on the left.

October 2, the left of the division attacks; the 1st Bn 308th Infantry, assisted by elements of the 307th Infantry and 306th MG Bn, penetrates the enemy position between the Bois de la Buironne and the Moulin de Charlevaux, but is surrounded.

October 7, division advances and re-establishes connection with this battalion.

October 8, division reaches the Rau des Noues in the Bois de Châtell, and the front now extends from 2 km southwest of Cbâtel-Chébéry to Etang de Poligny.

October 9, division pursues the retreating enemy, passes through the Bois des Quatrains and Bois de Lançon, and reaches a line from ¼ km south of La Besogne to the south slope of Hill 209; 82nd Division on right.

October 10, the enemy retreats to positions north of the Aire River; the division pursues and reaches a line from Marcq (excl.), through the southern limits of Chevières, to 1 km south of Grandpré; French 71st Division (French 38th Corps, French Fourth Army) on the left.

October 11–13, local actions occur.

October 14, division captures St. Juvin.

October 15, division changes direction from the north to the northwest, and the left of the division closes in on the Aire River.

Night of October 15–16, 78th Division begins the relief of the 77th Division.

October 16, 1st Bn 307th Infantry enters Grandpré, but units of the 78th Division complete its occupation.

October 16–30, division is concentrated near Pylône and Camp de Bouzon in corps reserve; rehabilitation.

October 31–November 1, elements of the division re-enter the front line and relieve part of the 82nd Division from the Ravin aux Pierres to the northwestern slope of Côte 182 north of St. Juvin.

November 1, division attacks north and reaches the high ground along the road 1 km east of Champigneulle, and, on the left, to beyond the Agron River astride the road from Champigneulle to St. Juvin; 80th Division on right, 78th Division on left.

Night of November 1–2, the enemy withdraws to the north.

November 2, division pursues and captures Champigneulle, and passes through Verpel, Thenorgues, and Harnicourt.

November 3, it passes through Autruche, Fontenoy, and St. Pierremont, and on November 4, occupies Oches.

November 5, division occupies La Berlière, Stonne and La Besace; its front now extends from La Besace (incl.), to south edge of Bois de Raucourt, thence along the road to les Huttes-d'Ogny Fme; 42nd Division is now on the left.

November 6, division resumes the pursuit northeast in the direction of the Meuse, establishes connection with the 1st Division (V Corps), which replaced the 80th Division on the right, and reaches the heights of the Meuse between Bois de Pourron and Chamblage Fme, with patrols at Villers-devant-Mouzon and Remilly-sur-Meuse.

November 7, division holds the line of the Meuse from Rouffy to Remilly-sur-Meuse, and advances its right to crest of Mont-de-Brune and east slope of Hill 275; 2nd Division (V Corps) on right.

November 8, division front is now along the Meuse from opposite Mouzon to Reinilly-sur-Meuse.

November 9–10, division relieves the 42nd Division, occupies the entire corps front, and establishes connection with the French 150th Infantry (French 40th Division, Fr. IX Corps, French Fourth Army) east of Pont-Maugis.

November 10–11, division holds the line of the Meuse from Mouzon (excl.) to Pont Maugis (excl.).

Post Armistice Activities

NOVEMBER 12, 1918–FEBRUARY 6, 1919

November 12, division is relieved of part its front by the French 48th Division, and moves to the vicinity of Sommauthe, Vaux-en-Dieulet, and La Besace.

November 14, division assumes command of the entire front of the V Corps, relieving troops of the 2nd and 89th Divisions, and engages in the enforcement of the armistice terms, salvage, and training.

November 17, the outpost positions of the 77th Division on east bank of the Meuse pass to the 90th Division.

November 20–24, division (less Arty) moves to Les Islettes Area; the 152nd Field Artillery Brig and 302nd Am Tn move to the vicinity of Grandpré.

November 26–December 5, division moves to the 9th (Châteauvillain) Training Area.

Return to the United States and Demobilization

FEBRUARY 7–MAY 9, 1919

February 7, division moves to Le Mans Area, American Embarkation Center.
February 9, 302nd TM Btry sails from Brest.
April 14, division moves to Brest.
April 17, DHQ, Hcf 153rd Infantry Brig, and 306th Infantry sail.
May 6, the last troops arrive at New York City. The demobilization at Camp Upton, on May 9, includes, DHQ, Hq 153rd Infantry Brig, Hq 154th Infantry Brig, and Hq 152nd Field Artillery Brig.

THE SEVENTY-EIGHTH DIVISION, NATIONAL ARMY

The 78th Division was organized at Camp Dix, New Jersey, with men enlisted from New Jersey, Delaware, northern New York and New England. The overseas movement took place between May 8, 1918, and June 11, 1918, when the last unit arrived in France. Major General Chase W. Kennedy organized the division and commanded it until April 20, 1918, when Major General James H. McRae took command. The 78th captured 432 prisoners. It was quiet 17 days and active 21 days. It advanced 21 kilometers. This division had 7,245 casualties. It had 1,384 battle deaths and 5,861 wounded. The division received 3,190 replacements.

155th Infantry Brigade

309th Infantry
310th Infantry
308th Machine Gun Battalion

156th Infantry Brigade

311th Infantry
312th Infantry
309th Machine Gun Battalion

153rd Artillery Brigade

307th Field Artillery
308th Field Artillery
309th Field Artillery
303rd Trench Mortar Battery

Divisional Troops

303rd Engineers
307th Machine Gun Battalion
303rd Field Signal Battalion

Trains

303rd Train Hdqs
303rd Military Police
303rd Ammunition Train
303rd Supply Train
303 Engineer Train
303rd Sanitary Train
Ambulance Cos and Field Hospitals 309–312

Record of Events

SECTORS WHERE THE SEVENTY-EIGHTH DIVISION WAS ENGAGED IN WARFARE

Limey sector, France, September 16 to October 5, 1918.
St. Mihiel offensive, France, September 16, 1918.
Meuse-Argonne offensive, France, October 16 to November 5, 1918.

Organization and Training in the United States

AUGUST 5, 1917–MAY 17, 1918

August 5, the War Department establishes the 78th Division, National Army, which is to be organized at Camp Dix, Wrightstown, New Jersey; drafts, anticipated for 1917, from Delaware, 1,202, New Jersey, 20,665, and New York, 21,160, are designed to furnish personnel.

August 13, the organization of DHQ is directed, and its commissioned personnel are ordered to report on or before August 15.

August 16, the commanding general of Camp Dix is directed to organize the division in accordance with the Tables of Organization of August 8, 1917.

August 23, Maj. Gen. Chase W. Kennedy assumes command.

August 25, the program for the draft of selective service men to camps is announced. During the last week in August the organization begins from a cadre of officers and men of the Regular Army, and from ORC and NA officers of the First Officers Training Camp at Madison Barracks.

September 5-10, the initial draft of 2,000 selective service men arrives at camp.

September 17, 200 additional men arrive; systematic training begins.

October 31, the division numbers about 16,000.

November 19-24, the last drafts of 1917 furnish the camp with 5,000.

November 30, transfers have reduced the division to less than half the authorized strength.

March 31, the division aggregates only 10,000, due to large transfers which exceed fresh drafts and other arrivals.

During April and May, transfers and drafts from New England, New York, New Jersey and Illinois complete the division.

May 11, the Adv Det sails from Philadelphia and arrives May 24 at Liverpool.

Movement Overseas

MAY 18-JUNE 12, 1918

May 18, division moves to the ports of embarkation of Boston, New York and Philadelphia.

May 19-21, DHQ and the infantry sail, and arrive May 31-June 5 in England.

May 27-June 6, all the artillery units, divisional troops, and trains sail, and arrive June 8-12 in England. The troops in England, after a brief stay in rest camps, proceed to Calais and Le Havre, the infantry to the former, the artillery to the latter.

Final Training and Operations

JUNE 4-NOVEMBER 11, 1918

June 4-August 20, training with the British in Flanders.

June 4-17, division (less Arty) detrains at Marquise and moves to the Lumbres Training Area, where it is affiliated with the British 34th Division.

June 8-August 21, division is under the administrative control of the II Corps.

June 12, 153rd Field Artillery Brig and 303rd Am Tn move to Camp de Meucon for training.

June 17, division (less Arty) is affiliated with the British 39th Division for training.

July 18, division (less Arty) moves to the vicinity of St. Pol-sur-Ternoise in the forward area of the British First Army, where it continues training.

August 17, 153rd Field Artillery Brig and 303rd Am Tn move to Toul and thence to Villers-en-Haye, where they are attached to the 90th Division.

August 20, division (less Arty) moves to the 11th (Bourbonne-les-Bains) Training Area.

August 25, division is ordered to join the First Army.

August 28, division (less Arty) moves to the 3rd (Bourmont) Training Area and on September 4 to the 2nd (Neufchâteau) Training Area.

August 28–September 11, 153rd Field Artillery Brig and 303rd Am Tn participate in the occupation of the Saizerais Sector, supporting the 90th Division.

September 10, division (less Arty) moves to the Bois de la Côte-en-Haye and Bois des Tranchées and thence, on September 11, to positions in the rear of the 2nd and 5th Divisions the Bois de Greney and Bois de la Rappe as a part of the reserve of the I Corps.

September 12–16, division (less Arty) participates in the St. Mihiel Operation.

September 12–16, division is in the reserve of the I Corps.

September 13, division (less Arty and Engrs) moves into the Bois d'Euvezin. The 153rd Field Artillery Brig and 303rd Am Tn support the 90th Division during this operation.

September 16–October 4, division (less Arty) occupies the Limey Sector (Lorraine).

Night of September 15–16, 155th Infantry Brig relieves the 2nd Division, except the artillery, from the Bois Blainchamp, through Moulin de Rembercourt and the eastern and northwestern edges of the Bois de la Montague, to a point 2 km northeast of Xammes.

Night of September 16–17, 156th Infantry Brig relieves the 5th Division, except the artillery, from la Souleuvre Fme to Bois de Blainchamp; 90th Division on right, 89th Division (IV Corps) on left. These positions are organized for defense and local actions take place.

September 17–October 4, 153rd Field Artillery Brig and 303rd Am Tn participate in the occupation of the Puvenelle Sector, supporting the 90th Division

October 4, the 89th and 90th Divisions relieve the 78th Division, which moves to the Forêt de la Reine.

October 5, division moves to Clermont-en-Argonne.

October 10, division, in reserve of the I Corps, moves into the Argonne Forest west of Montblainville.

October 10–November 5, division participates in the Meuse-Argonne Operation.

Night of October 15–16, division passes through the lines of the 77th Division along the front extending from Côte 182 near St. Juvin, through Chevières and Barbançon Fme, to Grandpré (incl.).

October 16, division attacks north, enters Clievières, and pushes its left across the Aire River, establishing contact with the French at Echaudé Fme; 82nd Division on right, French 71st Division (French 38th Corps, French Fourth Army) on left.

October 17, division enters the Bois des Loges and reaches the Fme des Grèves.

October 18, the right boundary is changed to a north and south line through the western outskirts of Champigneulle, and the front line is advanced to the vicinity of the Fme des Loges and to the Fme de Talma.

October 19, the front is advanced to high ground between Fme des Loges and Bellejoyeuse Fme; French 1st Dismounted Cavalry Division (French 38th Corps) is now on left.

October 20, the line in the Bois des Loges and near the Fme des Loges is withdrawn to the road from St. Juvin to Grandpré.

October 23, a series of attacks results in the capture of Talma (hill) and the Citadel of Grandpré.

October 25, division advances its line into the Bois de Bourgogne.

October 27, Grandpré is cleared of the enemy.

October 28–31, the position is consolidated.

October 31, 77th Division is on the right.

November 1, division again attacks, enters the Bois des Loges, and establishes its front in the Bois de Bourgogne 1 km north of Bellejoyeuse Fme.

November 2, the division pursues the retreating enemy and occupies the Bois des Loges, Beffu-et-Le Morthomme, Briquenay, and the western part of the Bois de Thénorgues.

November 3, the left boundary is changed to the line from Briquenay, through Germont, Brieulles-sur-Bar, and Les Petites-Armoises, to Tannay, the right boundary to the line from Authe to Stonne. The division pursues through Germont, Boult-aux-Bois, Belleville-sur-Bar, Authe, and Châtillon-sur-Bar and occupies Verrières and Brieulles-sur-Bar.

November 4, division occupies the Bois de Sy and Les Petites-Armoises; French 40th Division (French IX Corps) on left.

November 5, division clears the Bois de Sy, occupies Sy and Tannay, and is holding the southern slope of le Mont-Dieu and the high ground 1 km northeast of Tannay when the 42nd Division passes through its line between Sy and Tannay; the Division (less Arty) assembles near Verrières and Les Petites-Armoises.

November 5-8, 153rd Field Artillery Brig and 303rd Am Tn support the 42nd and 6th Divs in the Meuse-Argonne Operation.

November 6, division (less Arty) moves to camps west of Varennes-en-Argonne and on November 9 continues to the vicinity of Florent and Les Islettes.

Post Armistice Activities

NOVEMBER 11, 1918–APRIL 22, 1919

November 11, division (less Arty, which is assigned to the First Army) moves to the region south of Ste. Menehould.

November 12–December 7, 153rd Field Artillery Brig and 303rd Am Tn is attached to the 6th Division and to First Army.

November 16, division (less Arty) moves to the 21st (Semur) Training Area; training follows.

December 9, 153rd Field Artillery Brig and 303rd Am Tn rejoin.

April 20, 303rd TM Btry sails from St. Nazaire.

Return to the United States and Demobilization

APRIL 28–JUNE 9, 1919

April 23, 153rd Field Artillery Brig, 313th Am Tn, 307th, 308th, and 309th MG Bns, and part of the 303rd F Sig Bn move to Marseille.

April 26, the troops at Marseille begin to embark.

April 30, the remainder of the division moves to the Beautiran Area.

May 10, 311th Infantry sails from Bordeaux and other nearby units follow.

May 24, DHQ sails.

June 10, the last elements arrive at New York. The demobilization at Camp Dix includes, May 21, Hq 153rd Field Artillery Brig, May 26, Hq 156th Jnf Brig, June 3, Hq 155th Infantry Brig, and June 9, DHQ.

THE SEVENTY-NINTH DIVISION, NATIONAL ARMY

The 79th Division was organized at Camp Meade, Maryland, and was formed of men from Pennsylvania, Maryland, and the District of Columbia.

Large numbers of the men were transferred to southern divisions up to June 1918. This division trained nearly 80,000; only about 20,000 were retained. The overseas movement began July 9, 1918, and was completed August 3, when the last unit arrived in France. Major General Joseph E. Kuhn was in command of the division until the end. This division captured 1,077 prisoners. It was quiet 28 days and active 17 days. It advanced 19½ kilometers. Its total casualty loss was 6,750. It had 1,419 battle deaths and 5,331 wounded. It received 6,246 replacements,

157th Infantry Brigade

313th Infantry
314th Infantry
311th Machine Gun Battalion

158th Infantry Brigade

315th Infantry
316th Infantry
312th Machine Gun Battalion

154th Field Artillery Brigade

310th Field Artillery
311th Field Artillery
312th Field Artillery
304th Trench Mortar Battery

Divisional Troops

304th Engineers
310th Machine Gun Battalion
304th Field Signal Battalion
Headquarters Troop

Trains

304th Train Hdqs
304th Military Police
304th Ammunition Train
304th Supply Train

304th Engineer Train
304th Sanitary Train
Ambulance Cos and Field Hospitals 313–316

Record of Events

SECTORS WHERE THE SEVENTY-NINTH DIVISION WAS ENGAGED IN WARFARE

Meuse-Argonne offensive, France. September 24 to 30, 1918.
Meuse-Argonne offensive, France. October 8 to 25, 1918.
Meuse-Argonne offensive, France, October 29 to November 11, 1918.

Organization and Training in the United States

AUGUST 5, 1917–JULY 5, 1918

August 5, the War Department establishes the 79th Division, National Army, which is to be organized at Camp Meade, Annapolis Junction, Maryland; drafts, anticipated for 1917, from Maryland, 7,096, Pennsylvania, 32,643, and the District of Columbia, 929, are designed to furnish personnel.

August 13, the organization of DHQ is directed and its commissioned personnel are ordered to report on or before August 15.

August 16, the commanding general of Camp Meade is directed to organize the division in accordance with the Tables of Organization of August 8, 1917.

August 25, Maj. Gen. Joseph E. Kuhn assumes command; the program for the movement of selective service men to camps is announced. During the last week in August the organization, to include skeleton units, begins from a cadre of officers and men of the Regular Army, and from ORC and NA officers of the First Officers Training Camp at Fort Niagara.

September 19–24, the initial draft of about 17,000 selective service men arrive and join the division.

September 26–30, an additional 400 arrive. During October systematic training begins.

October 3–8, a draft of 2,000 arrives at the camp.

October 10, 6,000 leave the division for Camps Gordon and Hancock.

November 2–7, the last drafts of 1917 furnish the camp with 12,000.

November 30, the division aggregates over 20,000.

May 30, the division numbers 13,000. During June drafts, largely from New York, Ohio, Rhode Island, and West Virginia, and transfers complete the division, which has received an aggregate of over 80,000 men.

June 30, the Adv Det sails from Hoboken and arrives July 12 at Brest.

Movement Overseas

JULY 6–AUGUST 3, 1918

July 6, division moves to the ports of embarkation of Brooklyn, Hoboken, and Philadelphia.

July 8–10, division (less Arty and 304th Sup Tn) sails, and lands, July 15–21, at Brest.

July 31, 154th Field Artillery Brig (less Btry A 311th FA), 304th Am Tn, and 304th Sup Tn land at Liverpool and other British ports.

August 3, the last element of the division arrives at Liverpool. The 154th Field Artillery Brig, 304th Am Tn, and 304th Sup Tn proceed to La Havre and Cherbourg, after a brief stay in rest camps.

Final Training and Operations

JULY 19–NOVEMBER 11, 1918

Division (less Arty and 304th Sup Tn) moves to the 10th (Prauthoy) Training Area for training, the DHQ, 157th Infantry Brig, and divisional troops passing through the 12th (Mussy-sur-Seine) Training Area.

August 5, 154th Field Artillery Brig and 304th Am Tn move to Montmorillon for training.

August 11, 304th Sup Tn rejoins the division.

August 18, division is ordered to join the First Army.

August 23–September 9, division is under the administrative control of the VI Corps.

September 5, 154th Field Artillery Brig and 304th Am Tn move to La Courtine for training.

September 8, division (less Arty) moves to the Robert-Espagne Area.

September 10–13, division is under administrative control of the III Corps.

September 13, division (less Arty) moves to vicinity of Blercourt, and begins the relief of a portion of the French 157th Division from south of Haucourt to 800 in west of Avocourt.

September 15, division completes the relief of elements of the French 157th Division.

September 15–25, division (less Arty) occupies the Avocourt Sector (Lorraine).

September 20, division is ordered to join the First Army and the V Corps.

Night of September 21–22, troops of the 33rd Division occupy the outpost zone of the 79th Div.

September 23, troops of the 37th Division relieve the 157th Infantry Brig west of a point 2 km northeast of Avocourt in the Bois d'Avocourt, in the left half of the sector.

September 23–25, division prepares for the Meuse-Argonne Operation.

September 26, division attacks toward Montfaucon and the Bois de Cunel from its front in the Avocourt sector, captures Haucourt and Malancourt, and reaches a line from 1¼ km north of Malancourt along the northeastern edge of the Bois de Cuisy; 4th Division (III Corps) and on right, 37th Division on left.

September 26–30, division (less Arty) participates in the Meuse-Argonne Operation.

September 27, division captures Montfaucon and reaches a line from Côte 295 (excl.) to the slope ½ km northwest of Montfaucon.

September 28, division captures Nantillois, clears the enemy from the eastern part of the Bois de Beuge, temporarily penetrates the Bois des Ogons in of la Madeleine Fme, and establishes its front from Hill 274 south of Source de Wilpré, along the northern edge of Wood 268, to 1 km east of Cierges.

September 29, division resumes the attack, enters the Bois des Ogons and Wood 250, but finally withdraws to a defensive position along the ridge 300 in northwest of Nantillois and along the northern edge of the Bois d Beuge.

September 30, division is relieved by the 3rd Division and assembles in the vicinity of Malancourt.

October 3, division moves to the zone of the French II Colonial Corps north of St. Mihiel.

October 8, division, together with elements of the French 2nd Dismounted Cav Division and French 39th Division, relieves the 26th Division from Doncourt-aux-Templiers (excl.), through Saulx-en-Woëvre, to Fresnes-en-Woëvre (incl.); command passes to the 79th Division; local actions occur.

October 8–26, division (less Arty) occupies the Troyon Sector (Lorraine).

October 18, division relieves elements of the French 2nd Dismounted Cav Division in the Thillot Subsector.

October 26, division is relieved by the 33rd Division, moves to stations near Dieue-sur-Meuse, and passes to corps reserve.

October 26–November 11, division (less Arty) participates in the Meuse-Argonne Operation.

October 30–November 1, division relieves the 29th Division in the Grand-Montagne Sector and a portion of the 26th Division southeast thereof, along the line from 1¾ km west of Flabas, through Côte 360 in the Bois d'Ormont, Belleu Bois, Hill 361 in the Bois d'Etraye, to 1 km northwest of Hill

382 in Bois Plat-Chêne; 26th Division on right, French 15th Colonial Division on left.

November 3–6, division advances its left to positions on Hill 370 and on the southern slope of la Borne de Cornouiller (Hill 378).

November 7, division advances its left, through the enemy trenches at los Clairs-Chênes, reaching la Vaux-Rougieux ravine; the front now extends from 1¼ km north of Molleville Fme, through a point 1¼ km northeast of Sillon-Fontaine Fme, to ½ km east of Solférino Fme.

November 8, the sector is extended on the left to the Haraumont-Ecurey road; division attacks east and reaches the line from Bois de Moirey (excl.), through Etraye, north slope of la Côte d'Etraye, Revile (excl.), Bouillon Grêve, to Ecurey.

November 9, the front is reduced and now extends from the Bois de Moirey to Etraye.

November 9–11, division attacks, captures Crépion, Wavrille, Gibercy, and Ville-devant-Chaumont, and reaches a line from Chaumont-devant-Damvillers (incl.), along the high ground 1½ km west of Romagne-sous-les-Côtes, to 1½ km east of Gibercy.

Post Armistice Activities

NOVEMBER 12, 1918 – MAY 10, 1919

November 12, division (less Arty) establishes examining posts along armistice line and engages in the enforcement of the armistice terms, salvage, and training.

November 13, division relieves the French 15th Cl Division by extending its line to the left. The 154th Field Artillery Brig and 304th Am Tn move to the 9th (Châteauvillain) Training Area, and on November 24, to the 4th (Rimaucourt) Training Area.

November 18, division extends its area to Bezonvaux, and on November 20 to Fresnes-en-Woëvre, relieving the 6th Division.

December 10, certain units move to the Montmédy-Stenay Area to guard enemy materiel and maintain order.

December 26, division (less Arty) moves to the Souilly Area for training.

January 11, the artillery and ammunition train rejoin.

March 14, 304th TM Btry sails from St. Nazaire for the United States.

March 28, division moves to the 4th (Rimaucourt) Training Area.

April 19, 154th Field Artillery Brig moves to St. Nazaire.

April 21, division (less Arty and Engrs) moves to the Nantes Area.

Return to the United States and Demobilization

May 11–June 7, 1919

May 11, division begins to assemble at St. Nazaire.
May 13, 310th Field Artillery sails.
May 18, DHQ sails.
June 11, the last elements arrive at New York. The demobilization at Camp Dix includes, May 30, Hq 154th Field Artillery Brig, June 2, DHQ, June 6, Hq 158th Infantry Brig, June 7, Hq 157th Infantry Brig.

The Eightieth Division, National Army

The 80th Division was organized at Camp Lee, Virginia. The men were largely from Virginia, West Virginia and Western Pennsylvania. Major General Adelbert Cronkite commanded the division from September 9, 1917, until the end of the war. The division embarked from Newport News, where it arrived in its entirety through St. Nazaire, Bordeaux and Brest, June 19, 1918. It captured 1813 prisoners, was quiet one day and active 17. It advanced 80 kilometers. It suffered 6132 casualties, had 1132 battle deaths and 5000 wounded. It received 4,495 replacements.

159th Infantry Brigade

317th Infantry
318th Infantry
314th Machine Gun Battalion

160th Infantry Brigade

319th Infantry
320th Infantry
315th Machine Gun Battalion

155th Artillery Brigade

313th Field Artillery
314th Field Artillery
315th Field Artillery
305th Trench Mortar Battery

Divisional Troops

305th Engineers
313th Machine Gun Battalion
305th Field Signal Battalion

Trains

305th Train Hdqs
305th Military Police
305th Ammunition Train
305th Supply Train
305th Engineer Train
305th Sanitary Train
Ambulance Cos and Field Hospitals 317–320

Record of Events

SECTORS WHERE THE EIGHTIETH DIVISION WAS ENGAGED IN WARFARE

Picardy sector, France, July 25 to August 18, 1918.
St. Mihiel offensive, France, September 12 to 16, 1918.
Meuse-Argonne offensive, France, September 26 to 29, 1918.
Meuse-Argonne offensive, France, October 4 to 12, 1918.
Meuse-Argonne offensive, France, November 1 to 6, 1918.

Organization and Training in the United States

AUGUST 5, 1917–MAY 16, 1918

August 5, the War Department establishes the 80th Division, National Army, which is to be organized at Camp Lee, Petersburg, Virginia; drafts, anticipated for 1917, from Pennsylvania, 23,907, Virginia, 13,808, and West Virginia, 7,613, are designed to furnish personnel.

August 13, the organization of DHQ is directed, and its commissioned personnel are ordered to report on or before August 15.

August 16, the commanding general of Camp Lee is directed to organize the division in accordance with the Tables of Organization of August 8, 1917.

August 25, the program for the movement of selective service men to camps is announced.

August 27, Brig. Gen. Herman Hall assumes command. During the last week in August the organization begins from a cadre of officers and men of the Regular Army and from ORC and NA officers of the First Officers Training Camps.

September 5–10, the initial draft of 2,300 selective service men arrives at camp. Major General Adelbert Cronkite replaces Gen. Hall.

September 19–24, an additional 18,700 arrive. During October systematic training begins.

October 3–8, the last drafts of 1917 furnish the camp with 9,700.

October 31, the division aggregates over 20,000, and maintains this strength, notwithstanding large current gains and losses. During April and May drafts and transfers complete the division, which has received an aggregate of 40,000 men. May 10, the Adv Det sails from Hoboken and arrives May 23, at Brest.

Movement Overseas

May 17–June 9, 1918

May 17, the leading infantry units leave Camp Lee, and sail on May 18 from Newport News.

May 22 and 26, DHQ, the remaining infantry, the artillery and divisional units sail from Hoboken, Newport News, and Norfolk for Brest, Bordeaux, and St. Nazaire, arriving May 30–31 and June 8–9.

Final Training and Operations

June 2–November 11, 1918

June 2, division (less Arty and 305th Sup Tn) moves from Brest, St. Nazaire, and Bordeaux, via Calais, to the Samer Training Area.

May 31–August 23, division is under the administrative control of the II Corps.

June 10–July 3, division (less Arty and 305th Sup Tn) is affiliated with the British 16th (Irish) Division, British 34th Division, and British 117th Brig in the Samer Training Area.

June 10–August 18, training with the British in Flanders and Picardy.

June 13–16, 155th Field Artillery Brig and 305th Am Tn arrive at Redon, where they train until August 12.

July 4, division (less detached units) moves to the area of the British Third Army in the Artois Sector between Aveluy Woods and Arras; the 159th Infantry Brig is attached to the British IV and British V Corps, the 160th Infantry Brig to British VI Corps; training predominates.

July 23–August 7, division participates with the British in the occupation of the Artois Sector (Picardy). The troops are affiliated for training with the British Third Army, which is in line between Albert and Arras.

August 8, Somme offensive operation begins; units of division are, at times, in front line until August 18.

August 8–18, units of division (less Arty and 305th Sup Tn) participate in the Somme Offensive Operation.

August 15, 155th Field Artillery Brig and 305th Am Tn begin their training at Camp de Meucon.

Night of August 15–16, 2nd Bn 317th Inf, cooperating with a New Zealand battalion, advances about 2,400 yds. and occupies an enemy position east of Serre.

August 17, 320th Infantry takes over a British Guard Brigade sector with headquarters at Ransart.

August 19, division is relieved from the British Third Army; units are withdrawn from the front line except elements of 320th Inf; the troops move to the 14th (Aignay-le-Duc) Training Area, where they train.

August 25, division is ordered to join the First Army.

August 31, division (less Arty and 305th Sup Tn) continues, via Châtillon, to the vicinity of Stainville for further training.

September 7, division (less Arty) moves to the vicinity of Ligny-en-Barrois, Tronville-en-Barrois, and Nancois-le-Grand.

September 12–14, division (less Arty) is near Tronville in the reserve of the First Army during the St. Mihiel Operation.

September 13, 155th Field Artillery Brig and 305th Am Tn, coming from Camp de Meucon, revert to the division.

September 13–14, 320th Infantry and 315th MG Bn pass to the French II Colonial Corps, move to the vicinity of Woimbey, and are attached to the French 2nd Dismounted Cavalry Division in the St. Mihiel Operation; subsequently they rejoin the division.

September 14, division moves toward the Bois la Vile via Ippécourt and Osches, preparatory to the Meuse-Argonne Operation.

Night of September 21–22, 3rd Bn, 319th Infantry, relieves one battalion of the 33rd Division in the Béthincourt Sector.

September 24, the remainder of the 160th Infantry Brig moves toward Germonville to the Bois Bourrus.

Night of September 24–25, 159th Infantry Brig moves to Germonville, and the 160th Infantry Brig relieves troops of the 33rd Division in the Béthincourt Sector.

September 26–October 12, division participates in the Meuse-Argonne Operation.

September 26, division attacks with the 160th Infantry Brig from an east and west line south of Béthincourt, along the Tr Brody, Tr Kovel, and Tr d'Alsace, and occupies Béthincourt, Dannevoux, the Bois des Moriaux, and the Bois de Septsarges; division front is now along the Meuse from east of Dannevoux to south of Vilosnes-sur-Meuse, thence southwest to the northern edge of the Bois de Septsarges; 33rd Division on right, 4th Division on left.

September 27, division captures the Bois de Dannevoux; the 318th Infantry and one battalion of the 315th Field Artillery are detached and join the 4th Division.

September 28, division clears the Bois de la Côte Lémont.

Night of September 28–29, division (less Arty and 318th Infantry) is relieved by the 33rd Division, passes to the reserve of the III Corps and moves to a position near Montfaucon.

October 3, 155th Field Artillery Brig (less 2nd Bn, 315th Field Artillery, supporting the 4th Division until October 7), 305th Am Tn, and 318th Infantry (less 1st Bn) revert to the division.

Night of October 3–4, division moves into line between the 3rd and 4th Divisions near the southern edge of the Bois des Ogons and relieves troops of both these units.

October 4, division, with the 159th Infantry Brig in line from ½ km southwest of the Moulin de l'Etanche to 1 km northwest of Nantillois, attacks toward the Bois des Ogons; the line stabilizes south of the Bois des Ogons; 4th Division on right, 3rd Division (V Corps) on left.

October 5, 1st Bn, 318th Infantry, reverts to the division; the attack reaches the northern edge of the Bois des Ogons.

October 6–11, division, in a series of attacks, captures the Bois des Ogons, the western part of the Bois de Fays, and he western part of the Bois de Malaumont, and establishes a line from 1 km northeast of Cunel to 400 m south of that village.

Night of October 11–12, division (less Arty and 305th Engrs) is relieved by the 5th Division; the artillery and engineers continue in action with the III Corps, the artillery supporting the 5th Division until October 22, and then the 90th Division until November 11.

October 12–14, division (less detached units) moves via the Forêt de Hesse and Bois de Cuisy to Triaucourt and passes to the army reserve.

October 15–22, the division reorganizes.

October 23–24, division (less Arty) moves to the vicinity of Neuvilly and passes into corps reserve.

October 24–November 6, division (less Arty) again participates in the Meuse-Argonne Operation.

October 25–30, the division undergoes further rehabilitation and training.

Night of October 31–November 1, division relieves units of the 82nd Division along a front extending from 1 km south of St. Georges to 1½ km northeast of St. Juvin.

November 1, division, 160th Infantry Brig leading, attacks from the road between St. Georges and St. Juvin; the right of the attack mops up the western edge of St. Georges, captures Imécourt, reaches the road between Imécourt and Sivry-lès-Buzancy 1 km south of the latter town, and the advance elements reach the Fontaine des Parades; the left of the attack advances about 1 km; 2nd Division (V Corps) on right, 77th Division on left.

November 2, division advances through Alliépont and Sivry-lès-Buzancy, drives enemy from Buzancy, and establishes a front just north of Route Nationale No. 47 between the western edge of the Bois de Ia Folie and 1 km east of Harricourt.

November 3, division changes direction from the north to northeast, and advances to a front from 1½ km north of Fossé, les Tyrônnes Fme, Puits-Sartelles to 1 km east of St. Pierremont. **November 4,** division continues the advance and captures Vaux-en-Dieulet and Sommauthe.

November 5, division reaches the western outskirts of Beaumont, la Thibaudine Fme, Warniforêt, and a point 300 m east of La Bagnolle.

November 6, division advances to the general line, Beaumont and Yoncq, where the 1st Division passes through the 80th Division and the latter assembles near Sommauthe.

November 8, division (less detached units) moves to the south of Buzancy and on November 9 continues to the region of Cornay, Apremont, and Varennes-en-Argonne.

Post Armistice Activities
NOVEMBER 12, 1918–MARCH 29, 1919

November 11, division (less Arty) moves to the vicinity of Les Islettes and on November 18 to the 15th (Ancy-le-Franc) Training Area.

December 1–8, the division reorganizes.

December 6–7, 155th Field Artillery Brig rejoins.

December 9–March 19, training predominates.

February 12, 305th TM Btry sails from Brest.

Return to the United States and Demobilization
MARCH 30–JUNE 7, 1919

March 30, division moves to the Le Mans Area, American Embarkation Center.

May 9, division moves to Brest.
May 16, the leading elements sail from Brest.
May 17, DHQ leaves.
June 9, the last troops arrive at Boston. The demobilization includes, at Camp Lee, June 1, Hq 159th Infantry Brig, June 2, Hq 155th Field Artillery Brig, June 5, DHQ; at Camp Dix, June 7, Hq 160th Infantry Brig.

THE EIGHTY-FIRST DIVISION, NATIONAL ARMY

The 81st Division was organized at Camp Jackson, South Carolina. The members of the division were largely from North Carolina, South Carolina and Tennessee. Brigadier General Charles H. Barth organized the division and was in command until October 8, 1917, when he was relieved by Major General Charles A. Bailey. The overseas movement was completed between July 30 and August 26, 1918. This division captured 101 prisoners, was quiet 31 days, active no days, and advanced 5½ kilometers. It had 251 battle deaths and 973 wounded for a total of 1,224 casualties. It received 1,984 replacements.

161st Infantry Brigade

321st Infantry
322nd Infantry
317th Machine Gun Battalion

162nd Infantry Brigade

323rd Infantry
324th Infantry
318th Machine Gun Battalion

155th Field Artillery Brigade

316th Field Artillery
317th Field Artillery
318th Field Artillery
306th Trench Mortar Battery

Divisional Troops

306th Engineers
316th Machine Gun Battalion
306th Field Signal Battalion

Trains

306th Train Hdqs
306th Military Police
306th Ammunition Train
306th Supply Train
306th Engineer Train
306th Sanitary Train
Ambulance Cos and Field Hospitals 321–324

Record of Events

SECTORS WHERE THE EIGHTY-FIRST DIVISION WAS ENGAGED IN WARFARE

St. Die sector, France, September 20 to October 19, 1918.
Meuse-Argonne offensive, France November 7 to 11, 1918.

Organization and Training in the United States

AUGUST 5, 1917–JULY 12, 1918

August 5, the War Department establishes the 81st Division, National Army, which is to be organized at Camp Jackson, Columbia, South Carolina; drafts, anticipated for 1917, from Florida, 6,325, North Carolina, 15,974, and South Carolina, 10,081, are designed to furnish personnel.

August 13, the organization of DHQ is directed, and its commissioned personnel are ordered to report on or before August 15.

August 16, the commanding general of Camp Jackson is directed to organize the division in accordance with the Tables of Organization of August 8, 1917.

August 25, Brig. Gen. Charles H. Barth assumes command; the program for the movement of selective service men to camps is announced. During the last week in August the organization, to include skeleton units, begins from a cadre of officers and men of the Regular Army and from ORC and NA officers of the First Officers Training Camps.

September 5–10, the initial draft of 1,600 selective service men arrives at camp.

September 19–24, an additional 10,800 arrive. During September systematic training begins.

October 3–8, the last drafts of 1917 furnish the camp with 2,800. During October the greater part of the enlisted men are transferred, but fresh drafts arrive either direct or via Camps Gordon and Pike, from Alabama, Florida, Georgia, North Carolina, South Carolina and Tennessee, with the result that on October 31 the strength is nearly 12,000. During the winter further losses reduce the strength to fewer than 10,000.

May 16, the division (less Arty) moves to Camp Sevier. In May drafts of several thousand arrive. During June, drafts, including 8,000 from Alabama and 1,200 from New York, complete the division.

Movement Overseas

JULY 13–AUGUST 25, 1918

July 13, division moves via Camps Mills and Upton to the ports of embarkation of Boston, Brooklyn, Hoboken, New York, and Philadelphia.

July 30, Adv Det sails from New York, travels via England, and arrives on August 13 at Le Havre.

July 30, 31, and August 5, division (less 317th FA, 318th FA, 306th Am Tn, and 306th San Tn) sails, and arrives August 11, 12, and 15, in England.

August 7–9, the remaining units sail, and land, August 20–25, in England. The troops, after a brief stay in rest camps, proceed to Le Havre and Cherbourg.

Final Training and Operations

AUGUST 16–NOVEMBER 11, 1918

August 16, division (less Arty) moves to the 16th (Tonnerre) Training Area for training.

August 18, 156th Field Artillery Brig and 306th Am Tn arrive at Le Valdahon and the vicinity for training.

September 2–14, division is under the administrative control of the VI Corps.

September 14, division (less Arty) moves to the region about Bruyères in the zone of the French Seventh Army.

September 18, the leading units of the division, affiliated with the French 20th Division, enter the St. Die Sector, which extends from a point

¾ km south of Lusse to ½ km south of Allencombe, and relieve the 92nd Division.

September 18–October 1, division (less Arty) participates with the French in the occupation of the St. Die Sector (Lorraine).

September 18–November 1, division is under the administrative control of the VII Corps.

September 20, the command of the sector passes to the French 20th Division.

October 2, the 81st Division assumes command upon the relief of the French 20th Division; local actions occur.

October 2–19, division (less Arty) occupies the St. Die Sector (Lorraine).

October 17, the French 20th Division relieves the division in the southern subsector from ¾ km south of Lusse to 1 km southwest of Mémi.

October 19, the Polish 1st Division relieves the division in the northern part of the sector.

October 20, division moves to the Rambervilers Area and training follows.

October 31, division moves to the vicinity of Verdun-sur-Meuse, and, on November 2, proceeds to the Sommedieue Sector, where it becomes corps reserve.

November 2–11, division (less Arty) participates in the Meuse-Argonne Operation.

November 5, division begins the relief of the 35th Division, except 60th Field Artillery Brig and 110th Am Tn, from Bonzée-en-Woëvre, through Haudiomont, Châtilon-sous-Côtes, Moulainville-la-Basse, Fort de Vaux, to Ouvrage de Bezonvaux (excl.), 33rd Division (French II Colonial Corps) on right, French 10th Colonial Division on left.

November 7, the command of the front passes to the 81st Division.

November 9, French 10th Colonial Division relieves the Division in the left of the sector north of the Verdun-Etain road; the 81st Division attacks toward the northeast, enters Manheulles and the wooded areas of les Chairs-Chênes and la Noire-Haie, captures Moranville, and occupies the northern edge of the Bois de Moranville.

November 10, division captures Abaucourt and le Grand-Cognon and enters Grimaucourt-en Woëvre.

November 11, division resumes the attack, captures Grimaucourt-en-Woëvre and le Petit-Cognon, and advances to a line from a point 1 km southwest of Herméville to Abaucourt; minor gains are made northeast of Manheulies and in the southwestern corner of the Bois de Manheulles.

Post Armistice Activities

NOVEMBER 12, 1918–MAY 28, 1919

November 11–17, division (less Arty) maintains outposts along the armistice line.

November 18, division (less Arty) moves to the Souilly Area, and thence to the south, arriving on December 1 in the 12th (Mussy-sur-Seine) Training Area, where it is joined by the 156th Field Artillery Brig (less 316th FA) and 306th Am Tn; training follows. The 316th Field Artillery remains detached at St. Blin until March 21, and thereafter at Châteauvillain.

March 9, 306th TM Btry sails from St. Nazaire.

May 9, division (less 316th FA) moves to the Ballon Area, American Embarkation Center, Le Mans.

May 15, 316th Field Artillery rejoins.

Return to the United States and Demobilization

MAY 29–JUNE 23, 1919

May 21, the division moves to the ports of embarkation, the advance echelon of DHQ and the artillery to Brest, the remainder to St. Nazaire.

May 27, the leading artillery units sail. June 1, the advance echelon of DHQ sails.

June 24, the last element of the division arrives at Newport News. The demobilization includes, at Hoboken, June 11, DHQ; at Camp Devens, June 17, Hq 162nd Infantry Brig; at Camp Lee, June 11, Hq 156th Field Artillery Brig; at Camp Jackson, June 23, Hq 161st Infantry Brig.

THE EIGHTY-SECOND DIVISION, NATIONAL ARMY

The 82nd Division was organized at Camp Gordon, Georgia, from men of Georgia, Alabama and Tennessee. These original men were, however, mostly transferred to other divisions on October 10, 1917, and newly drafted men from Camps Devens, Upton, Dix, Meade and Lee were sent to the division in their place. In this division there were men from nearly every state but mostly from the Eastern states, The overseas movement which began April 25 was completed by the arrival of the last unit in France on June 1. Major General Eben Swift first commanded the division. He was succeeded May 9, 1918, by Brigadier General William P. Burnham, who continued in command until October 10, 1918, when Major General George B. Duncan succeeded him. On October 17, Major General William P. Burnham again took command and remained until November 7, when he was relieved by Major General George B. Duncan. The 82nd took 845 prisoners, was quiet 70 days and active 27. They advanced 17 kilometers. This division had 7546 casualties, 1398 battle deaths and 6248 wounded. The division received 8402 replacements.

163rd Infantry Brigade

325th Infantry
326th Infantry
320th Machine Gun Battalion

164th Infantry Brigade

327th Infantry
328th Infantry
321st Machine Gun Battalion

157th Field Artillery Brigade

319th Field Artillery
320th Field Artillery
321st Field Artillery
307th Trench Mortar Battery

Divisional Troops

307th Engineers
319 Machine Gun Battalion
317 Field Signal Battalion
Headquarters Troop

Trains

307th Train Hdqs
307th Military Police
307th Ammunition Train
307th Supply Train
307th Engineer Train

307th Sanitary Train
Ambulance Cos and Field Hospitals 325–328

Record of Events

SECTORS WHERE THE EIGHTY-SECOND DIVISION WAS ENGAGED IN WARFARE

Toul sector, France, June 26 to August 9, 1918.
Marbache sector, Toul, France, August 17 to September 11, 1918.
St. Mihiel offensive, France, September 12 to 16, 1918.
Meuse-Argonne offensive, France, October 6 to 31, 1918.

Organization and Training in the United States

AUGUST 5, 1917–APRIL 9, 1918

August 5, the War Department establishes the 82nd Division, National Army, which is to be organized at Camp Gordon, Atlanta, Georgia; drafts, anticipated for 1917, from Alabama, 5,596, Georgia, 18,337, and Tennessee, 14,528, are designed to furnish personnel.

August 13, the organization of DHQ is directed, and its commissioned personnel are ordered to report on or before August 15.

August 16, the commanding general of Camp Gordon is directed to organize the division in accordance with the Tables of Organization of August 8, 1917.

August 25, Maj. Gen. Eben Swift assumes command; the program for the movement of selective service men to camps is announced. During the first week in September the organization, to include skeleton units, begins from a cadre of officers and men of the Regular Army, and from ORC and NA officers of the First Officers Training Camp at Fort McPherson.

September 5–10, the initial draft of 1,900 selective service men arrives at camp.

September 19–24, an additional 12,400 arrive. During September systematic training begins.

October 3–8, the last drafts of 1917 furnish the camp with 4,300. During October nearly all National Army men from Alabama, Georgia, and Tennessee are transferred, the majority to the 30th, 31st, and 81st Divisions. Replacements, largely from the New England and Middle Atlantic States, join from Camps Devens, Dix, Lee, Meade, and Upton.

November 30, the division is virtually complete and systematic training is resumed. In March the winter losses are replaced by fresh drafts which come from Camps Devens, Dodge, Gordon, Travis, Upton and the depot brigade, aggregating 5,000, and by a contingent from Alabama, Georgia, and Tennessee, and the division is again complete.

Movement Overseas

APRIL 10–JULY 10, 1918

April 10, division moves via Camps Mills and Upton to the ports of embarkation of Boston, Brooklyn, and New York, en route to Liverpool.

April 16, Adv Det sails from New York and arrives on April 28.

April 25–May 7, DHQ, all the infantry units, Tn Hq and MP sail, and arrive May 7–25.

May 19, 157th Field Artillery Brig, 307th Am Tn, 307th Engrs and Tn, 307th F Sig Bn and 307th San Tn sail, and arrive May 31. The last unit, 307th Sup Tn, sails on June 28 and lands July 10. The troops, after a brief stay in rest camps, embark at Southampton for Le Havre.

Final Training and Operations

MAY 10–NOVEMBER 11, 1918

May 10–June 15, training with the British in Picardy.

May 10, division (less Arty, Engrs, 307th F Sig Bn, and trains) moves to the St. Valery-sur-Somme Training Area.

May 13–June 18, division is under the administrative control of the II Corps.

May 15–June 14, division (less detached units) trains with the British 66th Division.

June 3, 157th Field Artillery Brig and 307th Am Tn begin to arrive at Le Havre, and, on June 4, proceed to La Courtine for training.

June 3–4, 307th Engrs and Tn and 307th F Sig Bn arrive at Le Havre.

June 15, division (less detached units) moves to stations in and about Toul in the area of the French Eighth Army.

June 16–July 17, training with the French in Lorraine.

June 18–21, division is under the administrative control of the I Corps.

June 21–August 22, under the administrative control of the IV Corps.

June 23–25, all detached units, except the artillery, 319th MG Bn, and 307th Sup Tn, rejoin.

June 24, division (less detached units) moves to the Woëvre front, where it is affiliated with the French 154th Division in the Lagney Sector.

June 25, the leading battalions enter the line, which extends from the Forêt du Bois-le-Prêtre (incl.), through Regniéville (incl.), points 1 km north of Limey, 1 km north of Flirey, and 1 km north of Seicheprey, Marvoisin, la Tassenière on the Etang de Vargévaux 1 km west of Bouconville; the organization of the position and local actions follow.

June 25–July 17, division (less Arty, 319th MG Bn, and 307th Sup Tn) participates in the occupation of the Lagney Sector (Lorraine).

June 28, the command of the sector passes from the 26th Division to the French 154th Division; French 65th Division (French Eighth Army) on fight, French 34th Division (French Second Army) on left.

July 12, division assumes temporary command of the sector.

July 17, division (less Arty) relieves the last elements, except the artillery, of the French 154th Div; 319th MG Bn and 307th Sup Tn rejoin.

July 18–August 10, division (less Arty) occupies the Lucey Sector (Lorraine).

July 18, the sector is reduced by moving the right boundary to western outskirts of Remenauville and, as thus occupied, is called the Lucey Sector; the division assumes permanent command of this sector; French 64th Division (French 32nd Corps) is on the right, French 34th Division (French II Cl Corps) is on the left.

August 4, French 2nd Moroccan Division is on the right.

August 7, 1st Division is on the right.

August 10, division is relieved by the 89th Division and moves to the vicinity of Toul, and again, on August 12, toward the Marbache Sector.

Night of August 15–16, division begins the relief of the 2nd Division in the Marbache Sector, which extends from 1 km southeast of Port-sur-Seille, through Morville-sur-Seille, Losmenus, Pont-Mousson, to the Foret du Bois-le-Prêtre.

August 18, division is ordered to join the First Army.

August 19–September 11, division occupies the Marbache Sector (Lorraine).

August 19, division assumes command of the sector; the 157th Field Artillery Brig and 307th Am Tn move to this sector; French 32nd Division (French Eighth Army) on right, 1st Division on left.

August 20, French 125th Division is on the right.

August 22, 157th Field Artillery Brig assumes command of the sector artillery.

August 24, 90th Division is on the left.

September 12, this sector occupation merges into the St. Mihiel Operation.

September 12–16, division participates in the St. Mihiel Operation. The

82nd Division executes a holding mission in order to prevent hostile flanking action against the right of the First Army.

September 13, 163rd Infantry Brig and 327th Infantry raid and patrol to the northeast of Port-sur-Seille, toward Eply, in the Bois de Cheminot, Bois de la Voivrotte, Bois de la Tête-d'Or, and Bois Fréhaut; 328th Infantry, in connection with the attack of the 90th Division against the Bois-le-Prêtre, advances on the west of the Moselle River, and, in contact with the right of the 360th Infantry (90th Division), enters Norroy and reaches the heights just north of that town, where it consolidates its position.

September 15, 328th Infantry, in order to provide flank protection for the 90th Division, resumes the advance, reaches Vandières and the hill 400 in northwest thereof, but withdraws on the following day to the high ground 1¼ km north of Norroy.

September 17, the St. Mihiel Operation stabilizes.

September 17–20, division again occupies the Marbache Sector (Lorraine).

September 18, the sector is reduced when the 90th Division relieves the troops west of the Moselle River.

September 20, division is relieved by the French 69th Division, moves to the vicinity of Marbache and Bellevile, and on September 24, to stations near Triaucourt and Rarécourt in the area of the First Army.

September 26–October 2, division is in army reserve.

September 29–October 3, 327th Infantry is detached for duty with the I Corps and passes to the 28th Division.

September 30 and the Night of September 30–October 1, this regiment is in line between the 28th and 35th Divisions near Baulny. Subsequently it returns to bivouac near Varennes-en-Argonne.

October 3, division assembles near Varennes-en-Argonne prior to entering the line.

October 6–October 31, division participates in the Meuse-Argonne Operation.

Night of October 6–7, 164th Infantry Brig relieves troops of the 28th Division that are holding the front line from ½ km south of Flévilie to La Forge, along the eastern bank of the Aire River; the 163rd Infantry Brig remains in corps reserve.

October 7, division (less 163rd Infantry Brig) attacks the northeastern edge of the Argonne Forest, makes some progress toward Cornay, and occupies Hill 180 and Hill 223; 1st Division (V Corps) on right, 28th Division on left.

October 8, the division (less 163rd Infantry Brig) resumes the attack; the right enters Cornay, but later withdraws to the east and south of that town, the left reaches the southeastern slope of the high ground 2 km northwest of Châtel-Chéhery.

Night of October 8–9, 163rd Infantry Brig is released from corps reserve; the 326th Infantry relieves troops of the 28th Division on its left from 2 km west of Hill 223, through Drachen, to a point 2¼ km west of le Ménil Fme; 77th Division is on the left.

October 9, division resumes the attack and advances its left to a line from ½ km south of Pylône to the Rau de la Louvière.

October 10–31, division turns to the north and advances astride the Aire River to the region east of St. Juvin.

October 10, division relieves troops of the 1st Division on the fighting north of Fléville, as far as a new boundary extending north and south through Sommerance, attacks, captures Cornay and Marcq, and establishes the front, ½ km south of Sommerance, Martincourt Fme, Marcq (incl.).

October 11, the right of the division occupies Sommerance and the high ground 1 km north of la Rance Rau, the left advances to the railroad south of the Aire River.

October 12, 42nd Division (V Corps), on the right, relieves the troops in and near Sommerance.

October 14–15, division attacks, passes through part of the Hindenburg defensive position, and reaches a line just north of and parallel to the road from St. Georges to St. Juvin.

October 16, 78th Division is on the left.

October 18, division relieves elements of the 78th Division as far to the left as a north and south line slightly west of Marcq and Champigneulle.

October 21, division advances to the Ravin aux Pierres by means of local operations.

October 22–30, division consolidates its position.

October 31, division, except the artillery, is relieved by the 77th and 80th Divisions, and assembles in the Argonne Forest near Champ-Mahaut; the artillery supports the 80th Division along the right half of the former front until November 6.

November 2, division (less Arty) concentrates near La Chalade and Los Islettes, and, on November 4, moves to the 5th (Vaucouleurs) Training Area.

November 10, division (less Arty) moves to the 3rd (Bourmont) Training Area; the artillery concentrates near Les Islettes.

Post Armistice Activities

NOVEMBER 12, 1918–APRIL 21, 1919

November 16, division (less Arty) moves to the 10th (Prauthoy) Training Area.

November 18, 157th Field Artillery Brig and 307th Am Tn move to the vicinity of Ste. Menehould.
November 21–February 25, training predominates.
December 17, 157th Field Artillery Brig and 307th Am Tn rejoin.
February 9, 307th TM Btry sails from Brest for the United States.
February 26, division moves to the Bordeaux Area and trains.

Return to the United States and Demobilization

APRIL 22–MAY 27, 1919

April 22, the advance echelon of DHQ and the 307th Tn Hq sail. During May the balance of DHQ and the majority of the other troops follow.

June 6, the last element, a detachment of the 326th Infantry, arrives at New York. The demobilization includes, at Camp Upton, May 23, Hq 157th Field Artillery Brig, May 27, DHQ; at Camp Mills, May 25, Hq 164th Infantry Brig, May 26, Hq 163rd Infantry Brig.

THE EIGHTY-SEVENTH DIVISION, NATIONAL ARMY

This division did not participate in any combat while in France. Major General Samuel D. Sturgis remained in command until October 23, 1918, when he was relieved by Brigadier General William F. Martin.

173rd Infantry Brigade
345th Infantry
346th Infantry
335th Machine Gun Battalion

174th Infantry Brigade
347th Infantry
348th Infantry
336th Machine Gun Battalion

162nd Field Artillery Brigade
334th Field Artillery
335th Field Artillery

336th Field Artillery
312th Trench Mortar Battery

Divisional Troops

334th Machine Gun Battalion
312th Engineers
312th Field Signal Battalion
Headquarters Troop

Trains

312th Train Hdqs
312th Military Police
312th Ammunition Train
312th Supply Train
312th Engineer Train
312th Sanitary Train
Ambulance Cos and Field Hospitals 345–348

Organization and Training in the United States

AUGUST 5, 1917–JUNE 13, 1918

August 5, the War Department establishes the 87th Division, National Army, which is to be organized at Camp Pike, Little Rock, Arkansas; drafts, anticipated for 1917, from Alabama, 8,016, Arkansas, 10,267, Louisiana, 13,582, and Mississippi, 10,801, are designed to furnish personnel.

August 13, the organization of DHQ at Camp Pike is directed, and its commissioned personnel are ordered to report on or before August 15.

August 16, the commanding general of Camp Pike is directed to organize the division in accordance with the Tables of Organization of August 8, 1917.

August 25, Maj. Gen. Samuel D. Sturgis assumes command; the program for the movement of selective service men to camps is announced. During the last week in August the organization is begun from a cadre of officers and men of the Regular Army and from ORC and NA officers from the First Officers Training Camps.

September 5–10, the initial draft of 2,100 selective service men arrives at camp.

September 19–24, an additional 15,700 arrive. During September systematic training begins.

October 3–8, the last drafts of 1917 furnish 1,300. Prior to November

30 most of the enlisted men are transferred, including 3,000 to the 31st Division, 8,000 to the 39th Division, and 2,400 to the 81st Division.

January 31, the division approximates 23,000, drawn largely from the Middle West via Camps Custer, Dodge, Funston, Grant, Taylor, and Travis. Between January and June 40,000 fresh drafts arrive at Camp Pike, but departures aggregate over 30,000; the division loses more than 20,000.

June 30, the division approximates 15,000. In August a draft of 10,000, largely from New Jersey, New York and Pennsylvania, and other detachments completes the division.

Movement Overseas

JUNE 14–SEPTEMBER 16, 1918

June 14, division moves via Camp Dix to the ports of embarkation of Boston, Brooklyn, Montreal, New York, and Philadelphia.

August 16, the Adv Det sails from New York, and arrives August 28 at Liverpool.

August 23–31, the troops sail, and land September 3–16 in England, except 3rd Bn and Sup Co, 348th Infantry, which stop at Le Havre.

September 9, the SS *Persic*, carrying the Hq 174th Infantry Brig and 1st Bn 347th Infantry, is torpedoed, but the troops are transferred to other vessels. After a brief stay in rest camps the division proceeds to France via Le Havre and Cherbourg.

Activities Overseas

SEPTEMBER 6–DECEMBER 23, 1918

September 6, 162nd Field Artillery Brig and 312th Am Tn move to Bordeaux and the vicinity for duty with the SOS.

September 9, division (less Arty) moves to the Saintes-Pons Area.

September 16, the entire division passes to the SOS.

September 21, the divisional units which are assigned to Base Sections 1, 2, and 7 and the Intermediate Section, SOS, proceed to their respective stations where they engage in construction, guard, police, convoy, labor and other service of supply duties; the majority go to the Departments of Charente-Inférieure, Loir-et-Cher, Loire-Inférieure, Cher, and Gironde, but a few move to the Departments of Maine-et-Loire, Indre, Dordogne, Haute-Vienne, Vienne, and Morbihan; DHQ, Hq 173rd Infantry Brig, Hq 174th Infantry Brig, 312th Tn Hq and MP, and Hq 312th San Tn remain at Pons.

November 10, the troops at Pons move to the 12th Training Area at

Mussy-sur-Seine and later to Foulain and Luzy. Other headquarters are located as follows: 345th Infantry and 347th Infantry at Gièvres, 346th Infantry at Montoir, 348th Infantry at Camp Grange-Neuve, 334th MG Bn at Savenay, 335th MG Bn at Angers, 336th MG Bn at Nantes, 162nd Field Artillery Brig at Camp de Souge, 334th Field Artillery at Camp Baranquine, 335th Field Artillery at Montierchaume, 336th Field Artillery at La Rochelle, 312th TM Btry at Bassens, 312th Am Tn at Camp de Souge, 312th Engrs and Tn at Camp Génicart, 312th Sup Tn at St. Nazaire, and 312th F Sig Bn at Hennebont.

November 17, division is ordered to the base ports for the return.

December 6, DHQ and other units at Foulain and Luzy move to St. Nazaire and thence to Rezé, near Nantes.

Return to the United States and Demobilization

DECEMBER 24, 1918–MARCH 1, 1919

December 24, the leading element of the division, 347th Infantry, sails from Brest.

December 27–29, Hq 173rd Infantry Brig and Hq 174th Infantry Brig leave St. Nazaire and Hq 345th Infantry leaves Brest.

January 10, DHQ sails from St. Nazaire. In February other units sail from these ports and from Bordeaux, including, February 12, Hq 162nd Field Artillery Brig. Still other units follow at intervals. In July the 312th Sup Tn, the last element, sails, and arrives on July 22 at Newport News, Virginia. The demobilization at Camp Dix includes: February 5, Hq 174th Infantry Brig, February 8, Hq 173rd Infantry Brig, February 14, DHQ, March 1, Hq 162nd Field Artillery Brig.

THE EIGHTY-EIGHTH DIVISION, NATIONAL ARMY

The 88th Division was organized at Camp Dodge, Iowa, from men drawn from North Dakota, South Dakota, Minnesota, Nebraska, Illinois and Iowa. The overseas movement, which began August 8, 1918, was completed September 9, 1918, when the last unit arrived in France. The division was organized by Major General Edward H. Plummer. Major General William Weigel commanded the division in action. It captured 10 prisoners. It had 28 quiet days and zero active days. It had 118 casualties, 29 battle deaths and 89 wounded. It received 731 replacements.

175th Infantry Brigade

349th Infantry
350th Infantry
338th Machine Gun Battalion

176th Infantry Brigade

351st Infantry
352nd Infantry
339th Machine Gun Battalion

163rd Field Artillery Brigade

337th Field Artillery
338th Field Artillery
339th Field Artillery
313th Trench Mortar Battery

Divisional Troops

313th Engineers
337th Machine Gun Battalion
313th Field Signal Battalion
Headquarters Troop

Trains

313th Train Hdqs
313th Military Police
313th Ammunition Train
313th Supply Train
313th Engineer Train
313th Sanitary Train
Ambulance Cos and Field Hospitals 349–352

Record of Events

SECTORS WHERE THE EIGHTY-EIGHTH DIVISION WAS ENGAGED IN WARFARE

Center sector, Haute-Alsace, France, October 12 to November 4, 1918.
Meuse-Argonne offensive, France, November 9 to 11, 1918.

Organization and Training in the United States

AUGUST 5, 1917–JULY 30, 1918

August 5, the War Department establishes the 88th Division, National Army, which is to be organized at Camp Dodge, Des Moines, Iowa; drafts, anticipated for 1917, from Illinois, 9,366, Iowa, 12,749, Minnesota, 17,778, and North Dakota, 5,272, are designed to furnish personnel.

August 13, the organization of DHQ at Camp Dodge is directed, and its commissioned personnel ordered to report on or before August 15.

August 16, the commanding general of Camp Dodge is directed to organize the division in accordance with the Tables of Organization of August 8, 1917.

August 25, Maj. Gen. Edward H. Plummer assumes command; the program for the movement of selective service men to camps is announced. Late in August the organization, to include skeleton units, is begun from a cadre of officers and men of the Regular Army, and from ORC and NA officers of the First Officers Training Camp at Fort Snelling.

September 5–10, the initial draft of 2,200 selective service men arrives at camp.

September 19–24, an additional 18,000 arrive. During September systematic training begins.

September 30, the division aggregates 20,000. Transfers rapidly reduce the division and include, in October, 3,000 to the 34th Division and 1,000 to the 33rd Division; in November, 8,000 to the 87th Division.

January 31, the strength approximates 8,000. Between January and July more than 70,000 arrive at Camp Dodge but about 35,000 leave. In February the division receives drafts totaling 12,000 from Iowa and Minnesota, but subsequent losses exceed 16,000, the majority to the 82nd Division and others to the 30th, 33rd, 35th, and 90th Divisions.

April 30, the transfers to and from the division leave a strength of less than 8,500. During May and June more than 10,000 fresh drafts join, many from Missouri, Nebraska, and South Dakota. During July fresh drafts and transfers complete the division.

Movement Overseas

JULY 31–SEPTEMBER 9, 1918

July 31, division moves via Camps Mills and Upton to the ports of embarkation of Brooklyn, New York, Philadelphia, and Quebec.

August 5, Adv Det sails from New York, and lands August 12 at Liverpool.

August 8–17, division (less Hq 163rd Field Artillery Brig, 338th FA, 339th FA, 313th TM Btry, and 313th Sup Tn) sails, and arrives August 17–31 in England.

August 23–27, the remaining units sail, and land September 5 and 9 in England. The troops, after a brief stay in rest camps, proceed to Le Havre and Cherbourg.

Final Training and Operations

AUGUST 19–NOVEMBER 11, 1918

August 19, division (less Arty) moves to the 21st (Semur) Training Area for training.

September 2–14, division is under the administrative control of the VI Corps.

September 6, 163rd Field Artillery Brig and 313th Am Tn move to training areas, the brigade (less 338th FA) to Clermont-Ferrand and the vicinity, the 338th Field Artillery to Camp de Souge near Bordeaux; training follows.

September 14, division (less Arty) moves to the Héricourt Training Area for training.

September 15–November 7, division is under the administrative control of the VII Corps.

September 23–October 7, small detachments of the division train in line with troops of the French 38th Division in the Center Sector, which extends from the railroad 1 km west of Carspach, through Eglingen, to Spech-Bach Creek 3 km northwest of Ammertzwiller.

October 4, a part of the 313th Am Tn joins the division.

October 6, division (less Arty) moves to the Montreux-Château Training Area.

October 14, division (less Arty) participates in the occupation of the Center Sector (Alsace). During this period units of the division are affiliated with troops of the French 38th Division in this sector.

October 15–November 4, division (less Arty) occupies the Center Sector (Alsace).

October 15, division assumes command of the Center Sector.

October 24, division relieves the French 38th Division in the Fulleren Sector on the south, and thereby extends its front to a point in the Glücker-Wald 1½ km west of Hirtzbach; local actions follow.

November 4, division is relieved by the French 154th Division and moves to the vicinity of Belfort, and thence to the vicinity of Toul.

November 6, 175th Infantry Brig, detached, moves to region of

Minorville to become IV Corps reserve.

November 11, the last elements of the division arrive at Toul; training follows.

Post Armistice Activities

NOVEMBER 12, 1918–MAY 14, 1919

November 15, 313th Engrs and Tn move to the region north of Pont-a-Mousson for duty with the Second Army.

November 20, 313th Am Tn reverts to the division.

November 29, division (less Arty and Engrs) moves to the 1st (Gondrecourt) Training Area for training.

December 24–January 24, 163rd Field Artillery Brig (less 313th TM Btry) sails from Bordeaux for the United States.

December 28, 313th TM Btry follows from Brest.

January 10, 313th Engrs and Tn rejoin.

May 7, division (less Arty and Engrs) moves to La Suze Area, American Embarkation Center, Le Mans.

Return to the United States and Demobilization

MAY 15–JUNE 11, 1919

May 15, division moves to St. Nazaire, the engineers joining from the Gondrecourt Training Area.

May 19, 175th Infantry Brig sails, followed on May 20 by the 176th Infantry Brig, and on May 21 by DHQ.

June 6, the last elements of the division arrive at New York. The demobilization at Camp Dodge includes, January 21, Hq 163rd Field Artillery Brig, June 7, Hq 176th mt Brig, June 10, DHQ, and June 11, Hq 175th mt Brig.

THE EIGHTY-NINTH DIVISION, NATIONAL ARMY

The 89th Division was organized at Camp Fuston, Kansas, from men drawn from Missouri, Arizona, New Mexico, Colorado, Kansas, Nebraska, and South Dakota. The division was organized and trained by Major General Leonard Wood. When the division was sent overseas Brigadier General Frank L. Winn was placed in command. The overseas movement began May 24,

1918, and the unit arrived in France in June. On October 24, Major General William M. Wright was placed in command. For its good work during the Meuse-Argonne offensive, the 89th Division was chosen to become part of the Army of Occupation. This division captured 5061 prisoners. It was quiet 55 days, active 28. It advanced 48 kilometers. It had 7291 casualties, 1433 battle deaths, 5858 wounded and received 7669 replacements.

177th Infantry Brigade

353rd Infantry
354th Infantry
341st Machine Gun Battalion

178th Infantry Brigade

355th Infantry
356th Infantry
342nd Machine Gun Battalion

164th Field Artillery Brigade

340th Field Artillery
341st Field Artillery
342nd Field Artillery

Divisional Troops

314th Engineers
340th Machine Gun Battalion
314th Field Signal Battalion
Headquarters Troop

Train

314th Train Hdqs
314th Military Police
314th Ammunition Train
314th Supply Train
314th Engineer Train
314th Sanitary Train
Ambulance Cos and Field Hospitals 353–356

Record of Events

SECTORS WHERE THE EIGHTY-NINTH DIVISION WAS ENGAGED IN WARFARE

Lucey sector, Toul, France, August 10 to September 11, 1918.
St. Mihiel offensive, France, September 12 to 16, 1918.
Euvezin sector, Toul, France, September 17 to October 7, 1918.
Meuse-Argonne offensive, France, October 19 to November 11, 1918.

Organization and Training in the United States

AUGUST 5, 1917–MAY 20, 1918

August 5, the War Department establishes the 89th Division, National Army, which is to be organized at Camp Funston, Fort Riley, Kansas; drafts anticipated for 1917, from Arizona, 3,472, Colorado, 4,753, Kansas, 6,439, Missouri, 18,660, Nebraska, 8,185, New Mexico, 2,292, and South Dakota, 2,717, are designed to furnish personnel.

August 13, the organization of DHQ at Camp Funston is directed, and its commissioned personnel are ordered to report on or before August 15.

August 16, the commanding general of Camp Funston is directed to organize the division in accordance with the Tables of Organization of August 8, 1917. During the last week in August the organization is begun from a cadre of officers and men of the Regular Army, and from ORC and NA officers of the First Officers Training Camp at Fort Riley.

August 25, the program for the movement of selective service men to camps is announced.

August 27, Maj. Gen. Leonard Wood assumes command.

September 5–10, the initial draft of 2,200 selective service men arrives at camp.

September 19–24, an additional 18,600 arrive. During September systematic training begins.

October 3–8, the last drafts of 1917 furnish the camp with 17,300.

October 31, the division approximates 25,000. Between January and June the arrivals and departures at Camp Funston aggregate 20,000 each.

April 30, the division numbers 16,000, having been reduced by transfers to the 3rd, 4th, 35th, and other divisions. In May fresh drafts and transfers complete the unit.

Movement Overseas

May 21–July 8, 1918

May 21, Division moves, via Camp Mills and other stations, to the ports of embarkation of Boston, Brooklyn, Montreal, and New York.

June 4, Adv Det sails from New York and arrives June 11 at Liverpool.

June 4–5, DHQ and the infantry organizations sail, arriving June 16 and 21 at English ports.

June 12–28, all the artillery, divisional troops and trains sail, and arrive in English ports and Le Havre on June 25–July 10. The troops in England, after a brief stay in rest camps, proceed to Le Havre and Cherbourg.

Final Training and Operations

June 21–November 11, 1918

June 21, division (less Arty and 314th Sup Tn) moves to the 4th (Rimaucourt) Training Area for training.

July 4, 164th Field Artillery Brig and 314th Am Tn move to the vicinity of Ste. Hélène, Castelnau, and Le Taillan.

July 29, 314th Sup Tn rejoins.

August 3, 164th Field Artillery Brig and 314th Am Tn move to Camp de Souge, where they train. Division (less Arty) moves to the area of the French Eighth Army near Toul, and, on August 5, begins the relief of the 82nd Division in the Lucey Sector.

August 5–19, division is under the administrative control of the IV Corps.

August 10–September 11, division (less Arty) occupies the Lucey Sector (Lorraine).

August 10, division relieves the 82nd Division in this sector, which extends from Remenauville to Bouconville; local actions follow. The 1st Division is on the right, French 34th Division (French II Cl Corps) on the left.

August 12, French 39th Division (French II Cl Corps) is on the left.

August 18, division is ordered to join the First Army.

August 24, the 90th Division (I Corps) is on the right.

September 8–12, the sector is reduced; the 42nd, 1st, and French 39th Divisions, from right to left, occupy the western portion from a point 1¼ km northwest of Flirey, and the 2nd Division occupies the eastern portion from a point 1 km north of Limey.

September 12–16, division (less Arty) participates in the St. Mihiel Operation.

September 12, the sector occupation merges into the St. Mihiel Operation. Division attacks north, captures the Bois de Mort-Mare, Euvezin, and Bouillonville, and establishes a line from the west outskirts of Thiaucourt to la Fond-de-Mare, 1½ km south of Beney; 2nd Division (I Corps) on right, 42nd Division on left.

September 13–16, division continues the attack, captures Beney, Xammes, and Bois de Xammes, and reaches a line from 1½ km north of Xammes to 1 km south of Marimbois Fme.

September 15, 340th Field Artillery rejoins and supports the 177th Infantry Brig during the remainder of the operation.

September 16, 78th Division (I Corps) is on the right.

September 17–October 7, division occupies the Euvezin Sector (Lorraine). The line held by the division at the end of the St. Mihiel Operation constitutes the front of this sector.

September 18, IV Corps extends its sector to the right to include the front formerly held by the I Corps.

September 19, the remainder of the 164th Field Artillery Brig rejoins.

October 1, division relieves elements of the 42nd Division when the western boundary is moved to the southern corner of the Etang de Lachaussée; French 39th Division (French II Cl Corps) is on the left.

October 4, the sector is extended toward the east to a point 1½ km northeast of Jaulny, where the division relieves elements of the 78th Division; 90th Division is on the right; local actions follow.

October 7, division, except the artillery, is relieved by the 37th Division and assembles in the area northeast of Cominercy.

October 7–November 11, the artillery remains in the sector supporting the 37th Division until October 16, and, subsequently, the 28th Division.

October 9, division (less Arty) moves to the Récicourt Area.

October 12–November 11, division (less Arty) participates in the Meuse-Argonne Operation.

October 12–20, division is in the reserve of the V Corps, moving forward, October 12–14, behind the 32nd Division, which is attacking on the corps' front.

October 20, division relieves the 32nd Division from ½ km north of Romagne-sous-Montfaucon, through the small woods east of the Bois de Chauvignon, the northern edge of the Bois de Chauvignon, over Hill 262, the western edge of the Bois de Bantheyule, to ½ km northeast of la Tuilerie Fme; 5th Division (III Corps) on right, 42nd Division on left.

October 20–22, division clears the enemy from a part of the Bois de Bantheville after a stubborn resistance and reaches the northern and western edges of the woods.

October 22, 90th Division is on the right.
October 23–31, division consolidates its position and prepares to attack.
October 31, 2nd Division is on the left.
November 1, division attacks north-northeast, captures Rémonville and the Bois de Barricourt, and reaches a line west of Tuileries to southeast of La Follarde.
November 2–5, division advances through Barricourt, Tailly, Nouart, Bouclair, and Beaufort, reaching the Meuse from Laneuville-sur-Meuse to Pouilly.
November 7, division relieves units of the 2nd Division as far as a point south of Létanne.
November 10, units cross the Meuse west of Pouilly and reach the high ground north of that place.
November 11, divisional units cross the Meuse at Laneuville-sur-Meuse, occupy Stenay and a position northeast thereof; units on the left of the division occupy the Bois de Hache and Autréville.

Post Armistice Activities

NOVEMBER 12, 1918–MAY 4, 1919

November 11–24, division (less Arty) remains in vicinity of Stenay.
November 24–December 9, advance into Germany.
December 2, 164th Field Artillery Brig reverts to the division.
December 9, division arrives near Trier, via Belgium and Luxemburg.
December 10–May 4, division is stationed in Germany as a part of the Army of Occupation. After several readjustments, the divisional area includes the Kreise of Prüm, Bitburg, Trier Land, and Saarburg. The division trains and furnishes frontier and railway guards.
February 28, 314th TM Btry sails from St. Nazaire for the United States.

Return to the United States and Demobilization

MAY 5–JULY 12, 1919

May 5, division moves to Brest.
May 13, 314th Engrs and Tn sail from St. Nazaire.
May 15, 177th Infantry Brig sails.
May 31, the last elements arrive at New York. The demobilization includes, at Camp Funston, June 1, Hq 177th Infantry Brig, June 5, Hq 164th Field Artillery Brig, July 12, DHQ; at Camp Taylor, June 8, Hq 178th Infantry Brig.

The Ninetieth Division, National Army

The 90th Division was organized under the command of Major General Henry T. Allen at Camp Travis, Texas, from men drawn from Oklahoma and Texas. The overseas movement began in June 1918. The 358th Infantry paraded in England on July 4 before the Lord Mayor of Liverpool. The 90th Division shared with the 89th Division the honor of being the only National Army divisions selected for the Army of Occupation. The 90th Division captured 2412 prisoners, was quiet 42 days, active 26 and advanced 28½ kilometers. It suffered 7277 casualties and had 1392 battle deaths. It had 5885 wounded. The Division received 4437 replacements.

179th Infantry Brigade

357th Infantry
358th Infantry
344th Machine Gun Battalion

180th Infantry Brigade

359th Infantry
360th Infantry
345th Machine Gun Battalion

165th Field Artillery Brigade

343rd Field Artillery
344th Field Artillery
345th Field Artillery
315th Trench Mortar Battery

Divisional Troops

315th Engineers
343rd Machine Gun Battalion
315th Field Signal Battalion
Headquarters Troop

Trains

315th Train Hdqs
315th Military Police
315th Ammunition Train
315th Supply Train
315th Engineer Train
315th Sanitary Train
Ambulance Cos and Field Hospitals 357–360

Record of Events

SECTORS WHERE THE NINETIETH DIVISION WAS ENGAGED IN WARFARE

Villers-en-Haye sector, France, August 24 to September 11, 1918.
St. Mihiel offensive, France, September 12 to 16, 1918.
Puvenelle sector, France, September 17 to October 10, 1918.
Meuse-Argonne offensive, France, October 22 to November 11, 1918.

Organization and Training in the United States

AUGUST 5, 1917–JUNE 4, 1918

August 5, the War Department establishes the 90th Division, National Army, which is to be organized at Camp Travis, Fort Sam Houston, Texas; drafts for 1917 are from Oklahoma, 15,564, and Texas, 30,540.

August 13, the organization of DHQ at Camp Travis is directed, and its commissioned personnel are ordered, to report on or before August 15.

August 16, the commanding general of Camp Travis is directed to organize the division in accordance with the Tables of Organization of August 8, 1917.

August 25, Maj. Gen. Henry T. Allen assumes command; the program for the movement of selective service men to camps is announced. During the first week in September the organization is begun from a cadre of officers and men of the Regular Army, and from ORC and NA officers of the First Officers Training Qamp at Leon Springs.

September 5–10, the initial draft of 2,300 selective service men arrives at camp.

September 19–24, an additional 18,400 arrive. During September systematic training begins.

October 3–8, the last drafts of 1917 furnish the camp with 10,000.

October 31, the division approximates 22,500. Between January and June, 50,000 fresh drafts and transfers arrive at Camp Travis, but losses aggregate 35,000. Early in 1918 the division receives new drafts, many from Oklahoma and Texas. However, the transfers, many to Camps Doniphan, Hancock, Johnston, and Sheridan, reduce the strength to about 15,000 in April.

May 20–21, drafts from Illinois, Minnesota, North Dakota and South Dakota arrive from Camp Dodge.

May 31, the division approximates 24,000.

Movement Overseas

JUNE 5–JULY 17, 1918

June 5, division moves via Camp Mills to the ports of embarkation of Boston, Brooklyn, New York and Philadelphia.

June 13–20, the Adv Det, the Infantry (less 344th MG Bn), and the engineers sail, and arrive June 21–July 2 at Liverpool, except the Adv Det, 360th Infantry and two companies of 315th Engrs, which land at Southampton.

June 21, DHQ and 344th MG Bn sail, and land July 7–8 at Le Havre and London respectively.

June 28–July 6, the artillery, divisional troops, and trains sail; all except the 315th F Sig Bn, Hq 165th Field Artillery Brig, and 343rd Field Artillery land July 10, 15, and 17, at Liverpool, the 315th F Sig Bn lands July 10 at Avonmouth, and the other two units, July 16 at Manchester. The troops, after a brief stay in rest camps, proceed via Cherbourg and Le Havre.

Final Training and Operations

JUNE 24–NOVEMBER 11, 1918

June 24, division (less Arty and 315th Sup Tn) moves to the 14th (Aignay-le-Duc) Training Area for training.

July 19, 165th Field Artillery Brig and 315th Am Tn move to Camp Hunt at Le Courneau for training.

August 2, 315th Sup Tn rejoins.

August 17, division (less Arty) moves to the vicinity of Toul.

August 18, division is ordered to join the First Army.

August 18–21, division is under the administrative control of the IV Corps.

August 24–September 11, division (less Arty) occupies the Villers-en-Haye Sector (Lorraine).

August 24, division relieves the 1st Division in the Villers-en-Haye (formerly Saizerais) Sector from ¾ km northwest of Montrichard in the Forêt du Bois-le-Prêtre, through Fey-en-Haye; to ¼ km south of Remenauville; 82nd Division is on the right, 89th Division (IV Corps) is on the left; local actions follow.

September 10, the sector is reduced when the 2nd and 5th Divisions occupy the western portion of the sector; the new left boundary is 1 km east of Régniéville; 5th Division is on the left.

September 12–16, division (less Arty) participates in the St. Mihiel Operation.

September 12, division attacks north from the front line of the Villers-en-Haye Sector, advances into the Bois de Frière and Bois St. Claude, and establishes its left 1 km east of Viéville-en-Haye; 82nd Division on right, 5th Division on left.

September 13–15, division continues the advance, captures Villers-sous-Prény and the Bois des Rappes, and reaches a line from 1¼ km northwest of Vandières, through Côte 327, 1 km north of les Huit-Chemins in the Bois des Rappes, to a point 200 m south of la Souleuvre Fme.

September 16, division organizes the position.

September 17, the St. Mihiel Operation merges into sector occupation; 78th Division is on the left.

September 17–October 10, division (less Arty) organizes and occupies the Puvenelle Sector (Lorraine).

September 18, the sector is extended to Sablière on the east by the relief of elements of the 82nd Division; the new front extends from Sablière, north of Vandières, to Côte 327; local actions follow.

September 20, French 69th Division is on the right.

September 26, a demonstration is made in connection with the Meuse-Argonne Operation.

October 4, the sector is extended on the west to 1½ km south of Rembercourt-sur-Mad by the relief of elements of the 78th Division; the 89th Division extends its sector to the east and connects with the 90th Division.

October 7, the 37th Division is on the left.

October 9, the 92nd Division is on the right.

October 10, division is relieved by the 7th Division, and assembles in the reserve of the First Army near Toul.

October 13, division moves to the Nixéville Area.

October 18, division (less Arty and Engrs) moves into the Bois de Cuisy, 2 km west of Malancourt, in support of the 3rd and 5th Divisions.

October 19–November 11, division (less Arty) participates in the Meuse-Argonne Operation.

October 21–22, division relieves the 5th Division along the northern and western edges of the Bois des Rappes and along the spur running from the Bois de la Pultière to the northeastern outskirts of Romagnesous-Montfaucon; 3rd Division on right, 89th Division (V Corps) on left.

October 23, division attacks, captures Bantheville and Bonrrut, and reaches a line from the northern edge of the Bois des Rappes, north of Bourrut, to the slopes north of the Ravin dit Fosse-de-Balandre.

October 24 –November 1, a series of local engagements results in slight gains north of Andon Brook.

October 27, 5th Division is on the right.

November 1, division attacks and reaches a front extending from woods east of Fme de Chassogne, along the southern slopes of Côte 243, to the northern edge of Carpière Bois, 1¼ km north of Andevanne.

November 2–6, division advances through Villers-devant-Dum, Bois de Mont, Piois de Montigny, and the Bois de Tally, and reaches the Meuse from Sassey-sur-Meuse to 1½ km south of Laneuville-sur-Meuse.

Night of November 9–10, divisional units cross the Meuse at Sassey-sur-Meuse and reach Mouzay.

November 10, the crossing of the Meuse continues, at Sassey-sur-Meuse and Dun-sur-Meuse; divisional units reach the northeastern edge of the Bois du Chênois southwest of Baâlon, the Fme la Jardinelle, and enter Stenay.

November 11, division enters Baâlon and establishes its front on the heights northwest thereof, and along the eastern edge of Stenay.

Post Armistice Activities

NOVEMBER 12, 1918–MAY 16, 1919

November 12, division (less Arty) establishes outposts along the armistice line, and, on November 14, assumes part of the sector of the 5th Division.

November 17, the outposts are extended to Louppy (excl.), Baalon, Stenay, Inor, and Mouzon (excl.); a military police zone is established in front of the outpost line from Montmédy to Carignan; and the division is engaged in the enforcement of the armistice terms, salvage, and training.

November 22, 165th Field Artillery Brig, detached since June, rejoins.

November 23–25, division assembles near Velosnes, Montmédy, Batlon, and Jametz.

November 24, division, as part of the Army of Occupation, begins the march through Luxemburg, and the last elements arrive near Berncastel and Daun on December 27.

November 24–December 27, advance into Germany.

December 28–May 16, division is stationed in Germany as part of the Army of Occupation. After several readjustments the division occupies the Kreise of Daun, Wittlich, and Berncastel in the Regie Rungsbezirk of Trier, where it guards the railway system within its area; training predominates.

February 28, 315th TM Btry sails from St. Nazaire for the United States.

Return to the United States and Demobilization
MAY 17–JUNE 20, 1919

May 17, division moves to St. Nazaire.

May 28, Hq 165th Field Artillery Brig, 343rd and 345th MG Bns, and 343rd Field Artillery sail.

June 15, the last elements of the division arrive at Charleston, SC. The demobilization includes, at Camp Bowie, June 17, DHQ and Hq 180th Infantry Brig, June 20, Hq 165th Field Artillery Brig; at Camp Pike, June 18, Hq 179th Infantry Brig.

THE NINETY-FIRST DIVISION, NATIONAL ARMY

The 91st Division was organized from men of Alaska, Montana, Idaho, Nevada, Utah, Washington, California, and Oregon. The overseas movement was begun and completed during July 1918. It was commanded by Major General Harry A. Greene, August 25, 1917, to November 24, 1917; Brigadier General James A. Irons until December 23, 1917; Brigadier General Frederick S. Foltz until March 2, 1918; Major General Harry A. Greene until June 19, 1918; Brigadier General Frederick S. Foltz until August 31, 1918; and Major General William H. Johnson until November 11, 1918. The 91st Division captured 2,412 prisoners, was quiet 15 days and active 14. It advanced 34 kilometers. It suffered 5,778 casualties. It had 1414 battle deaths and 4364 wounded. It received 12,530 replacements.

181st Infantry Brigade

361st Infantry
302nd Infantry
347th Machine Gun Battalion

182nd Infantry Brigade

363rd Infantry
364th Infantry
348th Machine Gun Battalion

166th Field Artillery Brigade

346th Field Artillery
347th Field Artillery
348th Field Artillery
316th Trench Mortar Battery

Divisional Troops

316th Engineers
346th Machine Gun Battalion
316th Field Signal Battalion
Headquarters Troop

Trains

316th Train Hdqs
316th Military Police
316th Ammunition Train
316th Supply Train
316th Engineer Train
316th Sanitary Train
Ambulance Cos and Field Hospitals 361–364

Record of Events

SECTORS WHERE THE NINETY-FIRST DIVISION WAS ENGAGED IN WARFARE

St. Mihiel offensive, France, September 12 to 16, 1918.
Meuse-Argonne offensive, France, September 26 to October 4, 1918.
Meuse-Argonne offensive, France, October 8 to 12, 1918.
Ypres-Lys offensive, Belgium, October 31 to November 4, 1918.
Ypres-Lys offensive, Belgium, November 10 to 11, 1918.

Organization and Training in the United States

AUGUST 5, 1917–JUNE 20, 1918

August 5, the War Department establishes the 91st Division, National Army, which is to be organized at Camp Lewis, American Lake, Washington; drafts, anticipated for 1917, were from California, 23,060; Idaho, 2,287; Montana, 7,872; Nevada, 1,051; Oregon, 717; Utah, 2,370; Washington, 7,296; and Wyoming, 810.

August 13, the organization of DHQ at Camp Lewis is directed, and its commissioned personnel are ordered to report on or before August 15.

August 16, the commanding general of Camp Lewis is directed to organize the division in accordance with the Tables of Organization of August 8, 1917.

August 25, the program for the movement of selective service men to camps is announced.

August 26, Maj. Gen. Harry A. Greene assumes command. During the first week in September the organization, to include skeleton units, is begun from a cadre of officers and men of the Regular Army and from ORC and NA officers from the First Officers Training Camps.

September 5–10, the initial draft of 2,300 selective service men arrives at camp.

September 19–24, an additional 18,000 arrive. During September systematic training begins.

October 3–8, the last drafts of 1917 furnish the camp with 18,000.

October 31, the division approximates 26,000. Between January and June over 30,000 fresh drafts and transfers arrive at Camp Lewis, but losses aggregate 25,000. The division receives new men, but by March transfers reduce the strength to less than 20,000. During May and June the division is increased to 23,000.

Movement Overseas

JUNE 21–JULY 26, 1918

June 21, division moves via Camps Merritt and Mills to the ports of embarkation of Brooklyn, New York, and Philadelphia.

June 28, Adv Det sails, and arrives July 10 at Liverpool.

July 6–12, division (less 166th Field Artillery Brig, 316th Sup Tn, and 316th Tn Hq and MP) sails, and arrives July 17–23 at English ports and Glasgow.

July 14, 166th Field Artillery Brig, 316th Sup Tn, and 316th Tn Hq and MP sail, and arrive July 26 in England. Still other units land in France. The troops which land in England and Scotland, after a brief stay in rest camps, proceed via Cherbourg and Le Havre.

Final Training and Operations

JULY 21–NOVEMBER 11, 1918

July 21, division (less Arty) moves to the 8th (Nogent-en-Bassigny) Training Area for training.

July 28, 166th Field Artillery Brig moves to the vicinity of Clerinont-Ferrand and to the area south of Bordeaux for training, the 346th Field Artillery and 347th Field Artillery going to the latter.

August 18, division is ordered to join the First Army.

August 23–September 12, division is under the administrative control of the VI Corps.

September 6, division (less Arty) moves to the vicinity of Gondrecourt, and on September 10 to the Sorcy-sur-Meuse Area, where it is ready to support either the IV Corps or French II Colonial Corps in the St. Mihiel Operation.

September 13, division (less Arty) moves via the Vavincourt and Autré-court areas to the western part of the Forêt de Hesse, northeast of Neuvilly.

September 16–19, division is under administrative control of III Corps.

September 20, division begins to relieve the French 73rd Division, except in the outpost zone and center of resistance of Hermont, along the main line of resistance from ½ km north of La Cour, through Pont-des-4-Enfants and la Fonderie, to la Hardonnerie Fme (incl.).

September 22, division relieves the detachments of the French 73rd Division in center of resistance, Hermont.

September 22–25, division (less Arty) occupies the Aubréville Sector (Lorraine).

September 23, 37th Division relieves the 91st Division in Hermont and the latter prepares for the Meuse-Argonne Operation.

Night of September 25–26, division relieves the French troops in the outposts. The sector occupation merges into the Meuse-Argonne Operation.

September 26–October 4, division (less Arty) participates in the Meuse-Argonne Operation.

September 26, division, on the left of the V Corps, attacks toward Epinonville and Gesnes from the front line of the Aubréville Sector, advances through the Bois de Cheppy, enters Very, and after entering Epinonville occupies a line from ½ km southwest of Ivoiry, through a point ½ km southwest of Epinonville, to ½ km northwest of Very; 37th Division is on the right, 35th Division (I Corps) on the left.

September 27–30, division attacks; on September 28 it passes through Eclisefontaine and captures Exmorieux Fme, the Bois Communal de Cierges, the Bois Communal de Bauhiy, and Tronsol Fme, the left of the line extending south to 300 in northwest of Sérieux Fme;

September 29, division temporarily occupies Gesnes. **September 30,** it reaches a line from la Grange-aux-Bois Fme through a point 1 km west of Cierges, and Tronsol Fme (excl.), to northwest outskirts of Sérieux Fme, and organizes this position.

October 1, 1st Division is on the left.

October 2, division elements in zone of 1st Division north of Sérieux Fme are withdrawn.

October 4, division is relieved by the 32nd Division and moves to the Bois de Véry and Bois de Cheppy, where it passes to the reserve of the V Corps.

October 7, the 362nd Infantry is attached to the 1st Division, where it is needed as a reserve, and the 361st Infantry and 347th MG Bn are attached to the 32nd Division.

October 7–October 12, 181st Infantry Brig participates in the Meuse-Argonne Operation.

October 8, 181st Infantry Brig, after relieving the 128th Infantry (32nd Division) from Gesnes (excl.) to the northwestern edge of the Bois du Chêne-Sec (incl.), is attached to the 1st Division; 32nd Division on right, 1st Division on left.

October 9, 181st Infantry Brig advances to a line from Hill 255 (excl.), to Hill 269 (incl.).

October 10, division (less 181st Infantry Brig and Arty) moves by stages to the Nettancourt Area. The 181st Infantry Brig attacks, occupies Hill 255, and reaches a position in the Bois de Gesnes from ¼ km southwest of Hill 286 to 1¼ km southeast of la Musarde Fme, where it passes to the 32nd Division.

October 11, 181st Infantry Brig extends its left into the Bois de Romagne to a point ½ km south of la Musarde Fme, and resumes the attack, but without material gain.

October 12, 181st Infantry Brig is relieved by the 32nd Division and reverts to the 91st Division.

October 16, division (less Arty) is assigned to the Group of Armies of Flanders, moves to the Ypres–St. Jean Area, and from there, by stages, via the Roulers, Iseghem, and Desselghem areas to the vicinity of Waereghem east of the Lys River.

October 29–December 29, division is under administrative control of the II Corps.

October 30, division relieves the French 164th Division from ½ km east of Heirweg to Waereghem.

October 30–November 4, division (less Arty) participates in the Ypres-Lys Operation.

October 31, division attacks eastward and reaches a line extending from Steenbrugge, along the eastern edge of Spitaals-Bosschen to 1½ km west of Nokere; French 41st Division (French VII Corps) on right, French 128th Division (French VII Corps) on left.

November 1–3, division resumes the attack toward the southeast; November 1, it reaches the western outskirts of Audenarde and establishes a line from Bergwijk, through Kasteelwijk, to ½ km northwest of Bevere.

November 2, division captures Audenarde and advances its left towards Welden; November 3, it advances to a line from Petegem (excl.) to Audenarde (incl).

November 4, French 41st Division relieves the division, which moves to the area east of Vive–St. Eloi for rest.

November 4–11, 166th Field Artillery Brig forms a part of the army artillery in the Meuse-Argonne Operation and is in reserve in the St. Pierre and Brocourt Woods Cantoninents.

November 8, division moves to the vicinity of Olsene, Cruyshautem, and Oycke.

November 10, division, 182nd Infantry Brig leading, pursues; the 182nd Infantry Brig, with one regiment of field artillery attached, crosses the Scheldt at Audenarde and near Eyne, advances east and occupies a gap in the line between Cauwenberg and Moldergem; French 41st Division on right, French 12th Division on left.

November 11, 182nd Infantry Brig occupies Boucle–St. Blaise and advances to a line extending from Hoogstraet, through Boucle–St. Blaise, to 1 km southeast of Moldergem.

Post Armistice Activities

NOVEMBER 12, 1918–MARCH 15, 1919

November 11–18, division (less Arty) rests near Audenarde.

November 18, division (less Arty) moves to the Audenhove–Ste. Marie Area.

November 23, division (less Arty) moves by stages via the Dickelvenne Area to the Denterghem Area west of the Lys River, and thence, via the Roulers Area to vicinity of Poperinghe, where the last elements arrive on December 8.

December 2, 166th Field Artillery Brig (less 346th Field Artillery and 316th TM Btry) accompanies the Third Army into Germany as corps artillery of the VII Corps, and takes station in the Kreis Wittlich until February 11, when it returns to the United States.

December 22, division (less Arty) patrols the Franco-Belgian frontier west of Poperinghe from Beveren to Wàrànde.
December 27, division (less Arty) moves to La Ferté-Bernard Area, American Embarkation Center, Le Mans.
January 2, 346th Field Artillery sails from Brest for the United States.
February 23, 316th TM Btry sails from St. Nazaire.

Return to the United States and Demobilization

MARCH 16–MAY 13, 1919

March 16, division (less Arty) moves to St. Nazaire.
March 21, the leading Infantry units sail.
April 6, DHQ sails.
April 29, the last elements of the division arrive at New York. The demobilization includes, at Camp Kearny, April 19, Hq 181st Infantry Brig and Hq 166th Field Artillery Brig; at Camp Lewis, April 28, Hq 182nd Infantry Brig; at the Presidio of San Francisco, May 13, DHQ.

THE NINETY-SECOND DIVISION, NATIONAL ARMY

The 92nd division was organized at Camp's Dix, Meade, Upton, Dodge, Grant and Funston from colored National Army officers and men from all sections of the United States. Major General Charles C. Ballou commanded the division during most of its service. The 92nd captured 38 prisoners, was quiet 51 days and active two, and advanced 8 kilometers. It had 1642 casualties. It had 176 battle deaths and 1466 wounded. The division received 2920 replacements.

183rd Infantry Brigade
365th Infantry
366th Infantry
350th Machine Gun Battalion

184th Infantry Brigade
367th Infantry
368th Infantry
351st Machine Gun Battalion

167th Field Artillery Brigade

349th Field Artillery
350th Field Artillery
351st Field Artillery

Divisional Troops

307th Engineers
349th Machine Gun Battalion
325th Field Signal Battalion
Headquarters Troop

Trains

317th Train Hdqs
317th Military Police
317th Ammunition Train
317th Supply Train
317th Engineer Train
317th Sanitary Train
Ambulance Cos and Field Hospitals 365–368

Record of Events

SECTORS WHERE THE NINETY-SECOND DIVISION WAS ENGAGED IN WARFARE

St. Die sector, Vosges, France, August 29 to September 20, 1918.
Meuse-Argonne offensive, France, October 9 to November 11, 1918.

Organization and Training in the United States

OCTOBER 24, 1917–MAY 28, 1918

October 24, the War Department establishes the 92nd Division, National Army; colored selective service men from the United States at large are to be organized into the component units at various northern stations. General and field officers, and officers in the technical branches and in the field artillery above the grade of first lieutenant are to be white.

October 26, Brig. Gen. Charles C. Ballou is directed to organize the division in accordance with the Tables of Organization of August 8, 1917.

October 29, Brig. Gen. Ballou assumes command of the division with headquarters at Camp Funston, Fort Riley, Kansas. During November the organization begins and includes, at Camp Grant, Hq 183rd Infantry Brig, 365th Infantry, and 350th MG Bn; at Camp Upton, Hq 184th Infantry Brig, 367th Infantry, 351st MG Bn at Camp Dix, Hq 167th Field Artillery Brig, 349th and 350th Regts of FA, and 317th TM Btry at Camp Meade, 368th Infantry and 351st FA; at Camp Dodge, 366th Infantry; at Camp Sherman, 317th Engrs and 325th F Sig Bn; at Camp Funston, DHQ, Hq Troop, 349th MG Bn, and trains.

December 31, the division numbers about 20,000, a strength which is maintained. During the winter and spring systematic training is conducted. In May fresh drafts complete the division.

Movement Overseas

MAY 29–JULY 12, 1918

May 29, the troops from Camp Funston move to Camp Upton, where the larger part of the division, except the artillery, is concentrated prior to embarkation.

June 7, Adv Det sails from Hoboken, and arrives June 18 at Brest.

June 10–15, DHQ, the Infantry and the 349th Field Artillery sail, and arrive June 19 and 27 at Brest.

June 19–30, the remainder of the 167th Field Artillery Brig and the trains sail from Hoboken, and arrive June 26–July 12 at Brest and St. Nazaire.

Final Training and Operations

JUNE 24–NOVEMBER 11, 1918

June 24, the Infantry, except the 366th Infantry, moves to the 11th (Bourbonne-les-Bains) Training Area for training; the 366th Infantry follows a few days later.

July 3, 167th Field Artillery Brig arrives at Montmorillon for training.

August 12, division (less Arty), moves to Bruyères and the vicinity in the zone of the French Seventh Army.

August 12–19, division is under the administrative control of the V Corps, and, August 19–September 22, under the VII Corps.

August 13, 167th Field Artillery Brig moves to La Courtine and continues training.

August 23–30, division (less Arty) is affiliated with the French 87th Division, which relieves the 5th Division in the St. Die Sector. The front extends from a point ¾ km south of Lusse, in a northerly direction, to ½ km south of Allencombe.

August 30, division relieves the French 87th Division and assumes command; local actions follow.

August 30–September 20, division (less Arty) occupies the St. Die Sector (Lorraine)

September 20, division (less Arty) is relieved by the 81st Division and French 20th Division, command passing to the latter, and moves on September 21 to the region north of Triaucourt to join the First Army.

September 24, division (less 368th Infantry and Arty) assembles in the Argonne Forest northwest of Clermont; the 368th Infantry moves to the adjoining area of the French 38th Corps north of Ste. Menehould.

September 26–October 3, division (less Arty) participates in the Meuse-Argonne Operation.

September 26–30, division (less 368th Infantry and Arty) is in the wood northwest of Clermont as part of the reserve of the I Corps. The 368th Infantry, as part of the Groupement Durand which connects the First Army with the French Fourth Army, occupies the line from Côte 213 north of La Harazée to the northwestern edge of the Bois Carrè about 1½ km north of Vienne-le-Château; 77th Division (I Corps) on right, French 11th Cuirassiers, (French 1st Dismounted Cavalry Div, French 38th Corps), on left.

September 26, 368th Infantry attacks, and on September 28 reaches the line, Zepplin Trench, Tranchée de Tartarie.

September 29, French 9th Cuirassiers (French 1st Dismounted Cavalry Div, French 38th Corps) is on the left; division (less 183rd Infantry Brig) is ordered to the French 38th Corps, French Fourth Army, which is on the left.

September 30, 368th Infantry occupies Binarvile but later rejoins the division.

October 1–3, division (less 183rd Infantry Brig, Arty, and Engrs) is at the disposal of the French 38th Corps, and in reserve in the rear of the French 1st Dismounted Cavalry Division in the valley of Biesme Creek at Moiremont and at Camp du Souniat.

October 2, division (less detached units) reverts to the First Army, to be reserve of the I Corps. Troops of the 183rd Inf Brig and 317th Engrs, which are in the reserve of the First Army, are engaged in repairing roads.

October 4, division (less detached units) is directed to entrain for the area of the IV Corps.

October 6, division (less Arty) moves to the northwest of Nancy.

October 9–November 11, division occupies the Marbache Sector (Lorraine).

October 9, division (less Arty) relieves the French 69th Division along the front extending from Port-sur-Seille, through Morville-sur-Seille, and Lesmènils, to the eastern bank of the Moselle north of Pont-à-Mousson;

French 165th Division (French 32nd Corps, French Eighth Army) is on the right, 90th Division on the left.

October 10, 7th Division is on the left.

October 20, 349th and 350th Regts of Field Artillery rejoin and relieve troops of the 62nd Field Artillery Brig.

October 23, 7th Division (IV Corps) is on the left.

October 26, the sector is extended toward the west to Villers-sous-Prény and Prény (both excl); the 367th Infantry relieves elements of the 7th Division.

October 30, 351st Field Artillery rejoins.

November 10–11, division participates in the attack of the Second Army, occupies the Bois Cheminot, Bois de la Voivrotte and Bois Fréhaut.

Post Armistice Activities

NOVEMBER 12, 1918 – JANUARY 30, 1919

November 14, the French Tenth Army relieves the troops east of the Moselle and the division then assembles west of the Moselle; training predominates.

December 15, division moves to the Mayenne Area, American Embarkation Center, Le Mans, where it continues training.

Return to the United States and Demobilization

JANUARY 30 – MARCH 7, 1919

January 30, division moves to Brest.

February 1, the leading elements sail.

March 6, the last elements of the division arrive at New York. The mobilization includes, at Camp Meade, February 27, DHQ and Hq 167th Field Artillery Brig, March 7, Hq 184th Infantry Brig; at Camp Upton, March 7, 183rd Infantry Brig.

THE NINETY-THIRD DIVISION

The 93rd Division never functioned as a division within the AEF but separate infantry regiments saw considerable service with different French armies. The 93rd Division (colored National Guard) was filled to strength from National Army drafts. The overseas movement began on April 7, 1918, and was completed when the last unit arrived in France on April 22. The 369th, 370th, 371st and 372nd Infantry regiments were brigaded with the French and served as part of the French army. There was no artillery nor divisional troops nor trains, just the infantry. The division suffered 2,587 casualties. It had 574 battle deaths.

The sad story of this group of regiments was that the leadership of the AEF did not want any more "colored" troops under its command, so they offered the four infantry regiments to the French army, who gladly accepted them and utilized them vigorously. From all accounts they were as good as any of the regiments in the AEF.

Organization and Training in the United States
NOVEMBER 23, 1917–APRIL 6, 1918

November 23, the War Department directs the organization of the 185th and 186th Infantry Brigs (colored). The 185th Infantry Brig is to include the 369th Infantry (former 15th Infantry, NY National Guard) and the 370th Infantry (former 8th Infantry, Ill National Guard); the 186th Infantry Brig is to include the 371st Infantry, and the 372nd Infantry, the latter to be organized from colored National Guard units from Connecticut, District of Columbia, Maryland, Massachusetts, Ohio, and Tennessee. For purposes of administration the brigades are to be considered as a provisional division and Brig. Gen. Roy Hoffman is designated to command them; he is ordered to Camp Stuart, where the 372nd Infantry is to be formed.

December 1, the 370th Infantry is organized at Camp Logan and a colored Infantry regiment that had been organized at Camp Jackson from selective service men during the preceding October is designated the 371st Infantry. December 11, Brig. Gen. Hoffman arrives at Camp Stuart; on December 24, he assumes command of the provisional division.

January 1, the 372nd Infantry is organized.

January 5, the War Department designates the two brigades as the 93rd Division (Provisional) and orders the formation of a division staff. The minimum strength of about 9,000 under the Tables of Organization of August 15, 1917, is allowed; the staff are to be white officers. The division units train for field service.

March 10, the 370th Infantry joins at Camp Stuart, and on April 6, the 371st Infantry arrives.

Movement Overseas
DECEMBER 12, 1917–APRIL 22, 1918

December 12, the 369th Infantry (15th Infantry New York National Guard) sails from Hoboken, and arrives December 27, at Brest.

February 18, DHQ sails from Hoboken on the SS *George Washington* and arrives March 4 at Brest. Other troops sail from Newport News as follows, March 30, the 372nd Infantry, April 7, the brigade headquarters, 370th Infantry and 371st Infantry (less three companies).

April 14, the 372nd Infantry arrives St. Nazaire, and the other units on April 22 at Brest.

April 29, the last elements, three companies of the 371st Infantry, arrive at St. Nazaire.

Final Training and Operations

JANUARY 1–DECEMBER 12, 1918

The units of the division are to be affiliated with the French.

March 11, DHQ is established at Bar-sur-Seine (Aube) and retains administrative control until May 15, when it ceases to function and the personnel are assigned elsewhere. The four American regiments are reorganized to conform to the French tables of organization.

Activities of 369th, 371st, and 372nd Regts of Infantry Prior to the Meuse-Argonne Operation

369TH INFANTRY

January 1, 1918, the regiment moves to St. Nazaire and Camp Coëtquidan for duty with the SOS.

March 12, it proceeds to Givry-en-Argonne for training under the French 16th Division (French Fourth Army) and on March 15 establishes its headquarters at Herpont.

April 8–July 4, the regiment participates in the occupation of the Afrique Subsector (Champagne), north of Ste. Menehould, where its battalions are affiliated with battalions of the French 16th Division.

April 16, the regiment holds a 5 km front, extending from the western bank of the Aisne, through the Bois d'Hauzy, to Ville-sur-Tourbe, and, on April 29, assumes command of this sector.

Night of July 3–4, the regiment is relieved and withdraws to a second position north of Maffrécourt and Conrtemont, but keeps one battalion in an intermediate position near Berzieux.

July 15–18, the regiment participates in the Champagne-Marne Operation.

July 15, after assisting in stopping an attack against the front of the

French 16th Division, the regiment moves 6 km west to support the French 161st Division north of Minaucourt.

July 18, the regiment participates in the counterattack and recapture of the front line trenches by this division, and until July 22 it remains in support.

July 21–22, one battalion enters the front line in the Beauséjour subsector.

July 23–August 19, the regiment occupies the Calvaire Subsector (Champagne) from ¾ km south of Maisons-de-Champagne Fme to 1 km north of Beauséjour Fme, between Butte du Mesnil and Main de Massiges. Subsequently, it moves to St. Ouën, where it trains until September 7.

September 9, the regiment becomes an organic part of the French 161st Division.

September 11–15, the regiment occupies the Beauaêjour Subsector, which is in front of Butte du Mesnil and extends from 1 km north of Beauséjour Fme to 1¾ km northeast of Le Mesnil-lês-Hurlus.

September 14–16, the regiment is relieved and moves to the Somme-Bionne Area preparatory to the Meuse-Argonne Operation.

371st Infantry

April 26, the regiment moves to the vicinity of Rembercourt-aux-Pots, where it trains under the French XIII Corps until June 6. It then becomes an organic part of the French 157th Division and as such is at the disposal of the French 68th Division near Verdun-sur-Meuse.

June 11–September 14, the regiment participates in the occupation of the Verdun Sector (Lorraine).

June 11, it occupies a reserve position west of Béthelainville in support of the French 68th Division, and on June 23 in an Avocourt subsector west of Hill 304.

July 14, the regiment moves to the right and on July 16 occupies the adjoining Favry subsector, the left of Sector 304, but still retains a part of the Avocourt subsector and a command post at Verrières; a reorganization of the sector and patrolling follow.

September 14, the regiment is relieved and moves, via Heiltz-l'Evêque, to the Somnie-Bionne Area, where it arrives September 24, preparatory to the Meuse-Argonne Operation.

372nd Infantry

April 21, the regiment moves to Condé-en-Barrios, where it trains under the French XIII Corps until May 26. It then joins the French 63rd Division, which occupies a sector between the Aire River and Le Four de Paris.

May 26, the regiment enters the divisional area and takes station near Futeau.

May 26–July 15, the regiment participates in the occupation of the Aire Sector (Lorraine).

June 4, it moves into the front line and on June 7 assumes command of the Argonne-Ouest Subsector, where it trains in the front line.

June 21, the regiment is assigned to the French 35th Division.

June 27–July 1, it relieves the French 123rd Infantry in a VaiIquois subsector and on July 1 assumes command.

July 2, the regiment becomes an organic part of the French 157th Division.

July 14, the French 157th Division is relieved from the Aire Sector and moves near Grange-le-Comte Fme for rest; the regimental headquarters goes to Lochêres.

July 16–September 14, the regiment participates in the occupation of the Verdun Sector (Lorraine). The regiment, in Division reserve, occupies a second position near Béthelainville until July 24, when it enters Subsector 304, and on July 26, relieves the French 92nd Infantry; the reorganization and consolidation of the subsector follows.

September 9, the regiment is relieved by the 129th Infantry (33rd Division) and moves to the Bois de Brocourt.

September 13, it proceeds via Brienne-le-Château and Vitry-le-Francois to Hans, where it arrives on September 24, preparatory to the Meuse-Argonne Operation.

Activities of 369th, 371st, and 372nd Regts of Infantry During the Meuse-Argonne Operation

September 26–October 8, the 369th Infantry (French 161st Division) and the 371st Infantry and 372nd Infantry (French 157th Division) participate in the Meuse-Argonne Operation.

September 26, the French IX Corps (French Fourth Army), with the French 2nd Moroccan and French 161st Divisions abreast and French 157th Division in reserve, attacks toward Challerange, Marvaux, and Vieux from the sector front, which extends from near Main de Massiges to a point east of Mesnil-lês-Hurlus. The 369th Infantry (French 161st Division) advances from the Ravin d'Hébuterne, captures Ripont, and occupies a front of ¾ km just north of that village; French 163rd Infantry on the right, French 2nd Moroccan Division on the left.

September 27, the 369th Infantry reaches the slopes north of Fontaine-en-Dormois.

September 28, the French 157th Division enters on the left of the French 161st Division; the 371st Infantry advances to 400 m south of le Pied; the 372nd Infantry captures the western part of Bellevue Signal Ridge and reaches a position south of Bussy Fme; the 369th Infantry advances against resistance to the southern slope of Bellevue Signal Ridge; the French 163rd Infantry is in line between the 369th and 372nd regiments. September 29, the 372nd Infantry attacks Séchault but retires and reorganizes south of Bussy Fme; the 369th Infantry, with parts of the 372nd Infantry, captures Séchault and reaches a line just northeast of that village; the 371st Infantry captures Ardeuil and Montlauxelles and establishes a line from Moulin Moya-Ston to la Croix Cavilliers.

September 30, the 369th Infantry advances to a line one km south of les Rosiers Fme; the 371st Infantry captures Trières Fme, 2 km south of Monthois.

Night of September 30–October 1, the 369th Infantry is relieved and placed in division reserve. October 1, the 372nd Infantry relieves the 371st Infantry, which passes to the division reserve. October 2, the 372nd Infantry attacks and reaches a line across the Séchault-Monthois road ¾ km south of Monthois, where it remains in position.

Night of October 7–8, the French 157th Division is relieved.

Activities of 369th, 371st, and 372nd Regts of Infantry Subsequent to Withdrawal from the Meuse-Argonne Operation

369TH INFANTRY

October 7, the 369th Infantry (French 161st Division) moves to Vitryle-François and passes to corps reserve.

October 8, rehabilitation begins.

October 14, it moves to the Belfort Area and then to the vicinity of Thann.

October 17–November 11, the regiment, stationed at Wesserling and St. Amarin, participates in the occupation of a Thur sub-sector (Alsace), which is part of a sector between Limbach and Metzeral held by the French 161st Division (French Seventh Army).

November 17, the regiment moves with the French 161st Division (French Second Army, now in the Army of Occupation) to the Rhine, and on November 18 takes station at and near Blodelsheim.

December 12, the regiment is relieved from duty with the French Army and on December 17 moves to the Bellort Area.

371ST AND 372ND REGTS OF INFANTRY

October 7, the 371st Infantry and 372nd Infantry, part of the French 157th Division, assemble near Beauséjour Fme, north of Minaucourt, and

October 11–12 move via Vahny and Ste. Menehould to the vicinity of Corcieux.

October 13–November 11, these regiments, with the French 333rd Infantry, occupy the Anould Sector (Alsace), which lies between Weiss Creek and Fave Creek and extends from Tête-des-Faux, through Le Bonhoznme, Tête-du-Violu, and Wisembach to Frapelle; the 371st Infantry enters a Bonhomme subsector, and the 372nd Infantry enters Subsector B, near Wiseinbach.

November 17, the regiments move to the Bruyères Area. **December 20,** when the French 157th Division is disbanded, the regiments revert to GHQ, AEF.

Operations of 370th Infantry Overseas

April 25–November 11, 1918

April 25, the regiment moves to Grandvillars where it passes to the French Seventh Army and is attached to the French 73rd Division for training.

May 19, the regiment is transferred to the French 133rd Division and continues training.

June 1, it joins the French 10th Division (French XL Corps), which is occupying a sector between the Swiss border and the Rhine-Rhône Canal.

June 12, the regiment moves via Nançois-le-Petit to Lignières and on June 17 joins the French 34th Division (French Second Army), which is occupying a sector between Etang de Vargévaux and Les Paroches.

June 17–July 5, the regiment participates in the occupation of the St. Mihiel Sector (Lorraine).

June 22, it enters a Han-sur-Meuse-Bislée subsector, southwest of St. Mihiel.

July 1, the regiment begins to withdraw from the sector aiid occupies a reserve position in support of the French 34th Division, (French II Colonial Corps).

July 5, the regiment moves via Les Islettes to the vicinity of Auzéville, where it joins the French 36th Division (French XIII Corps, French Second Army).

July 7–August 18, the regiment participates in the occupation of the Aire Sector (Lorraine), which extends from the Bois d'Avocourt to the Aire River.

July 7, the regiment passes to the division reserve near Auzéville, but elements serve successively in the front line near Vauquois.

August 15, the regiment is relieved from duty with the French 36th Division and moves by stages to Rampont, where on August 18, it entrains for the Bar-le-Duc Area and further training.

September 1, the regiment moves via Betz to the vicinity of La Ferté-Milon, where it arrives on September 4 and passes to the French 59th Division (French Tenth Army).

September 14, the regiment moves with the French 59th Division to the Vauxaillon Area, where it stays in the division reserve until September 22.

September 15–October 13, the regiment participates in the Oise-Aisne Operation.

September 17–22, four companies, attached to troops of the French 232nd and French 325th Regts of Infantry (French 59th Division, French 18th Corps) participate in attacks against Mont-des-Singes and the northeastern spur of the Moisy plateau.

September 24, the regiment enters the front line between Champ-Vailly and Ecluse, where it engages in local actions; French 325th Infantry on the right, French 31st Division (French 16th Corps) on the left.

September 28–October 4, the regiment, during a general attack of the French 59th Division, is engaged at Ecluse, Fme de la Rivière and near Mont-des-Singes, assists in driving the enemy north of the Oise-Aisne Canal, and establishes a line south of the canal from Ecluse to the Pinon-Brancourt road.

October 5–11, patrolling continues.

October 6, French 16th Corps now commands the French 59th Division.

October 12, the regiment, participating in a general attack, crosses the canal and Ailette River, advances into the Bois de Mortier, and occupies the Tranchée du Bronze and Tranchée de l'Acier, northeast of the Fme de la Rivière.

October 13, the regiment, in the division reserve, approaches Cessières.

October 14, the French 59th Division passes to the army reserve, but the regiment remains, reorganizes, and trains near Cessières.

October 27, the French 59th Division is placed at the disposal of the French 18th Corps (French Third Army).

October 28–November 11, the regiment participates in the Oise-Aisne Operation.

Night of October 27–28, the French 59th Division moves to the front near Grandlup-et-Fay, northeast of Laon, where, on October 30, it relieves the French 127th Division.

October 30–November 4, the 370th Infantry is in division support near Chantrud Fme.

Night of November 4–5, the enemy is withdrawing to the Antwerp-Meuse line.

November 5, the regiment, advancing in line with the French 59th Division, which is in pursuit of the enemy, reaches the vicinity of St. Pierremont.

November 6, it advances northeasterly and drives the enemy from the Bois du Val–St. Pierre, reaching a position east of Nampcelles-la-Cour.

November 8, it captures Beaumé and stops south and southwest of Aubenton with its left along the railroad.

November 9, the regiment reaches Pont-d'Any. On November 10, it is north of Eteignieres, and on November 11, the vicinity of Gué-d'Hossus, ¾ km north of Rocroi, across the Belgian border.

November 12, the regiment withdraws to an area northeast of Aubenton and then to the north of Laon.

November 16, the headquarters is at Barenton-sur-Serre.

December 10, the regiment moves by stages to an area north of Helms; the division headquarters is at Villers-Franqueux.

December 13, the regiment is relieved from duty with the French 59th Division and goes to Soissons.

Return to the United States and Demobilization

DECEMBER 13, 1918–MARCH 11, 1919

The regiments move to the American Embarkation Center, Le Mans. December 23, the 370th Infantry leaves the Soissons Area; December 31, the 369th Infantry leaves the Belfort Area; January 1–2, the 371st Infantry and 372nd Infantry leave the Bruyères Area.

January 9, the troops move to Brest.

February 2, the 369th Infantry and 370th Infantry sail, arriving at New York on February 12 and February 9, respectively.

February 3, the 371st and 372nd Infantry sail, arriving at Hoboken on February 11. The troops pass through Camp Upton and are demobilized, February 28, 369th Infantry at

Camp Upton, and 371st Infantry at Camp Jackson, March 6, 372nd Infantry at Camp Sherman, March 11, 370th Infantry at Camp Grant.

The following divisions were not utilized in combat activities but served as replacement units or Depot Divisions.

EIGHTH DIVISION, REGULAR ARMY

The Eighth Division was organized at Camp Fremont, California, from men of the regular army, August 3, 1918. Major General William S. Graves, with his staff and 5000 men and 100 officers were transferred to Siberia. Major General Eli A. Holmich succeeded General Graves in command of the division. The overseas movement began October 30, 1918. The 8th Artillery Brigade, the 8th Infantry Brigade, with the 16th Infantry Brigade headquarters and the 319th Engineers were the only organizations of this division that went to France. These troops became the garrison of Brest and assisted in making the huge camps where troops were embarked. After the Armistice, the 8th Infantry and the 2nd Battalion of the 7th Field Artillery of the 1st Division became American forces in Germany under General Allen. They were not involved in any combat operations. This division was labeled a Depot Replacement and Labor Division.

115th Infantry Brigade

12th Infantry
62nd Infantry
23rd Machine Gun Battalion

16th Infantry Brigade

8th Infantry
13th Infantry
24th Machine Gun Battalion

8th Field Artillery Brigade

2nd Field Artillery
81st Field Artillery
83rd Field Artillery
8th Trench Mortar Battalion

Divisional Troops

22nd Machine Gun Battalion
319th Engineers
320th Field Signal Battalion
Headquarters Troop

Trains

8th Train Hdqs
8th Military Police
8th Ammunition Train
8th Supply Train
319th Engineer Train
8th Sanitary Train
Ambulance Cos and Field Hospitals 11, 31, 32, 43

Organization and Training in the United States

DECEMBER 17, 1917–OCTOBER 17, 1918

December 17, the War Department directs the organization at Camp Fremont of the 8th Division, Regular Army, in accordance with the Tables of Organization of August 8, 1917. The 16th Infantry Brig comprising the 8th and 13th Regts of Infantry then at Camp Fremont, together with the 12th Infantry and the 62nd Infantry (formed from personnel of the 12th Infantry in 1917), which arrive early in January, form the nucleus.

January 2–April 4, the machine gun battalions are formed from personnel of the infantry regiments; the trains, except the 8th Sup Tn which comes from Camp Johnston, are organized. In May a draft of 8,000 arrives and raises the strength to 22,000 officers and men.

January 4, the skeleton organization of the 319th Engrs (formed from the 3rd Engrs) arrives from the Hawaiian Dept.

January 5, Col. Elmore F. Taggart, 12th Infantry, assumes temporary command of the division; the 15th Infantry Brig is organized; systematic training begins.

January 6, 320th F Sig Bn arrives from Camp Dodge.

February 14, units of the 8th Field Artillery Brig, which includes the 2nd FA, 81st Field Artillery (organized from the 23rd Cav in 1917), and 83rd Field Artillery (organized from the 25th Cav in 1917), begin to arrive.

February 18, Hq 8th Field Artillery Brig is formed.

June 30, 8th Field Artillery Brig moves to Fort Sill for training at the Firing Center.

August 3, the transfer of about 100 officers and 5,000 men to the Siberian Expeditionary Force is ordered. In September the arrival of drafts from several camps completes the division.

September 11, 319th Engrs and Tn move to Camp Upton, sail September 25 from New York, arrive October 7 at Liverpool and October 13 at Le Havre, and proceed to Brest, where they begin the construction of Pontanezen Barracks.

Movement Overseas

OCTOBER 18–NOVEMBER 9, 1918

October 18, division (less 319th Engrs and Tn) moves from Camp Fremont and Fort Sill to Camp Mills.

October 27, Adv Det sails from Hoboken, and arrives November 3 at Brest.

October 28, 31, and November 2, DHQ, Hq 16th Infantry Brig, 8th Infantry, and 8th Field Artillery Brig sail from Hoboken and New York, arriving on November 9 at Brest. The 15th Infantry Brig, 13th Infantry, 22nd and 24th MG Bns, 320th F Sig Bn, and Tns remain at Camp Mills.

Activities Overseas

NOVEMBER 10, 1918–JULY 15, 1919

November 10, the division commander, accompanied by his staff, takes command of Base Section No. 5, SOS, at Brest.

November 12, Hq 16th Infantry Brig and the 8th Infantry move to the Pons-Saintes Training Area; training and police duty follow.

November 14, 8th TM Btry moves to Vitrey.

November 15, 8th Field Artillery Brig (less 8th TM Btry) moves to Ploermel; camp duties.

November 19–27, a part of the division staff is at Pons.

November 25, Hq 16th Infantry Brig ceases to function, and on the 27th units of this brigade join the permanent garrison of Camp Pontanezen, Brest.

November 28, part of the troops in France are ordered to return to the United States.

July 10, 8th Infantry is attached to the Army of Occupation and is moved from Brest to Coblenz.

Return to the United States

DECEMBER 25, 1918 – AUGUST 31, 1919

December 25, 8th TM Btry sails from Brest.

January 4, 8th Field Artillery Brig (less 8th TM Btry) leaves Brest, arrives January 18 at Hoboken, and moves to Camp Mills.

August 15, 319th Engrs and Tn sail from Brest, and arrive August 27 at Hoboken.

August 24, DHQ Detachment follows.

Activities in the United States and Demobilization

NOVEMBER 10, 1918 – SEPTEMBER 15, 1919

November 25, 12th Infantry moves to Camp Stuart.

December 1, 13th Infantry moves to Camp Merritt, and other units in the United States, except artillery, move to Camp Lee.

January 17, the demobilization of emergency personnel and units in the United States is ordered.

January 20, 8th Field Artillery Brig leaves Camp Mills, and arrives January 22 at Camp Knox. February 23, 62nd Infantry is detached. During February the demobilization is completed, and includes on February 25 the Hq 15th Infantry Brig. Subsequently, September 5, DHQ Detachment is demobilized. The 8th Field Artillery Brig remains active for the time being.

THE THIRTY-FIRST DIVISION, NATIONAL GUARD

The 31st Division was made up from National Guard units of Alabama, Georgia and Florida at Camp Walter, Georgia. The overseas movement began September 16, 1918, and concluded November 9, 1918. Upon arrival in France the unit was made a replacement division and sent to Le Mans Area. Thereafter it existed only as a skeleton division, its personnel being sent as replacements to other divisions. The generals in command at different times were Major General Francis J. Kernan, Brigadier General John L. Hayden, Major General Frances H. French, and Major General Le Roy S. Lyon.

61st Infantry Brigade

121st Infantry
122nd Infantry
117th Machine Gun Battalion

62nd Infantry Brigade

123rd Infantry
124th Infantry
118th Machine Gun Battalion

56th Field Artillery Brigade

116th Field Artillery
117th Field Artillery
118th Field Artillery
106th Trench Mortar Battery

Divisional Troops

116th Machine Gun Battalion
106th Engineers
106th Field Signal Battalion
Headquarters Troop

Trains

106th Train Hdqs
106th Military Police
106th Ammunition Train
106th Supply Train
106th Engineer Train
106th Sanitary Train
Ambulance Cos and Field Hospitals 121–124

THE THIRTY-FOURTH DIVISION, NATIONAL GUARD

The 34th Division was composed of National Guard units of Iowa, Minnesota, Nebraska, and North Dakota and South Dakota. It was organized at Camp Cody, New Mexico. The overseas movement began September 16, 1918, and was completed October 24, 1918. The division was broken up after its arrival in France and ceased to function as a division. Its commanders were Major General Augustus P. Blocksom, Major General William R. Smith, Major General Beaumont B. Buck and Brigadier General John A. Johnson.

67th Infantry Brigade

133rd Infantry
134th Infantry
126th Machine Gun Battalion

68th Infantry Brigade

135th Infantry
136th Infantry
127th Machine Gun Battalion

59th Field Artillery Brigade

125th Field Artillery
126th Field Artillery
127th Field Artillery
109th Trench Mortar Battery

Divisional Troops

125th Machine Gun Battalion
109th Engineers
109th Field Signal Battalion
Headquarters Troop

Trains

109th Train Hdqs
109th Military Police

109th Ammunition Train
109th Supply Train
109th Engineer Train
109th Sanitary Train
Ambulance Cos and Field Hospitals 133–136

Organization and Training in the United States

JULY 15, 1917–AUGUST 19, 1918

July 15, the National Guard units of Iowa, Minnesota, Nebraska, North Dakota, and South Dakota are called into federal service.

July 18, the War Department designates National Guard troops of Iowa, Minnesota, Nebraska, North Dakota and South Dakota to form the 34th Division. Camp Cody, Deming, New Mexico, is selected for the training.

August 3, the War Department directs the concentration and organization of the division at Camp Cody.

August 5, the National Guards of Iowa, Minnesota, Nebraska, North Dakota and South Dakota are drafted into federal service.

August 19, the concentration at Camp Cody begins.

August 25, Maj. Gen. Augustus P. Blocksom assumes command; the 67th Infantry Brig is organized and ultimately includes the 1st Iowa and 5th Nebraska Regts of Infantry, detachments of the 2nd Iowa Infantry, of separate companies of Iowa Infantry, of the 1st Iowa Cav, and of the 4th and 6th Regts of British Infantry; the 68th Infantry Brig is organized and ultimately includes the 1st and 2nd Regts of Minnesota Infantry and 2nd Squadron 1st SD Cav.

September 28–October 5, division is reorganized in accordance with the Tables of Organization of August 8, 1917.

October 1, the 59th Field Artillery Brig is organized and ultimately includes the 3rd Minnesota and 4th British Regts of Infantry the 1st Iowa Field Artillery and a detachment of the 2nd Iowa Infantry.

October 29, systematic training begins. During October and November drafts aggregating 5,000 arrive from Camps Dodge and Funston. The losses through May 10 aggregate about 4,000. In June the division loses nearly all trained personnel in order to meet the requirements of the AEF automatic replacement system. Subsequently, replacements arrive, the majority drawn from Arizona, Colorado, Kansas, New Mexico, Oklahoma, and Texas, which complete the division during August.

Movement Overseas

AUGUST 20–OCTOBER 24, 1918

August 20, the division (less Arty) moves via Camp Dix to the ports of embarkation of Brooklyn and New York.

September 9, Adv Party sails from New York.

September 13, 59th Field Artillery Brig moves from Fort Sill to Camp Upton.

September 16–25, DHQ, part of the 67th Infantry Brig, the 125th MG Bn, 59th Field Artillery Brig, and 109th Engrs and Tn sail, and arrive September 29–October 9, at Liverpool, except the 126th Field Artillery, which lands in Scotland. The remaining units are quarantined at Camp Dix until October 12. The last unit leaves New York on October 17 and arrives October 24 in England. The troops stay a short time in rest camps and then proceed via Cherbourg and Le Havre.

Activities Overseas

OCTOBER 4–DECEMBER 22, 1918

October 4, division (less Arty, Engrs, 109th Sn Tn, and 109th Tn Eq and MP) moves to the Labrède Area for training.

October 7, 109th Engrs and Tn move from Cherbourg to the Mesves-Bulcy Area and engage in construction.

October 11, 59th Field Artillery Brig (less 109th TM Btry) moves to the St. Laurent-de-Médoc Area, the 109th TM Btry to Vitrey, and the 109th Am Tn to Camp de Souge, for training.

October 17, orders direct that the division be skeletonized, but subject to reconstitution. Upon arrival in the Labrède Area some units are reduced to an average strength of 25 while others remain at full strength.

October 29, the division is ordered reduced to a record cadre as its reconstitution is no longer contemplated.

November 2, the 126th Field Artillery moves to Camp de Souge for training and the 109th Sn Tn and 109th Tn Eq and MP leave the ports for Le Mans.

November 6, units in the Labrède Area move to Le Mans. At Le Mans units are transferred to the 2nd Depot Division and further skeletonized; a Division Record Cadre of 14 officers and 95 men represents DHQ, the infantry brigade headquarters, the infantry regiments, machine gun battalions, and train headquarters and military police; the 109th Sn Tn forms a separate cadre; the surplus personnel are classified for other assignment; the 109th F Sig Bn moves to the Signal Corps Replacement Depot at Cour-Cheverny.

November 13, 59th Field Artillery Brig (less 126th Field Artillery and 109th TM Btry), organized as corps artillery and destined for the VIII Corps, moves to the Artillery Training Center at Clermont-Ferrand.

November 26, 109th Sup Tn, moving from Le Mans via St. Nazaire, arrives at Nantes for convoy duty. November 27, 59th Field Artillery Brig (less detachments) moves from Clermont-Ferrand to the vicinity of Ambarès-et-Lagrave, where the 126th FA, Division Record Cadre, and 109th Sn Tn Cadre join.

Return to the United States and Demobilization
DECEMBER 23, 1918 – FEBRUARY 18, 1919

December 23, the 59th Field Artillery Brig (less TM Btry) moves to Camp Génicart near Bordeaux.

December 24, the artillery sails from Bordeaux, followed, December 30, by the 109th TM Btry from Brest.

January 6–7, Division Record Cadre and part of the 109th Sn Tn sail from Bordeaux.

April 18, 109th F Sig Bn, and, June 10, the Motor Bn of the 109th Am Tn, follow.

June 17, 109th Engrs and Tn sail from St. Nazaire, and arrive June 29 at Newport News. The demobilization includes, at Camp Dodge, January 24, Eq 59th Field Artillery Brig; at Camp Grant, February 18, Record Cadre.

THE THIRTY-EIGHTH DIVISION, NATIONAL GUARD

The 38th Division was formed from the National Guard of West Virginia, Kentucky and Indiana at Camp Shelby, Mississippi. The overseas movement occurred in October 1918. Upon its arrival in France it was broken up and ceased to function as a combat division. The commanders in succession were Major General William H. Sage, Brigadier General Edward M. Lewis, Brigadier General Henry H. Whitney and Brigadier General William V. Judson.

75th Infantry Brigade
149th Infantry
150th Infantry
138th Machine Gun Battalion

76th Infantry Brigade

151st Infantry
152nd Infantry
139th Machine Gun Battalion

63rd Field Artillery Brigade

137th Field Artillery
138th Field Artillery
139th Field Artillery

Divisional Troops

113th Engineers
113th Field Signal Battalion
137th Machine Gun Battalion
Headquarters Troop

Trains

113th Train Hdqs
113th Military Police
113th Ammunition Train
113th Supply Train
113th Engineer Train
113th Sanitary Train
Ambulance Cos and Field Hospitals 149–152

Organization and Training in the United States

JULY 15, 1917–SEPTEMBER 10, 1918

July 15, the National Guard of West Virginia is called into federal service.

July 18, the War Department designates National Guard troops of Indiana and Kentucky to form the 38th Div, but this is amended later to include troops of West Virginia National Guard. Camp Shelby, Hattiesburg, Mississippi, is selected for the training.

August 3, the War Department directs the concentration and organization of the division at Camp Shelby.

August 5, the NG units of Indiana, Kentucky, and West Virginia are drafted into federal service. During August the concentration at Camp Shelby begins.

August 25, Maj. Gen. William H. Sage assumes command.

September 4, the 75th Infantry Brig is organized and ultimately includes the 2nd Kentucky and 2nd West Virginia Regts of Infantry, and detachments of the 1st Kentucky, 3rd Kentucky, and 1st West Virginia Regts of Infantry.

September 18, the 76th Infantry Brig is organized and ultimately includes the 1st and 2nd Regts of Indiana Infantry and detachments of the 3rd and 4th Regts of Indiana Infantry and of 1st Indiana Cav.

September 19, division is reorganized in accordance with the Tables of Organization of August 8, 1917.

October 1, the 63rd Field Artillery Brig is organized and ultimately includes the 3rd Ind Infantry (less MG Co) and detachments of the 4th Ind Infantry of 1st Kentucky Infantry, and of Indiana Cav; systematic training begins. During November the division reaches a strength of 24,000, including a draft of 100 officers and 2,000 men from the 84th Division.

June 30, the division numbers only 19,000. During the summer drafts of 1,800, including some from Illinois, and 6,000 from Arkansas, Louisiana, and Mississippi complete the division.

Movement Overseas

SEPTEMBER 11–OCTOBER 25, 1918

September 11, the division moves via Camp Mills to the ports of embarkation of Brooklyn, Montreal, New York, and Quebec.

September 15, 113th Engrs and Tn sail from New York, and arrive September 28 at Brest.

September 17, Adv Det sails from New York, and arrives September 29 in England.

October 2, DHQ, Hq 75th Infantry Brig, 149th Infantry, and 138th MG Bn sail from New York, and land October 9 at Southampton.

October 4–14, the remainder of the division follows via England; the majority land on October 17, a few on October 18, and the last part of the 151st Infantry on October 25. These units stay a short time in rest camps and then proceed via Cherbourg and Le Havre.

Activities Overseas

OCTOBER 2–NOVEMBER 28, 1918

October 2, 113th Engrs and Tn, assigned to the Advance Section, SOS, move from Brest to the departments of Côte-d'Or, Haute-Maine, and Vosges, with headquarters at Latrecey.

October 13, division (less Arty, and 113th Engrs and Tn) moves to the Nantes Area.

October 17, orders direct that the division be skeletonized.

October 23, 63rd Field Artillery Brig (less 113th TM Btry which goes to Vitrey) moves to Ploërmel.

October 29, division is ordered reduced to a record cadre.

November 2, division (less Arty, 113th Engrs and Tn, 113th F Sig Bn, and 113th Sn Tn), consisting of 11,000 officers and men, moves from the Nantes Area to Le Mans to be skeletonized.

November 5, to Camp de Meucon for training.

November 8, 113th F Sig Bn moves to the Signal Corps Replacement Depot at Cour-Cheverny.

November 11, 113th San Tn moves to St. Aignat-des-Noyers, where it is skeletonized. The Division Record Cadre of eight officers and 102 men is formed at Le Mans to represent the skeletonized units, which include the DHQ, 75th Infantry Brig, 76th Infantry Brig, 137th MG Bn, and 113th Tn Hq and MP. The surplus personnel pass through the classification camp of the 2nd Depot Division for other assignment.

November 19, 113th Sup Tn moves to Bordeaux for convoy and other duty with the SOS.

November 24, the motorized section of the 113th Am Tn arrives at Marseille.

Return to the United States and Demobilization

NOVEMBER 29, 1918–MARCH 8, 1919

November 29, the Division Record Cadre moves from the Le Mans Area, via Camp de Meucon, and the 63rd Field Artillery Brig and Animal Section of the 113th Am Tn from the latter place to Brest.

December 9, the Division Record Cadre sails, followed December 13 17 by 63rd Field Artillery Brig (less 113th Tm Btry) and, December 26, by the Animal Section of the 113th Am Tn.

January 4, 113th TM Btry, and, January 8, the Record Cadre of the 113th San Tn sail.

February 15, 113th Engrs and Tn move to the Departments of Cote d'Or, Haute-Maine, and Meurthe-et-Moselle, where, February 18, they are attached to the 7th Div.

April 23, 113th F Sig Bn leaves for Bordeaux.

April 24, 1st Bn 113th Engrs moves to Konz for duty with the 89th Division.

May 24, 113th Engrs concentrates in Le Mans Area, embark, June 12, at Brest, and arrives June 19 at Hoboken.

July 31, the last element, part of the 113th Am Tn, arrives at New York. The demobilization includes, at Camp Taylor, January 8, Division Record Cadre; at Fort Benjamin Harrison, January 18, Hq 63rd Field Artillery Brig.

THE THIRTY-NINTH DIVISION, NATIONAL GUARD

The 39th Division was made up of the National Guard of Arkansas, Mississippi and Louisiana at Camp Beauregard, Louisiana. The overseas movement was completed on September 7, 1918. Upon its arrival in France the division was designated as the 5th Depot Division and ordered to the St. Florent area. The unit trained personnel to be used as replacements. The division was commanded by Major General Henry C. Hodges, Jr.

77th Infantry Brigade

153rd Infantry
154th Infantry
141st Machine Gun Battalion

78th Infantry Brigade

155th Infantry
156th Infantry
142nd Machine Gun Battalion

64th Field Artillery Brigade

140th Field Artillery
141st Field Artillery
142nd Field Artillery
114th Trench Mortar Battery

Divisional Troops

140th Machine Gun Battalion
114th Engineers

114th Field Signal Battalion
Headquarters Troop

Trains

114th Train Hdqs
114th Military Police
114th Ammunition Train
114th Supply Train
114th Engineers Train
114th Sanitary Train
Ambulance Cos and Field Hospitals 153–156

Organization and Training in the United States

July 18, 1917–July 30, 1918

July 18, the War Department designates National Guard troops of Arkansas, Louisiana, and Mississippi to form the 39th Division. Camp Beauregard, Alexandria, Louisiana, is selected for the training.

August 3, the War Department directs the concentration and organization at Camp Beauregard.

August 5, the National Guard units of Arkansas, Louisiana, and Mississippi are drafted into federal service. During August the concentration at Camp Beauregard is begun.

August 25, Maj. Gen. Henry C. Hodges, Jr., assumes command; the infantry brigades are organized and ultimately include the 77th Infantry Brig, the 1st and 3rd Regts of Arkansas Infantry, the MG Co of 2nd Arkansas Infantry, and detachments of the 1st Louisiana and 2nd Mississippi Regts of Infantry, 78th Infantry Brig, the 1st Mississippi Infantry and detachments of the 1st Louisiana and 2nd Mississippi Regts of Infantry.

September 1, the 64th Field Artillery Brig is organized and ultimately includes the 1st Louisiana and 1st Mississippi Regts of FA, and the 2nd Arkansas Infantry (less MG CQ).

September 24, 300 ORC officers are ordered to join from the 84th Division.

September 27, division is reorganized in accordance with the Tables of Organization of August 8, 1917.

October 17, systematic training begins.

November 9–14, drafts from Arkansas, Louisiana, and Mississippi, aggregating 9,000, arrive from the 87th Division and increase the strength to

22,000. During May 5,600 are transferred, but in June 11,000 replacements arrive, including 7,000 from Camp Taylor. During July additional personnel from Camps Pike, Taylor, and Travis complete the division.

Movement Overseas

July 31–September 12, 1918

July 31, the division moves via Camps Merritt, Mills, and Stuart to the ports of embarkation of Hoboken, Newport News, and New York.

August 5, Adv Det sails from New York, and arrives August 12 at Liverpool.

August 6, 77th Infantry Brig sails, and arrives August 18 at Brest.

August 18, DHQ sails, and arrives August 27 at Brest.

August 22–31, the remaining units sail and arrive September 3–12 at Brest.

Activities Overseas

August 22–November 29, 1918

August 14, division is designated as the 5th Depot Division.

August 22, division (less Arty, which goes to a training area) moves to the Charost and Mehun-sur-Yêvre Area southwest of Bourges, where the reorganization begins.

September 3–October 29, division functions as the 5th Depot Division.

During September the 114th Engrs and Tn and 114th F Sig Bn are assigned as army and corps troops; the remaining units, except artillery, 114th Sn Tn, and 141st MG Bn are reduced to training cadres whose duties are to receive, train, equip, and forward replacements of both officers and men for the infantry, including machine gun units, and for ammunition and supply trains; a classification camp is established. During September and October the surplus personnel are transferred as replacements.

October 2, 141st MG Bn is designated as a corps anti-aircraft machine gun battalion, and, October 9, moves to the anti-aircraft school at Langres for training. The division forwards 10,156 replacements.

October 29, orders direct that the division be skeletonized.

November 2, units of the 5th Depot Division move to St. Aignan-Noyers where they are skeletonized and the surplus personnel are transferred to the 1st Depot Division for use as replacements.

November 18, a Division Record Cadre, with officers and selected men from each unit, is designated to represent DHQ, the infantry regiments, 140th and 142nd MG Bns, 114th Suk Tn and 114th Tn Hq.

Final Training and Operations of Detached Units

64TH FIELD ARTILLERY BRIG AND 114TH AM TN

September 9, the artillery moves to Messac and the vicinity for training, and, September 24, proceeds to the Artillery Training Center at Camp Coëtquidan for further instruction.

November 8, 64th PA Brig (less 141st PA, 2nd and 3rd Bns 142nd PA, and 114th TM Btry) moves to the artillery school at Le Valdahon.

141ST MG BN

October 9, this battalion moves to and trains at the anti-aircraft artillery school at Langres until November 29.

114TH ENGRS AND TN

September 23, this regiment is ordered to Clermont-en-Argonne for duty with the First Army.

October 4, it arrives in the army area.

October 4–November 11, the regiment participates in the Meuse-Argonne Operation, where it serves with the First Army and I and V Corps, engaging primarily in road construction. November 18–20, the regiment salvages materiel in the region near Germont, Harricourt, and Buzancy. Subsequently, it stays at Froidos and Ligny-le-Châtel.

114TH F SIG BN

September 27, the battalion moves to St. Aignan Noyers, and later to Chitenay, for duty with the 1st Depot Division.

November 9, the battalion moves to Ippécourt and the vicinity for duty in the area of the First Army, where it remains until March 19.

114TH SAN TN (LESS 156TH AMB CO AND 156TH F HOSP)

November 9, the train (less detached units) moves to Souilly for duty with the VII Corps and participates with it in the advance into, and the occupation of, Germany.

January 20, the train becomes the VII Corps San Tn.

Return to the United States and Demobilization

NOVEMBER 30, 1918–MAY 1, 1919

November 30, the Division Record Cadre moves from St. Aignan-Noyers to St. Nazaire, where the 141st MG Bn joins.

December 19, a part of the 114th Am Tn sails from St. Nazaire, followed,

December 20, by the Division Record Cadre and 141st MG Bn. Other units follow and include, January 9, 114th TM Btry from Brest, April 20, 114th Engrs from Brest, and April 8–June 3, 64th PA Brig from Brest, Marseille, and St. Nazaire. The last element, the VII Corps San Tn, formerly the 114th San Tn, sails June 21 from Brest and arrives June 30 at Boston. The demobilization includes, at Camp Beauregard, January 23, Division Record Cadre; at Camp Shelby, May 1, Hq 64th Field Artillery Brig.

THE FORTIETH DIVISION, NATIONAL GUARD

The 40th Division was organized at Camp Kearney, California, from the National Guard of Arizona, New Mexico, Colorado, Utah, Nevada and California. It completed its overseas movement August 28, 1918. Upon its arrival in France the unit was made a replacement division and became the 6th Depot Division at La Guerche Area. Major General Frederick S. Strong commanded.

79th Infantry Brigade
157th Infantry
158th Infantry
144th Machine Gun Battalion

80th Infantry Brigade
159th Infantry
160th Infantry
145th Machine Gun Battalion

65th Field Artillery Brigade
143rd Field Artillery
144th Field Artillery
145th Field Artillery
115th Trench Mortar Battery

Divisional Troops
143rd Machine Gun Battalion
115th Engineers

115th Field Signal Battalion
Headquarters Troop

Trains

115th Train Hdqs and Military Police
115th Ammunition Train
115th Supply Train
115th Engineers Train
115th Sanitary Train
Ambulance Cos and Field Hospitals 157–160

Organization and Training in the United States

JULY 18, 1917–JULY 25, 1918

July 18, the War Department designates National Guard troops of Arizona, California, Colorado, Nevada, New Mexico, and Utah, to form the 40th Division. Camp Kearny, Linda Vista, California, is selected for the training.

August 3, the War Department directs the concentration and organization of the division at Camp Kearny.

August 5, the National Guard units of Arizona, California, Colorado, New Mexico and Utah are drafted into federal service. During August the concentration at Camp Kearny begins.

August 25, Maj. Gen. Frederick S. Strong assumes command; the brigades are organized and ultimately include 79th Infantry Brig, the 1st Colorado and 1st Arizona Regts of Infantry and detachments of the 1st New Mexico Infantry and 1st Colorado Cav; 80th Brig, the 2nd, 5th and 7th Regts of California Infantry and a detachment of California Cav; 65th Field Artillery Brig, the 1st and 2nd California and 1st Utah Regts of FA, and the MG Co. of 2nd Colorado Infantry.

September 24, division is reorganized in accordance with the Tables of Organization of August 8, 1917. During September and October systematic training begins; more than 200 officers of the ORC and NA join. During October and November drafts aggregating 9,000 from Camps Lewis and Funston complete the division. However, subsequent transfers amount to over 8,000. During June and July 10,000 men from Camp Lewis and 6,000 from California again complete the division, but the training is incomplete at the time of embarkation.

Movement Overseas

JULY 26–AUGUST 31, 1918

July 26, the division moves via Camp Mills to the ports of embarkation of Boston, Brooklyn, Montreal, New York, and Philadelphia.

August 5, Adv Det sails from New York, and arrives August 12, at Liverpool.

August 7–11, the division (less Arty, 115th Sup Tn, 115th F Sig Bn, and 115th San Tn) sails, and arrives August 17–25 in England.

August 13–16, the remaining units follow and land, August 28–31, in England. The troops stay a short time in rest camps and then proceed via Cherbourg and Le Havre.

Activities Overseas

AUGUST 22–DECEMBER 14, 1918

August 16, division is designated the 6th Depot Division.

August 22, division (less Arty, which goes to Camp de Souge for training) moves to La Guerche-sur-l'Aubois and the vicinity.

August 28, the creation of the 6th Depot Division is announced.

August 30–October 29, division functions as the 6th Depot Division.

August 30, division reorganizes as the 6th Depot Division to receive, train, equip, and forward replacements, both officers and men, for the infantry, including machine gun units, and the ammunition and supply trains. During September the division is reduced; 7500 replacements are sent to the 28th, 32nd, and 77th Divisions; training cadres are established; and the training of replacements is begun.

September 20, 115th F Sig Bn is transferred to the II Corps Signal School and arrives September 22 near Châtilbon-sur-Seine. September 25, 157th, 158th, and 159th F Hosps are transferred to the VI Corps, and on September 27 the 115th Engrs and Tn follow.

October 14, 115th F Sig Bn moves to the Toul Area and, on October 16 joins the Second Army.

October 16, a classification camp with capacity of 5,000 opens at La Guerche-sur-l'Aubois and within the month returns 11,000 former hospital cases to their organizations.

October 23, a total of 16,327 replacements have been forwarded.

October 24, division is designated as a replacement unit.

October 30, 158th Infantry and 144th MG Bn move to Chelles to form a regional replacement depot for the First Army, where, on November 4, they absorb the III Corps Replacement Bn.

October 30–December 4, the 6th Depot Division functions as a Regional Replacement Unit.

October 31, 159th Infantry and 143rd MG Bn move to the vicinity of Saleux to form a regional replacement depot for the II Corps, and subsequently absorb the II Corps Replacement Bn.

November 4, the remaining units of the 6th Depot Division arrive at Revigny.

November 7, an advance replacement depot, organized from the I and V Corps Replacement Bns, opens at Grangele-Comte.

November 8, division establishes a regional replacement depot at Revigny and a temporary classification camp with a capacity of 700 at Contrisson, in order to return hospital cases and stragglers to the First, Second, and Third Armies, and to equip men who go on leave from combat divisions.

December 5, the First Army Replacement Bn and Third Army Replacement Bn are organized at Contrisson and the Second Army Replacement Bn at Chelles to assume the duties of the Division at Revigny and Chelles.

December 8–26, the 65th Field Artillery Brig sails from Bordeaux for United States.

December 14, the units at Revigny, Chelles, and Saleux are relieved and made subject to the orders of the SOS for the return.

Return to the United States and Demobilization

DECEMBER 15, 1918–JUNE 30, 1919

January 6, the units in the Revigny Area join parts of the former Depot Division at Beautiran in the Bordeaux Area. The division receives 8,800 casualties for transportation to the United States.

February 20, troops move from the Beautiran Area to Camp Génicart.

March 6, the leading infantry troops sail from Bordeaux and other units follow at intervals.

June 25, 115th F Sig Bn leaves Brest.

July 19, the last element, a part of the 115th Engrs, arrives at New York. The demobilization includes, at Camp Kearny, April 20, DHQ, April 27, Hq 79th Infantry Brig and Hq 80th Infantry Brig; at Camp Lewis, June 30, Hq 65th Field Artillery Brig.

THE FORTY-FIRST DIVISION, NATIONAL GUARD

The 41st Division was organized at Camp Greene, North Carolina, from the National Guard units of Oregon, Washington, Montana, Utah and Wyoming. The overseas movement which began October 18, 1917, was completed December 9, 1917, when the last unit arrived in France. It was designated as the 1st Depot Division and sent to the St. Aignan Area. It was then broken up and used for instruction or replacement of combat divisions at the front. The 66th Artillery Brigade served as Corps and Army Artillery throughout its service in France and was active at Marne-Aisne, St. Mihiel and Meuse-Argonne offensives. The 41st Division while serving as the 1st Depot Division from January 1, 1918, to December 31, 1918, sent for 263,395 replacements. The commanders were Major General Hunter Liggett, Brigadier General George LeRoy Irwin, Brigadier General Richard Coulter, Brigadier General Robert Alexander, Brigadier General William S. Scott, Major General John E. McMann and Brigadier General Eli Cole, U.S. Marine Corps.

81st Infantry Brigade

161st Infantry
162nd Infantry
147th Machine Gun Battalion

82nd Infantry Brigade

163rd Infantry
164th Infantry
148th Machine Gun Battalion

66th Field Artillery Brigade

146th Field Artillery
147th Field Artillery
148th Field Artillery
116th Trench Mortar Battery

Divisional Troops

146th Machine Gun Battalion
116th Engineers

116th Field Signal Battalion
Headquarters Troop

Trains

116th Train Hdqs and Military Police
116th Ammunition Train
116th Supply Train
116th Engineer Train
116th Sanitary Train
Ambulance Cos and Field Hospitals 161–164

Organization and Training in the United States

JULY 18, 1917–NOVEMBER 25, 1917

July 18, the War Department designates National Guard troops of Idaho, Montana, Oregon, Washington, and Wyoming to form the 41st Division. Camp Fremont, Palo Alto, California, is originally selected for the training.

July 25, the National Guard units of Oregon, Washington, and Wyoming are called into federal service.

August 3, the War Department directs the concentration and organization of the division at Camp Fremont, but this is subsequently changed to Camp Greene, Charlotte, North Carolina.

August 5, the National Guard units of Colorado, Idaho, Montana, North Dakota, New Mexico, Oregon, South Dakota, Washington, Wyoming and the District of Columbia are drafted into the federal service.

September 3, units from these states begin to arrive at Camp Greene.

September 18, Maj. Gen. Hunter Liggett assumes command.

September 19, the division is reorganized in accordance with the Tables of Organization of August 8, 1917; the brigades are organized; systematic training begins. The brigades ultimately include, 81st Infantry Brig, the 3rd Oregon and 2nd Washington Regts of Infantry and detachments of the 3rd D.C., 2nd Idaho, and 2nd North Dakota Regts of Infantry and of Washington Cav; 82nd Infantry Brig, the 2nd Montana and 1st North Dakota Regts of Infantry, and detachments of the 3rd D.C., 2nd North Dakota, and 4th South Dakota Regts of Infantry; 66th Field Artillery Brig, detachments of Colorado, New Mexico, Oregon, and Washington Regts of FA, of the 2nd Idaho, 2nd North Dakota, 3rd Wyoming, and 4th South Dakota Regts of Infantry, and of Oregon Cav.

October 22, the division moves to Camp Mills, where the concentration is completed.

November 10–20, 8,000 men from the 91st Division complete this unit.

December 16, the elements still in the United States move to Camp Merritt.

Movement Overseas

NOVEMBER 26, 1917–FEBRUARY 6, 1918

November 26, the leading units sail from Hoboken and arrive December 11, at St. Nazaire. December 13, DHQ, 81st Infantry Brig, and the trains (less 116th Engr Tn) sail from Hoboken, and arrive on December 27 and 28, at Brest.

December 15–January 11, 66th Field Artillery Brig (less 148th FA) and the remaining infantry sail, and arrive December 25–January 19 at Liverpool except the 116th TM Btry, which lands at St. Nazaire.

February 6, the last element arrives abroad.

Activities Overseas

DECEMBER 8, 1917–JANUARY 23, 1919

December 8, 1917, division is designated as the Replacement Division, I Corps.

December 20, 1917–January 17, 1918, division moves to La Courtine, and January 9–24 proceeds to the St. Aignan and Noyers Area. It forwards about 2,800 replacements.

January 15, 1918, division is re-designated as the Base and Training Division, I Corps. The Base and Training Division, which is reduced to a training cadre strength by forwarding the surplus personnel as replacements, includes DHQ, Hq Troop, Hq 82nd Infantry Brig, 163rd Infantry (less nine companies), 146th MG Bn, parts of the 147th and 148th MG Bns, 116th Am Tn, 116th F Sig Bn, Hq and one company of the 116th Sup Tn, and an ambulance company and field hospital of the 116th San Tn, a total of 198 officers and 5,454 men. Other units, which are detached, include certain infantry and machine gun troops which are sent to schools and to duty with the SOS; the 116th Engrs and Tn sent to Selles-sur-Cher and then to Angers, where on January 23, they form a replacement depot under the 1st Depot Division and forward a total of 29,000 engineer replacements; the 66th Field Artillery Brig (less 147th FA) sent to Camp de Souge and Libourne for training; and the 147th FA, a part of which is sent to La Courtine, where it functions as a field artillery replacement unit from February to June, the remainder to school duty and the 116th TM Btry sent to the school at Langres.

January 20–April 11, division is under the administrative control of the I Corps. During February and March the Divisional area of St. Aignan and Noyers is divided into five districts, a classification camp and salvage plant are established, training schools for specialists are opened, infantry training battalions are organized, and systematic training is begun.

March 5, 1918, unit is re-designated as the Depot Division, I Corps.

April 11, in addition to its duties as Depot Division, unit begins to function as the replacement division for the entire AEF, and it so functions until early in August, when the 2nd Depot Division (83rd Division) assumes a part of the duties.

April 11–July 12, additional schools for specialists, a school for field officers, cavalry training units, labor companies, an Infantry Training Regiment, a Military Specialists Holding Company, and a Disciplinary Barracks are organized; the 146th, 147th, and 148th MG Bns are reassembled to train replacements for machine gun units; the 162nd Infantry (less 2nd Bn in England) and the skeleton units of the 164th Infantry rejoin; and the 116th F Sig Bn trains and forwards about 4,000 Signal Corps replacements.

July 13, 1918, division is re-designated as the 1st Depot Division, AEF.

August 31, 161st Infantry rejoins and absorbs the 1st Training Regt. In September there are four infantry regiments, three machine gun battalions, one supply train, one ammunition train, ten schools, and some troops of the Marine Corps engaged in training and forwarding replacements.

In November a squadron of cavalry is added.

November 8, division receives the personnel of the 3rd and 5th Depot Divisions for disposal as replacements. During the operations in France the division organizes 41 Depot Labor Cos, 51 Prisoner of War Escort Cos, 40 Casual Cos, Leave Area Detachments, and various other units; forwards 185,811 replacements, and returns 102,461 casuals to their organizations. December 26, the 1st Depot Division is abolished and the 41st Division is recreated by the reassignment of the original units.

Final Training and Operations of Detached Units

66TH FIELD ARTILLERY BRIG
(LESS 147TH FIELD ARTILLERY AND 116TH TM BTRY)

This brigade concentrates at Camp de Souge during January and February 1918 for training.

July 3–6, the troops move to the Château-Thierry front where they serve under the I Corps.

July 8–14, the 148th Field Artillery and July 9–14, the 146th Field

Artillery participate in the occupation of the Château-Thierry Sector under the French Sixth Army.

July 15–18, the brigade participates in the Champagne-Marne Operation as French 38th Corps artillery, July 18–August 6, in the Aisne-Marne Operation as I Corps artillery, and, August 7–12, in the Vesle Sector as I Corps artillery.

August 12, the brigade moves to a rear area near La Ferté-sous-Jouarre.

August 20, the brigade passes to the artillery of the First Army, and the headquarters moves to Dieue-sur-Meuse.

August 26, the 146th and 148th Regts of Field Artillery are in the St. Mihiel Area.

September 12–16, the 146th Field Artillery supports the V Corps and the 148th Field Artillery supports the IV and I Corps in the St. Mihiel Operation.

September 16, Hq 66th Field Artillery Brig moves to Sivry-la-Perche.

September 26–November 11, the brigade, which is with the artillery of the First Army until November 6 and thereafter with the III Corps, participates in the Meuse-Argonne Operation. **December 2,** the brigade passes to the Third Army and proceeds to Germany for duty with the Army of Occupation.

May 9, the brigade passes to the SOS for the return to the United States, and, on May 25, moves to St. Nazaire.

147TH FA

Various units are stationed initially at Abainville, Gondrecourt, La Courtine, and Saumur. In June the 1st Bn leaves Saumur for duty with the 26th Division, participates June 13–22 in the occupation of the Toul-Boucq Sector, and later joins the 32nd Division. Early in July the regiment (less Btry F) assembles under the 57th Field Artillery Brig (32nd Division) at Belfort, and participates July 1–22 in the occupation of the Centre Sector; August 1–6, in the Aisne-Marne Operation near Château-Thierry; August 7–17, in the occupation of the Fismes Sector supporting the 28th Division; August 18–September 6, in the Oise-Aisne Operation supporting the 28th Division until September 1 and thereafter the French Moroccan Division; September 22–25, in the occupation of the Avocourt Sector supporting the 79th Division; and in the Meuse-Argonne Operation, September 26–30, supporting the 79th Division, September 30–October 6, supporting the 3rd Division, October 6–19, supporting the 32nd Division, October 19–November 6, supporting the 89th Division, and then as part of the artillery of the First Army until November 11.

April 8, the regiment is released for return to the United States.

116TH TM BTRY

This battery, detached, serves January through September 1918 at the Army Trench Artillery School, Langres; September 9–December 17, at 4th Army Trench Artillery Center, Vitrey; and December 1918–February 1919 at St. Sébastien, in the area of the 41st Division; then returns to the United States.

Return to the United States and Demobilization

JANUARY 24–JUNE 28, 1919

January 24, the division, numbering about 16,000, moves to Brest.
January 28, the leading unit, 164th F Hosp, sails from Marseille.
February 3, DHQ and the leading infantry troops sail from Brest; other infantry and divisional troops follow.
April 14, 147th Field Artillery moves from Amanty to Brest and sails on May 1.
May 25, 66th Field Artillery Brig (less 147th FA) moves to St. Nazaire and arrives June 15, at Brooklyn.
June 30, the last element of the division, a detachment of the 66th Field Artillery Brig, arrives at Charleston. The demobilization includes, at Camp Dix, February 22, DHQ and Hq 82nd Infantry Brig, March 3, Hq 81st Infantry Brig; at Camp Lewis, June 28, Hq 66th Field Artillery Brig.

THE SEVENTY-SIXTH DIVISION, NATIONAL ARMY

The 76th Division was made up of National Army drafts from Maine, New Hampshire, Vermont, Rhode Island and Connecticut. It was trained at Camp Devens, Massachusetts. The overseas movement began July 5, 1918, and was completed later that month upon the unit's arrival in France. The unit was made a Depot Division and ordered to St. Aignan Area. It was broken up and its personnel was used as replacement for combat divisions at the front. The division was commanded by Major General Harry F. Hodges and Brigadier General William Wiegel.

151st Infantry Brigade

301st Infantry
302nd Infantry
302nd Machine Gun Battalion

152nd Infantry Brigade

303rd Infantry
304th Infantry
303rd Machine Gun Battalion

151st Field Artillery Brigade

301st Field Artillery
302nd Field Artillery
303rd Field Artillery
301st Trench Mortar Battery

Divisional Troops

301st Machine Gun Battalion
301st Engineers
301st Field Signal Battalion
Headquarters Troop

Trains

301st Train Hdqs
301st Military Police
301st Ammunition Train
301st Supply Train
301st Engineer Train
301st Sanitary Train
Ambulance Cos and Field Hospitals 301–304

Organization and Training in the United States

AUGUST 5, 1917–JULY 2, 1918

August 5, the War Department establishes the 76th Division, National Army, which is to be organized at Camp Devens, Ayer, Massachusetts; drafts, anticipated for 1917, from Connecticut, 10,977, Maine, 1,821, Massachusetts, 20,586, New Hampshire, 1,204, New York, 5,840, Rhode Island, 2,211, and Vermont, 1,049, are designed to furnish personnel.

August 13, the organization of DHQ is directed, and its commissioned personnel are ordered to report on or before August 15.

August 16, the commanding general of Camp Devens is directed to organize the division in accordance with the Tables of Organization of August 8, 1917.

August 25, Maj. Gen. Harry F. Hodges assumes command; the program for the movement of selective service men to camps is announced. During the last week in August the organization, to include skeleton units, begins from a cadre of officers and men of the Regular Army, and from ORC and NA officers of the First Officers Training Camps.

September 5–10, the initial draft of 2,000 selective service men arrives at camp.

September 19–24, an additional 17,500 arrive. In September, systematic training begins.

October 3–8, the last drafts of 1917 furnish the camp with 17,500.

October 31, the division numbers about 22,000. During the winter fresh drafts and transfers arrive, but are exceeded by the losses which include, in November alone, 3,600, the majority of whom go to the 82nd Division.

March 31, the division aggregates less than one-half the authorized strength. In April and June new drafts and transfers complete the division.

June 28, the Adv Det sails from New York, and arrives July 10 at Liverpool.

Movement Overseas

JULY 3–AUGUST 8, 1918

July 3, division moves to the ports of embarkation of Boston, Brooklyn, Halifax, New York, and Montreal.

July 5–6, DHQ and the 151st Infantry Brig sail.

July 12–August 8, division arrives at English ports. It proceeds, after a brief delay in rest camps, to Bordeaux, Cherbourg, and Le Havre.

July 14, while en route, the unit is designated as a Depot Division.

July 16, all troops are en route except two batteries of the 301st FA.

Activities Overseas

JULY 19–NOVEMBER 17, 1918

July 19, division (less 302nd Infantry and 151st Field Artillery Brig) moves to the St. Amand-Mont-Rond Area; the 302nd Infantry and 151st Field Artillery Brig go to Bordeaux and the vicinity.

August 3–November 7, division (less 302nd Infantry and 151st Field Artillery Brig) is reorganized to conform to the organization of a depot division; five districts are established and assigned to the 301st Infantry, 303rd

Infantry, 304th Infantry, 301st MG Bn and 301st Engrs, respectively; units of the division except the 301st F Sig Bn and 301st Engrs and Tn, are reduced to a training cadre strength; about 7,000 men leave as replacements for other divisions. During its existence as a Depot Division it receives, trains, equips, and forwards 19,971 replacements (officers and men) for infantry, machine gun, ammunition train, and supply train units. August 25, 301st F Sig Bn moves to St. Geosmes.

September 9, 301st Engrs and Tn, having been assigned to the IV Corps, move to Toul where they join that corps.

October 29, division (less DHQ and Hq Troop, 151st Field Artillery Brig, 301st Engrs and Tn, 301st F Sig Bn, and 301st Sup Tn) is ordered skeletonized.

November 7, the depot organization of the division ceases, and the 76th Division absorbs the depot personnel; the 151st Infantry Brig, 152nd Infantry Brig, 301st MG Bn, 301st Am Tn, 301st Tn Hq and MP, move to the area of the 1st Depot Division (41st Division) at St. Aignan-Noyers, where the units are skeletonized, a record cadre of 11 officers and 84 men is formed, and the surplus personnel are classified for assignment to other organizations.

November 13, 301st Sup Tn moves to St. Aignan-Noyers. **November 17,** 301st San Tn (less 304th Amb Co and F Hosp, skeletonized) is attached to the IV Corps.

Final Training and Operations of Detached Units

302ND INFANTRY

July 17, the regiment moves from Le Havre to Bordeaux and the vicinity (Bordeaux, St. Sulpice, Camp Génicart, and Pengueux) where it remains until October 8, when it reverts to the division at St. Amand-Mont-Rond.

151ST FIELD ARTILLERY BRIG

August 5, the brigade (less 303rd FA) moves to the vicinity of Bordeaux, the 303rd Field Artillery to Clermont-Ferrand. September 5, 301st Field Artillery and 302nd Field Artillery move to Camp de Souge for training.

November 2–11, 151st Field Artillery Brig (less 301st FA) participates in the occupation of the St. Mihiel Sector as corps artillery with the French II Colonial Corps and French XVII Corps.

November 15, the brigade (less 301st FA) is attached to the IV Corps and, on November 17, passes into the reserve of the Second Army.

November 26, the brigade (less 301st FA) is assigned to the IX Corps (Second Army).

January 8, 151st Field Artillery Brig (less 301st FA) is relieved and proceeds from St. Mihiel and Rupt-en-Woevre to Camp de Souge, where it remains until March 19, when it moves to Bordeaux, preparatory to embarkation.

301ST ENGRS AND TN

The regiment and train participate as corps troops, September 12–16, in the St. Mihiel Operation, and, September 17–November 11, in the occupation of the Toul Sector.

November 17, the regiment and train move with the IV Corps to Germany as part of the Army of Occupation and remain in the Coblenz Area until May 27, when they move to St. Nazaire for embarkation.

301ST F SIG BN

September 24, the battalion leaves St. Geosmes en route to the front.

September 25–November 11, the battalion participates in the occupation of the Marbache Sector, serving with the VI Corps. It remains in the vicinity of Marbache until December 24. Thereafter it functions as corps troops (VI Corps) in Lorraine, the Grand Duchy of Luxemburg, and in the department of Meurthe-et-Moseile until April 27, when it proceeds to Brest for embarkation.

301ST SUP TN

November 20, the train moves from St. Aignan-Noyers to Le Havre. It is engaged in routine and convoy duties in the SOS at various stations until May 24, when half of the train sails from Le Havre; the remainder follows on June 13 from St. Nazaire.

301st San Tn.

November 17, the train (less 304th Amb Co and F Hosp), attached to the IV Corps, moves to Germany as part of the Army of Occupation and remains in the Coblenz Area until May 27, when it moves to St. Nazaire preparatory to embarkation.

Return to the United States and Demobilization

NOVEMBER 27, 1918–MAY 5, 1919

November 25, division (less detached units) moves to St. Nazaire.
November 27, DHQ and Hq Troop embark at St. Nazaire.
December 28, 301st Field Artillery sails from Brest.
April 13, the remainder of the 151st Field Artillery Brig sails from Bordeaux.

July 11, 301st Sup Tn, the last element of the division, arrives at Newport News. The demobilization at Camp Devens includes, January 14, DHQ (skeletonized), February 25, Hqs 151st and 152nd Infantry Brigs (skeletonized), May 5, Hq 151st Field Artillery Brig.

THE EIGHTY-THIRD DIVISION, NATIONAL ARMY

The 83rd Division was organized at Camp Sherman, Ohio, from National Army drafts from Ohio and West Virginia. The overseas draft, which began June 4, 1918, was completed by the arrival of the last unit in France June 21, 1918. It was designated as a depot division upon its arrival in France and sent to the Maus Area. Here the division was broken up and artillery brigade and engineer and signal troops were sent forward as corps and army charges. The rest of the division was trained as replacements for combat divisions at the front. The division was commanded by Major General Edwin F. Glenn for its entire existence.

165th Infantry Brigade
329th Infantry
330th Infantry
323rd Machine Gun Battalion

166th Infantry Brigade
331st Infantry
332nd Infantry
324th Machine Gun Battalion

158th Field Artillery Brigade
322nd Field Artillery
323rd Field Artillery
324th Field Artillery
308th Trench Mortar Battery

Divisional Troops
322nd Machine Gun Battalion
308th Engineers

308th Field Signal Battalion
Headquarters Troop

Trains

308th Train Hdqs
308th Military Police
308th Ammunition Train
308th Supply Train
30th Engineer Train
308th Sanitary Train
Ambulance Cos and Field Hospitals 329–332

Organization and Training in the United States

AUGUST 5, 1917–MAY 23, 1918

August 5, the War Department establishes the 83rd Division, National Army, which is to be organized at Camp Sherman, Chilhicothe, Ohio; drafts are anticipated for 1917, from Ohio, 38,773, and Pennsylvania, 4,309, to furnish personnel.

August 13, the organization of DHQ is directed, and its commissioned personnel are ordered, to report on or before August 15.

August 16, the commanding general of Camp Sherman is directed to organize the division in accordance with the Tables of Organization of August 8, 1917.

August 25, Maj. Gen. Edwin F. Glenn assumes command; the program for the movement of selective service men to camps is announced. During the last week in August the organization begins from a cadre of officers and men of the Regular Army, and from ORC and NA officers of the First Officers Training Camp at Fort Benjamin Harrison.

September 5–10, the initial draft of 2,100 selective service men arrives at camp.

September 19–24, an additional 17,200 arrive. During September systematic training begins.

October 3–8, a draft of 13,000 arrives at the camp.

October 31, the division approximates 22,800.

December 14–19, the last drafts of 1917 furnish 900 to the camp.

March 31, the winter losses have exceeded arrivals and the division numbers fewer than 17,000. During April and May drafts, largely from Kentucky, Ohio, and Pennsylvania, complete the division.

Movement Overseas

MAY 24–JUNE 28, 1918

May 24, division moves via Camps Merritt and Mills to the ports of embarkation of Boston, Hoboken, New York, and Philadelphia.

June 4, Adv Det sails from New York and lands June 11 in England.

June 4–14, the troops sail, and land June 15–28 in England. After a brief stay in rest camps, the division goes to Le Havre and Cherbourg.

Activities Overseas

JUNE 19, 1918–JANUARY 8, 1919

June 19, DHQ, 331st Infantry and 332nd Infantry move to the 8th (Nogenten-Bassigny) Training Area.

July 1, 329th Infantry, 330th Infantry, the machine gun battalions, 308th F Sig Bn, and 308th Sup Tn move to Le Mans Area.

June 27, division is designated as a depot division. The 332nd Infantry, 158th Field Artillery Brig, 308th Am Tn, 308th Engrs, 308th F Sig Bn, 308th TM Btry, and 308th San Tn are detached and serve as army and corps troops.

July 2–10, training of divisional units in the 8th (Nogent-en-Bassigny) Training Area is supervised by the IV Corps.

July 30, division (less detached units) concentrates in Le Mans Area.

August 1, division begins to function as the 2nd Depot Division. During its existence 195,221 replacements, officers and men, drawn from personnel from the United States and casuals at large, are trained for the infantry, including machine gun units, ammunition trains and supply trains, and are forwarded to the advance zone.

August 12, 49th Infantry joins the division, replacing the detached 332nd Infantry. The Ecommoy Area, the city of Le Mans, the Forwarding Camp, the Belgian Camp, the Classification Camp, and the Spur Camp gradually come under the control of this 2nd Depot Division. Its district is divided into the following five areas for administrative purposes, La Suze (331st Infantry), Laigné-en-Belin (330th Infantry), Ecommoy (329th Infantry), Conlie (49th Infantry), and Mayet (the three machine gun battalions). During October there is a maximum of 45,000 troops in the area.

December 15–31, the American Embarkation Center, an organization which is formed at this time, relieves the 2nd Depot (83rd) Division.

Final Training and Operations of Detached Units

332ND INFANTRY AND 331ST F HOSP

July 25, these units move via Marseille to Villafranca, Custoza, and Sommacompagna, Italy.

August 12, they proceed to Valeggio and train. Early in October the regiment moves to the north of the Treviso and makes frequent marches in the rear of the Piave River front.

October 27–28, the regiment assists in establishing bridgeheads at the Piave River.

October 28–November 4, 332nd Infantry participates in the Vittorio-Veneto Operation (Italy).

October 30, this regiment, as part of the Italian 31st Division (British 14th Corps, Tenth Italian Army), participates in the pursuit of the Austrians from the Piave to the Tagliamento River; the 2nd Bn crosses the Tagliamento under fire and reaches Villaorba on November 4, when the Austrian armistice becomes effective.

November 21, 2nd Bn 332nd Infantry arrives at Cattaro and sends troops into Montenegro.

November 24, Hq and the 1st Bn 332nd Infantry move to Treviso, the 3rd Bn moves to Fiume.

March 28–29, the regiment assembles at Genoa.

March 29–April 4, these troops sail for the United States, the first contingent sails from Genoa on March 29, the second contingent from Marseille on March 29 and April 4.

158TH FIELD ARTILLERY BRIG AND 308TH AM TN

June 27, these troops move to the vicinity of Guipry and Maure-de-Bretagne.

August 13, they continue to Camp Coëtquidan for further training.

September 18, they move to the vicinity of Bar-le-Duc.

September 26–November 11, 158th Field Artillery Brig and 308th Am Tn participate in the Meuse-Argonne Operation.

September 26, 322nd FA, 308th TM Btry, and 308th Am Tn support the 91st Division.

September 26–30, 158th F.A. Brig is attached to the 32nd Division, and later it is assigned to the V Corps as artillery.

October 2, 158th Field Artillery Brig is attached to the 29th Division and supports, October 8–28, the French 18th Division and 29th Division in Meuse-Argonne Operation.

308TH ENGRS AND TN

June 20, these troops are on duty with the SOS.

July 22, they are attached to the I Corps and serve as corps engineers.

July 28–August 6, 308th Engrs and Tn participate in the Aisne-Marne Operation.

August 12, they are attached to the III Corps.

August 18–September 9, 308th Engrs and Tn participate in the Oise-Aisne Operation.

September 26–November 11, 308th Engrs and Tn participate in the Meuse-Argonne Operation. Subsequently they form part of the Army of Occupation in Germany.

May 16, 308th Engrs and Tn are relieved from the III Corps and on May 24 proceed to the American Embarkation Center, Le Mans.

308TH F SIG BN

July 7, this battalion is attached to the III Corps and functions as the corps signal battalion.

August 7–17, 308th F Sig Bn participates in the Vesle Sector.

August 18–September 8, in the Oise-Aisne Operation.

September 26–November 11, in the Meuse-Argonne Operation. It forms part of the Army of Occupation in Germany for the remainder of its service with the III Corps.

Return to the United States and Demobilization

JANUARY 9–OCTOBER 8, 1919

January 9, all units of the former 2nd Depot Division move to Brest.

January 12, DHQ and the leading troops sail, and arrive January 21 at Hoboken.

May 5, 158th Field Artillery Brig sails from Brest.

August 5, the last elements of the division arrive at New York. The demobilization at Camp Sherman includes, February 11, Hq 166th Infantry Brig, February 12, Hq 165th Infantry Brig, May 24, Hq 158th Field Artillery Brig, October 8, DHQ.

THE EIGHTY-FOURTH DIVISION, NATIONAL ARMY

This is another division that was, as the reports state, to be "skeletonized" not long after its arrival in France. As far as can be determined, none of its units was in combat during its existence. Major General Wilber C. Hale was the division's commanding officer until November 14, 1918.

167th Infantry Brigade

333rd Infantry
334th Infantry
326th Machine Gun Battalion

168th Infantry Brigade

335th Infantry
336th Infantry
327th Machine Gun Battalion

159th Field Artillery Brigade

325th Field Artillery
326th Field Artillery
327th Field Artillery
309th Trench Mortar Battery

Divisional Troops

325th Machine Gun Battalion
309th Engineers
309th Field Signal Battalion
Headquarters Troop

Trains

309th Train Hdqs
309th Military Police
309th Ammunition Train
309th Supply Train

309th Engineer Train
309th Sanitary Train
Ambulance Cos and Field Hospitals 333–336

Organization and Training in the United States

AUGUST 5, 1917–AUGUST 19, 1918

August 5, the War Department establishes the 84th Division, National Army, which is to be organized at Camp Taylor, Louisville, Kentucky; drafts are anticipated for 1917 from Illinois, 10,573, Indiana, 17,510, and Kentucky, 14,236, to furnish personnel.

August 13, the organization of DHQ is directed, and its commissioned personnel are ordered, to report on or before August 15.

August 16, the commanding general of Camp Taylor is directed to organize the division in accordance with the Tables of Organization of August 8, 1917.

August 25, Brig. Gen. Wilbur E. Wilder assumes temporary command; the program for the movement of selective service men to camps is announced. During the last week in August the organization begins from a cadre of officers and men of the Regular Army, and from ORC and NA officers of the First Officers Training Camps at Forts Benjamin Harrison and Sheridan.

September 5–10, the initial draft of 2,100 selective service men arrives at camp.

September 19–24, an additional 17,000 arrive.

October 3–8, the last drafts of 1917 furnish the camp with 8,400. During October systematic training begins.

October 6, Maj. Gen. Harry C. Hale assumes command until October 31, 1918.

October 31, the division aggregates 18,500. The October–December losses aggregate 9,000, including drafts of 2,000 each to the 38th and 87th Divisions; the gains include 500 junior officers from the Second Officers Training Camps. During the winter drafts arrive, but in March several thousand men leave the division.

May 1, the division numbers fewer than 12,000. During May drafts totaling 17,000 reach camp from Indiana, Kentucky, and Ohio, but 5,300 leave.

June 6, the division (less Arty, which is at the Field Artillery Firing Center, West Point, Kentucky) moves to Camp Sherman. During July and August drafts arrive and complete the division. For the most part they are from Ohio, but include a contingent of 1,700 North Dakota and Montana, and from Camp Dodge.

Movement Overseas

AUGUST 20–OCTOBER 25, 1918

August 20, Division (less Arty) moves to Camp Mills en route to England and Scotland via Brooklyn, New York, and Quebec.

August 25, 157th Field Artillery Brig moves from West Point, Kentucky, to Camp Mills.

August 27, Adv Det sails from New York and arrives September 3 at Liverpool.

September 1–4, the infantry, except Hq 168th Infantry Brig, two battalions of the 336th Infantry and the 326th MG Bn, sail, and arrive September 9–16 at Liverpool.

September 9, 159th Field Artillery Brig and divisional troops and trains, except the TM Btry, Sup Tn, and Am Tn, sail from New York and arrive September 21 and 22 at Liverpool and Glasgow.

September 12–17, and October 14, the remaining units sail, and arrive at British ports September 25–October 2 and October 25. After a brief stay in English rest camps the troops proceed to France via Le Havre and Cherbourg.

Activities Overseas

SEPTEMBER 13–DECEMBER 30, 1918

September 13, Division (less Arty) moves to the West Perigueux Area for training.

September 26, 159th Field Artillery Brig (less 309th TM Btry and 309th Am Tn) moves to Camp de Souge; the 309th Am Tn follows on October 12. The 309th TM Btry moves to Vitrey for training.

October 3, division is ordered skeletonized, but with a view to reconstitution.

October 9, about 10,000 men from the infantry, including machine gun units, are transferred to the 1st Depot Division for use as replacements, which reduces these units to an average strength of 25.

October 22, 309th Engrs and Tn move to St. Nazaire for duty with the SOS.

October 29, division (less 159th Field Artillery Brig, 309th Engrs, 309th F Sig Bn, and trains) is ordered reduced to record cadre strength, as the reconstitution is no longer contemplated, and directed to proceed to Le Mans for the absorption of the surplus personnel by the 2nd Depot Division.

November 3, 309th F Sig Bn leaves for the Signal Corps Replacement Depot at Cour-Cheverny.

November 5, DHQ, 167th and 168th Infantry Brigs, 325th MG Bn, 308th Tn Hq and MP move to Le Mans Area, where they are further skeletonized.

November 10, a Division Record Cadre of 7 officers and 93 enlisted men is formed at Le Mans and the surplus personnel are classified for reassignment.

November 11, some elements of the 309th San Tn move from Perigueux to St. Aignan-Noyers for skeletonization by the 1st Depot Division.

November 25, Division Record Cadre is ordered from Le Mans Area to Camp de Souge to join the 159th Field Artillery Brig for return to the United States.

*Return to the United States
and Demobilization*

DECEMBER 31, 1918–JULY 26, 1919

December 31, 309th TM Btry sails from Brest.

January 6, Division Record Cadre, 309th San Tn Cadre, and Hq 159th Field Artillery Brig sail from Bordeaux. The remainder of the artillery and the 309th Am Tn follow prior to February 2.

April 21, 309th F Sig Bn sails. The last troops of the division, part of the 309th Engrs, arrive on July 18 at New York. The demobilization at Camp Zachary Taylor includes, January 26, Hq 159th Field Artillery Brig, July 26, Division Record Cadre.

THE EIGHTY-FIFTH DIVISION, NATIONAL ARMY

This was another division included in the decision to be skeltonized. A portion was sent to North Russia in an attempt, originated by the British and French, to stop the nation becoming a Soviet state.

169th Infantry Brigade

337th Infantry
338th Infantry
329th Machine Gun Battalion

170th Infantry Brigade

339th Infantry
340th Infantry
330th Machine Gun Battalion

160th Field Artillery

328th Field Artillery
329th Field Artillery
330th Field Artillery
310th Trench Mortar Battery

Divisional Troops

328th Machine Gun Battalion
310th Engineers
310th Field Signal Battalion
Headquarters Troop

Trains

310th Train Hdqs
310th Military Police
310th Ammunition Train
310th Supply Train
310th Engineer Train
310th Sanitary Train
Ambulance Cos and Field Hospitals 337–340

Organization and Training in the United States

AUGUST 5, 1917–JULY 10, 1918

August 5, the War Department establishes the 85th Division, National Army, which is to be organized at Camp Custer, Battle Creek, Michigan; drafts, anticipated for 1917, from Michigan, 23,309, and Wisconsin, 5,695, are designed to furnish personnel.

August 13, the organization of DHQ is directed, and its commissioned personnel are ordered to report on or before August 15.

August 16, the commanding general of Camp Custer is directed to organize the division in accordance with the Tables of Organization of August 8, 1917.

August 25, Maj. Gen. Joseph T. Dickman assumes command; the program for the movement of selective service men to camps is announced. During the last week in August the organization, to include skeleton units, begins from a cadre of officers and men of the Regular Army, and from ORC and NA officers of the First Officers Training Camps.

September 5–10, the initial draft of 1,800 selective service men arrives at camp.

September 19–24, an additional 14,400 arrive. During September systematic training begins. In October the division loses about 2,000. In November a draft of 10,800 arrives at the camp and the division attains a strength of 20,000. Between January and July over 50,000 arrive at Camp Custer, but more than 30,000 leave, many passing through the division.

April 30, fewer than 12,000 are in the division.

During May, 7,600 join the division from the depot brigade.

June, fresh drafts, including 2,500 from Camp Grant, and 1,500 from Camp Taylor drawn largely from Illinois, Indiana, and Kentucky, complete the division.

Movement Overseas

JULY 11–AUGUST 11, 1918

July 11, division moves via Camp Mills to the ports of embarkation of Boston, Brooklyn, New York, and Philadelphia.

July 14, Adv Det sails from New York, and arrives July 26 at Liverpool.

July 21–22, DHQ, the infantry, except the 340th Infantry and 330th MG Bn, the divisional troops and part of the trains sail, and arrive August 3, in England.

July 23–31, 160th Field Artillery Brig, the remaining infantry units, and the trains sail, and arrive August 6–11, in England, except part of the 340th Infantry, which goes to Le Havre. After a brief stay in English rest camps, the various units except the 339th Infantry, 1st Bn 310th Engrs, 337th Amb Co, and 337th F Hosp, proceed to Le Havre and Cherbourg; these excepted troops go to North Russia.

Activities Overseas

AUGUST 8, 1918–MARCH 8, 1919

July 28, division is designated as the 4th Depot Division.

August 11, division (less Arty and units in England) moves to the area of Pouilly-sur-Loire, Sancerre, and Cosne.

August 14–October 29, division functions as the Depot Division, Intermediate Section, SOS. The 160th Field Artillery Brig, 339th Infantry, 310th Engrs, 310th F Sig Bn, 310th TM Btry, 310th Am Tn are detached and serve either in the North Russian Expedition or as corps and army troops. The remainder of the division is reduced to training cadre strength of about 250 officers and 4,000 men, organized as the 4th Depot Division. This Depot Division establishes a classification camp at Cosne. It receives, trains, equips, and forwards officer and enlisted replacements for the infantry, including machine gun units and ammunition and supply trains. Prior to October 24, when it is re-designated the Regional Replacement Depot for the Second Army, it forwards 3,948 replacements.

October 30, the former Depot Division (less 337th Infantry, 3rd Bn 340th Infantry, 329th MG Bn, detached) moves to vicinity of Toul. The various organizations function as regional replacement sub-depots for all arms and services, receiving, uniforming, arming, and equipping casuals and the personnel evacuated from hospitals. The division absorbs the corps replacement battalions and utilizes the surplus personnel as replacements.

October 30–January 12, division functions as the Regional Replacement Depot, Second Army.

December 9, a provisional battalion is organized to relieve the division.

December 13, General Dickman is replaced in command of the division by Maj. Gen. James Parker, among many other later commanding officers.

December 25, division is released for return to the United States.

January 13, DHQ, Hq 169th Infantry Brig, Hq 170th Infantry Brig, 337th Infantry, 338th Infantry, 340th Infantry, 328th MG Bn, 329th MG Bn, 330th MG Bn, 310th Tn Hq, 85th Division MP Co, 310th Sup Tn and 310th San Tn, a total of 229 officers and 4,095 men, move to Le Mans Area.

January 15–March 8, division is in Le Mans Area (American Embarkation Center).

February 20, 160th Field Artillery Brig reverts to the division. The division receives replacements and aggregates 20,000 at the time of departure.

February 28, 310th TM Btry sails from St. Nazaire.

Final Training and Operations of Detached Units

339TH INFANTRY, 1ST BN 310TH ENGRS, 337TH AMB CO, AND 337TH F HOSP FORM THE AEF IN NORTH RUSSIA

August 9, these units are detached from the 85th Division, designated as the American Expeditionary Forces, North Russia, and form part of an allied expeditionary force under British command.

160TH FIELD ARTILLERY BRIG AND 310TH AM TN

August 12, the artillery moves from Le Havre and Cherbourg to Camp Coetquidan for training.

October 22, the brigade moves to the 4th (Rimaucourt) Training Area.

October 29, the 328th Field Artillery is attached to the VI Corps and serves with the 167th Field Artillery Brig (92nd Div) from October 31 to November 11 in the Marbache Sector (Lorraine). The 329th Field Artillery is attached to the IV Corps and the 1st Bn supports the 7th Division and the 2nd Bn supports the 28th Division from October 31 to November 11 in a defensive sector (Lorraine).

November 4, the 330th Field Artillery is attached to the VI Corps but remains at Rimaucourt with the Advance Section, SOS. The greater part of the 1st Am Tn is sent to the 1st Depot Division for use as replacements.

November 15, the brigade (less 330th FA) assembles at Pont-à-Moussou for training.

December 17, 310th TM Btry is detached.

January 13, 328th Field Artillery and 329th Field Artillery are attached to the 7th Division, and, on February 1, to the 91st Division, but, February 20, they revert to the 85th Division, 2nd Bn 310th Engrs.

September 9, this battalion is attached to the V Corps and participates, September 12–16, in the St. Mihiel Operation, September 22–25, in the occupation of a defensive sector (Lorraine) near Récicourt, and, September 26–November 11, in the Meuse-Argonne Operation.

November 22, the battalion is assigned to the VII Corps (Third Army) and serves with the Army of Occupation.

310TH F SIG BN

August 24, this battalion joins the IV Corps near Toul, where, August 26–September 11, it serves the front line divisions in a defensive sector (Lorraine), September 12–16, participates in the St. Mihiel Operation, and, September 17–November 11, again serves in a defensive sector.

November 17, the battalion, as part of the IV Corps, joins the Third Army and serves with the Army of Occupation.

Return to the United States and Demobilization

MARCH 9–APRIL 24, 1919

March 9, division (less 339th Infantry, 310th TM Btry, 310th Engrs, 310th F Sig Bn, 337th Amb Co, and 337th F Hosp) moves to Brest.

March 23, DHQ and certain units of the 337th Infantry sail, and other troops soon follow.

August 17, the last element of the division, a detachment of the 310th Sup Tn, arrives at Hoboken. The demobilization at Camp Custer includes, April 16, Hq 169th Infantry Brig, April 18, DHQ, April 23, Hq 160th Field Artillery Brig, and April 24, Hq 170th Infantry Brig.

THE EIGHTY-SIXTH DIVISION, NATIONAL ARMY

This division is another selected to be skeletonized, but not until October 13, 1918, after they arrive overseas. Major General Thomas H. Barry, who had been selected to command this division, is replaced by Brigadier General, later Major General, Charles H. Martin on March 21, 1918.

171st Infantry Brigade

341st Infantry
342nd Infantry
332nd Machine Gun Battalion

172nd Infantry Brigade

343rd Infantry
344th Infantry
333rd Machine Gun Battalion

161st Field Artillery Brigade

331st Field Artillery
332nd Field Artillery
333rd Field Artillery
311th Trench Mortar Battery

Divisional Troops

331st Machine Gun Battalion
311th Engineers
311th Field Signal Battalion
Headquarters Troop

Trains

311th Train Hdqs
311th Military Police
311th Ammunition Train
311th Supply Train
311th Engineer Train
311th Sanitary Train
Ambulance Cos and Field Hospitals 341–344

Organization and Training in the United States

AUGUST 5, 1917–AUGUST 17, 1918

August 5, the War Department establishes the 86th Division, National Army, which is to be organized at Camp Grant, Rockford, Illinois; drafts, anticipated for 1917, from Illinois, 31,714, and Wisconsin, 7,181, are designed to furnish personnel. August 13, the organization of DHQ at Camp Grant is directed, and its commissioned personnel are ordered, to report on or before August 15.

August 16, the commanding general of Camp Grant is directed to organize the division in accordance with the Tables of Organization of August 8, 1917.

August 25, Maj. Gen. Thomas H. Barry assumes command; the program for the movement of selective service men to camps is announced. During the last week in August the organization is begun from a cadre of officers and men of the Regular Army, and from ORC and NA officers of the First Officers Training Camp at Fort Sheridan.

September 5–10, the initial draft of 2,000 selective service men arrives at camp.

September 19–24, an additional 15,500 arrive. During September systematic training begins.

October 3–8, the last drafts of 1917 furnish the camp with 7,700, but 5,400 leave the division for the 33rd Division. **October 31,** the division has slightly more than 21,000. Between January and August more than 100,000 fresh drafts arrive at the camp, many joining the division, but the transfers aggregate 80,000, including 8,000 to the 33rd Division, 4,500 to the 4th Division, 2,500 to the 85th Division, 1,000 to Camp Johnston, and large contingents to the ports of embarkation.

April 30, the division approximates 10,000.

May 14, the 161st Field Artillery Brig moves to Camp Robinson, Wisconsin, for special training. The division is gradually increased and finally drafts and transfers from the depot brigade, many from Illinois and Minnesota, furnish the full complement in the month of August.

Movement Overseas

AUGUST 18–OCTOBER 9, 1918

August 18, the division (less Arty) moves via Camps Upton and Mills to the ports of embarkation of Brooklyn and New York.

September 4, the 161st Field Artillery Brig moves from Camp Robinson to Camp Mills. The troops sail for English and Scottish ports.

September 8, the Adv Det and part of the 343rd Infantry sail, and arrive on September 21 at Liverpool.

September 9, DHQ, the infantry, and 311th Engrs and Tn sail, arriving Sept. 21–22.

September 17, the 161st Field Artillery Brig, 311th San Tn, and some divisional troops sail and land September 29 and October 2.

September 25 and October 2, the 311th Am Tn and 311th Sup Tn sail, arriving October 7 and 9, respectively. The troops proceed via Le Havre and Cherbourg after a short stay in rest camps.

Activities Overseas

SEPTEMBER 24–DECEMBER 24, 1918

September 24, the division (less Arty) moves to the East Bordeaux Area for training.

October 3, the division is ordered skeletonized, but with a view to reconstitution; certain organizations are to be reduced to an average cadre strength of 25.

October 4, the 161st Field Artillery Brig (less 3 11th TM Btry) moves to Camp Hunt and the 311th TM Btry moves to Vitrey for training.

October 7–8, the division transfers about 7,500 from the rifle companies to the 2nd Depot Division for replacement purposes.

October 19, the 311th Engrs and Tn move to Bassens for duty with the SOS.

October 20, the division transfers about 1,200 from the machine gun battalions to the 2nd Depot Division.

October 29, the division is ordered reduced to a record cadre strength, as the prospect of reconstitution is abandoned.

November 8, the division (less 161st Field Artillery Brig, 311th Am Tn, 311th Engrs and Tn, 311th F Sig Bn, and 311th San Tn) moves to Le Mans.

The division (less 311th Sup Tn and detached units) is further skeletonized; a Division Record Cadre of 9 officers and 107 men is formed to represent DHQ, the infantry brigade headquarters, the infantry regiments, the machine gun battalions and the train headquarters and military police; and the surplus personnel are classified for other assignment.

November 9, the 311th F Sig Bn goes to the Signal Corps Replacement Depot at Cour-Cheverny.

November 13, the 311th San Tn moves to St. Aignan Noyers for further reduction by the 1st Depot Division.

November 27, the Division Record Cadre moves from Le Mans to Le Courneau, where it joins the 161st Field Artillery Brig.

Return to the United States and Demobilization
December 25, 1918 – January 30, 1918

December 25, Hq 161st Field Artillery Brig, 333rd FA, and a part of the Division Record Cadre sail from Bordeaux. Other troops follow, the last artillery sailing February 2.

June 13, the 311th Engrs and Tn leave Bordeaux.

August 9, the last element of the division arrives at New York. The demobilization at Camp Grant includes, January 20, Hq 161st Field Artillery Brig, January 30, Division Record Cadre.

Organizations Not Assigned To Divisions

First Corps Artillery Park

Champagne-Marne defensive, France, July 15 to 18, 1918.
Aisne-Marne offensive, France, July 18 to August 6, 1918.
Château-Thierry sector, France, August 7 to 17, 1918.
Oise-Aisne offensive, France, August 18 to September 10, 1918.
Verdun sector, France, September 12 to 25, 1918.
Meuse-Argonne offensive, France, September 26 to November 11, 1918.

Second Corps Artillery Park

Aisne-Marne offensive, France, August 4 to 6, 1918.
Vesle sector, France, August 7 to 17, 1918.

Oise-Aisne offensive, France, August 18 to 21, 1918.
St. Mihiel offensive, France, September 12 to 15, 1918.
Meuse-Argonne offensive, France, September 26 to November 11, 1918.

Third Corps Artillery Park

Meuse-Argonne offensive, France, October 30 to November 11, 1918.

Fourth Corps Artillery Park

Toul sector, France, October 30 to November 11, 1918.

First Army Artillery Park

St. Mihiel offensive, France, September 12 to 16, 1918.
Meuse-Argonne offensive, France, September 26 to November 11, 1918.

Forty-Second Artillery, Coast Artillery Corps

Belfort sector, France, April 19 to November 11, 1918. 1st Battalion.
Champagne sector, France, April 29 to July 14, 1918, 3rd Battalion.
Champagne-Maine defensive, France, July 15 to 18, 1918 3rd Battalion.
Champagne sector, France, July 18 to September 21, 1918. 3rd Battalion.

Forty-Third Artillery, Coast Artillery Corps

Toul sector, France, April 22 to August 12, 1918.
2nd Battalion, April 22 to August 12, 1918.
3rd Battalion (Battery F), May 25 to August 12, 1918.
St. Mihiel offensive, France.
3rd Battalion (Battery F), September 12 to 16, 1918.
Meuse-Argonne offensive, France.
1st Battalion, September 26 to November 11, 1918.
3rd Battalion, September 26 to November 11, 1918.

Forty-Fourth Artillery, Coast Artillery Corps

Toul sector, France, April 20 to June 30, 1918.
Batteries A, B, April 20th to June 24, 1918.
Batteries E, F, April 20th to June 30, 1918.
Champagne-Marne defensive, France, Batteries A, B, E, F, July 15 to 18, 1918.

Champagne sector, France, Batteries A, B, E, F, July 19 to August 23, 1918.
Haute-Alsace sector, France, Batteries C, D, April 20 to August 21, 1918.
St. Mihiel offensive, France, Batteries A, B, C, D, B, F, September 12 to 16, 1918.
Meuse-Argonne offensive, France, Batteries A, B, C, D, B, F, September 26 to November 11, 1918.

Fifty-First Artillery, Coast Artillery Corps

Toul sector, France.
1st Battalion, April 10 to September 11, 1918.
2nd Battalion, April 15 to September 11, 1918.
Verdun sector, France.
3rd Battalion, April 27 to September 11, 1918.
September 17 to October 26, 1918.
St. Mihiel offensive, France.
1st, 2nd and 3rd Battalions, September 12 to 16, 1918.
Thiacourt sector, France.
1st Battalion, September 17 to November 11, 1918.
3rd Battalion, September 17 to October 29, 1918.
Meuse-Argonne offensive, France.
3rd Battalion, October 27 to November 11, 1118

Fifty-Second Artillery, Coast Artillery Corps

Champagne sector, France, 3rd Battalion, April 9 to July 14, 1918.
Aisne-Marne defensive, France, 3rd Battalion, July 15 to 17, 1918.
Champagne sector, France, 3rd Battalion, July 18 to September 25, 1918.
Argonne sector, France, 1st Battalion, August 27 to September 6, 1918.
St. Mihiel offensive, France, 1st Battalion, September 12 to 16, 1918.
Meuse-Argonne offensive, France, September 26 to November 11, 1918.
Battery A, September 26 to October 20, 1918.
Batteries B, E, and F, September 26 to October 10, 1918.
Batteries C and D, September 26 to November 11, 1918.

Fifty-Third Artillery, Coast Artillery Corps

St. Mihiel offensive, France, 1st, 2nd and 3rd Battalions, September 12 to 16, 1918.
Meuse-Argonne offensive, France, 1st and 3rd Battalions and Battery D, September 26 to November 9, 1918.

Fifty-Fifth Artillery, Coast Artillery Corps

Vesle sector, France, 1st, 2nd and 3rd Battalions, August 9 to 17, 1918.
Oise-Aisne offensive, France, 1st, 2nd and 3rd Battalions, August 18 to September 9, 1918.
Meuse-Argonne offensive, France, 1st, 2nd and 3rd Battalions, September 26 to November 11, 1918.

Fifty-Sixth Artillery, Coast Artillery Corps

Vesle sector, France, 1st Battalion, August 11 to 17, 1918.
Oise-Aisne offensive, France.
1st Battalion, August 18 to September 7, 1918.
2nd Battalion, August 21 to September 5, 1918.
Meuse-Argonne offensive, France.
1st Battalion, October 4 to November 11, 1918.
2nd Battalion, September 26 to November 11, 1918.
3rd Battalion, September 26 to November 11, 1918.

Fifty-Seventh Artillery, Coast Artillery Corps

Toul sector, France, 2nd Battalion, May 22 to September 11, 1918.
St. Mihiel offensive, France, 1st, 2nd and 3rd Battalions, September 12 to 16, 1916.
Meuse-Argonne offensive, France, 1st, 2nd and 3rd Battalions, September 26 to November 11, 1918.

Fifty-Eighth Artillery, Coast Artillery Corps

Marbache sector, France.
1st Battalion, October 20 to November 11, 1918.
2nd Battalion, November 2 to 11, 1918.
3rd Battalion, November 9 to 11, 1918.

Fifty-Ninth Artillery, Coast Artillery Corps

St. Mihiel offensive, France, 2nd and 3rd Battalions, September 12 to 14, 1918.
Meuse-Argonne offensive, France.
1st Battalion, September 26 to November 8, 1918.
2nd Battalion, September 26 to November 6, 1918.
3rd Battalion, September 26 to November 9, 1918.

Sixtieth Artillery, Coast Artillery Corps

St. Mihiel offensive, France.
1st Battalion, September 12 to 14, 1918.
2nd Battalion, September 14.
3rd Battalion, September 14.
Meuse-Argonne offensive, France, 1st, 2nd and 3rd Battalions, September 26 to November 11, 1918.

Sixty-Fifth Artillery, Coast Artillery Corps

St. Mihiel offensive, France, 1st and 2nd Battalions, September 12 to 16, 1918.
Meuse-Argonne offensive, France, 1st and 2nd Battalions, September 26 to November 11, 1918.
Marbache sector, France, 3rd Battalion, October 25 to November 11, 1918.

First Gas Regiment (Formerly the 30th Engineers)

1st British Army sector, March 3 to April 22, 1918.
Company A, March 3 to April 22, 1918.
Company B, March 1 to April 22, 1918.
Toul sector, France, May 26 to June 18, 1918.
Company A, May 26 to June 25, 1918.
Company B, May 22 to June 18, 1918.
Château-Thierry sector, France, June 25 to July 17, 1918.
Company B, June 25 to July 17, 1918.
Company D, June 29 to July 17, 1918.
Aisne-Marne offensive, France, Companies B and D, July 18 to August 6, 1918.
Vesle sector, France, Companies B and D, August 6 to 13, 1918.
St. Mihiel offensive, France, Companies A, B, C, D, E, F, September 12 to 16, 1918.
Meuse-Argonne offensive, France, Companies A, B, C, D, E, F, September 26 to November 11, 1918.

First Battalion, Trench Artillery

Aisne-Marne offensive, France, Batteries A, B, C, and D, July 13 to August 6, 1918.
St. Mihlel offensive, France.
Batteries A and B, September 12 to 15, 1918.
Batteries C and D, September 12 to 16, 1918.
Thiacourt sector, France, Batteries C and D, September 17 to October 20, 1918.

Meuse-Argonne offensive, France.
Batteries A and B, September 26, to November 11, 1918.
Batteries C and D, October 30 to November 11, 1918.

Second Cavalry

Toul sector, France, April 14 to May 7, 1918.
1st Squadron, April 14 to 24, 1918.
Troops F and G, April 14 to May 7, 1918.
Troop H, April 14 to May 6, 1918.
Troop I, April 14 to May 1, 1918.
Troops K and L, April 14 to 30, 1918.
Troop M, April 14 to 23, 1918.
Alsne-Marne offensive, France.
July 18 to August 6, 1918.
Troops A and C, July 18 to August 6, 1918.
Troop I, August 3 to 6, 1918.
Toul sector, France, August 7 to September 11, 1918.
Troops A and C, August 7 to September 11, 1918.
Troops B, D, F, and H, August 24 to September 11, 1918.
Troop G, July 12 to September 11, 1918.
St. Mihiel offensive, France, September 12 to 16, 1918.
1st Squadron, September 12 to 16, 1918.
Troops F, G, and H, September 12 to 16, 1918.
Toul sector, France, September 17 to 25, 1918.
Troops B, D, F, and H, September 17 to 26, 1918.
Troop G, September 17 to November 11, 1918.
Meuse-Argonne offensive, France, September 26 to November 11, 1918.
1st Squadron, September 26 to November 11, 1918.
Troops F, H, I, and M, September 26 to November 11, 1918.

First Anti-Aircraft Battalion

St. Mihiel offensive, France, September 12 to 16, 1918.
Meuse-Argonne offensive, France, September 26 to November 11, 1918.

Second Anti-Aircraft Battalion

St. Mihiel offensive, France, September 12 to 16, 1918.
Meuse-Argonne offensive, France, September 26 to November 11, 1918.

First Anti-Aircraft Machine Gun Battalion

St. Mihiel offensive, France, September 12 to 16, 1918.
Meuse-Argonne offensive, France, September 26 to November 11, 1918.

Second Anti-Aircraft Machine Gun Battalion

Meuse-Argonne offensive, France, September 26 to November 11, 1918.

One Hundred-Fifteenth Field Signal Battalion

Toul sector, France, October 16 to November 11, 1918.

Three Hundred First Field Signal Battalion

Marbache sector, France, September 25 to November 11, 1918.

Eleventh Engineers (Standard Gauge Railway)

Somme sector, France, August 18 to November 19, 1917.
December 5, 1917 to January 29, 1918.
Battles near Cambrai, France, November 20 to December 4, 1917.
Lys defensive, April 9 to 27, 1918.
North Picardy sector, France, April 28 to June 13, 1918.
St. Mihiel offensive, France, September 12 to 16, 1918.
Toul sector, France, September 17 to November 11, 1918.
Company A, September 17 to November 11, 1918.
Company B, September 17 to November 11, 1918.
Company C, September 17 to October 12, 1918.
Meuse-Argonne offensive, France, September 26 to November 11, 1918.
Company D, September 26 to November 11, 1918.
Company E, September 26 to November 11, 1918.
Company F, September 26 to November 11, 1918.
Company C, October 12 to November 11, 1918.

Twelfth Engineers (Light Railway)

Somme sector, France, August 21 to November 19, 1917; December 6, 1917 to March 20, 1918.
Companies A, B, D, E, and F, April 7 to 17, 1918.
Company C, April 7 to 28, 1918.

Battles near Cambrai, France, November 20 to December 4, 1917.
Somme defensive, France, March 21 to April 6, 1918.
North Picardy sector, France, Companies A, B, D, E, and F, April 22 to July 26, 1918.
Company C, April 28 to July 25, 1918.
Baccarat sector, France, July 29 to August 24, 1918.
St. Mihiel offensive, France, September 12 to 16, 1918.
Meuse-Argonne offensive, France, September 26 to October 9, 1918.
Toul sector, France, October 13 to November 11, 1918.

Thirteenth Engineers (Standard Gauge Railway Operation)

Verdun sector, France, September 12, 1917 to November 11, 1918.

Fourteenth Engineers (Light Railway)

Arras-Bapaume sector, France, August 21, 1917, to March 20, 1918; April 7 to May 20, 1918.
Somme defensive, France, March 21 to April 6, 1918.
Aise-Marne offensive, France, August 2 to 6, 1918.
Alsne-Marne sector, France, August 7 to 17, 1918.
Oise-Aisne offensive, France, August 18 to September 10, 1918.
Meuse-Argonne offensive, France, September 26 to November 11, 1918.

Fifteenth Engineers (Standard Gauge Railway)

St. Mihiel offensive, France, Companies B and F, September 12 to 16, 1918.
Meuse-Argonne offensive, France, Companies B and F, September 26 to November 11, 1918.

Sixteenth Engineers (Standard Gauge Railway)

Lys defensive, Belgium, April 9 to 27, 1918.
North Picardy sector, France, April 28 to June 17, 1918.
Meuse-Argonne offensive, France, October 25 to November 11, 1918.

Twenty-First Engineers (Light Railway)

St. Mihiel offensive, France, September 12 to 16, 1918.
Meuse-Argonne offensive, France, October 9 to November 11, 1918.

Twenty-Second Engineers (Light Railway)

Meuse-Argonne offensive, France, Companies C, D, E, F, K, L, and M, September 26 to November 11, 1918.

Twenty-Third Engineers (Highway)

Toul sector, France, Company A, February 23 to July 20, 1918.
Company B, May 9 to 25, 1918. Company C, February 23 to September 11, 1918.
Company D, June 20 to 23, 1918.
Company G, September 1 to 11, 1918.
Company I, August 29 to September 11, 1918.
St. Mihiel offensive, France, Companies C, G, H and I, September 12 to 16, 1918.
Meuse-Argonne offensive, France.
Company A, September 26 to November 11, 1918.
Company D, October 25 to November 11, 1918.
Company E, October 28 to November 11, 1918.
Company F, October 27 to November 11, 1918.
Company H, September 26 to November 11, 1918.
Company K, October 30 to November 11, 1918.
Company L, September 26 to November 11, 1918.
Company M, October 27 to November 11, 1918.
Tool sector, France, Companies C, G, and I, September 16 to November 11, 1918.

Twenty-Fourth Engineers (Supply and Shop)

Toul sector, France, Companies C, E, and F, August 27 to September 11, 1918.
St. Mihiel offensive, France, Companies C, D, E, and F, September 12 to 16, 1918.
Meuse-Argonne offensive, France, September 26 to October 12, 1918.
Company A, September 26 to October 12, 1918.
Company B, October 2 to 11, 1918.
Company C, September 26 to October 11, 1918.
Company D, October 14 to November 11, 1918.
Company E, September 26 to October 11, 1918.
Company F, September 26 to October 12, 1918.
Toul sector, France.
Company A, October 13 to November 11, 1918.
Company B, October 12 to November 11, 1918.
Company C, October 12 to November 11, 1918.
Company D, October 14 to November 11, 1918.

Company K, October 12 to November 11, 1918.
Company F, October 13 to November 11, 1918.

Twenty-Fifth Engineers (General Construction)

Meuse-Argonne offensive, France.
Company A, September 26 to November 11, 1918.
Company B, September 26 to November 11, 1918.
Company C, September 26 to November 11, 1918.
Company D, September 28 to November 11, 1918.
Company E, September 27 to November 11, 1918.
Company F, September 28 to November 11, 1918.

Twenty-Sixth Engineers (Water Supply)

St. Mihiel offensive, France, Companies B, E. and F, September 12 to 16, 1918.
Meuse-Argonne offensive, France.
September 26 to November 11, 1918.
Company C, October 2 to November 11, 1918.
Company D, September 26 to November 11, 1918.
Company E, September 30 to November 11, 1918.
Company F, September 26 to November 11, 1918.
Toul sector, France.
Company A, September 26 to November 11, 1918.
Company B, May 30 to November 11, 1918.

Twenty-Seventh Engineers (Mining)

Meuse-Argonne offensive, France,
A, September 26 to November 11, 1918.
B, September 26 to November 11, 1918.
C, September 26 to November 11, 1918.
D, October 24 to November 11, 1918.
E, October 24 to November 11, 1918.
F, October 24 to November 11, 1918.

Twenty-Eighth Engineers (Quarry)

Toul sector, France, Companies A and B, August 10 to September 11, 1918.
St. Mihiel offensive, France, Companies A, B, and E, September 12 to 16, 1918.

Meuse-Argonne offensive, France, Companies C and F, September 26 to November 11, 1918.

Twenty-Ninth Engineers (Surveying and Printing)

Aisne-Marne defensive, France, Companies B and C, July 15 to 18, 1918.
Tool sector, France, Companies B, C, and I, July 18 to September 11, 1918.
St. Mihiel offensive, France, Companies B, C, D, and I, September 12 to 16, 1918.
Toul sector, France, Companies D, K, and M, September 17 to November 11, 1918.
Meuse-Argonne offensive, France, Companies B, C, and I, September 26 to November 11, 1918.

Thirty-Seventh Engineers (Electrical and Mechanical)

St. Mihiel offensive, France, September 12 to 16, 1918.
Meuse-Argonne offensive, France, Companies C, E, and F, September 26 to November 11, 1918.
Toul sector, France, Companies A, B, and D, October 9 to November 11, 1918.

Fortieth Engineers (Camouflage)

Aisne-Marne offensive, France, 1st Battalion, July 18 to August 6, 1918.
St. Mihiel offensive, France, 1st Battalion, September 12 to 16, 1918.
Meuse-Argonne offensive, France, September 26 to November 11, 1918.

Fifty-Sixth Regiment Engineers (Searchlight)

St. Mihiel offensive, France, Companies A and B, September 12 to 16, 1918.
Meuse-Argonne offensive, France.
Company A, September 26 to November 11, 1918.
Company B, September 26 to November 11, 1918.
Company C, October 19 to November 11, 1918.
Toul sector, France, Companies C and H, October 5 to November 11, 1918.

Six Hundred-Second Engineers

St. Mihiel offensive, France, Companies A, B, and C, September 12 to 14, 1918.

Meuse-Argonne offensive, France, Companies A, B, and C, September 26 to November 11, 1918.

Six Hundred Third Engineers

Meuse-Argonne offensive, France, October 29 to November 11, 1918.

Six Hundred-Fourth Engineers

Meuse-Argonne offensive, France, October 28 to November 11, 1918.

First Pioneer Infantry

Aisne-Marne offensive, France, July 26 to August 6, 1918.
Oise-Alsne offensive, France, August 18 to September 10, 1918.
Meuse-Argonne offensive, France, September 24 to November 11, 1918.

Third Pioneer Infantry

Meuse-Argonne offensive, France, September 26 to November 11, 1918.

Fifty-First Pioneer Infantry

St. Mihlel offensive, France, September 12 to 16, 1918.
Toul sector, France, September 26 to November 11, 1918.

Fifty-Second Pioneer Infantry

St. Mihiel sector, France, 1st Battalion, August 18 to 24, 1918.
Meuse-Argonne offensive, France, September 26 to November 11, 1918.

Fifty-Third Pioneer Infantry

St. Mihiel offensive, France, 1st Battalion, September 12 to 16, 1918.
Meuse-Argonne offensive, France, September 24 to November 11, 1918.

Fifty-Fourth Pioneer Infantry

Meuse-Argonne offensive, France, September 26 to November 11, 1918.

Fifty-Sixth Pioneer Infantry

Meuse-Argonne offensive, France, September 30 to November 11, 1918.

Fifty-Ninth Pioneer Infantry

Verdun sector, France, September 29 to October 10, 1918.
Meuse-Argonne offensive, France, October 18 to November 11, 1918.

Eight Hundred-Second Pioneer Infantry

Meuse-Argonne offensive, France, October 3 to November 11, 1918.

Eight Hundred-Third Pioneer Infantry

Toul sector, France, October 22 to November 11, 1918.

Eight Hundred-Fourth Pioneer Infantry

Marbache sector, France, October 7 to November 11, 1918.

Eight Hundred-Fifth Pioneer Infantry

Meuse-Argonne offensive, France, October 3 to November 11, 1918.

Eight Hundred-Sixth Pioneer Infantry

Meuse-Argonne offensive, France, October 3 to 9, 1918.

Eight Hundred-Seventh Pioneer Infantry

Meuse-Argonne offensive, France, September 26 to November 11, 1918.

Eight Hundred-Eighth Pioneer Infantry

Meuse-Argonne offensive, France, October 1 to November 11, 1918.

Fifty-First Telegraph Battalion

Vosges sector, France, September 12 to November 11, 1918.

Fifty-Second Telegraph Battalion

Aisne-Marne offensive, France, August 4 to August 6, 1918.
Vesle sector, France, August 7 to 17, 1918.
Oise-Aisne offensive, France, August 18 to September 9, 1918.
Meuse-Argonne offensive, France, September 26 to November 11, 1918.

Fifty-Fifth Telegraph Battalion

Vosges sector, France, Companies D and E, June 20 to August 20, 1918.
St. Mihiel sector, France, August 26 to September 11, 1918.
St. Mihiel offensive, France, September 12 to 16, 1918.
Meuse-Argonne offensive, France, September 26 to November 11, 1918,

Four Hundred First Telegraph Battalion

St. Mihiel offensive, France, September 12 to 16, 1918.
Meuse-Argonne offensive, France, September 26 to November 11, 1918.

Four Hundred Fifth Telegraph Battalion

St. Mihiel offensive, France, September 12 to 16, 1918.
Toul sector, France, September 17 to November 11, 1918.

Four Hundred Sixth Telegraph Battalion

Toul sector, France, February 28 to March 21, 1918.
Château-Thierry sector, France, June 23 to July 14, 1918.
Champagne-Marne defensive, France, July 15 to 18, 1918.
Aisne-Marne offensive, France, July 18 to August 6, 1918.
Toul sector, France, August 20 to September 11, 1918.
St. Mihiel offensive, France, September 12 to 16, 1918.
Verdun sector, France, September 20 to 25, 1918.
Meuse-Argonne offensive, France, September 26 to November 11, 1918.

Four Hundred Ninth Telegraph Battalion

Toul sector, France, October 19 to November 11, 1918.

Four Hundred Eleventh Telegraph Battalion

Aisne-Marne offensive, France, July 29 to August 6, 1918.
St. Mihiel offensive, France, September 12 to 16, 1918.
Meuse-Argonne offensive, France, September 26 to November 11, 1918.

Four Hundred Twelfth Telegraph Battalion
(Served with British Army)

Dickebush Lake and Scherpenberg sectors, Belgium, July 9 to August 30, 1918.
Vpres-Lys offensive, August 31 to September 2, 1918.
Somme offensive, France, September 27 to October 21, 1918.

Four Hundred Seventeenth Telegraph Battalion

Marbache sector, France, September 25 to November 11, 1918.

Four Hundred Nineteenth Telegraph Battalion

Toul sector, France, October 27 to November 11, 1918.

Three Hundred First Battalion, Tank Corps
(Served with British Army)

Somme offensive, France, September 29, October 8, 17, and 28, 1918.

Three Hundred Forty-Fourth Battalion, Tank Corps

St. Mihiel offensive, France, September 12 to 15, 1918.
Meuse-Argonne offensive, France, September 26 to October 14, 1918.

Three Hundred Forty-Fifth Battalion Tank Corps

St. Mihiel offensive, France, September 12 to 15, 1918.
Meuse-Argonne offensive, France, September 26 to October 14, 1918.

First Corps Observation Group, Air Service, First Army

1st Corps Observation Squadron

Toul sector, France, April 4 to June 28, 1918.
Aisne-Marne sector, France, July 1 to 14, 1918.

Champagne-Marne defensive, France, July 15 to 18, 1918.
Aisne-Marne offensive, France, July 18 to August 6, 1918.
Vesle sector, France, August 7 to 12, 1918.
Toul sector, France, August 26 to September 11, 1918.
St. Mihiel offensive, France, September 12 to 16, 1918.
Toul-Verdun sector, France, September 17 to 25, 1918.
Meuse-Argonne offensive, France, September 24 to November 11, 1918.

12TH CORPS OBSERVATION SQUADRON

Toul sector, France, May 10 to June 12, 1918.
Baccarat (Luneville) sector, France, June 13 to 28, 1918.
Aisne-Marne sector, France, June 30 to July 14, 1918.
Champagne-Marne defensive, France, July 15 to 18, 1918.
Aisne-Marne offensive, France, July 18 to August 6, 1918.
Vesle sector, France, August 7 to 12, 1918.
Tool sector, France, August 22 to September 11, 1918.
St. Mihiel offensive, France, September 12 to 16, 1918.
Meuse-Argonne offensive, France, September 24 to November 11, 1918.

50TH CORPS OBSERVATION SQUADRON

St. Mihiel offensive, France, September 12 to 16, 1918.
Toul-Verdun sector, France, September 17 to 23, 1918.
Meuse-Argonne offensive, France, September 26 to November 11, 1918.

Third Corps Observation Group, Air Service, First Army

88TH CORPS OBSERVATION SQUADRON

Toul sector, France, May 30 to July 5, 1918.
Aisne-Marne sector, France, July 7 to 14, 1918.
Champagne-Marne defensive, France, July 15 to 18, 1918.
Aisne-Marne offensive, France, July 18 to 30, 1918.
Vesle sector, France, August 7 to September 8, 1918.
St. Mihiel offensive, France, September 12 to 16, 1918.
Meuse-Argonne offensive, France, September 26 to November 11, 1918.

90TH CORPS OBSERVATION SQUADRON

Toul sector, France, June 16 to September 11, 1918.
St. Mihiel offensive, France, September 12 to 16, 1918.
Meuse-Argonne offensive, France, September 26 to November 11, 1918.

199TH SQUADRON — USED AS AIR PARK

Meuse-Argonne offensive, France, September 26 to November 11, 1918.

Fourth Corps Observation Group, Air Service, Second Army

8TH CORPS OBSERVATION SQUADRON

St. Mihiel offensive, France, September 12 to 16, 1918.
Toul sector, France, September 26 to November 11, 1918.

135TH CORPS OBSERVATION SQUADRON

Toul sector, France, August 9 to September 11, 1918.
St. Mihiel offensive, France, September 12 to 16, 1918.
Toul sector, France, September 17 to November 11, 1918.
168th Corps Observation Squadron
Toul sector, France, October 12 to November 11, 1918.

Fifth Corps Observation Group, Air Service, First Army

99TH CORPS OBSERVATION SQUADRON

Toul sector, France, June 22 to July 1, 1918.
St. Die sector, France, July 19 to August 24, 1918.
St. Mihiel offensive, France, September 12 to 16, 1918.
Meuse-Argonne offensive, France, September 26 to November 11, 1918.

104TH CORPS OBSERVATION SQUADRON

St. Mihiel offensive, France, September 12 to 16, 1918.
Meuse-Argonne offensive, France, September 26 to November 11, 1918.

1ST AIR PARK — FORMERLY 183RD SERVICE SQUADRON

Champagne-Marne defensive, France, July 15 to 18, 1918.
Aisne-Marne offensive, France, July 18 to August 6, 1918.
Vesle sector, France, August 7 to 20, 1918.
St. Mihiel offensive, France, September 12 to 16, 1918.
Meuse-Argonne offensive, France, September 24 to November 11, 1918.

Sixth Corps Observation Group, Air Service, Second Army

354TH CORPS OBSERVATION SQUADRON

Toul sector, France, October 28 to November 11, 1918.

Seventh Corps Observation Group, Air Service, First Army

258TH CORPS OBSERVATION SQUADRON

Vosges sector, France, October 31 to November 10, 1918.

First Army Observation Group, Air Service, First Army

9TH ARMY OBSERVATION SQUADRON — NIGHT

Toul sector, France, August 30 to September 11, 1918.
St. Mihiel offensive, France, September 12 to 16, 1918.
Meuse-Argonne offensive, France, September 26 to November 11, 1918.

24TH ARMY OBSERVATION SQUADRON

St. Mihiel offensive, France, September 12 to 16, 1918.
Meuse-Argonne offensive, France, September 26 to November 11, 1918.

91ST ARMY OBSERVATION SQUADRON

Toul sector, France, June 3 to September 11, 1918.
St. Mihiel offensive, France, September 12 to 16, 1918.
Meuse-Argonne offensive, France, September 26 to November 11, 1918.

186TH ARMY OBSERVATION SQUADRON

Meuse-Argonne offensive, France, November 5 to 11, 1918.

First Day Bombardment Group, Air Service, First Army

11TH DAY BOMBARDMENT SQUADRON

St. Mihiel offensive, France, September 14 to 16, 1918.
Toul sector, France, September 17 to 24, 1918.
Meuse-Argonne offensive, France, September 26 to November 11, 1918.

20TH DAY BOMBARDMENT SQUADRON

St. Mihiel offensive, France, September 14 to 16, 1918.
Toul sector, France, September 17 to 28, 1918.
Meuse-Argonne offensive, France, September 26 to November 11, 1918.

96TH DAY BOMBARDMENT SQUADRON

St. Mihiel offensive, France, September 12 to 16, 1918.
Toul sector, France, September 17 to 23, 1918.
Meuse-Argonne offensive, France, September 26 to November 11, 1918.

166TH DAY BOMBARDMENT SQUADRON
Meuse-Argonne offensive, France, October 18 to November 11, 1918.

Second Day Bombardment Group, Air Service, Second Army

163RD DAY BOMBARDMENT SQUADRON
Toul sector, France, November 5 to 11, 1918.

First Pursuit Group, Air Service, First Army

27TH PURSUIT SQUADRON
Toul sector, France, June 2 to 25, 1918.
Aisne-Marne sector, France, June 30 to July 14, 1918.
Champagne-Marne defensive, France, July 15 to 18, 1918.
Aisne-Mainne offensive, France, July 18 to August 6, 1918.
Vesle sector, France, August 7 to 29, 1918.
Toul sector, France, September 1 to 11, 1918.
St. Mihiel offensive, France, September 12 to 16, 1918.
Verdun Sector, France, September 17 to 25, 1918.
Meuse-Argonne offensive, France, September 26 to November 11, 1918.

94TH PURSUIT SQUADRON
Toul sector, France, April 14 to June 29, 1918.
Aisne-Marne sector, France, June 30 to July 14, 1918.
Champagne-Marne defensive, France, July 15 to 18, 1918.
Aisne-Marne offensive, France, July 18 to August 6, 1918.
Vesle sector, France, August 7 to 17, 1918.
Toul sector, France, September 4 to 11, 1918.
St. Mihiel offensive, France, September 12 to 16, 1918.
Verdun Sector, France, September 17 to 25, 1918.
Meuse-Argonne offensive, France, September 26 to November 11, 1918.

95TH PURSUIT SQUADRON
Toul sector, France, May 10 to June 27, 1918.
Aisne-Marne sector, France, July 1 to 14, 1918.
Champagne-Marne defensive, France, July 15 to 18, 1918.
Aisne-Marne offensive, France, July 18 to August 6, 1918.
Vesle sector, France, August 7 to 17, 1918.
Toul sector, France, September 3 to 11, 1918.
St. Mihiel offensive, France, September 12 to 16, 1918.

Verdun sector, France, September 17 to 25, 1918.
Meuse-Argonne offensive, France, September 26 to November 11, 1918.

147TH PURSUIT SQUADRON

Toul sector, France, June 2 to 27, 1918.
Aisne-Marne sector, France, June 29 to July 14, 1918.
Champagne-Marne defensive, France, July 15 to 18, 1918.
Aisne-Marne offensive, France, July 18 to August 6, 1918.
Vesle sector, France, August 7 to 13, 1918.
Toul sector, France, September 4 to 11, 1918.
St. Mihiel offensive, France, September 12 to 16, 1918.
Verdun Sector, France, September 17 to 25, 1918.
Meuse-Argonne offensive, France, September 26 to November 11, 1918.

185TH PURSUIT SQUADRON — NIGHT

Meuse-Argonne offensive, France, October 18 to November 11, 1918.

4TH AIR PARK — FORMERLY 218TH SERVICE SQUADRON

Toul sector, France, September 1 to 11, 1918.
St. Mihiel offensive, France, September 12 to 16, 1918.
Toul sector, France, September 17 to 25, 1918.
Meuse-Argonne offensive, France, September 26 to November 11, 1918.

Second Pursuit Group, Air Service, First Army

13TH PURSUIT SQUADRON

Toul sector, France, August 10 to September 11, 1918.
St. Mihiel offensive, France, September 12 to 16, 1918.
Toul-Verdun sector, France, September 17 to 22, 1918.
Meuse-Argonne offensive, France, September 26 to November 11, 1918.

22ND PURSUIT SQUADRON

Somme defensive, France, March 21 to April 6, 1918.
Amiens sector, France, April 7 to June 24, 1918.
Toul sector, France, August 21 to September 11, 1918.
St. Mihiel offensive, France, September 12 to 16, 1918.
Meuse-Argonne offensive, France, September 26 to November 11, 1918.

49TH PURSUIT SQUADRON

Toul sector, France, August 16 to September 11, 1918.
St. Mihiel offensive, France, September 12 to 16, 1918.

Toul sector, France, September 17 to 23, 1918.
Meuse-Argonne offensive, France, September 26 to November 11, 1918.

139TH PURSUIT SQUADRON

Toul sector, France, June 30 to September 11, 1918.
St. Mihiel offensive, France, September 12 to 16, 1918.
Toul-Verdun sector, France, September 17 to 23, 1918.
Meuse-Argonne offensive, France, September 26 to November 11, 1918.

5TH AIR PARK — FORMERLY 279TH SERVICE SQUADRON

Meuse-Argonne offensive, France, October 31 to November 11, 1918.

Third Pursuit Group, Air Service, First Army

28TH PURSUIT SQUADRON

Somme defensive, France, March 21 to April 6, 1918.
Lys defensive, France, April 9 to 27, 1918.
Ypres sector, Belgium, April 28 to June 24, 1918.
Tool sector, France, September 2 to 11, 1918.
St. Mihiel offensive, France, September 12 to 16, 1918.
Meuse-Argonne offensive, France, September 26 to November 11, 1918.

93RD PURSUIT SQUADRON

Toul sector, France, August 11 to September 11, 1918.
St. Mihiel offensive, France, September 12 to 16, 1918.
Meuse-Argonne offensive, France, September 26 to November 11, 1918.

103RD PURSUIT SQUADRON

Champagne sector, France, February 19 to April 9, 1918.
Aisne sector, France, April 11 to 30, 1918.
Ypres-Lys sector, Belgium, May 2 to June 29, 1918.
Toul sector, France, July 5 to September 11, 1918.
St. Mihiel offensive, France, September 12 to 16, 1918.
Meuse-Argonne offensive, France, September 26 to November 11, 1918.

213TH PURSUIT SQUADRON

Toul sector, France, August 14 to September 11, 1918.
St. Mihiel offensive, France, September 12 to 16, 1918.
Meuse-Argonne offensive, France, September 26 to November 11, 1918.

2ND AIR PARK — FORMERLY 360TH SERVICE SQUADRON

Toul sector, France, July 27 to September 11, 1918.
St. Mihiel offensive, France, September 12 to 16, 1918.
Meuse-Argonne offensive, France, September 26 to November 1918.

Fourth Pursuit Group, Air Service, Second Army

17TH PURSUIT SQUADRON

St. Quentin-Arras sector, France, February 11 to March 20, 1918.
Somme defensive, France, March 21 to April 6, 1918.
Amiens-Arras sector, France, April 7 to June 20, 1918.
Nieuport-Ypres sector, Belgium, July 15 to August 18, 1918.
Somme offensive, France, August 21 to October 28, 1918.

141ST PURSUIT SQUADRON

Toul sector, France, October 23 to November 11, 1918.

148TH PURSUIT SQUADRON

Somme defensive, France, March 21 to April 6, 1918.
Albert St. Omer sector, Belgium, April 7 to June 30, 1918.
Nieuport-Ypres sector, Belgium, July 20 to August 11, 1918.
Somme offensive, France, August 12 to October 28, 1918.

6TH AIR PARK — FORMERLY 822ND SERVICE SQUADRON

Toul sector, France, October 31 to November 11, 1918.

First Corps Balloon Group, Air Service, First Army

1ST BALLOON COMPANY

Baccarat sector, France, April 19 to July 16, 1918.
Aisne-Marne offensive, France, July 20 to August 6, 1918.
Vesle sector, Finance, August 7 to 13, 1918.
Toul sector, France, August 29 to September 11, 1918.
St. Mihiel offensive, France, September 12 to 16, 1918.
Meuse-Argonne offensive, France, September 24 to October 17, 1918.

2ND BALLOON COMPANY

Toul sector, France, March 5 to June 27, 1918.
Aisne-Marne sector, France, July 2 to 14, 1918.
Champagne-Marne defensive, France, July 15 to 18, 1918.

Aisne-Marne offensive, France, July 18 to August 6, 1918.
Vesle sector, France, August 7 to 12, 1918.
Toul sector, France, August 29 to September 11, 1918.
St. Mihiel offensive, France, September 12 to 16, 1918.
Meuse-Argonne offensive, France, September 26 to November 10, 1918.

5th Balloon Company

Toul sector, France, August 1 to September 3, 1918.
St. Mihiel offensive, France, September 12 to 16, 1918.
Meuse-Argonne offensive, France, October 18 to November 10, 1918.

Third Corps Balloon Group, Air Service, First Army

3rd Balloon Company

Baccarat sector, France, August 1 to September 4, 1918.
Meuse-Argonne offensive, France, September 26 to October 24, 1918.
Meuse-Argonne offensive, France, November 1 to 11, 1918.

4th Balloon Company

Toul sector, France, April 12 to August 1, 1918.
Aisne-Marne offensive, France, August 4 to 6, 1918.
Vesle sector, France, August 7 to September 8, 1918.
Verdun sector, France, September 16 to 25, 1918.
Meuse-Argonne offensive, France, September 26 to November 11, 1918.

9th Balloon Company

Toul sector, France, August 16 to September 11, 1918.
St. Mihiel offensive, France, September 12 to 16, 1918.
Meuse-Argonne offensive, France, September 26 to November 11, 1918.

42nd Balloon Company

St. Mihiel offensive, France, September 12 to 16, 1918.
Meuse-Argonne offensive, France, October 24 to November 11, 1918.

Fourth Corps Balloon Group, Air Service, Second Army

15th Balloon Company

Toul sector, France, October 9 to November 11, 1918.

16th Balloon Company

Toul sector, France, September 26 to November 11, 1918.

69th Balloon Company

Toul sector, France, August 20 to September 5, 1918.
St. Mihiel offensive, France, September 12 to 16, 1918.
Toul sector, France, September 17 to November 11, 1918.

Fifth Corps Balloon Group, Air Service, First Army

6th Balloon Company

Toul sector, France, August 1 to 29, 1918.
St. Mihiel offensive, France, September 12 to 16, 1918.
Meuse-Argonne offensive, France, September 26 to October 16, 1918.

7th Balloon Company

Toul sector, France, July 25 to August 28, 1918.
St. Mihiel offensive, France, September 12 to 16, 1918.
Meuse-Argonne offensive, France, September 26 to November 11, 1918.

8th Balloon Company

Toul sector, France, August 3 to 18, 1918.
St. Mihiel offensive, France, September 15 to 16, 1918.
Meuse-Argonne offensive, France, September 26 to November 11, 1918.

12th Balloon Company

St. Mihiel offensive, France, September 12 to 16, 1918.
Meuse-Argonne offensive, France, September 30 to October 7, 1918.
Meuse-Argonne offensive, France, October 16 to November 11, 1918.

Sixth Corps Balloon Group, Air Service, Second Army

10th Balloon Company

Toul sector, France, September 4 to 11, 1918.
St. Mihiel offensive, France, September 12 to 16, 1918.
Toul sector, France, September 17 to November 11, 1918.

Army Balloons, First Army

11th Balloon Company

St. Mihiel offensive, France, September 12 to 16, 1918.
Meuse-Argonne Offensive, France, September 26 to November 11, 1918.

43rd Balloon Company

Toul sector, France, August 18 to September 11, 1918.
St. Mihiel offensive, France, September 12 to 16, 1918.
Meuse-Argonne offensive, France, September 26 to November 11, 1918.

Third Air Park (Formerly 255th Service Squadron)

Flight A, attached to 2nd Pursuit Group.
Flight B, attached to 1st Army Observation Group.
Flight C, attached to 4th Corps Observation Group.
Toul sector, France, September 1 to 11, 1918.
St. Mihiel offensive, France, September 12 to 16, 1918.
Toul sector, France
Flight A, September 17 to 22, 1918.
Flight C, September 17 to November 11, 1918.
Meuse-Argonne offensive, France, September 26 to November 11, 1918.
Flights A and B.

Appendix: AEF Units Cited by the French High Command

From Colonel De Chambrun and Captain De Marenches, *The American Army in the European Conflict*. New York: Macmillan, 1919, pages 410–19.

Third Infantry Brigade (2nd Division)

In the course of operations north of the Marne, from June 1 to July 2, 1918, under General Lewis, the Third Infantry Brigade stormed the village of Vaux and La Roche Wood. It took an important share in the victorious offensive, the result of which was to compel the enemy to evacuate the soil of France and to sue for an armistice.

Fourth Infantry Brigade (Marines) (2nd Division)

In the course of heavy fighting, this brigade was rushed to a part of the front that was being violently attacked by the enemy. It had no sooner entered into line than the brigade, in conjunction with French troops, checked a violent attack launched on an important sector of Allied positions. Afterward, on its own account, it undertook a succession of successful offensive operations under General James G. Harbord.

Operating in closest liaison, its two regiments and its machine gun battalion, after twelve days of incessant fighting (from June 2 to June 13) succeeded in making an advance of a mile to a mile and a half on a two mile and a quarter front over difficult ground, capturing during their advance important quantities of material and taking two strongholds of paramount importance: the village of Bouresches and the strongly fortified Belleau Wood.

Sixty-third Infantry Brigade (32nd Division)

Composed of the 125th and 126th Regiments, this brigade was involved in the fighting around Juvigny on August 28, 1918. Immediately upon arriving on the battlefield it assumed the offensive, surprised the enemy and demoralized it. In hand-to-hand fighting it emerged victorious in spite of repeated enemy counter-attacks. It pushed back the foe to the vicinity of Terny-Sorny and vanquished him, thus affording powerful aid to the French troops who were nearby during the attacks, which took place from August 30 to September 1.

Sixty-fourth Infantry Brigade (32nd Division)

French soldiers fighting in the neighborhood of the 64th paid it sincere tribute by calling it "The Terrible Brigade." Composed of the 127th and 128th Infantry Regiments, it stormed the village of Juvigny on August 30, and on August 31 and September 1 continued its advance, constantly maintaining its superiority over the enemy notwithstanding severe losses, checking most violent counter-attacks, and fighting for three days without rest or pause, and almost without food.

5th Regiment of Infantry (Marines) (2nd Division)

Engaged unexpectedly in the offensive of July 18, 1918, during a very dark night on unknown and difficult ground, for two days the 5th Regiment displayed remarkable vigor and tenacity without allowing itself to be discouraged either by hardships or difficulty of supply. It pushed back the enemy to a depth of seven miles, capturing 2,700 prisoners, twelve cannon, and several hundred machine guns. This regiment was commanded by Colonel Logan H. Feland.

5th Regiment of Infantry (Marines)

The 5th Regiment took part in the operations engaged in Champagne during October 1918 by the Fourth Army. It participated on October 3 in the attack on the strong enemy positions between the White Hills and Medeah Farm and pushed forward to St. Etienne a Ames, thus making an advance of three miles and a half. It captured several thousand prisoners, cannon, machine guns, and important quantities of war material.

This attack, together with that of the French divisions, compelled the enemy to evacuate both banks of the Suippe and the high ground around Notre Dame-des-Champs.

6th Regiment of Infantry (Marines) (2nd Division)

Engaged unexpectedly in the offensive of July 18, 1918, during a very dark night on unknown and difficult ground, for two days this unit displayed remarkable vigor and tenacity without allowing itself to be discouraged either by hardships or difficulty of supply. The 6th Regiment pushed back the enemy to a depth of seven miles, capturing 2,700 prisoners, twelve cannon, and several hundred machine guns. It was commanded by Colonel Logan H. Feland (Col. Harry Lee). It took part in the operations in Champagne during October 1918, by the Fourth Army and participated October 3 in the attack on the strong enemy positions between the White Hills and Medeah Farm. The unit pushed forward to Saint-Étienne-à-Arnes, thus making an advance of three miles and a half. It captured several thousand prisoners, cannon, machine guns, and important quantities of war material. This attack, together with that of the French divisions, compelled the enemy to evacuate both banks of the Suippe and the high ground around Notre Dame-des-Champs.

9th Regiment of Infantry (2nd Division)

Under command of Colonel (Leroy S.) Upton, the 9th Regiment engaged unexpectedly in the offensive of July 18, 1918, during a very dark night on unknown and difficult ground. For two days it displayed remarkable vigor and tenacity without allowing itself to be discouraged either by hardships or difficulty of supply. It pushed back the enemy to a depth of seven miles, capturing 2,700 prisoners, twelve cannon, and several hundred machine guns.

It participated in the Fourth Army's operations in Champagne during October 1918 and was part of the attack on the strong enemy positions between the White Hills and Medeah Farm on October 3, and pushed forward to Saint-Étienne-à-Arnes, thus making an advance of three miles and a half. It captured several thousand prisoners, cannon, machine guns, and important quantities of war material. This attack, with that of the French divisions, compelled the enemy to evacuate both banks of the Suippe and the high ground around Notre Dame-des-Champs.

18th Regiment of Infantry (1st Division)

On July 18, 1918, under the energetic leadership of its commander, Colonel Frank Parker, it elicited the admiration of all the neighboring units in taking by storm all the objectives assigned to it absolutely without check and in spite of severe casualties. During the days following it continued to display the same aggressive spirit and determination. In October 1918, under the excellent leadership of Colonel Charles A. Hunt, assisted by a body of officers of the first order, the 18th Regiment displayed the same qualities of abnegation, launching desperate attacks on powerful positions and succeeded in throwing back the enemy.

23rd Regiment of Infantry (2nd Division)

Engaged unexpectedly in the offensive of July 18, 1918, during a very dark night on unknown and difficult grounds, for two days the 23rd Regiment displayed remarkable vigor and tenacity, pushing the enemy back seven miles while disregarding hardships. It captured 2,700 prisoners, twelve cannon, and several hundred machine guns. This regiment was commanded by Colonel Paul B. Malone.

23rd Regiment of Infantry

This regiment took part in the Fourth Army operations in Champagne during October 1918. It participated on October 3 in the attack on the strong enemy positions between the White Hills and Medeah Farm and pushed forward to Saint-Étienne-à-Arnes, making an advance of three miles and a half, capturing several thousand prisoners, cannon, machine guns, and important quantities of war material.

28th Regiment of Infantry

On May 28, 1918, with Colonel H.E. Ely (Col. Edward R. Stone) in command, this unit attacked a strongly fortified village and reached all objectives and retained the ground conquered in spite of repeated counter-attacks.

30th Regiment of Infantry (3rd Division)

One of the old original regiments of the American Army, this unit under Colonel Edmund L. Butts withstood the main onslaught of the German attack of July 15, 1918, on the front of the army corps to which it had been assigned. Under heavy artillery fire which entailed severe losses, the 30th Regiment checked the enemy's drive and re-established its initial positions after capturing more than two hundred prisoners.

38th Regiment of Infantry (3rd Division)

Under Colonel Ulysses G. McAlexander, the 38th regiment resisted the German assault of July 15, 1918. Attacked on its front and outflanked on both wings, it maintained its position on the banks of the Marne according to orders received to that effect, hurled back an enemy superior in numbers and captured two hundred prisoners.

39th Regiment of Infantry (4th Division)

Attached to a division entrusted with the defense of the sector, this regiment was called upon to take part in a battle on the day following its arrival in the line. Under the command of Colonel Frank C. Bolles, it displayed remarkable bravery in the course of its baptism of fire. It captured the Crêsnes Thickets, the town of Norroy, an enemy battery, important quantities of trench equipment, machine guns and over a hundred prisoners.

104th Regiment of Infantry (26th Division)

In the course of the fighting on April 10, 12, and 13, the 104th Regiment was subjected to heavy bombardment and attacked by powerful German forces. It succeeded in checking a dangerous enemy advance, energetically counter-attacking with the bayonet and taking prisoners. It recaptured the trenches which it had been forced to abandon in the course of the enemy's initial assault.

125th and 126th Regiments of Infantry (32nd Division)

These units are mentioned in general orders concerning the Sixty-third Brigade.

127th and 128th Regiments of Infantry (32nd Division)

These regiments are mentioned in orders concerning the Sixty-fourth Brigade.

369th Regiment of Infantry (93rd Division)

Led by Colonel Hayward, who, though wounded, insisted on retaining command of his regiment during action, by Lieutenant Colonel Pickering, an officer of coolness and courage, by Major Cobb (killed), by Major Spencer (severely wounded), by Major Little, an excellent leader, the 369th Regiment of American infantry, which, in the September attacks of 1918 was for the first time under fire, captured strong and vigorously defended enemy entrenchments, stormed the village of Sechault, and took prisoners, six cannon, and large numbers of machine guns.

371st Regiment of Infantry (93rd Division)

Under command of Colonel Miles, this regiment launched an attack on an obstinately defended position, captured it after desperate fighting and under exceptionally heavy machine gun fire. Continuing its advance, in spite of enemy artillery fire that entailed severe losses, the unit captured many prisoners besides cannon, machine-guns, and important quantities of material.

372nd Regiment of Infantry (93rd Division)

Under command of Colonel Tupes, the 372nd Regiment launched an attack on an obstinately defended position, captured it after heavy fighting under exceptional machine-gun fire. Continuing its advance despite enemy artillery fire and severe losses, it captured many prisoners, besides cannon, machine guns, and important quantities of material.

12th Regiment of Artillery (2nd Division)

This regiment assisted the Second Division's attack on July 18 southwest of Soissons, firing at close range. The guns were boldly pushed forward, following the advancing infantry and inflicted severe losses on the enemy.

After the relief of the infantry of the Second Division on July 20, the 12th Regiment valiantly fought side by side with the Fifty-eighth and Twelfth French Divisions, helping the infantry in the course of their unceasing attacks and more especially on July 21 during the assault on Hartennes.

15th Regiment of Artillery (2nd Division)

On July 18, 1918, at the southwest of Soissons, pushing its guns ahead upon the heels of the advancing infantry, it inflicted heavy losses on the enemy. The Second Division having been relieved on July 20, the 15th Regiment was successively ordered to sustain the Fifty-eighth and Twelfth French Divisions with which it fought, and in the course of the frequent counter-attacks launched by these two divisions and, more especially during the assault on Hartennes (July 21), officers and enlisted men of the regiment fought valiantly.

17th Regiment of Artillery (2nd Division)

The 17th Regiment aided the attack of the Second Division on July 18 southwest of Soissons. Always impatient to push forward the guns and in spite of heavy enemy bombardment, it constantly inundated the foe under a terrific destruction fire from its 155s. After the Second Division had been relieved on July 20, it remained in line sustaining the Fifty-eighth and Twelfth French Divisions. Officers and enlisted men displayed remarkable energy in the courageous accomplishment of all the missions entrusted to them; during the continuous attacks launched by the French divisions, they inflicted severe losses on the enemy, and displayed, amid dangers and hardships of all kinds, high valor and extraordinary tenacity.

2nd Regiment of Engineers (2nd Division)

With Colonel William A. Mitchell in command, this regiment engaged unexpectedly in the offensive of July 18, 1918, during a very dark night on unknown and difficult ground; for two days it displayed remarkable vigor and tenacity without allowing itself to be discouraged by hardships or difficulty of supply. It pushed back the enemy to a depth of seven miles, capturing 2,700 prisoners, twelve cannon, and several hundred machine guns.

2nd Regiment of Engineers

This unit played a part in the operations undertaken in Champagne in October 1918. On October 3, during the attack on the White Hills and Medeah Farm, it aided in the advance of the infantry as far as Saint-Étienne-à-Arnes. Thanks to the assistance which it afforded to the infantry operation it became possible to eject the enemy from the banks of the Suippe and from the high ground around Notre Dame-des-Champs.

302nd Regiment of Engineers (77th Division)

With Colonel Sherill in command, on September 6, 1918, this regiment constructed a bridge over the Vesle River in three hours, the work being carried out under constant artillery fire. The success of this feat rendered it possible for the French artillery to cross the river at the very start of operations and contributed to the success of the offensive then under way.

1st Battalion, 102nd Regiment of Infantry (26th Division)

Under Col. Hiram I. Bearss, U.S. Marine Corps, this unit rushed aggressively into the battle and after desperate fighting triumphed over the enemy greatly superior in number and entrenched in concrete shelters backed by great masses of machine guns and a powerful artillery. It stormed a village and maintained its positions throughout the day, notwithstanding four enemy counter-attacks.

4th Machine Gun Battalion (2nd Division)

On the evening of July 18, 1918, near Vierzy, this battalion assisted in the attack delivered by the Third Brigade. In the course of an advance with an attacking infantry, it overcame the resistance of the enemy. By the destruction of strongly enforced machine gun nests, it gave valuable help to the infantry by occupying the objectives gained and holding them against powerful counter-attacks.

5th Machine Gun Battalion (2nd Division)

On the evening of July 18, 1918, near Vierzy, this battalion assisted in the attack delivered by the Third Brigade. In the course of an advance with an attacking infantry, it overcame the resistance of the enemy. By the destruction of strongly enforced machine gun nests, it held the objective against powerful counter-attacks.

6th Machine Gun Battalion (Fourth Brigade, Second Division)

This battalion was mentioned in general orders concerning the Fourth Brigade (Marines).

6th Machine Gun Battalion

After a long journey in trucks and a night march over difficult roads, this battalion, on July 18, 1918, rushed into battle in the vicinity of Vierzy and aided in consolidating the position captured that day. On the morning of the nineteenth it pushed forward in the open, under a rain of artillery and machine-gun fire, and helped in the assault against the enemy's reinforced positions. Confronted with resistance and counter-attacks, it organized and held the positions the infantry had just gained.

7th Machine Gun Battalion (3rd Division)

This battalion prevented the enemy from crossing the Marne, and in the course of fierce fighting, especially on May 31 and June 1, contested the northern suburbs of Château-Thierry foot by foot, inflicting tremendous losses upon the enemy.

119th Machine Gun Battalion (32nd Division)

This unit fought for four days in the vicinity of Juvigny; it was hit hard by the enemy bombardment but pushed forward checking counterattacks and inflicting serious losses. It gave powerful assistance in the capture of Juvigny and in retaining the conquered positions.

1st Anti-aircraft Battalion

Under its commander, Major Cushing, this unit made itself conspicuous through the excellent results on the Marne and the Moselle.

2nd Field Signal Battalion (1st Division)

Having received orders to repair the telephone lines in a dangerous zone, the battalion worked all night under a heavy bombardment of gas shells with severe losses.

The following organizations also obtained mention in the general orders of the French High Command:

1st Battery, 1st Anti-aircraft Battalion.
Company F, 9th Regiment of Infantry.
Company G, 9th Regiment of Infantry.
Company I, 9th Regiment of Infantry.
Company L, 9th Regiment of Infantry.
Company C, 370th Regiment of Infantry.
Company B, 30th Regiment of Engineers.
Company C, 56th Regiment of Engineers (Searchlights).
Battery D, 17th Regiment of Artillery.
Battery B, 53rd Regiment of Artillery.
Battery H, 53rd Regiment of Artillery.
308th Battery, Trench Artillery.
2nd Platoon, Stokes Trench Mortars, 102nd Infantry.
2nd Platoon, Company B, 168th Infantry.
Shenkel Platoon, Company B, 111th Infantry.
Benz Platoon, Company A, 111th Infantry.
Pioneer Platoon, Trench Mortar Battery, 168th Infantry.
1st Platoon, Company B, 168th Infantry.
1st Platoon, Company C, 308th Infantry.
2nd Platoon, Company C, 308th Infantry.
Air Squadron 91.
Air Squadron 94.
Air Squadron 103 (Lafayette), three citations.

NOTES

Preface

1. George C. Marshall, *Memoirs of My Services in the World War 1917–1918* (Boston: Houghton Mifflin, 1976), p. 138.

Text

1. Much of this section was derived from William Jannen, Jr., *The Lions of July: Prelude to War, 1914*, and Holger H. Herwig, *The First World War: Germany and Austria-Hungary 1914–1918*.
2. Much of the text in this section has been derived from May, *The World War and American Isolation, 1914–1917*, and Venzon, *The United States in the First World War: An Encyclopedia*, pp. 794–96.
3. Trask, *The AEF and Coalition Warmaking, 1917–1918*, pp. 5–6.
4. Crowell, *America's Munitions 1917–1918*, pp. 158–190.
5. Shipley Thomas, *The History of the A.E.F.*, pp. 27–28.
6. Ibid., p. 28. The salutation was really spoken by Col. Charles E. Stanton, an Army officer in his party.
7. Ibid., pp. 29–32.
8. The first division to land was, of course, the First Infantry Division. Much of the above was derived from Thomas, *The History of the A.E.F.*, and De Chambrun, *The American Army in the European Conflict*.
9. The Germans had not met this kind of accuracy since the early days of 1914 when facing the then insignificant British army, which also had previously placed great importance on rifle training.
10. Much of this section was derived from Tucker, *The European Powers in the First World War: An Encyclopedia*.
11. The Germans expected to occupy certain parts of Belgium and several French colonies. The Allies had entirely different ideas, none of which planned for Germany to continue being a leading nation.
12. Tucker, pp. 295–96.
13. Shipley Thomas, *The History of the A.E.F.*, pp. 55–57.
14. "Sturm Truppen," rather derisively known to the Allies as "Hindenburg's Traveling Circus," was a body of picked German shock troops, whose duty it was to deliver predatory raids at intervals. They were obstinate fighters and were usually reinforced by a strong support of artillery.
15. Much of the preceding has been derived from De Chambrun, Thomas, Venzon, and Browne, among others.

16. I read that someplace in the past but cannot now remember exactly what my source was and have not been able to locate that as a fact. I believe it is a fact and for that reason have included it. It is just another example of the guilty reasoning of all the participants.

17. Venzon, p. 371.

18. I could not locate the original of the quote. My source was Browne, *The American Army in the World War*, p. 59.

19. Albertus Catlin, "*With the Help of God and a Few Marines*," p. 138.

20. Mainly derived from Trask, pp. 73–74.

21. Thomas, pp. 61–62.

22. Much of the preceding was derived from Venzon, pp. 622–23.

23. Browne, *The American Army in the World War*, p. 64.

24. Ibid., p. 623. The 3rd deservedly became known as the "Rock of the Marne."

25. Pershing, *Final Report*, p. 35.

26. Thomas, pp. 118–122. Unfortunately, this would not be the only time in this war when American troops would be left in the lurch.

27. Hertling, a Bavarian, had reluctantly accepted the role of German chancellor on 1 November 1917 and resigned on 2 October 1918. He believed the war was a disaster.

28. Much of the above has been derived from Clark, *Devil Dogs: Fighting Marines of World War I*; Venzon, pp. 565–56; and Clark, *The Second Infantry Division in World War I*.

29. Johnson and Hillman, *Soissons 1918*, p. 137.

30. Thomas, pp. 177–79.

31. Ibid., pp. 182–83.

32. Bearss was extremely successful. He later was promoted to command the 51st Infantry Brigade, though still but a Marine colonel. He would finally receive promotion to brigadier general twenty years later.

33. Browne, p. 90.

34. The above mostly derived from Hallas, *Squandered Victory*; Clark, *Second Division*; Thomas; De Chambrun; Pershing, *Final Report of the First Army*; and Trask.

35. This was in direct violation of an agreement with the French command that the French would have that town as their objective. That was where the main French army surrendered to the Germans in 1870.

36. The above mostly derived from Clark, *Second Division*; Thomas; De Chambrun; Hunter Liggett, *Report of the First Army*; and Trask.

37. Clark, *Devil Dogs*.

38. Ayres, *The War with Germany: A Statistical Summary*, p. 113.

39. Browne and Pillsbury, *The American Army in the World War: A Divisional Record*, pp. 38–39.

40. Browne and Pillsbury, *The American Army in The World War*, all the transportation data, pp. 38–42.

41. Thomas, *The History of the A.E.F.*, p. 69.

42. Leonard P. Ayres, *The War with Germany: A Statistical Summary*, p. 105.

43. Browne and Pillsbury, *The American Army in The World War*, pp. 46–47.

44. Leonard P. Ayres, *The War with Germany: A Statistical Summary*, p. 119.

45. Leonard P. Ayres, *The War with Germany: A Statistical Summary*, p. 122.

46. Browne and Pillsbury, *The American Army in the World War*, p. 52.

BIBLIOGRAPHY

Encyclopedias
Tucker, Spencer C., ed. *The European Powers in the First World War.* New York: Garland, 1996.
Venzon, Anne C., ed. *The United States in the First World War.* New York: Garland, 1995.

Periodicals
Colby, Elbridge. "The March of the 26th." *Infantry Journal* 47 (1940).
United States Army. *The Indian* (2nd Division magazine). various issues from author's collection.

Books
Addison, James Thayer. *The Story of the 1st Gas Regiment.* Boston: Houghton Mifflin, 1919.
Akers, Herbert H. *History of the 3rd Battalion, Sixth Regiment, U.S. Marines.* Hillsdale, Mich.: Akers, MacRitchie and Hurlbut, 1919.
Albertine, Connell. *The Yankee Doughboy.* Boston: Branden Press, 1968.
American Battle Monuments Commission. *American Armies and Battlefields in Europe.* Washington, D.C.: U.S. Government Printing Office, 1938.
_____. *1st Division, Summary of Operations in the World War.* Washington, D.C.: U.S. Government Printing Office, 1944.
_____. *2nd Division, Summary of Operations in the World War.* Washington, D.C.: U.S. Government Printing Office, 1944.
_____. *4th Division, Summary of Operations in the World War.* Washington, D.C.: U.S. Government Printing Office, 1944.
_____. *26th Division, Summary of Operations in the World War.* Washington, D.C.: U.S. Government Printing Office, 1944.
_____. *42nd Division, Summary of Operations in the World War.* Washington, D.C.: U.S. Government Printing Office, 1944.
_____. *78th Division, Summary of Operations in the World War.* Washington, D.C.: U.S. Government Printing Office, 1944.
_____. *82nd Division, Summary of Operations in the World War.* Washington, D.C.: U.S. Government Printing Office, 1944.
_____. *89th Division, Summary of Operations in the World War.* Washington, D.C.: U.S. Government Printing Office, 1944.
_____. *90th Division, Summary of Operations in the World War.* Washington, D.C.: U.S. Government Printing Office, 1944.

Amerine, William Henry. *Alabama's Own in France.* New York: Eaton and Gettinger, 1919.
Annual Report of the Secretary of War: 1919. Washington: U.S. Government Printing Office, 1919.
Army Times, editors of *The Yanks Are Coming.* New York: G.P. Putnam's Sons, 1960.
Ayres, Leonard P. *The War with Germany: A Statistical Summary.* Washington, D.C.: U.S. Government Printing Office, 1919.
Bach, Christian A. *The 4th Division in the World War.* Garden City, N.Y.: Country Life Press, 1920.
Baker, Newton D. *Annual Report of the Secretary of War, 1919.* Washington, D.C.: 1919.
Barnett, Correlli. *The Swordbearers.* New York: William Morrow, 1964.
Barron, Elwyn A., ed. *Deeds of Heroism and Bravery.* New York: Harper & Brothers, 1920.
Benwell, Harry A. *History of the Yankee Division.* Boston: Cornhill, 1919.
Berry, Henry. *Make the Kaiser Dance.* Garden City, N.Y.: Doubleday, 1978.
Bogert, George D. *Let's Go.* San Francisco: H. S. Cracker, 1927.
Braim, Paul F. *The Test of Battle: The American Expeditionary Force in the Meuse-Argonne Campaign.* Shippensburg, PA: White Mane, 1998.
Broughton, Van Tuyl. *History of the 11th Engineers.* New York: J.J. Little and Ives, 1926.
Broun, Heywood. *The A.E.F.* New York: D. Appleton, 1918.
Brown, William. *The Adventures of an American Doughboy.* Tacoma, Wash.: Press of Smith Kinney, 1919.
Browne, G. Waldo, and Rosecrans W. Pillsbury. *The American Army in the World War: A Divisional Record of the American Expeditionary Forces in Europe.* Manchester, NH: Overseas Book Company, 1921.
Bullard, R.L. *Personalities and Reminiscences of the War.* New York: Doubleday, Page, 1925.
Bullard, R.L., with B. Reeves. *American Soldiers Also Fought.* New York: Longmans, Green, 1936.
Callaway, A.B. *With Packs and Rifles.* Boston: Meador, 1929.
Carter, Eliot A. *Lanes of Memory.* Boston: Privately printed, 1963.
Carter, Russell Gordon. *The 101st Field Artillery, A.E.F.: 1917–1919.* Boston: Houghton Mifflin, 1940.
Casey, Robert J. *The Cannoneers Have Hairy Ears.* New York: J. H. Sears, 1927.
Chase, Joseph Cummings. *Soldiers All.* New York: George H. Doran, 1920.
Chastaine, Ben H. *History of the 18th U.S. Infantry, 1st Division: 1812–1919.* New York: Hymans, 1920.
Cheseldine, Raymond Minshall. *Ohio in the Rainbow.* Columbus, Ohio: F.F. Heer, 1924.
Clark, George B. *Devil Dogs: Fighting Marines of World War I.* Novato, CA: Presidio, 1999.
_____. *The Second Infantry Division in World War I: A History of the American Expeditionary Force Regulars, 1917–1919.* Jefferson, NC: McFarland, 2007.
Cline, Thomas S. *The Story of the 16th Infantry in France.* Montabauer-Frankfurt: Martin Flock, 1919.
Codman, Charles. *Contact.* Boston: Little, Brown, 1937.
Coffman, Edward M. *The War to End All Wars.* New York: Oxford University Press, 1968.
_____. *The Hilt of the Sword: The Career of Peyton C. March.* Madison: University of Wisconsin Press, 1966.
Cole, Robert B. *The History of the 39th U.S. Infantry During the World War.* New York: Joseph D. McGuire, 1919.
Collins, Louis Loren. *History of the 151st Field Artillery.* Saint Paul, Minn.: McGill Wanner, 1924.
Colonna, Benjamin A. *The History of Company B, 311th Infantry in the World War.* Freehold, N.J.: Transcript Printing House, 1922.
Cooke, James J. *Pershing and His Generals: Command and Staff in the AEF.* Westport, CT: Praeger, 1997.

Cowing, Kemper F. *Dear Folks at Home*. Boston: Houghton Mifflin, 1919.
Crazier, Emmet. *American Reporters on the Western Front*. New York: Oxford University Press, 1959.
Crowell, Benedict. *America's Munitions 1917–1918*. Washington, D.C.: U.S. Government Printing Office, 1919.
Cushing, Harvey. *From a Surgeon's Journal*. Boston: Little, Brown, 1936.
Cushing, John T. *Vermont in the World War 1917–1919*. Burlington, Vt.: Free Press Printing, 1928.
Cutchins, John A. *History of the 29th Division Blue and Gray: 1917–1919*. Philadelphia: Press of McCalla, 1921.
Dawes, Charles G. *A Journal of the Great War*. 2 vols. Boston: Houghton Mifflin, 1921.
De Chambrun, Col., and Captain De Marenches. *The American Army in the European Conflict*. New York: Macmillan, 1919.
Derby, Richard. *Wade in Sanitary!* New York: G.P. Putnam's Sons, 1919.
Dickman, Joseph T. *The Great Crusade*. New York: D. Appleton, 1927.
Dienst, Charles F. *They're from Kansas: History of the 353rd Infantry Regiment, 89th Division*. Wichita: Eagle Press, 1921.
Duane, James T. *Dear Old K*. Boston: Thomas Todd, 1922.
Duffy, Francis P. *Father Duffy's Story*. Garden City, N.Y.: Garden City Publishing, 1919.
Edwards, Frederick. *Fort Sheridan to Montfaucon*. Deland, Fla: B.O. Painter, 1954.
Emmett, Christopher. *Give Way to the Right*. San Antonio: Naylor, 1934.
English, George H. *History of the 89th Division, U.S.A.* Denver: Smith Brooks, 1920.
Ettinger, Albert M., and A. Churchill Ettinger. *A Doughboy with the Fighting 69th: A Remembrance of World War I*. New York: Pocket Books, 1992.
Farrell, Thomas F. *A History of the 1st U.S. Engineers*. Coblenz: n.p., 1919.
Fifield, James H. *The Regiment: A History of the 104th U.S. Infantry A.E.F., 1917–1919*. Springfield, Mass.: n.p., 1946.
Fleming, Thomas. *The Illusion of Victory: America in World War I*. New York: Basic Books, 2003.
Foch, Ferdinand. *The Memoirs of Marshall Foch*. New York: Doubleday, 1931.
Ford, Bert. *The Fighting Yankees Overseas*. Boston: Norman B. McPhail, 1919.
Foster, Pell W. *A Short History of Battery B, 12th Field Artillery*. New York: Privately printed, 1921.
Frothingham, Thomas G. *The American Reinforcement in the World War*. Garden City, N.Y.: Doubleday, Page, 1927.
Fuess, Claude M. *Phillips Academy Andover in the Great War*. New Haven: Yale University Press, 1919.
George, Albert G. *Pictorial History of the Twenty-sixth Division United States Army*. Boston: Ball, 1920.
George, Herbert C. *A Farrier in Arms*. New York: Pageant, 1953.
Gibbons, Floyd. *And They Thought We Wouldn't Fight*. New York: George H. Doran, 1918.
Gowenlock, Thomas R. *Soldiers of Darkness*. Garden City, N.Y.: Doubleday, Doran, 1937.
Hagood, Johnson. *The Services of Supply*. Boston: Houghton Mifflin, 1927.
Hallas, James H. *Squandered Victory: The American First Army at St. Mihiel*. Westport, CT: Praeger, 1995.
Hamilton, Craig, and Louise Corbin. *Echoes from Over There: By the Men of the Army and Marine Corps who Fought in France*. New York: Soldier's Publishing, 1919.
Hamin, Elizabeth C. *In White Armor*. New York: Knickerbocker Press, 1919.
Harbord, James G. *America in the World War*. Boston: Houghton Mifflin, 1933.
———. *The American Army in France*. Boston: Little, Brown, 1936.
———. *Leaves from a War Diary*. New York: Dodd, Mead, 1925.
Hart, Liddell. *A History of the World War, 1914–1918*. Boston: Little, Brown, 1935.

_____. *The Real War, 1914–1918.* Boston: Little, Brown, 1930.
_____. *Reputations Ten Years After.* Boston: Little, Brown, 1928.
Hartney, Harold B. *Up and at 'Em.* Harrisburg: Stackpole Sons, 1940.
Hauslee, W.M. *Soldiers of the Great War.* Washington, D.C.: Soldiers Record Publishing Association, 1920.
Havlin, Arthur C. *The History of Company A, 102nd Machine Gun Battalion, 26th Division, A.E.F.* Boston: Privately printed, 1928.
Herwig, Holger H. *The First World War, Germany and Austria-Hungary, 1914–1918.* London: Arnold, 1997.
Herzog, Stanley J. *The Fightin' Yanks.* Stamford, Conn.: Cunningham, 1922.
Hills, Ratcliffe M. *War History of the 102nd Regiment U.S. Infantry.* Hartford, Conn.: Privately printed, 1924.
Hinman, Jesse R. *Ranging in France with Flash and Sound.* Portland, Ore.: Dunham, 1919.
Hitz, Benjamin D. *A History of Base Hospital 32.* Indianapolis: n.p., 1922.
Hogan, Martin J. *The Shamrock Battalion of the Rainbow.* New York: D. Appleton, 1919.
Holden, Frank A. *War Memories.* Athens, GA: Athens Book Co., 1922.
Holt, Tonie and Valmai. *Battlefields of the First World War: A Traveller's Guide.* London: Pavilion Books, 1995.
Hopper, James. *Medals of Honor.* New York: John Day, 1929.
Hoyt, Charles B. *Heroes of the Argonne.* Kansas City, Mo.: Franklin Hudson, 1919.
Hudson, James J. *Hostile Skies.* Syracuse, N.Y.: Syracuse University Press, 1968.
Hughes, W.C. *History of E Battery, 319th Field Artillery.* C.M. Maiberger, n.d.
Huidekoper, Frederic Louis. *The History of the 33rd Division, A.E.F.* Springfield, Ill.: State Historical Society, 1921.
Hungerford, Edward. *With the Doughboy in France.* New York: Macmillan, 1920.
Jannen, William Jr. *The Lions of July: Prelude to War, 1914.* Novato, CA: Presidio Press, 1996.
Johnson, Clarence W. *The History of the 321st Infantry.* Columbia, R.I.: Bryan, 1919.
Johnson, Douglas V. II, and Rolfe L. Hillman, Jr. *Soissons, 1918.* College Station: Texas A&M University Press, 1999.
Johnson, Douglas W. *Battlefields of the World War.* London: Oxford University Press, 1921.
Johnson, Thomas M. *Without Censor.* Indianapolis: Bobbs-Merrill, 1928.
Kean, Robert W. *Dear Marraine, 1917–1919.* n.p. Privately printed, 1969.
Kelly T. Howard. *What Outfit Buddy?* New York: Harper and Brothers, 1920.
Kenamore, Clair. *From Vauquois Hill to Exermont: A History of the 35th Division.* St. Louis: Guard, 1919.
Kernan, William F. *History of the 103rd Field Artillery.* Providence, R.I.: Remington, n.d.
Kurtz, Leonard P. *Beyond No Man's Land.* Buffalo, N.Y.: Foster and Stewart, 1937.
La Branche, Ernest E. *An American Battery in France.* Worcester, Mass.: Belisle, 1923.
Lambert, Joseph I. *One Hundred Years with the Second Cavalry.* Fort Riley, KS: Capper, 1939.
Langer, William L. *Gas and Flame in World War I.* New York: Alfred A. Knopf, 1965.
Langille, Leslie. *Men of the Rainbow.* Chicago: O'Sullivan, 1933.
Lavine, A. Lincoln. *Circuits of Victory.* Garden City, N.Y.: Doubleday, Page, 1921.
Lejeune, John A. *The Reminiscences of a Marine.* Philadelphia: Dorrance, 1930.
Liggett, Hunter. *A.E.F. Ten Years Ago in France.* New York: Dodd, Mead, 1928.
_____. *Commanding an American Army.* Boston: Houghton Mifflin, 1925.
Lonergan, Thomas C. *It Might Have Been Lost.* New York: G. P. Putnam's Sons, 1929.
MacArthur, Charles G. *War Bugs.* Garden City, N.Y.: Doubleday, Doran, 1929.
MacArthur, Douglas. *Reminiscences.* New York: McGraw-Hill, 1964.
MacLean, William P. *My Story of the 130th F.A.* Topeka, KS: Boys Industrial School, 1920.
March, Peyton C. *The Nation at War.* Garden City, NY: Doubleday, Doran, 1932.

Marshall, Conrad. *History of M Company, 357th Infantry, 1917–1919.* Carnegie, Okla.: Carnegie Herald, 1919.
Marshall, George C. *Memoirs of My Services in the World War.* Boston: Houghton Mifflin, 1976.
Masseck, C.K. *Official Brief History of the 89th Division U.S.A., 1917–1918–1919.* n.p., 1919.
Maurer, Maurer. *The U.S. Air Service in World War I.* 4 vols. Washington, D.C.: U.S. Government Printing Office, 1979.
May, Ernest R. *The World War and American Isolation 1914–1917.* Cambridge, MA: Harvard University Press, 1959.
McCarthy, William B. *Memories of Troop A, Company D, 102nd Machine Gun Battalion.* New Haven: Tuttle Morehouse and Taylor, 1919.
McClellan, Edwin N. *The United States Marine Corps in World War I.* Washington, D.C.: Historical Branch, U.S. Marine Corps, 1920.
McIntyre, Colby L. *The Old Man of the 103rd.* Houlton, Me.: Aroostook Print Shop, 1940.
Meehan, Thomas F. *History of the 78th Division in the World War, 1917–18–19.* New York: Dodd, Mead, 1921.
Metcalf, Clyde H. *A History of the United States Marine Corps.* New York: G.P. Putnam's Sons, 1939.
Miller, Henry R. *The 1st Division.* Pittsburgh: Crescent, 1920.
Mitchell, William. *Memoirs of World War I.* New York: Random House, 1960.
Morrow, George L. *The 58th Infantry in the World War.* n.p., 1919.
Moss, Jas. A., and Harry S. Howland. *America in Battle, With Guide to the American Battlefields in France and Belgium.* Menasha, Wis.: Geo. Banta, 1920.
Mozley, George. *Our Miracle Battery.* Lowell, Mass.: Sullivan Brothers, 1920.
Murray, Williamson. *Military Adaptation in War: With Fear of Change.* Cambridge: Cambridge University Press, 2011.
Nelson, John. *A Brief History of the Fighting Yankee Division, A.E.F.* Worcester, Mass.: n.p., 1919.
Nettleton, George H. *Yale in the World War.* 2 vols. New Haven: Yale University Press, 1925.
New York Life Insurance Co. *NYLIC War Stories, Being a Brief Record of the Service in the Great War of Soldiers, Sailors, Marines Who Went from the Home Office of the NYLIC.* New York: n.p., 1920.
O'Connor, Richard. *Black Jack Pershing.* Garden City, N.Y.: Doubleday, 1961.
Ottosen, P.H. *Trench Artillery, A.E.F.* Boston: Lothrop, Lee and Shepard, 1931.
Palmer, Frederick. *America in France.* New York: Dodd, Mead, 1918.
_____. *John J. Pershing: General of the Armies.* Harrisburg: Military Service Publishing, 1948.
_____. *Newton D. Baker: America at War.* New York: Dodd Mead, 1931.
Payne, Robert. *The Marshall Story.* New York: Prentice-Hall, 1951.
Peixotto, Ernest. *The American Front.* New York: Charles Scribner's Sons, 1919.
Pershing, John J. *Final Report of General John J. Pershing.* Washington, D.C.: U.S. Government Printing Office, 1920.
_____. *My Experiences in the World War.* 2 vols. New York: Frederick A. Stokes, 1931.
_____. *Report of the First Army, American Expeditionary Forces: Organization and Operations.* Fort Leavenworth: General Services Schools Press, 1923.
Pollard, James B. *The 47th Infantry, A History, 1917–1918–1919.* Saginaw, Mich.: Seemann and Peters, 1919.
Pottle, Frederick A. *Stretchers.* New Haven: Yale University Press, 1929.
Powell, Alexander. *The Army Behind the Army.* New York: Charles Scribner's Sons, 1919.
Putnam, Eben. *Report of the Commission on Massachusetts' Part in the World War.* Boston: Commonwealth of Massachusetts, 1931.
Ranlett, Louis F. *Let's Go!* Boston: Houghton Mifflin, 1927.

Reilly, Henry. *Americans All, the Rainbow at War.* Columbus, Ohio: F.F. Hear, 1936.
Rendinell, J.B., and George Pattullo. *One Man's War.* New York: J.H. Sears, 1928.
Reynolds, Quentin. *They Fought for the Sky.* New York: Rinehart, 1957.
Rickenbacker, Eddie V. *Fighting the Flying Circus.* Garden City, N.Y.: Doubleday, 1965.
Rogers, Horatio. *The Diary of an Artillery Scout.* North Andover, Mass.: Privately printed, 1975.
Roosevelt, Theodore, Jr. *Average Americans.* New York: G.P. Putnam's Sons, 1919.
Rudin, Harry R. *Armistice 1918.* New Haven: Yale University Press, 1944.
Samson, Henry T. *The War Story of C Battery, 103rd Field Artillery.* Norwood, Mass.: Pimpton Press, 1920.
Schauble, Lambert. *The First Battalion, 406th Telegraph.* Philadelphia: Redfield, Kendrick-Odell, 1921.
Schurman, Jacob G. *A History of the 309th Regiment of Infantry.* New York: n.p., 1919.
Searcy, Earl B. *Looking Back.* Springfield, Ill.: Journal Press, 1921.
Sibley, Frank P. *With the Yankee Division in France.* Boston: Little, Brown, 1919.
Sirois, Edward D. *Smashing Through the World War with Fighting Battery C, 102nd F.A.* Salem, Mass.: Meet Press, 1919.
Skillman, Willis R. *The A.E.F.* Philadelphia: George W. Jacobs, 1920.
Society of the Fifth Division. *The Official History of the 5th Division, U.S.A. in the World War, 1917–1919.* New York: Wynkoop, Hallenbeck, Crawford, 1919.
Society of the 1st Division. *History of the First Division during the World War, 1917–1919.* Philadelphia: John C. Winston, 1922.
Spaulding, Oliver L., and J.W. Wright. *The 2nd Division American Expeditionary Force in France, 1917–1919.* New York: Hillman Press, 1937.
Stackpole, Markham W. *World War Memoirs of Milton Academy.* Cambridge, Mass.: Riverside Press, 1940.
Stallings, Laurence. *The Doughboys.* New York: Harper and Row, 1963.
Stansbury, Henry D. *Maryland's 117th Trench Mortar Battery in the World War.* Baltimore: John D. Lucas, 1942.
Stewart, Lawrence. *Rainbow Bright.* Philadelphia: Dorrance, 1923.
Strickland, Daniel W. *Connecticut Fights.* New Haven: Quinnipiac, 1930.
Stringer, Henry R., ed. *Heroes All!* Washington, D.C.: Fassett, 1919.
Taber, John H. *The Story of the 168th Infantry.* 2 vols. Iowa City: State Historical Society of Iowa, 1925.
Taylor, Emerson G. *New England in France.* Boston: Houghton Mifflin, 1920.
Thomas, Lowell. *This Side of Hell.* Garden City, N.Y.: Doubleday, Doran, 1932.
———. *Woodfill of the Regulars.* Garden City, N.Y.: Doubleday, Doran, 1929.
Thomas, Shipley. *The History of the A.E.F.* New York: George H. Doran, 1920.
Toland, John. *No Man's Land.* Garden City, N.Y.: Doubleday, 1980.
Tompkins, Raymond S. *The Story of the Rainbow Division.* New York: Boni and Liveright, 1919.
Trask, David F. *The AEF and Coalition Warmaking, 1917–1918.* Lawrence: University Press of Kansas, 1993.
U.S. Army. *The Americans in the Great War: Volume 1. The Second Battle of the Marne.* Clermont-Ferrand, France: Michelin & Cie, 1920.
———. *The Americans in the Great War: Volume 2. The Battle of St. Mihiel.* Clermont-Ferrand, France: Michelin & Cie, 1920.
———. *The Americans in the Great War. Volume 3. Meuse-Argonne Battle.* Clermont-Ferrand, France: Michelin & Cie, 1920.
———. *Field Orders First Army Corps.* n.p., n.d.
———. *The Genesis of the First American Army.* Washington, D.C.: U.S. Government Printing Office, 1929.

———. *Histories of 251 Divisions of the German Army which Participated in the War.* Washington, D.C.: U.S. Government Printing Office, 1920.
———. *History of the 101st United States Engineers, A.E.F., 1917–1919.* Cambridge, Mass.: University Press, 1926.
———. *History of the 102nd Field Artillery.* Boston: Lawrence, 1927.
———. *History of the 103rd Infantry, 1917–1919.* Boston: H.I. Hymans, 1919.
———. *A History of the 2nd Regiment of Engineers.* Cologne: M. DuMont Schauberg, 1919.
———. *History of the 6th Machine Gun Battalion.* Neuwied on the Rhine: n.p., 1919.
———. *History of the 3rd Division, United States Army in the World War.* Cologne: M. Du Mont Schauberg, 1919.
———. *Illinois in the World War: An illustrated History of the 33rd Division.* Chicago: States Publications Society, 1921.
———. *The Immortal Yankee Division, 1917–1919.* Boston: n.p.
———. *The 9th U.S. Infantry in the World War.* n.p., n.d.
———. *Official History of the 82nd Division, American Expeditionary Forces, 1917–1919.* Indianapolis: Bobbs-Merrill, 1919.
———. *Order of Battle of the United States Land Forces in the World War (General Headquarters, Armies, Army Corps, Services of Supply and Separate Forces).* Washington, D.C.: U.S. Government Printing Office, 1988.
———. *Order of Battle of the United States Land Forces in the World War (Divisions).* Washington, D.C.: U.S. Government Printing Office, 1988.
———. *Order of Battle of the United States Land Forces in the World War (War Department, Posts, etc.).* Washington, D.C.: U.S. Government Printing Office, 1988.
———. *Records of the 2nd Division (Regular).* 9 vols. Washington, D.C.: Army War College, 1927.
———. *Summaries of Intelligence, First Army, American Expeditionary Forces.* 2 volumes. n.p., 1918.
———. *Summary of Operations, First Army, American Expeditionary Forces, Aug. 9–Nov. 11, 1918.* n.p., n.d.
———. *United States Land Forces in the World War, 1917–1919.* 17 vols. Washington, D.C.: U.S. Government Printing Office, 1948.
United States. *Decorations, United States Army 1862–1926: A List of Awards of the Congressional Medal of Honor, the Distinguished Service Cross and the Distinguished Service, Medal Awarded Under the Authority of the Congress of the United States.* Washington, D.C.: U.S. Government Printing Office, 1927.
Viereck, George S. *As They Saw Us.* Garden City, N.Y.: Doubleday, Doran, 1919.
Wainwright, Philip S. *History of the 101st Machine Gun Battalion.* Hartford, CT: 101st Machine Gun Battalion Association, 1922.
Westover, Wendell. *Suicide Battalions.* New York: G.P. Putnam's Sons, 1929.
Wilson, Dale E. *Treat 'Em Rough!* Novato, Calif.: Presidio, 1990.
Winterich, John T. *Squads Write!* New York: Harper and Brothers, 1931.
Wise, Frederic M. *A Marine Tells It to You.* New York: J.H. Sears, 1929.
Wise, Jennings C. *The Turn of the Tide: American Operations at Cantigny, Château-Thierry and the Second Battle of the Marne.* New York: Henry Holt, 1920.
Wrentmore, Ernest L. *In Spite of Hell.* New York: Greenwich, 1958.

INDEX

Aisne Defensive and Belleau Wood 2, 22–23, 24, 36, 42, 53, 70, 74, 82
Aisne Marne Offensive 30–39, 53, 60, 65, 70, 76, 82, 85, 86, 90, 92, 93, 94, 115, 117, 119, 130, 133, 134, 149, 152, 153, 182, 185, 186, 191, 193, 260, 282, 286, 296
Alexander, Maj. Gen. Robert 190, 282
Allen, Maj. Gen. Henry T. 238, 239, 262
American Army units: 1st Army 41, 42, 62, 65, 67, 68, 76, 78, 86, 94, 96, 101, 120, 140, 156, 161, 168, 173, 174, 186, 187, 200, 202, 205, 211, 222, 223, 235, 240, 241, 246, 252, 277, 280, 282, 286; I Corps 63, 66, 67, 68, 73, 75, 76, 79, 85, 92, 99, 101, 108, 117, 118, 119, 132, 133, 134, 151, 152, 153, 155, 168, 183, 185, 187, 192, 194, 200, 201, 221, 223, 235, 236, 246, 252, 284, 285, 286, 296; II Corps 91, 125, 127, 131, 136, 144, 145, 146, 147, 159, 166, 178, 192, 199, 210, 221, 247, 280, 281; III Corps 64, 66, 75, 86, 87, 88, 94, 95, 133, 152, 153, 155, 161, 167, 205, 206, 212, 236, 246, 280, 286, 296; IV Corps 65, 66, 76, 77, 102, 118, 120, 163, 177, 179, 184, 185, 193, 200, 221, 232, 235, 236, 240, 241, 246, 252, 253, 290, 291, 294, 304; V Corps 66, 67, 68, 78, 79, 87, 95, 100, 139, 140, 145, 152, 155, 161, 167, 168, 178, 196, 205, 212, 213, 223, 224, 236, 242, 246, 247, 251, 277, 281, 286, 295, 304; VI Corps 107, 112, 172, 205, 216, 231, 246, 280, 291, 304; 1st Division 16, 17, 18, 24, 31, 32, 33, 34, 35, 36, 40, 41, 42, 44, 48, 52, 59–69, 76, 79, 87, 117, 118, 120, 135, 151, 155, 161, 169, 186, 187, 196, 213, 222, 223, 224, 235, 241, 247, 262, 335, 340; Second Division 18, 22, 24, 31, 32, 33, 34, 35, 44, 45, 47, 65, 68, 69–80, 84, 101, 118, 132, 173, 188, 196, 200, 213, 222, 235, 236, 237, 333, 334, 335, 337, 338, 339; Third Division 22, 24, 25, 26, 27, 28, 30, 37, 75, 80–89, 95, 96, 102, 103, 132, 133, 133, 134, 152, 153, 154, 155, 206, 242, 286, 336, 339; Fourth Division 38, 86, 87, 88, 89–97, 102, 103, 119, 134, 153, 161, 162, 185, 186, 193, 206, 212, 336; Fifth Division 44, 76, 77, 87, 88, 95, 96, 97–104, 155, 156, 200, 212, 236, 241, 242, 251; Sixth Division 105–109, 122, 124, 207; Seventh Division 102, 109–114, 135, 136, 178, 241, 253, 304; Eighth Division (Depot Division) 262–265; Twenty-sixth NG Division 17, 18, 40, 41, 42, 52, 63, 66, 75, 94, 100, 108, 112, 114–123, 132, 133, 141, 152, 185, 206, 207, 222, 286, 336, 338; Twenty-seventh NG Division 123–129, 145, 146, 147, 161; Twenty-eighth NG Division 129–136, 145, 146, 147, 161; Twenty-ninth NG Division 121, 137–141, 162, 206, 295; Thirtieth NG Division 126, 127, 128, 141–148; Thirty-first NG Division (Depot Division) 227, 265–266; Thirty-second NG Division 18, 37, 38, 67, 68, 80, 86, 87, 93, 94, 102, 103, 133, 134, 146, 148–157, 162, 178, 186, 187, 236, 247, 286, 295, 296, 334, 336, 339; Thirty-third NG Division 39, 73, 88, 95, 104, 127, 140, 147, 157–164, 178, 179, 205, 206, 211, 212, 230, 257, 306; Thirty-fourth NG Division 230, 267–270; Thirty-fifth NG Division 66, 107, 134, 135, 145, 163, 164–170, 217, 223, 246; Thirty-sixth NG Division 78, 170–174; Thirty-seventh NG Division 101, 112, 135, 145, 146, 154, 175–180, 193, 206, 236, 241, 246; Thirty-eighth NG Division 31, 270–274;

Fortieth NG Division (Depot Division) 278–281; Forty-first NG Division 282–287; Forty-second NG Division 17, 25, 28, 36, 37, 38, 66, 67, 78, 86, 87, 93, 119, 133, 152, 155, 180–189, 193, 196, 202, 224, 236; Seventy-sixth NA Division 116, 287–292; Seventy-seventh NA Division 25, 38, 68, 79, 80, 94, 100, 134, 153, 177, 184, 188, 189–197, 201, 213, 224, 252, 280, 338; Seventy-eighth NA Division 77, 101, 102, 188, 195, 197–202, 224, 236, 241; Seventy-ninth NA Division 87, 95, 108, 109, 121, 122, 128, 141, 154, 161, 163, 178, 202–208, 286; Eightieth NA Division 39, 68, 79, 87, 95, 102, 161, 162, 195, 196, 208–214, 224; Eighty-first NA Division 108, 109, 163, 169, 214–218, 220, 227, 252; Eighty-second NA Division 65, 67, 76, 108, 118, 135, 187, 195, 201, 213, 218–225, 230, 235, 241, 289; Eighty-third NA Division (Depot Division) 285, 292–296; Eighty-fourth NA Division 272, 275, 297–300; Eighty-fifth NA Division 300–305, 306; Eighty-sixth NA Division 159, 305–308; Eighty-seventh NA Division 225–228, 275; Eighty-eighth NA Division 159, 228–232; Eighty-ninth NA Division 44, 65, 66, 76, 77, 79, 103, 108, 145, 155, 163, 178, 186, 187, 188, 196, 200, 222, 232–237, 238, 241, 242, 273, 286; Ninetieth NA Division 44, 65, 76, 88, 96, 101, 102, 103, 104, 112, 178, 196, 200, 212, 222, 223, 230, 235, 236, 237, 238–243, 253; Ninety-first NA Division 66, 67, 136, 154, 155, 162, 168, 169, 178, 243–249, 284, 295, 304; Ninety-second NA Division 112, 194, 217, 241, 249–253; Ninety-third Division 49, 253–261

American organizations not assigned to divisions: 1st Air Park — Formerly 183rd Service Squadron 324; 2nd Air Park — Formerly 360th Service Squadron 329; Third Air Park — Formerly 255th Service Squadron 332; 4th Air Park — Formerly 218th Service Squadron 327; 5th Air Park — Formerly 279th Service Squadron 328; 6th Air Park — Formerly 822nd Service Squadron 329; First Anti-aircraft Battalion 313, 314; Second Anti-aircraft Battalion 313, 314; First Army Artillery Park 309; Forty-second Artillery, Coast Artillery Corps 309; Forty-third Artillery, Coast Artillery Corps 309; Forty-fourth Artillery, Coast Artillery Corps 309–310; Fifty-first Artillery, Coast Artillery Corps 310; Fifty-second Artillery, Coast Artillery Corps 310; Fifty-third Artillery, Coast Artillery Corps 310; Fifty-fifth Artillery, Coast Artillery Corps 311; Fifty-sixth Artillery, Coast Artillery Corps 311; Fifty-seventh Artillery, Coast Artillery Corps 311; Fifty-eighth Artillery, Coast Artillery Corps 311; Fifty-ninth Artillery, Coast Artillery Corps 311; Sixtieth Artillery, Coast Artillery Corps 312; Sixty-fifth Artillery, Coast Artillery Corps 312; First Corps Artillery Park 308; Second Corps Artillery Park 308–309; Third Corps Artillery Park 309; Fourth Corps Artillery Park 309; 1st Balloon Company 329; 2nd Balloon Company 329–330; 3rd Balloon Company 330; 4th Balloon Company 330; 5th Balloon Company 330; 6th Balloon Company 331; 7th Balloon Company 331; 8th Balloon Company 331; 9th Balloon Company 330; 10th Balloon Company 331; 11th Balloon Company 331; 12th Balloon Company 331; 15th Balloon Company 330; 16th Balloon Company 330; 42nd Balloon Company 330; 43rd Balloon Company 332; 69th Balloon Company 331; First Battalion, Trench Artillery 312–313; 11th Day Bombardment Squadron 325; 20th Day Bombardment Squadron 325; 96th Day Bombardment Squadron 325; 163rd Day Bombardment Squadron 326; 166th Day Bombardment Squadron 326; Second Cavalry 313; Eleventh Engineers (Standard Gauge Railway) 314; Twelfth Engineers (Light Railway) 314–315; Thirteenth Engineers (Standard Gauge Railway Operation) 315; Fourteenth Engineers (Light Railway) 315; Fifteenth Engineers (Standard Gauge Railway) 315; Sixteenth Engineers (Standard Gauge Railway) 315; Twenty-first Engineers (Light Railway) 315; Twenty-second Engineers (Light Railway) 316; Twenty-third Engineers (Highway) 316; Twenty-fourth Engineers (Supply and Shop) 316–317; Twenty-fifth Engineers (General Construction) 317; Twenty-sixth Engineers (Water Supply) 317; Twenty-seventh Engineers (Mining) 317; Twenty-eighth Engineers (Quarry) 317–318; Twenty-ninth Engineers (Surveying and Printing) 318; Thirty-seventh Engineers (Electrical and Mechanical) 318; Fortieth Engineers (Camouflage) 318; Fifty-sixth Engineers (Searchlight) 318; Six Hundred-second Engineers 318; Six Hundred-third Engineers 319; Six Hundred-fourth Engineers 319; One Hundred-Fifteenth Field Signal Battalion 314; Three Hundred First Field Signal Battalion 314; First Gas Regiment 312; 1st Observation Squadron 322–323; 9th Army Observation Squadron – Night 325; 24th Army Observation Squadron 325; 91st Army Observation Squadron 325; 186th Army Observation Squadron 325; 8th Corps Observation Squadron 324; 12th Corps Observation Squadron 323; 50th Corps Observation Squadron 323; 88th Corps Observation Squadron 323; 90th Corps Observation Squadron 323; 99th Corps Observation Squadron 324; 104th Corps Observation Squadron 324; 135th Corps Observation Squadron 324; 258th Corps Observation Squadron 325; 354th Corps Observation Squadron 324; First Pioneer Infantry 319; Third Pioneer Infantry 319; Fifty-first Pioneer Infantry 319; Fifty-second Pioneer Infantry 319; Fifty-third Pioneer Infantry 319; Fifty-fourth Pioneer Infantry 319; Fifty-sixth Pioneer Infantry 319; Fifty-ninth Pioneer Infantry 320; Eight Hundred-second Pioneer Infantry 320; Eight Hundred-third Pioneer Infantry 320; Eight Hundred-fourth Pioneer Infantry 20; Eight Hundred-fifth Pioneer Infantry 320; Eight Hundred-sixth Pioneer Infantry 320; Eight Hundred-seventh Pioneer Infantry 320; Eight Hundred-eighth Pioneer Infantry 320; 13th Pursuit Squadron 327; 17th Pursuit Squadron 329; 22nd Pursuit Squadron 327; 27th Pursuit Squadron 326; 28th Pursuit Squadron 328; 49th Pursuit Squadron 327–328; 93rd Pursuit Squadron 328; 94th Pursuit Squadron 326; 95th Pursuit Squadron 326–327; 103rd Pursuit Squadron 328; 139th Pursuit Squadron 328; 141st Pursuit Squadron 329; 147th Pursuit Squadron 327; 148th Pursuit Squadron 329; 185th Pursuit Squadron – Night 327; 213th Pursuit Squadron 328; Three Hundred-first Battalion, Tank Corps 322; Three Hundred forty-fourth Battalion, Tank Corps 322; Three Hundred forty-fifth Battalion, Tank Corps 322; 199th Squadron – Used as Air Park 324; Fifty-first Telegraph Battalion 320; Fifty-second Telegraph Battalion 321; Fifty-fifth Telegraph Battalion 321; Four Hundred-first Telegraph Battalion 321; Four Hundred-fifth Telegraph Battalion 321; Four Hundred-sixth Telegraph Battalion 321; Four Hundred-ninth Telegraph Battalion 321; Four Hundred-eleventh Telegraph Battalion 322; Four Hundred-twelfth Telegraph Battalion 322; Four Hundred-seventeenth Telegraph Battalion 322; Four Hundred-nineteenth Telegraph Battalion 322

Baccarat Sector 17, 24–25, 38, 176, 177, 181, 183, 184, 191, 193
Bailey, Maj. Gen. Charles A. 214
Ballou, Maj. Gen. Charles C. 249, 250
Bamford, Brig. Gen. Frank E. 59, 114
Barry, Maj. Gen. Thomas H. 305, 306
Barth, Brig. Gen. Charles H. 109, 111, 214, 215
Bell, Maj. Gen. George, Jr. 157, 159
Bell, Maj. Gen. J. Franklin 190, 191
Blocksom, Maj. Gen. Augustus P. 267, 268
British Army units: First Army 132, 145, 200; Second Army 192; Third Army 126, 145, 192, 210, 211; Fourth Army 127, 145, 166; Fifth Army 83; III Corps 127, 160; IV Corps 210; V Corps 210; VI Corps 210; IX Corps 128, 146, 147; XIII Corps 128, 147; XIV Corps 295; XIX Corps 166; Australian Corps 127, 160; 1st Australian 146; 2nd Australian 146; 3rd Australian 127; 4th Australian 160; 1st Div. 128, 147; 2nd Div. 192; 6th Div. 126, 128, 145, 147; 12th Div. 127; 14th Div. 145; 16th Div. 92, 210; 18th Div. 127; 25th Div. 128, 147; 30th Div. 126; 33rd Div. 145; 34th Div. 126, 131, 199, 210; 35th Div. 145; 38th Div. 166; 39th Div. 144, 192, 200; 41st Div. 126; 42nd Div. 192; 46th Div. 146; 49th Div. 145; 50th Div. 128; 58th Div. 160; 66th Div. 125, 221; 74th Div. 127
Brown, Brig. Gen. Preston 81
Buck, Maj. Gen. Beaumont B. 63, 81, 267
Bullard, Maj. Gen. Robert B. 59
Bundy, Maj. Gen. Omar 69
Burnham, Brig. Gen. William P. 218–219

Cameron, Gen. George H. 89, 90
Champagne-Marne Defensive 22, 24, 25–30, 53, 70, 77, 82, 84, 85, 94, 115, 119, 130, 132, 134, 153, 173, 181, 182, 184, 185, 193, 255, 256, 286
Clement, Maj. Gen. Charles M. 129, 130
Cole, Brig. Gen. Eli, USMC 282
Coulter, Brig. Gen. Richard 282
Cronkite, Maj. Gen. Adelbert 208, 210

Dickman, Maj. Gen. Joseph F. 80, 82, 302, 303
Doyen, Brig. Gen. Charles A., USMC 69
Duncan, Maj. Gen. George B. 190, 219

Edwards, Maj. Gen. Clarence B. 114, 116
Ely, Maj. Gen. Hanson E. 97
Erwin, Brig. Gen. James B. 105, 106

Foch, Gen. Ferdinand 13, 30, 39, 41, 42, 51, 52
Foltz, Brig. Gen. Frederick S. 243
French, Maj. Gen. Frances H. 265
French Army units: First Army 62, 63, 64; Second Army 43, 73, 94, 169, 194, 222, 258, 259; Third Army 64, 260; Fourth Army 28, 77, 173, 187, 194, 195, 196, 201, 252, 255, 257; Fifth Army 63, 74, 134; Sixth Army 74, 85, 92, 93, 117, 119, 120, 193, 286; Seventh Army 151, 184, 216, 251, 259; Eighth Army 62, 65, 76, 117, 168, 184, 192, 221, 222, 231, 253; Ninth Army 119; Tenth Army 64, 75, 85, 92, 153, 253, 260; 4th Cavalry Div. 74, 84; II Colonial Corps 63, 73, 120, 121, 135, 136, 163, 169, 179, 206, 211, 217, 222, 235, 236, 246, 259, 290; 10th Colonial Div. 63, 75, 84, 85, 94, 108, 118, 122, 169, 217; 15th Colonial Div. 73, 88, 94–95, 103, 120, 121, 141, 156, 162, 169, 207; I Corps 65, 94, 118, 153; II Corps 92, 93, 185; III Corps 75, 85, 86, 152, 153, 194; V Corps 134; VI Corps 63, 64; VII Corps 17, 92, 93, 179, 185, 247, 248; IX Corps 17, 62, 63, 64, 78, 187, 196, 201, 257; X Corps 64, 73; XI Corps 77, 78, 117, 193; XIII Corps 256, 259; XV Corps 76; XVI Corps 260; XVII Corps 73, 88, 94, 121, 135, 140, 161, 162, 290; XVIII Corps 260; XX Corps 64, 75; XXI Corps 25, 74, 77, 184, 185; XXX Corps 75, 153, 179; XXXII Corps 62, 63, 65, 73, 76, 222; XXXIII Corps 163, 169; XXXVII Corps 185, 253; XXXVIII Corps 74, 75, 84, 93, 118, 119, 133, 152, 153, 185, 195, 201, 252, 286; XL Corps 139, 259; 1st Dismounted Cav. Div. 195, 201, 252; 2nd Dismounted Cav. Div. 94, 120, 121, 206, 211; 1st Div. 108, 174; 3rd Div. 64; 4th Div. 86, 92, 152; 5th Div. 179; 7th Div. 78, 173; 9th Div. 134, 151, 152; 10th Div. 84, 151, 152, 259; 11th Div. 179; 12th Div. 76, 179, 184, 248; 13th Div. 184, 185; 14th Div. 18, 183; 16th Div. 255, 256; 18th Div. 62, 121, 140, 141, 161, 162, 295; 20th Div. 84, 85, 132, 134, 216, 217, 252; 21st Div. 77, 78, 100, 117; 22nd Div. 78, 117, 167, 174; 26th Div. 121, 122; 28th Div. 86; 31st Div. 260; 32nd Div. 76, 86, 222; 33rd Div. 73, 92, 135; 34th Div. 73, 118, 222, 235, 259; 35th Div. 257; 36th Div. 259, 260; 38th Div. 75, 140, 231; 39th Div. 65, 75, 85, 118, 119, 120, 121, 132, 133, 135, 163, 178, 185, 187, 206, 235, 236; 40th Div. 187, 196, 201; 41st Div. 18, 92, 184, 247, 248; 43rd Div. 74, 185; 45th Div. 63; 47th Div. 62; 48th Div. 196; 51st Div. 117, 132; 52nd Div. 73, 185; 53rd Div. 139, 140, 152, 174; 58th Div. 76; 59th Div. 153, 260, 261; 60th Div. 64; 61st Div. 77, 117, 174, 184, 192, 193; 62nd Div. 93, 94, 100, 134, 184, 185, 193; 63rd Div. 256; 64th Div. 65, 76, 153, 222; 65th Div. 118, 222; 66th Div. 153; 68th Div. 256; 69th Div. 63, 65, 102, 118, 223, 241, 252; 70th Div. 100; 71st Div. 195, 201; 73rd Div. 74, 78, 85, 132, 133, 134, 168, 173, 246, 259; 77th Div. 100; 79th Div. 169; 87th Div. 101, 251, 252; 89th Div. 65; 120th Div. 134, 161, 194; 125th Div. 27, 85, 132, 133; 127th Div. 153, 260; 128th Div. 18, 179, 183, 184, 248; 131st Div. 73, 107, 108, 168, 177; 132nd Div. 179, 185; 133rd Div. 259; 151st Div. 117, 139, 140, 152; 152nd Div. 63, 64; 153rd Div. 65; 154th Div. 118, 221, 222, 231; 157th Div. 161, 205, 256, 257, 258; 161st Div. 256, 257, 258; 162nd Div. 63, 108; 164th Div. 18, 74, 86, 92, 134, 183, 185, 193, 194, 247; 165th Div. 253; 166th Div. 64; 167th Div. 74, 75, 77, 118, 119, 185; 170th Div. 77, 184, 185; 1st Moroccan 31, 32, 63, 64, 65, 75, 286; 2nd Moroccan 65, 222, 257

Glenn, Maj. Gen. F. 292, 293
Gordon, Maj. Gen. Walter P. 105
Graves, Maj. Gen. William S. 262

Index 355

Greble, Maj. Gen. John E. St. John 170, 172
Greene, Maj. Gen. Harry A. 243, 245

Haan, Brig. Gen. William G. 148
Haig, Field Marshal Douglas 8, 29, 51
Hale, Mag Gen. Wilbur C. 297, 298
Hall, Brig. Gen. Herman 209
Harbord, Maj. Gen. James G. 69
Hay, Maj. Gen. William H. 129
Hayden, Brig. Gen. John L. 265
Hines, Maj. Gen. John L. 89
Hodges, Maj. Gen. Harry F. 287, 289
Hodges, Maj. Gen. Henry C., Jr. 274, 275
Holmich, Brig. Gen. Eli A. 262

Irons, Brig. Gen. James A. 243
Irwin, Brig. Gen. George Leroy 282

Joffre, Marshal Joseph Jacques Césaire 13
Johnson, Brig. Gen. John A. 267
Johnson, Maj. Gen. William H. 243
Judson, Brig. Gen. William V. 267

Kennedy, Maj. Gen. Chase W. 197
Kernan, Maj. Gen. Francis J. 265
Kuhn, Maj. Gen. Joseph E. 203, 204

Lejeune, Maj. Gen. John A., USMC 69
Lewis, Gen. Edward M. 142, 270
Liggett, Maj. Gen. Hunter 282, 283
Lyon, Maj. Gen. LeRoy S. 265

Mann, Maj. Gen. William A. 180, 182
Martin, Maj. Gen. Charles H. 305
Martin, Brig. Gen. William F. 225
McMann, Maj. Gen. John E. 282
McManor, Maj. Gen. James E. 97
McRae, Maj. Gen. James H. 197
Menoher, Maj. Gen. Charles T. 180
Meuse-Argonne Offensive and Blanc Mont 1, 39, 41, 43–45, 46, 53, 60, 66, 67, 70, 77, 78, 82, 87, 90, 95, 98, 102, 106, 108, 110, 115, 127, 128, 130, 134, 135, 138, 140, 143, 146, 149, 154, 156, 158, 161, 162, 163, 165, 168, 169, 171, 173, 176, 178, 182, 187, 191, 194, 198, 201, 202, 204, 206, 209, 211, 212, 215, 217, 220, 223, 229, 233, 234, 236, 239, 241, 244, 246, 247, 248, 250, 252, 255, 256, 257, 258, 277, 282, 286, 295, 296, 304
Montdidier-Noyon Defensive 22, 23–24, 25, 39, 53, 60, 63, 64
Morrison, Maj. Gen. John F. 143
Morton, Maj. Gen. Charles G. 137
Muir, Maj. Gen. Charles H. 98, 129

O'Ryan, Maj. Gen. John 123, 124

Parker, Brig. Gen. Frank 59
Parker, Maj. Gen. James 148, 150, 303
Pershing, Gen. John J. 12, 13, 14, 16, 27, 30, 31, 39, 40, 41, 42, 43, 44, 47, 51, 52
Pétain, Marshal Henri-Phillipe 8, 14, 39
Plummer, Maj. Gen. Edward H. 228, 230

Read, Maj. Gen. George W. 142
Rhodes, Maj. Gen. Charles D. 180

Sage, Maj. Gen. William H. 270, 272
St. Mihiel Offensive 18, 38, 39–43, 52, 53, 60, 65, 66, 70, 73, 76, 82, 87, 90, 94, 95, 98, 101, 115, 120, 143, 145, 161, 168, 169, 173, 182, 186, 198, 200, 206, 209, 211, 220, 222, 223, 234, 235, 236, 239, 241, 244, 246, 259, 282, 286, 290, 291, 304
Scott, Brig. Gen. William S. 282
Sibert, Maj. Gen. William L. 59
Smith, Maj. Gen. William R. 170, 176, 267
Strong, Maj. Gen. Frederick S. 278, 279
Sturgis, Maj. Gen. Samuel D. 225, 226
Summerall, Brig. Gen. Charles P. 59
Swift, Maj. Gen. Eben 218, 220

Traub, Maj. Gen. Peter M. 164

Weigel, Maj. Gen. William 228, 287
Whitney, Brig. Gen. Henry H. 270
Whittlesey, Lt. Colonel Charles 190
Winn, Brig. Gen. Frank Linn 232–233
Wood, Maj. Gen. Leonard 232, 234
Wright, Maj. Gen. William M. 164, 165, 233

www.ingramcontent.com/pod-product-compliance
Lightning Source LLC
Chambersburg PA
CBHW051206300426
44116CB00006B/451